The Riddle
o f
Human Rights

The Riddle of Human Rights

Gary Teeple

Department of Sociology and Anthropology
Simon Fraser University

Garamond Press
Aurora, Ontario

Printed and bound in Canada

Cover art work courtesy of Juan M. Sánchez

Published 2004 in Canada by Garamond Press Ltd,
63 Mahogany Court, Aurora, Ontario L4G 6M8

National Library of Canada Cataloguing in Publication

Teeple, Gary, 1945-
    The riddle of human rights / Gary Teeple.

Includes bibliographical references and index.
ISBN 1-55193-041-2 (bound).—ISBN 1-55193-039-0 (pbk.)

    1. Human rights. I. Title.

JC571.T43 2004   341.4'8   C2004-902223-7

Garamond Press gratefully acknowledges the support of the Department of Canadian Heritage, Government of Canada, and the support of the Ontario Media Development Corporation of the Government of Ontario.

Dedicated to the memory of my grandmothers
Hilma Walden and Meeta Teeple

Other Works by Gary Teeple

Capitalism and the National Question in Canada (ed.) 1972

Marx's Critique of Politics, 1984

Globalization and the Decline of Social Reform, 1995
(revised and expanded, 2000)

La globalization du monde et le déclin du réformisme social, 2004

Contents

Preface

Because the claims and entitlements known as human rights embrace all the key social, economic, and political relations belonging to a capitalist system, they make any systematic and comprehensive attempt to analyze them a near-impossible undertaking. For this reason my intent from the outset was restricted to drawing out only some of the most significant aspects of these rights and subjecting them to a critical analysis. There are, then, many issues concerning human rights that are not addressed here, but I hope at least there is an argument that constitutes a framework for their consideration.

This book is offered as one of many contributions to the critical assessment of the fundamental ethics and ideological rationalization of contemporary capitalism. Above all, I have endeavoured to show that capitalism never could honour the rights it has claimed as its ideals and that global capitalism has outgrown human rights as the ethical and ideological precepts of an earlier stage in capitalist development. The main thrust of the argument is that in this shift to global accumulation of capital the rights that once had a certain practical and theoretical validity for some are being more or less rapidly eclipsed, undermined, usurped, and pervasively violated as a consequence of the expansion of the very system that gave rise to them. Despite their proclamation as absolutes, these rights have always been contradictory in nature and relative to a stage of development of capitalism – characteristics that point to their transient nature and, it follows, to the inevitability of their passing. During the roughly half-century of the declared existence of human rights, a substantial part of humanity has never possessed most of these rights; and even where they still exist in some measure, they are increasingly becoming mere abstractions, as the powers that be show their contempt for this set of ideals from the past – ideas that in fact never were and could never have been fully realized.

A draft of this book was completed in the spring of 2001. After receiving several reviews I began revising and editing it in the late summer, and then the unforeseen events of September 11 occurred. It was immediately obvious that a book on human rights could not be published in the midst of this crisis without an understanding of what was happening. In the United States and throughout the world, the following few months saw the widespread abrogation of civil and political rights and the almost universal legislating of draconian emergency laws. I began over the next year to study the attacks of 9/11 and the aftermath, and produced a book-length manuscript, clearly too long for inclusion here as a chapter and indeed involving a different analytical focus. The last chapter of this book gives some sense of the argument that I have made regarding the meaning of September 11 and its relation to human rights.

Acknowledgements

There are several friends and colleagues and other readers whom I want to thank – in particular, Herbert Adam, Sol Benatar, Ken Fish, Marilyn Gates, Harry Glasbeek, Wolf-Dieter Narr, and John Whitworth. All of them read one draft or another of the manuscript, with the exception of the last chapter. They gave me detailed, constructive criticisms of the text, which made me reconsider parts of the argument and forced me to clarify several points. Their comments came from varying political and disciplinary perspectives and ranged from specific details to the most far-reaching philosophical questions about human rights. They gave much of their time, made very thoughtful comments, and offered encouragement. I owe them a great deal of gratitude for giving me their insights and for their interest. While not all of their criticisms and suggestions were incorporated, the book certainly is better for their efforts.

Juan Sánchez created the art that graces the cover. I am flattered that he agreed to do it and pleased to have art as criticism as part of this book.

Robert Clarke did the editing; but as usual there was far more to his editing than mere grammar and punctuation. He was, as ever, astute, clear, demanding, an exacting critic, and a pleasure to work with. The final shape of the book owes much to his understanding and critical eye.

Peter Saunders of Garamond Press was, of course, central to this project. His encouragement and his patience underlie the work presented here, but he was also an incisive and critical reader and editor of the text. He has been a force for academic publishing in this country – a point too little mentioned, but a fact that I and many others are grateful for. For his efforts on this manuscript I owe him many thanks.

More than central was Monica Escudero, whose love and patience and reassurance and support were always present. As a partner, lover, friend, and critic, she was always there; it is difficult to imagine writing this book without her support and presence.

Introduction

The idea of a single world order embracing all of humanity and resting on fundamental principles of human conduct has been a matter of philosophical speculation since antiquity. It was only in the aftermath of World War II, however, that such an idea, complete with specific standards of conduct, was actually proclaimed as universal and attempts made to realize it. Its manifestations came in the form of the United Nations' Charter and the Universal Declaration of Human Rights – documents affirming certain principles asserted as being fundamental to human relationships and as constituting the ideals of an emerging world order.

Although declared as absolutes, these "human rights" have, from the beginning, been the subject of considerable conflict over interpretation and enforcement. They cannot be said, moreover, ever to have been wholly respected or upheld. Despite often-repeated claims made for their universality and equality, the administration of these rights has always been highly skewed in favour of some; and the violation of others in varying ways and degrees has been ubiquitous. In the world today, the principles of most human rights appear to be increasingly transgressed, subordinated, or usurped. In general human rights seem to be more in decline than ascendant. The seeming promise of the postwar years, of a world based on clearly established human rights, lies unfulfilled, denied by the realities of contradictory interests and seemingly irreconcilable differences.

While there is little doubt today that we are on the verge of the realization of a single integrated world economy, this configuration is far from being the "peaceable kingdom" or "perpetual peace" of the political philosophers. The realization of a full range of human rights appears to be still no more than a distant goal. Indeed, the consolidation of the global economy and regulatory structures seems to be taking place more in the violation than in the realization of human rights. Everywhere, the powers that be employ all the means that circumstances allow, fair and foul, to achieve the dominance of certain interests over others. Instead of respect for human rights for all, the world is witness to dispossession, confiscation and theft of real property, and the gradual denial of a wide range of rights, by both legal authorities and transnational corporations. It would be difficult to argue that human rights prevail on the world stage and not the principle of might is right.

At the same time, many thousands of organizations and millions of people are dedicated to defending, advancing, and clarifying these rights – within an accelerating struggle to have human rights respected and an accompanying expansion in consciousness about their nature and violation. This expanding conflict and growing consciousness go hand in hand, although not as a simple progression towards achieved rights and discerning clarity. Despite continuing violations and systematic obfuscation and rationalization of the violations, the demands for these rights and the consciousness surrounding their nature continue to grow.

On the Use of the Concept of Human Rights

The intent of this book is to challenge the concept of human rights – to show that the contradictions that characterize human rights reflect the conflicts inherent in capitalist society, lead to the pervasive violation of those rights, and make respect for them impossible, particularly in this era of global capitalism. In general the intent is to argue that human rights as spelled out in the Universal Declaration of Human Rights are not *human* rights – that is, they are not elemental, inherent, or universal, but rather time-bound and relative to a particular mode of production. To be sure, they are a set of rights with a certain reality, but the qualifier "human" obfuscates the relativity. The existence and concept of human rights are quintessentially ideological: they take what is and assert that as the truth.

For this reason the original manuscript of this book had quotation marks around each use of the concept to indicate that the term was to be read as contested – that the usual meaning of the concept was not the meaning that I was attributing to it. The problem in writing such a critique as this is that the concept of human rights is so widely accepted and deeply held as a reference to something genuinely human that readers may automatically understand the concept, when written without quotation marks, in the ideological sense – that is, as if human rights really were a set of human absolutes. This common understanding of the concept is generally unquestioned and assumed to be normal and is therefore very difficult to disengage from. For editorial reasons we decided against the repetition of quotation marks, and we urge readers to bear in mind that the meaning of human rights throughout this text is always contested.

Unlike any time since World War II, the conditions of the world at the outset of the twenty-first century present a paradox: the systemic and systematic violation of these rights by the very governments that declare them as absolutes. This contradiction obliges us to reconsider the meaning of human rights, to re-examine what they are, to ask why they remain constantly in question and why they conflict with other forms of right. The very inconsistency of their meaning and application also demands that we inquire into their future and that we question their viability as the principles of the emerging world order. The dilemma also raises doubts about whether the full realization of human rights is even abstractly possible, which leads in turn to questions about their presumed irreproachable integrity and about the existing structure of a world order that appears only to allow for the contested dominance of some rights over others.

THE RIDDLE

The first relatively coherent and comprehensive assertion of human rights comes in the ringing declarations of the American and French revolutions of the eighteenth century. Those documents laid out the fundamentals, casting human rights as individual claims resting on private property. Indeed, the individual right to private property was pre-eminent. It was a right that informed the principles and practice of all other rights: to freedom of speech, assembly, and religion, to the vote and election, to security and protection under law, to the rule of law, and even to life.

Following the social and national struggles of the nineteenth and early twentieth centuries, these rights were gradually extended from what were privileges for certain property owners to entitlements for other classes, strata, and groups – including slaves, workers, ethnic minorities, women, and colonial subjects. Wherever these rights were attained, however, the possibility of exercising them continued to depend by and large on the holding of wealth, on having the financial means to exercise those rights. They were, moreover, largely restricted by national definitions and enforcement; rarely did they reach beyond the borders of the nations that proclaimed them, except as models of a stage of political development for emerging nation-states.

Their transnational extension came in 1948, when the United Nations proclaimed the Universal Declaration of Human Rights (UDHR). (See appendix.) That document marked a significant step by extending eighteenth-century abstract national individual rights to the whole world and affirming the individual, along with the state, as a subject in international law.[1] It also signalled a qualitative advance in the development of human self-consciousness: never before had an international forum openly declared all humans everywhere to be "equal." Once limited to the constitutions of a small number of nation-states, the claimed equality of humans was now proclaimed to be a universal truth. The acknowledgement that all humans were human marked an enormous change over pre-war attitudes and practice in which the colonization, enslavement, annihilation, and dispossession of whole populations had been justified by various doctrines of inferior and superior peoples. Indeed, this assertion of universal rights and a universal subject forms a watershed in human history and consciousness.

Despite the historic nature of this step in the development of consciousness, the UDHR declared humans to be equal only in a certain respect: as *possessors* of a set of rights. The UDHR was not claiming an equality of wealth, or of equal access to public goods and services; and it was not claiming an equality in the means of realizing these human rights. It claimed only an equality in the *possession* of individual rights – humans were declared to be equal as humans only in the circumscribed and abstract sense of all holding the same rights as individuals. The rights of the UDHR, then, are deceptive; their possession does not mean that everyone is actually equal or can in fact exercise or benefit from those rights.

As significant as this new self-awareness was, moreover, the human rights set forth in the UDHR were from the outset a matter of debate; the very casting of these rights was achieved only after considerable contention amongst the national representatives commissioned to define them.[2] Ever since, the definition and interpretation of civil, political, and social rights have remained intractable issues, with considerable inconsistencies in principle, legal status, and application.

The key civil and political rights included in the UDHR, for instance, are now found in most liberal democracies, but not in all modern constitutions. Several articles in the UDHR, moreover, proclaim the existence of certain "economic, social and cultural" rights, but those same rights do not appear, for example, in the U.S. Bill of Rights or, for that matter, in most other national declarations. Different groups, classes, courts of law, and nations, furthermore, have held varying interpretations of most, if not all, of the civil, political, and social rights of the UDHR. For some organizations, such as the United Nations, human rights are defined as universal; for others, such as the American Anthropological Association, the universality of rights remains in question.[3] Each of these rights, furthermore, also has its own history – and one not yet finished because the definitions and interpretations continue to evolve.[4] Demands for new rights – for women, children, indigenous peoples, environmental protection, animals – continue to emerge and find formal expression.

The legal status of rights also has inconsistencies. Some rights have juridical meaning only within nation-states; other rights imply transnational relations. Within a nation, some rights, in particular civil and political rights, are integral to political constitutions and considered fundamental to the system; other rights, usually social rights, have no such status. Some rights are legally binding on certain constituencies; other rights are not. As with their definition, the legal status of human rights can be and has been contested; it changes over time, and interpretations vary.

Inconsistencies are also to be found in the use or application of rights. Most obviously, the political left and right wings both make appeals for the defence of human rights and justify actions on the same grounds. The U.S. government composes a list of countries purportedly violating human rights, but at the same time stands accused by many, including Human Rights Watch, United Nations committees, and Amnesty International, of a "persistent and widespread pattern of human rights violations" within its own boundaries.[5] It is also accused by many of these same organizations of committing numerous violations abroad. Diverse social movements and organizations work for human rights, but they define those rights in different ways: some include demands for fundamental and comprehensive changes to the social systems they work within; others, such as Amnesty International, eschew criticism of the system and focus on individuals and particular violations of certain civil and political rights. Human rights commissions or tribunals in various countries, moreover, adjudicate a variable range of civil, political, and social rights with varying powers and resources. At the global level, the few mechanisms that exist for the advancement or enforcement of human rights are highly circumscribed in their mandates and budgets. Despite the declared universality of human rights, there is no single authoritative transnational mechanism, with a corresponding universal access for individuals (the main subject) or collectivities, or with the supranational powers to enforce their practice, prosecute violators, and adjudicate transgressions.[6]

Numerous debates, many philosophical differences, and seemingly unanswerable questions, then, surround the phenomena of human rights. Their definition is not at all a settled matter, their legal status across jurisdictions and their uses and enforcement are blatantly inconsistent, and their violation is common. If it has been established in international forums that all humans are abstractly equal in the possession of these rights, there is little agreement on anything else about them, and patently limited respect for them. For those who attempt to fathom their meaning or work for their realization, they remain problematic, even enigmatic; they continue to be demands whose implicit intent is not entirely clear. Why are they considered inherent and absolute and yet violated everywhere? Why are they defined as universal and yet cannot find a universal definition? To embark on an analysis of human rights is to confront the inconsistencies, contradictions, and truths and untruths that they contain; it is to explore what can be described as abstract statements that epitomize the modern condition in the form of a riddle.

THE ARGUMENT

This critique of human rights rests on the fact that they are a product of history. A brief review of their origins (Chapter I) is intended to clarify the different kinds of rights that are found under the rubric of human rights and to establish that they are the product of several centuries of struggle and represent the balance of power between material interests in a given type of social formation, rather than being god-given or inherent in the human condition.

Near the end of the era of the national development of capital, human rights were given their first coherent, formal, and international definition in 1948, and were proclaimed to be not just the abstract ethical statement of a given system, but the very essence of humanity. They were defined as absolutes, just as in all historical eras the corresponding rights have been cast as sanctified or absolute in some way. Given this, we argue that far from being inherent, indivisible, inalienable, and universal, human rights are in fact relative to a particular mode of production and its corresponding contradictions (Chapter II).

If we are to understand the relativity of human rights, their changing nature, and the source of their contradictions, we also need to explore the nature of rights in themselves and what they reflect (Chapter III). Far from being independent social variables, the character and content of human rights derive from other relationships in civil society. Indeed, the belief that they are absolute goes far to obscure and veil their own nature and the social and economic inequalities that characterize civil society. Here we examine some of the most significant contradictions within human rights, and between human rights and real life, in order to clarify the relative nature of rights and to grasp how they disguise and conceal the iniquities of society as marketplace.

This same line of argument continues with respect to rights outside the capitalist mode of production (Chapter IV). The contrasting of human rights with the kinds of rights found in other systems of production or social and economic conditions – that is, in social formations of socialized capital, Third World nations,[7] or the Fourth World – indicates again that they are relative to a mode of production.

If they are relative, then, the issue of the widespread apparent consensus on support for human rights must be addressed (Chapter V). The fact that those on both the left and the right of the political spectrum often find themselves promoting causes in the name of human rights requires explanation. The contradictory nature of the rights included under the rubric of human rights goes a long way to explaining this paradox, but an analysis of what passes for the defence of human rights reveals that what is often thought to be progressive for subordinate classes and peoples is double-edged and not infrequently negative. Although certain organizations, such as Human Rights Watch and Amnesty International, assume an apparently unassailable moral high ground as critics of injustice, we argue that, however much they may draw attention to some violations, they remain supporters of the prevailing property relations of a particular social formation; their self-defined mandates obscure the meaning and significance of social rights, not to mention the rights of women, children, Aboriginals, and marginal peoples, and the rights necessary to protect the environment. Similarly, they cloud the reasons as to why, in certain instances, subordinated classes or peoples are forced to take up arms to defend themselves against corporate or state oppression.

Given all these contradictions and inconsistencies and the growing ramifications of globalization, the future of human rights comes into question (Chapter VI). With the shift in the principal site of capital accumulation from the national to the global, the struggle for rights has begun to undergo a similar shift – although it generally remains within the framework of human rights. The development of rights at the global level entails for the most part only the development of corporate private rights; other components of human rights remain largely restricted to national or regional jurisdictions. Maintaining the pre-eminence of corporate rights has cost humanity and nations dearly; and to assuage the trauma and veil the realities, authorities have employed officially sanctioned "truth commissions" and ad hoc tribunals. As an alternative to the obvious legal and judicial shortcomings of these mechanisms, a majority of nations in the United Nations in 1998 established the framework for an International Criminal Court; but the development of that body too has been hampered by a lack of independence, a restricted mandate, a circumscribed structure, and opposition from the U.S. government.

As a conclusion to the argument, we take up the issue of human rights as representing possible principles for the future (Chapter VII). If they served as the principles for the expansion of capital throughout the world in the second half of the twentieth century, the question now is about how the struggle over rights reflects the new conditions of the twenty-first century. The nature of global capitalism is qualitatively different from that of national capitalism; and the relative power of transnational corporations (TNCs) will continue to bring about the retrenchment and subordination of the entire range of civil, political, and social rights that characterized the industrial nations after World War II. Even the United Nations, once central to the postwar advance of liberal-democratic principles, is now openly promoting the goal of global free trade, implying the pre-eminence of the rights of transnational corporations. Yet, despite the increasing UN support of corporate rights, the struggle for rights by subordinate classes and peoples and for protection of the environment continues. Given the global context for these struggles and demands, the present age, more than ever, allows us to grasp the underlying meaning of human rights.

By their nature rights are historically relative, and the human rights of the twentieth century are no different. If the UDHR of 1948 marks a watershed in the development of human consciousness – in the simple recognition that all humans possess a common element – the events and aftermath of September 11, 2001, also mark a historical turning point – the proof of the relativity of human rights (Chapter VIII). September 11 and its outcome signify that the rights of the UDHR cannot be realized within the framework of global capitalism. The terror of 9/11 and the response to it constitute the violent announcement of the great dilemma of the twenty-first century: the inherent contradictions in human rights can no longer persist as compromises. Globalization is the assertion of the pre-eminence of corporate civil rights over all other rights; it is a process that undermines and usurps the civil, political, and social rights of non-corporate sectors everywhere, leaving few options for governing by legitimate means.

Modes of Production

The concept of *mode of production* refers to the structured ways in which human needs are satisfied in a given era. Every mode comprises a labour process (raw materials, instruments of production, and labour) and a social division of labour (reflected in a set of property relations). Prior to the current development of science and technology, nature (or geography) always played a significant role in circumscribing or framing human needs and their satisfaction.

The *capitalist mode of production* rests on a highly productive array of instruments and a complex social division of labour, within a system of private property. It has two dominating features: first, all that is produced is produced as commodities, that is, as private property for exchange; second, the direct purpose of and underlying motive for production are to make a profit. Although the satisfaction of needs is the reason that production takes place at all, that is not the immediate goal of production under capitalism.

CHAPTER I
The Diverse Origins

Although the nature of human rights has long been in question, there has at least been a general acceptance that the rights comprise three distinct categories: civil, political, and social. Each of the categories – as well as the many rights subsumed within them – have different histories, and have emerged in different periods.[1] Indeed, the categories are sometimes referred to as "two generations" of rights – with civil and political rights the first generation, and "economic, social, and cultural," as the United Nations refers to them, the second. We refer to this second broad category as "social rights." Some commentators have recently suggested a "third generation" as "group" or "collective" rights; although there is limited consensus on the meaning, this category often refers to one or several of Aboriginal rights, environmental rights, and the rights to development and to peace.

The one thing all the categories have in common is an association with the arrival and maturation of a capitalist class and the subsequent rise of a working class and the modern state. As coherent sets of rights, they do not exist outside of these developments; they are born with these classes; and they reflect the abstract principles of contested property relations in capitalist social formations.

The arrival of civil and political rights in their modern form came with the political revolutions of the eighteenth and nineteenth centuries, which announced the pre-eminence of a capitalist class and its property relations and completed the resolution of a decaying feudal system into two arenas: the state and civil society, the spheres of public affairs and private interests. This division was ensconced in the modern liberal-democratic constitution. Civil rights, or the "rights of man," by and large define the relations between conflicting individual interests in civil society. Political rights, or the "rights of the citizen," define the relation between the individual and the state. Social rights reflect the consequences of class conflict in a system in which the social product is distributed via the market or the "price mechanism," and in which corporations need to socialize the costs of one or the other aspect of reproduction.

Civil Society

Much has been written about civil society in the last few years. Here the concept refers to the sphere of diverse particular interests framed by the role of the state. The state is defined as the embodiment of the "general interest" in the form of the formalized property relations that prevail in civil society. These relations are derived mainly from the sphere of production and exchange, but they embrace the activities of all particular interests. Civil society, by contrast, comprises not only individuals, clubs, trade unions, churches, non-governmental organizations (NGOs), and gangs, but also, most importantly, corporations and workers. All interact within the bounds of the legal structure – laws, policies, and regulations – the abstracted property framework embodied in the state.

Although the concept has been used recently as a synonym for social movements, the "people," the "nation," or networks of NGOs – that is, various non-corporate sectors – that use makes it into a concept that defies precise definition, makes it into a thing in itself, obscures a relation to the state, and ignores the role of corporations in defining property relations. This widespread use constitutes a significant disservice to the conceptualization of global power relations and to the building of critical awareness and movements of resistance.

The use of the concept in this book implies that the state and civil society demand each other, that one cannot be conceived without the other. On the one hand, the elements of civil society act as particular interests, while on the other hand, the state embodies and defends the "whole," the abstracted framework of prevailing relations of property derived from civil society. When one or another of the parts of civil society acquires sufficient collective power to threaten the existence of another part or to challenge the state as the embodiment of the "whole," this dichotomous relation between state and civil society is itself threatened. The corporations as the collective power of capital and the trade unions or social movements as the collective power of living capital comprise the main contenders in this challenge.

Civil Rights

Civil rights, the first of the categories to appear historically, reflected the new property relations found in the emerging marketplace society. They provided an impetus and foundation for the rule of law – the antithesis of the arbitrary and personal rule of the then-presiding absolute monarchs or ecclesiastic authorities. They served to counter the rights and privileges of precapitalist property forms: namely, feudal rights and obligations, and customary and premodern statutory law. In contradistinction to feudal relations, they imply a definition of the human as found in civil society – that is, as an isolated individual, equal in the possession of the "rights necessary for individual freedom."[2] To be formalized in law they required a new kind of state as their embodiment.

Typically, civil rights are rights to liberty, property, security, and justice; but this *liberty* is that of the individual without regard to the social; it is *property* as private property; *security* as state protection of individual rights, private possessions, and the person; and *justice* as the vindication of the outcome of unequal property relations. The rights to freedom of speech, assembly, movement, and faith are similarly cast as civil rights within a framework of private property. Most of these rights can only be realized with the expenditure of money. As a whole they encapsulate the fundamental principles of civil society, the arena of market relations, the sphere of individual interest. They reflect the fundamental relations of production and exchange of private property.

The Rule of Law

The rule of law refers to a form of governance in which the citizenry is ruled under the authority of a constitution and associated laws and not by arbitrary or unaccountable rulers. The principles that characterize rule of law generally comprise the following: everyone is subject to the ordinary law of the land; all legal action is to be carried out "in the ordinary manner and courts of the land"; the judiciary is independent of the executive and of non-public remuneration; and civil rights are the source of a nation's constitution (not the consequence) and the object of judicial enforcement. Articles 6-11 of the Universal Declaration of Human Rights (UDHR) cover many of these points.

As a principle standing in opposition to arbitrary rule, the rule of law is historically progressive; but given that the law in a capitalist society is the codification of the property relations that produce enormous material inequalities, the principle of rule of law in this system stands as another means to perpetuate that inequality.

The origin of civil rights lies in individual commodity production and in the phenomenon of contract as the legal mechanism of exchange and distribution. (Civil rights have little meaning in modes of production that do not include private production or ownership of commodities.) Civil rights define the individual as abstracted from the community; in fact, there is no community implied in the concept except as the sum of the parts or as the abstract property framework embodied in the state. Civil rights belong to the individual as the "economic man" of classical economics, the idealization of the independent commodity producer, defined by rights to the individual's own labour-power and product of labour, and to private possession of the means of production. Society here is understood as entailing merely the rules of the marketplace, the regulations within which independent commodity producers, exercising "rational choice," exchange their products in their own self-interests. (It follows that those outside "economic" relations were, and in some cases still are, not considered to possess civil rights.) The purpose of life in such a society is simply the self-interested pursuit of wealth and power, a pursuit that necessarily comes at the expense of others and is guaranteed by the state in upholding civil rights.

Civil rights, then, are the rights of the individual as the personification of private property. They reflect the tenets of civil society as marketplace society; as such they form the rationale of the liberal-democratic state.[3] They are the principles that guide the actions of the state, mark the character of its constitution, inform its legislation, and constitute the object of security matters. It is for these reasons that the liberal state makes the declaration of the "rights of man," that is, civil rights, the preface to its constitution.

POLITICAL RIGHTS

Political rights define the relation of the individual in civil society to the state, the embodiment of the framework of the prevailing property relations; they are the "rights of the citizen." In general, they are limited to the right to vote, to be elected, to reform or amend the constitution if elected, and "to petition the government," all of which presume periodic elections. Implied in political rights is the right to insurrection[4] as a means of responding to a government that violates the principles that frame the constitution – that is, the rights of private property – but that right is never extended to a population impoverished and degraded by the consequences of the accumulation of private property in the hands of a few. In these circumstances, insurrection in the name of the common good would spell the end of private property, and hence of the divide between civil society and state.

The history of modern political rights is the history of the decline of property qualifications over these rights. The first persons to have political "voice," to have influence in an otherwise arbitrary government, were those able to demand it by virtue of ownership rights and the power entailed in those rights, namely, the ability to mobilize armed forces or the obligations accruing from economic relations, especially money lending. Later, in premodern parliaments, the bourgeoisie as a class gained political rights by virtue of its financial and commercial power. With the dissolution of feudalism, these rights were progressively extended to owners of the means of production and resources of specified smaller amounts. Only in the nineteenth century did the extension of political rights to all males in the industrial countries, by dint of the pressure of the organized working classes, begin to take place; and only in the twentieth century were those rights extended to women. With that extension came the arrival and definition of modern citizenship.[5]

The precondition of modern citizenship was the Industrial Revolution, which forced the growth of the modern nation-state. The expansion of capital to create domestic and overseas markets required a standing army and navy, which could be secured only through an increase in the national debt – which in turn gave rise to the need for an expanded tax base – and a legitimate means of enlisting troops. Numerous local and regional loyalties and identities, moreover, had to be transformed into a single national character. Coincident with these new conditions, the Industrial Revolution forced a broad transformation of property relations. During the nineteenth century the dispossession of the majority of the population of their means of production was gradually completed; forcing precapitalist subordinate classes and strata to become members of the working class or farm labourers. As an emerging element in civil society, the new working classes were without political rights; yet they were confronted by the demands of the state (taxes, military service, identity) within a property framework that favoured and defended corporate private property over property as labour-power. Much of the class conflict in this period, then, took the form of the struggle for civil rights and the franchise. By winning the franchise, the purported right to participate in the formation of public policy, the working classes were made to feel part of a system whose raison d'être was alien to it.

In the nineteenth and twentieth centuries, political rights were gradually extended to include all those able to sell their labour-power. Although political rights acquired the appearance of belonging to all regardless of property rights, private property remained the underlying principle. The legal foundation of personhood, and so of citizenship, is the right to possess as an individual; and the presupposition of citizenship is a civil society, a marketplace society, divorced from the state. In feudal times, the state and civil society were not completely separate. Some classes were at once "political" – that is, they had a political role by virtue of the class ("estate" is the proper name of this class with inherent political rights). Modern political systems are marked by the complete separation of the state from civil society – no political privileges, all are equal as individuals before the state – but this was not always so.

In most of the industrial nations the working classes had won the political rights belonging to constitutions grounded in civil rights in the first half of the twentieth century, but this victory gave them a political voice within a property framework that did not represent their interests – except as social reforms, as forms of countervailing rights. Liberal democracy constitutes the representative mechanisms for a civil society defined by a prevailing form of private property, with national and local peculiarities shaped by its history of class development and social conflict. As the prevailing form, corporate private property defines the chief relations of the system, while the conflict between different class demands, especially between those of capital and labour, lends the system its distinctive features. The rights to elect and be elected, then, are rights to participate in a government that must *in principle* represent the interests of the pre-eminent form of private property; they are rights within a framework of privileged private corporate property. By and large, the government legislates privilege as right, while the interests of the non-corporate sectors find expression more as compromises, concessions, or exceptions.

SOCIAL RIGHTS

These concessions, or countervailing rights, comprise the category of social rights, and they constitute diverse reforms with varied histories. Typically, they include a range of subsidized health services, state-financed primary and secondary education, social security mechanisms (such as disability and old age pensions, and unemployment and occupational accident insurance), employment standards, and trade union rights, including the right to strike. Although many of these rights existed in Europe and the United States before World War II, their most comprehensive and coherent development came in the postwar era in the shape of the Keynesian welfare state (KWS), the high point of social reformism within industrial nations.

Social rights arose with the coming of the working class; they reflect the exercise of the prevailing corporate private rights, which usurps land and other means of production from individual proprietors – allowing private rights to exist in the abstract but being largely unrealizable except as corporate private rights. The consequent dependence of the working classes on wage-labour – the subjection of the non-owners to the owners of the means of production – means that their rights as workers are not only subordinate but also contradictory to those of the corporation. This dependence also means that the chronic, and periodically large-scale, shortages of work that characterize capitalism always leave some and frequently many workers without the ability to satisfy their elementary needs. From this condition springs the demand for social reforms to protect workers from the vagaries of the labour market and corporate arbitrariness, and to allow for their social reproduction in periods of economic crisis.[6]

Chronic class conflict and the consequences of systemic economic inequality only partially account for the origin of social rights. Some of these rights spring more from the inability of capital relations to embrace all aspects of societal reproduction and the ensuing need for state subsidization or the "socialization" of the associated costs.

Whatever their origin, social rights in a system dominated by corporate private rights always represent compromises to the prevailing principles. They are rights dependent on state regulation and provision of goods and services, and therefore they contradict the principles of private property. Typically they are found in four arenas of government intervention: in the labour market (minimum-wage laws, unemployment insurance, trade union rights); in the workplace itself (employment standards, health and safety standards, collective bargaining); in the reproduction of the labour force (medicare, education, and the provision of food, shelter, and clothing); and in support of those defined as "unproductive" (child care, child benefits, old age pensions). These are the rights that infringe on such civil rights as individual "liberty," security of property, and justice as the vindication of the rights of private property.[7] For this reason, there is rarely any constitutional guarantee of social rights, or any state obligation to provide them. Their existence depends on class pressure and state legislation and provisionally funded programs; they are a product of the conditions and class tensions of an era and so constitute the short-term policies of presiding governments. For the most part, social rights do carry legal entitlement, but that entitlement is very much dependent on the political persuasion of the party in power and the history of class relations. All social rights are subject to the discretionary powers of the legislators in a way that constitutionally guaranteed civil and political rights usually are not.

For this reason, the exercise of many social rights comes with a price. The receiving of social assistance, for instance, has often been conditional on the loss of the ability to exercise certain civil and political rights. If to be a citizen is to be defined by private property rights, at the very least with regard to labour-power, then to be unemployed or unemployable can imply the forfeiture of "personhood" and therefore dignity and the means to exercise certain rights. While most social rights in the industrial nations today still have legal entitlement, their administration is often associated with an overriding sense of lost "personhood" for the recipient. Since the 1980s, however, even this legal entitlement has been systematically stripped away to remove the legal reality and sentiment of a right. To be more consistent with the rights of private property, although not with the ethos, many social rights have been transformed into forms of charity – a form of income redistribution in which rights become the privileges of donors.

It is an obvious irony that advocates of a system of private property and self-interest should want to place many social rights into the category of charity, thereby making those rights dependent on the altruism, empathy, and social conscience of citizens – that is, on individuals who are seen by these same advocates of private property as being defined by selfishness, egoism, and greed.

THE UNIVERSAL DECLARATION OF HUMAN RIGHTS

The first international expression of these three groups of rights in a coherent manner came with the United Nations' Charter and in particular the Universal Declaration of Human Rights (UDHR), which remain the seminal global expression of the equal status of all humans – albeit only as possessors of certain rights. No other similar document, not even from the League of Nations after World War I, precedes the Declaration. It was advanced by the Allied nations, the victors in World War II, and it is usually seen as reflecting in part the outcome of the Nuremberg and Tokyo War Crimes Tribunals. More broadly it has been seen as a statement of principles countering the restrictive nationalist ideologies, military aggression, and widespread atrocities associated with the governments of Fascist Italy, Nazi Germany, and Imperial Japan from the 1930s to 1945.[8]

While the UDHR may be taken as the assertion of certain principles as universal in response to the beliefs and actions of the Axis powers, the Declaration contains another significant embedded meaning. The Allied powers were not, after all, free of guilt in regard to militarism, beliefs in superiority, and abuses of subject peoples prior to the war. The colonies of Britain, Holland, France, and Belgium, and the client regimes of the United States, were more than familiar with military invasion, forced labour, and the destruction of ways of life and the lives of hundreds of thousands of innocent people prior to the 1930s (not to mention afterwards). The Allies, moreover, were not free of guilt in their wartime actions or postwar treatment of prisoners. The reason that Britain declared war in 1939 had nothing to do with the Axis atrocities, for the worst of those acts had not yet been committed.

The reason for declaring war in the first place more likely rests in the kind of political rule that had developed in the Axis nations. Underlying the formation of these autocratic governments were historical conditions that had not allowed for the full establishment of the relations between the state and civil society that had come to characterize liberal democracy.[9] Instead, in all three cases the state assumed a primacy over a fractious civil society, with significant spheres of precapitalist property relations that worked against the premise of a liberal-democratic state. This primacy took the form of the arbitrariness of absolute leaders; but absolutism creates a dilemma for capital because it is the negation of the rule of law, the rule of the abstracted relations of private property that underlies the liberal-democratic capitalist system.

Although many large corporations in both the Allied and Axis countries benefited from, and supported, these totalitarian governments, especially where the working classes through socialist or communist parties threatened to win political power, the contradiction of the principle of the rule of law by the principle of absolutism made for an uneasy relationship. However advantageous the corporate sector finds dictatorship or even totalitarianism from time to time, it can be tolerated only as an interim or temporary political form as long as capital remains relatively competitive. Despite beneficial reciprocal relations between corporate capital and the Axis regimes, once the state had defined itself as independent, as the embodiment of an "organic unity," its policies were then derived from ideas and philosophies (such as racial superiority and historical destiny) that were not necessarily related to the market, to the economy. The proclaimed "unity" of the social formation meant that civil and political rights, representative mechanisms, social organizations, and even religious institutions became seen as unnecessary and were fashioned accordingly, restricted, or abolished. No longer mere figureheads or managers for a framework of private property, the leaders now danced more or less to their own tune. It followed that arbitrary political pre-eminence put into question the primacy of corporate right.[10] The personal power of dictatorial leaders displaced the impersonal authority of politicians as managers of a property framework.[11]

By contrast, where civil society evolved into developed capitalist relations, the state framed these property relations with the rule of law. The relation between state and civil society here, taking the form of liberal democracy, allowed prevailing property rights to dominate in public policy. Liberal democracy is a political system that allows for more or less reform within the property umbrella of prevailing individual or corporate rights. Leadership here amounts to managing the general framework of the activities of the predominant corporations, while the ensuing class conflict is met with sufficient concessions or coercion to keep the system stable. The property relations remain as pre-eminent while the leaders, as administrators of the framework, come and go.

The UDHR, then, can be seen as a statement against autocratic rule, particularly against leaders who would exercise personal, national, religious, or ethnic ideas over economic rights. What the UDHR does is enunciate the principles that arise from the conflicts that characterize civil society and underlie the relation between the state and civil society. It constitutes the evolving ethical code of modern capitalism, in which is guaranteed the primacy of the economic by declaring individual (and by extension, corporate) rights as inherent, inalienable, and universal. Article 17 states, "Everyone has the right to own property alone …" By contrast, social rights were never made absolute or justiciable, as were civil rights. Article 22 states that "the right to social security" is limited "in accordance with the organization and resources of each State." Social rights were probably included at that time as a way of mitigating class struggle and so facilitating social reproduction in the postwar capitalist nation-state, as well as of providing a "human face" to the system that had failed in the 1930s and now increasingly faced the growth of socialism in the USSR, Eastern Europe, and throughout the former and remaining colonial world.

By most accounts, the UDHR has become part of customary law in international accords, treaties, and agreements; and by ratifying its two associated covenants, most states have bound themselves to respect the rights[12] found in these three documents, sometimes known together as the International Bill of Rights. Nonetheless, the nature of the two covenants (which were adopted by the UN in 1966, but not "entered into force" until 1976) reflect the relative importance given to the different subsets of human rights. On the one hand, the International Covenant on Economic, Social and Cultural Rights, which covers broad social rights, has no mechanism for enforcement and no complaint mechanism. Signatory nations to this covenant are obliged only to work towards its fulfilment "progressively" as their "maximum available resources" allow. If a nation has not ratified the accord, such as in the case of the United States, it has no such obligation.

Signatories to the International Covenant on Civil and Political Rights, on the other hand, are supposed to guarantee that these rights are "immediately enforceable." And this covenant has an Optional Protocol that allows the citizens of nations that have signed it to make representations to the UN Human Rights Commission. This "communication" with the Commission must be from an individual or representative who has allegedly suffered "a consistent pattern of gross violations" of one or more of the listed civil or political rights; it cannot come from a group or class of individuals. The final outcome is but a statement of views on changes to be made; there is no means of enforcement. Despite such limitations, the government of the United States waited years to sign the International Covenant on Civil and Political Rights, and did so then only after several reservations and declarations were made about it. Washington ratified it only in 1992.

This covenant at least provides a complaint mechanism, however circumscribed and complicated, for violations of civil and political rights, a mechanism that does not exist for violations of social rights. Even so, there is no legal aid offered to make these representations to this UN Commission; and what happens after such a communication has been made and received would constitute a travesty of most systems of judicial procedure.[13] It is probably safe to assume that the UN Human Rights Commission was never intended to be an expedient mechanism for the enforcement or advancement of human rights.[14] The Western powers, particularly the United States, well aware of their own discriminatory laws, preferred to treat human rights as distant goals rather than as justiciable standards.[15] The UN Commission has also never been free of political lobbying and partisan influence in its operation, even after the establishment of a UN High Commissioner for Human Rights in 1993.

The UDHR not only was a response to past and present threats but also provided a guide to the future in the making. Just as at the birth of the modern nation-state, when the principles underlying the capitalist mode of production and its liberal-democratic political form were heralded, so too in the immediate postwar period the principles of a new world order were proclaimed. In declaring that all humans inherently possessed civil and political rights, the UDHR was necessary as the ethical rationale for the expansion of capital across the world; it implied a system of private property for all and an end to colonialism, a world open to international corporate exploitation.

In fact, the UDHR can be seen as part of the "global enabling framework" established in the postwar period.[16] The economic structure of a global system of capitalism was first posed in 1944 at the Bretton Woods conference with the formation of the International Monetary Fund (IMF) and the World Bank, both designed to facilitate not only the reconstruction of capitalism after the war but also the economic exploitation of the postcolonial world. In 1947 these agencies were complemented by the creation of the General Agreement on Trade and Tariffs (GATT), a body intended to begin the formal removal of all barriers to trade and commerce between nations. The promotion of a political foundation for a global system was the function of the United Nations, formed in 1945. The principles of liberal democracy, as the political form corresponding to the capitalist mode of production, constituted the UN ideal and the goal of UN activities in the postcolonial world. But the framework lacked a statement of its fundamental principles, and this the UDHR provided in 1948 by declaring that the ethical precepts of capitalism were fundamental to all humans and by formally proclaiming that these rights were possessed by the people of the world.

The origins of human rights as we know them, then, do not rest in some sort of "social contract" purportedly countering a hypothetical "state of nature," or in moral imperatives, or in abstract principles of justice, or in ideal notions of human dignity or respect, or in fundamental human values. These rights are the compromised and evolving outcome of conflict and struggle between classes, strata, genders, and peoples over several centuries. In their present form they constitute the continually developing principles of a particular system; as the ethical basis of the relations of capital, they were promoted after World II in the form of the UDHR to enhance the legitimacy of capitalism, to help secure capitalist relations in the defeated nations, to counter socialism, and to retain the postcolonial nations within the emergent global capitalist system.

Despite the inherent relation of human rights to the capitalist mode of production, and their consequent political use and individualistic premise, there is embedded in the UDHR the first universal and authoritative proclamation of the oneness, the totality, the ecumenical nature of humanity, albeit as so many atomized individuals. For the first time in history, human beings everywhere were declared to be human beings, although it was as beings defined in the image of a particular system. In this dichotomy lies the fundamental paradox of the UDHR – a declaration of historical particularity in the guise of universality.

CHAPTER II

The Absolutes

It is no small irony that, despite their diverse historical origins, their reflection of capitalist ethics at a certain stage, and the continuing debates over their meaning, human rights have always been declared as absolutes. They are held up as defining what it means to be human; and they are characterized as equal in their possession, inherent in all individuals, indivisible, inalienable, and universal. An understanding of the meaning of human rights requires an examination of all of these claims.

THE HUMAN IN HUMAN RIGHTS

Implied in the concept of human rights is an unspoken presupposition about what it means to be *human*. In the context of human rights, to be human is merely to possess rights – and not just any rights, but the civil and political rights spelled out in liberal-democratic charters and declarations. The nature of the rights possessed defines the nature of the holders; these are individual rights held by individuals as sovereign beings; they define human relations as external, contractual, and self-interested. The human in the context of human rights, then, is nothing but the way the human being appears in a society based on contractual relations; it is the human defined as isolated individual, as whole unto itself, as singularity, as an unrelated atom; it is not the human as a social being, as a product of social relations, whose chief characteristic is relations to others. Social rights, though they may sometimes complement civil and political rights, are not usually considered a necessary part of the definition of human.

The citizens of liberal democracies are easily convinced that the concept of human being is simply a matter of self-relatedness because it reflects the central element of their reality. That is, the principles of their daily lives are based on contractual, self-interested relations that define the system in which they live and that must be followed if they are to maintain their material existence. The concept merely takes as human the character of exchange relations in capitalist society; and so the human in human rights is a concept specific to a mode of production that supposedly applies to all. To call the rights associated with the marketplace "human," then, is simply to assert something as being universal when it is actually historically specific.

People born into capitalist societies are made over in this image and live in a society that reinforces such relations. They are socialized to believe in the truth of a notion of human that belies the process of socialization itself. Made in the image of the marketplace, members of society are prevented from seeing that this concept of human precludes the entire range of social characteristics associated with human meaning derived from relationships – love, honour, passion, joy, dedication, loyalty, affection, selflessness, friendship, consideration. In a market society, these qualities often become the butt of jokes or the signs of naiveté; they are completely unrelated and inconsequential to life in a capitalist society.

The definition, moreover, excludes all those human beings who do not possess all civil and political rights. Until after World War II, this exclusion extended not only to women – to half of the adult population of the industrial world – but also, more generally, to the majority of the rest of the world – namely, to Aboriginal and colonized peoples. Even now, in practice, a sizable minority remains outside this definition of human being, despite the declared inclusive nature of human rights. Children have never been included as human beings in this definition. To be human only as a possessor of certain rights is to make being a human the privilege of some – namely, those who are fully liable in contractual relations in civil society, the arena of the pursuit of private interests in capitalist systems.

THE ASSERTION OF EQUALITY

Central to the historical significance of human rights declarations is the assertion of the *equality of rights*. To proclaim that all human beings are equal is to reject, in the definition of humans, all notions of religious, national, ethnic, gender, and other differences and inequalities that once were, and in some places still are, meaningful. More specifically, the assertion of equality means that with respect to the possession of civil and political rights a person's social status is of no consequence. As a counter to feudal rights at the time of the formation of the modern nation-state, that assertion was revolutionary, reflecting the principles of the ascendant bourgeoisie. After World War II, it was again necessary to proclaim universal equality not only as an antidote to the crimes perpetuated in the name of the racist ideologies that justified the military expansion, atrocities, and labour policies of the Axis powers, but also as an aid to opening the European colonial empires to international, and more particularly U.S., investment.

The notion of equality, however, is only an abstraction; no two humans are equal in any empirical way. The equality claimed for human rights applies only to the equal possession of rights; and there are two major limitations to this equality. One is that all rights remain abstractions unless people have the means to realize them and live in a system in which they can be realized. The other is that not all humans qualify as possessors of rights; those who are marginal to or outside capitalist relations or dependent on others – for example, indigenous peoples, Roma, children, and (still in many countries) women – are often excluded. Nonetheless, the idea of the equality of all can be see as a halting first step towards the recognition that all humans have something in common, even though it is posed as the possession of abstract rights rather than their social nature and creative potential.

RIGHTS AS INHERENT

Human rights are often declared to be *natural* or *inherent in the individual,* which is one way of portraying them as timeless, immanent, and independent of external causes, to establish them as absolutes. But far from being natural, these rights not long ago did not exist; indeed, they could hardly be dreamed of. Their evolution began not much more than a few centuries ago, and their existence as a coherent set is only about a half-century old. They are no more natural or inherent than was the divine right of kings; and in medieval Europe the belief in this right was as earnest and pervasive as the current belief in human rights.

Civil rights, as a product of a system of contract relations, were initially called "natural" or "eternal" to sanctify the demands of a capitalist class in the face of feudal privilege and obligations, as a means of proclaiming the principles of a new age. Their history makes it clear that they are relative to a particular mode of production and to the changing class struggles that characterize the evolution of that mode. The most cursory knowledge of the historical development of civil rights cannot be reconciled with the view that we are "born" with these rights.

Political rights similarly are a product of the arrival of private property as the prevailing form of holding land or goods, and the consequent separation of the social formation into two spheres: civil society and the state. Political rights, tied to the possession of private property rights, brought an end to the political privileges of the estates of medieval Europe. The gradual extension of these rights through the reduction of property qualifications brought into being modern political rights, but this development is the consequence of decades of struggle; political rights in themselves have nothing to do with anything natural to or inherent in human beings.

The same can be said about social rights; they too are a product of social struggle over a long period. But there is another point to be made here: social rights arise as a counter to prevailing corporate private rights, as demands for alleviation of the worst effects of capitalism or as a product of "market failure" or incapacity of some sort. Their structure usually involves the state creation of indemnity funds for redistribution comprising a portion of wages, and collected as taxes, premiums, and deferred income. As a product of the state, they always embody an element of socialized capital, capital outside the realm of private accumulation; as such they stand in opposition to the principle of private corporate rights. In other words, the first- and second-generation rights contradict each other, which means that one side in theory at least cannot be inherent.

In practice, as we have seen, no human rights are inherent. All three forms of rights have been and remain in a constant process of challenge, contestation, denial, rejection, and evolution; and this condition belies any suggestion of a natural or inherent status. All were initially fought for: civil and political rights were won from feudal institutions; social rights were won from private corporate rights. All evolve through struggle once the principle has been won. Civil and political rights were gradually extended to workers, Jews, women, indigenous peoples, Roma, and other minorities through the eighteenth to twentieth centuries; and social rights reached the pinnacle of their development in the welfare state of the late twentieth century. These rights are portrayed as only partially inherent in children. "Minors" are still seen as the possessions of their parents or wards of the state until they reach the age of "majority," when they are deemed able to become possessors of private rights.

RIGHTS AS INDIVISIBLE AND INALIENABLE

When human rights are said to be *indivisible*, the term is usually taken to mean that each category of right is equally important, that one category cannot be ranked above another or promoted above others, or violated in the interests of any other. The evidence suggests, however, that the component parts of human rights are continually being divided. Even the two main covenants outlining the first and second generations of rights point to significant differences in their status. Moreover, the two main human rights organizations, Amnesty International and Human Rights Watch, play roles defined by a dramatic differentiation between civil and political rights *and* social and other rights. The neo-liberal policies that inform government practice around the world are intended to undermine or eliminate social rights while leaving in place formal political and civil rights. The definition, promotion, and enforcement of human rights everywhere have always divided those rights into separate spheres with differential treatment.

In another reference to their supposedly absolute nature, human rights, in particular civil and political rights, are also commonly called *inalienable*. This condition implies that they cannot be surrendered, or taken away – their "ownership" cannot be transferred to another. Human rights, however, are continuously alienated in all kinds of ways, both legal and illegal. For the most part they are alienated by mainstream institutions and structures that represent or embody prevailing corporate rights.

Indeed, the alienation of the human rights of much of the world's population is an integral part of the global and national systems of capital accumulation. In the already profound and still growing inequality in the resources to realize these rights, for instance, those who have little or no revenue have few rights in practice – their rights are usurped by the structure of economic inequality itself. From the perspective of the corporation, in which the power of ownership is concentrated, the demand for human rights for all is answered in the paraphrase of an infamous line: let them eat abstractions.

The rights held by dominant capitalist classes around the world also impinge on or even contradict the rights held by other classes or groups. Because the state embodies the prevailing property relations, moreover, governments are often the most prevalent violators of human rights. This alienation of the rights of their own citizens is but a normal outcome of the contradictory nature of classes and their rights and the need to uphold the prevailing rights at the expense of the rights of non-corporate sectors. Every industrial nation has its own numerous examples of the abrogation of the civil, political, and social rights of its citizens in the name of upholding civil order, the framework of corporate private property. In many Third World countries, more often than not with the assistance of the U.S. government, state violations of human rights have led to lengthy periods of state terror: Chile, Argentina, and Guatemala are only a few among many examples.[1]

Similarly, on the global level, the structure of property relations and their institutional embodiment in a supranational "enabling framework" underlie large-scale violations of human rights around the world. The World Bank, IMF, and the World Trade Organization (WTO), in particular, all transgress and infringe on the rights of national states and their citizens.[2] They do this in the normal course of their activities, which is to facilitate international trade and create a global regulatory framework for administering economic relations on a transnational level. That framework is, to be clear, an administrative structure for capital alone – for corporate private rights and not for the exercise of any other rights included in various declarations or charters of human rights. The neo-liberal and structural adjustment policies that these institutions promote, demand, and enforce are all destructive of a wide range of human rights and of national rights and environmental regulations legislated by sovereign governments. Typically, structural adjustment policies have called for a retrenching of the public sector (which has meant the cutback of health, education, and social service programs and employment in this sector), the expansion of agricultural exports (which has meant the dispossession of farmers from the land and the decline of production for domestic use), and the devaluation of the national currency (which has made the price of goods and services extremely expensive for the lower strata of the working classes). Corporate rights for the most part stand in contradiction to all other rights.

The very structure of global trade – that is, the inequality of trade relations – also leads to enormous indebtedness, widespread corruption, and environmental destruction in Third World countries; and all of these conditions have consequences for the exercise of human rights.[3] The trade liberalization in agricultural products demanded of many Third World countries, for instance, can destroy whole ways of life when producers are confronted with the massively subsidized products of the United States and Europe.[4] Transnational corporations (TNCs), moreover, regularly violate civil and political rights around the world – so much so that they have given rise to numerous attempts at formulating codes of conduct to provide at least some protection to the economic, cultural, and political integrity of host nations and their citizens.[5] When nations resist subordination to the pre-eminence of corporate right, they face the possibility of military intervention by those states (in particular, the United States, Britain, and France) that most clearly represent the interests of TNCs. Unilateral interventions by the United States provide obvious examples of the enforcement of transnational corporate rights in violation of national civil, political, and social rights.[6]

Many charters, conventions, and declarations of human rights, moreover, include at least one clause that sets limits to the exercise of human rights – limits that can be determined by the government of the day. Even though the ability to legislate and enforce these limits may be conditional, the civil, political, and social rights proclaimed by a state can still be restricted by that same state. The same document declaring these rights to be inalienable often contains clauses that allow them to be alienated.[7]

THE ASSERTION OF UNIVERSALITY

Along with equality, the assertion of the *universality* of human rights stands at the heart of their historical significance – the claim that these rights are accorded to all humans everywhere. The declarations of equality and universality represent enormous historical steps because they assert opposition to all forms of discrimination – in fact, to any social, cultural, or biological element that distinguishes or separates human beings from one another. The notions of equality and universality together imply that we are all the same except for our respective achievements in life – notions that embody a clear denial and negation of the justifications underlying all forms of discrimination. Despite its significance in advancing this understanding, the purported universality is one of the most debated absolutes claimed for human rights

To be sure, the notion of universality implies that all humans share something, but what this sharing means within the realm of human rights is contradictory. If what we share is the possession of individual rights, then to have these individual rights in common is simply to celebrate the principle of separation from others as our "bond." It is of historic significance that the humans in human rights are made abstract equals, but what we "share" – what makes us equal – is the right to our isolation from each other.

The declaration of universality, moreover, runs into difficulty when we survey the full scope of claims to being human. Given that human rights are accorded to humans only as individual possessors of rights, they preclude multifarious social dimensions from the definition of human. The universality of human rights, moreover, does not extend to children, because in the world of human rights children are not "persons" in law. In a world of commodity production, universality would appear to apply only after the age at which a person becomes legally liable in a contract relation. Women the world over are also denied in law or in practice the full range of human rights.[8] The claim of universality is only defensible if one is willing to omit children and others who are not legally "persons" and to dismiss the social character of humanity and other notions of right belonging to other modes of production.

Despite obvious problems with the claim, the purported universality of human rights has a special importance for the governments of the dominant capitalist nations, which have strongly promoted the principle. In 1993 the World Conference on Human Rights in Vienna concluded with a declaration that one writer described as stating "categorically and repeatedly" that "the universal nature" of the rights and freedoms outlined was "beyond question" and that they were "universal, indivisible and interdependent and interrelated." The declaration indicated that "democracy, development and respect for human rights and fundamental freedoms are interdependent and mutually reinforcing."[9] The conference was heralded by Western states as "a victory for the universality of human rights." A short examination of these claims of victory helps to clarify why the West is so insistent on promoting the universality of human rights. The "democracy" referred to is liberal democracy, the political form that guarantees a framework of prevailing private (corporate) property while allowing for the appearance of the sovereignty of citizens. There is no sense of democracy as a participatory tool in the workplace or in the making of public policy. The "development" referred to is capitalist development, economic growth as capital accumulation; there is no suggestion that development might take place in the form of state capital or socialized capital directly controlled by working people. "Respect for human rights and fundamental freedoms" is respect for civil and political rights – the rights underlying liberal democracy and the capitalist mode of production. The reference does not suggest respect for social rights, that is, countervailing rights that most benefit working classes and subordinate peoples. Here, then, in the concept of human rights we can see relativity cast as universality.

For these reasons, the banner of human rights has been an important part of U.S. foreign policy. Especially after the Vietnam War, it has been used to rationalize U.S. activities around the world in opposing the threat of socialism or even national capitalist development to the unfettered movement of international capital. It has been used to justify U.S. intervention when it was needed to guarantee corporate interests. For U.S. foreign policy, human rights and "democracy" have become instruments rather than goals.[10]

The purported universality of human rights is, moreover, compromised in two significant ways. First, in a system of private property, the exercise of many rights requires the financial means to do so, and thus the relative amount of personal wealth determines the degree to which many rights can be exercised. Second, in any system the exercise of rights depends on the existence of corresponding mechanisms for their defence and advancement, and prosecution and adjudication of violations. When these mechanisms do not exist or only nominally exist, or exist mainly for some rights and not for others, the possibility of exercising rights is correspondingly limited.

The reality of the universality of human rights, then, is not possible to argue; and that is why it is usually merely asserted as if an existing truth. Human rights as defined in the UDHR are the abstract expression of the economic, political, and ethical principles of capitalist nations; before capitalism no such rights existed (except as evolving rights reflecting the rise of capitalist relations), and where capitalism does not exist, neither do these rights. They appear now to be more and more widespread because of the geographic expansion of the relations of capital that increasingly encompass most of the world. The declaration of the universality of human rights is the declaration of the principles of a particular mode of production that has long aspired to be universal, and is now on the verge of being so.

THE RELATIVITY OF HUMAN RIGHTS

The "triumph of capitalism" has not precluded a debate on the universality of human rights. A host of nations in Asia, Africa, and the Middle East, as well as many indigenous peoples, have made arguments that these rights are relative. Most of the reported objections to the notion of universality rest on the argument that these rights are the reflection of Western, Judeo-Christian values – a contention that has not met with much by way of effective refutation.

Some Third World nations have used the argument of relativism to justify child labour, the absence of labour and environmental standards, and political arbitrariness. The "comparative advantage" of these nations, runs the argument, depends on cheap labour and material resources and authoritarian government, and the application of human rights strictures would undermine these trade advantages vis-à-vis the industrial countries. Such a position is probably accurate, but it points to the incompatibility of human rights and the expansion of capital. Economists imbued with the morality of capital justify such arguments and make poverty and environmental despoliation into "comparative advantage." In 1991 World Bank economist (later president of Harvard) Lawrence Summers stated: "I think the economic logic behind dumping a load of toxic waste in the lowest wage country is impeccable .... I've always thought that underpopulated countries in Africa are vastly underpolluted."[11] The only beneficiaries of the "comparative advantage" of being poor and underdeveloped, and of the conscious violation of human rights, are the people in power in these nations and the TNCs that exploit the labour and resources.

Other Third World leaders have made a "communitarian" or "cultural" argument in reaction to the individualistic premise of the UDHR. Although the values of parts of the non-industrial world do continue to have a certain communal basis, that condition frequently becomes an argument for the presumption by the state to act on behalf of the "community" and to suppress political opposition to its abuse or illegitimate seizure of power. This argument has not been convincingly realized in the defence or respect of cultural integrity; rather, it has materialized as part of the use of state power to serve the interests of national elites and/or TNCs.[12]

Others have argued that human rights and the implicit liberal democracy, if set in place, would merely promote the divisions of ethnicity or tribe or religion, and make Third World countries all the more difficult to govern. The not infrequent use of such divisions, however, to maintain authoritarian or arbitrary rule in many of these countries raises suspicions about such an argument.[13]

Still, the argument for the relativity of rights should not be dismissed because it has been used to justify the abuse of power or the circumscription of rights in certain countries. Some governments may argue for relativity and some for universality, but no country is free of continuing violations. No government can point to the universal adherence of human rights under its jurisdiction.

Another source of the argument comes from nations interested in defending forms of national development that do not conform to the demands of TNCs. When countries take up policies of national development and public ownership or other non-corporate forms of property holding and industrial management, they can experience difficulties with the strict application of civil and/or political rights. Social rights and other forms of generalized power may be emphasized in their stead. Under Allende in 1970-73 Chile attempted one of many examples of national development. Its efforts embodied an instance of a certain national relativity of rights, while the U.S.-inspired coup d'état in 1973 was an example of the imposition of the universality of certain civil rights, in the form of corporate rights. It would appear that the United States sacrificed the universality of national political rights in order to abrogate social and other national rights and to make pre-eminent transnational corporate civil rights.[14] Here again was relativity parading as universality – which is the essence of Western states' insistence on the universality of human rights.

The argument for relativism also comes from those indigenous peoples who maintain non-capitalist modes of production, live in ways marginal to the relations of capital, or have been dispossessed of their means of production (land, water, wildlife). In general, they argue for property relations that are based not on individual ownership rights but on collective rights.[15] The demand for Aboriginal rights always implies non-alienable group rights over a certain territory – a form of right not compatible with a system of alienable private property. Any assertion of collective rights runs counter to the premise of individualism in the human rights of the capitalist mode of production.

If there is no reality to the declared universality of human rights, the continuing emphatic insistence on the claim raises the question of its meaning. Taken literally, it is but a corporate caricature of what it means to be human extended to the world; the human in human rights is the loneliest of atoms. Taken metaphorically, however, the claim of universality was the clarion call of a new age after World War II, an age in which capital began to throw off its national dress in order to continue to expand and to confront the growing appeal of socialism by offering its citizens more rights within the framework of corporate private property.

Before 1945 the Soviet Union was one of the very few nations that could at least make claims for universal rights for its citizens and national and ethnic groups, although we now know that the reality for its citizens did not correspond. In the West, some nations did make national declarations on civil and political rights, but assertions of universality were never matched in legal statutes or common practice; and the expansion of capital as national corporations outside the nation-state was often justified on grounds of implicit or explicit superiority of nationality, race, religion, or ethnicity. In this expansion, however, national capitals collided with other national capitals, resulting in the two devastating world wars. The end of World War II signified the beginning of the end of national capitals struggling for supremacy and the arrival of the era of the expansion of capital as such – the global corporation *sans* nationality, on the world stage.

The UDHR represents the implicit recognition that capital could no longer expand with its national prejudices and restrictions. It marked the call of the growing capitalization of the world by a capital increasingly generating itself at the global level. The declared universality of human rights reflected the aspiration of capital freeing itself from its national shells and from a world divided into colonies and spheres of influence. The so-called "economic, social and cultural" rights were included in the UDHR because that document emerged in the context of the lessons of World War II, the social unrest of the 1930s, and the postwar growth of socialism, but Western governments generally did not consider the declaration of those rights to be much more than the promulgation of fine-sounding phrases.[16] In the UDHR the relativity of the rights of modern capitalism was proclaimed as universal.

In general, the inconsistencies, limits, and restrictions found in the absolutes claimed for human rights suggest that they only exist relative to a mode of production and to changes in that mode. It is the most obvious of historical observations to say that rights are different in different modes of production. It is for this reason that rights can and do collide when different modes overlap or are "articulated" – which continues to be the case now, with the corporate rights of global capitalism confronting social rights, Aboriginal rights, customary and religious practices, and rights that arise in a system of socialized capital. By their nature, rights have no absolute qualities.

Within any given mode of production, rights, more specifically, are the reflection of the contestation over the production and distribution of the social product; they embody class or group relations and conflict.[17] From this it follows that all rights evolve over time. Even the continuing insistence on the universality of the UDHR merely corresponds to the ongoing pursuit of the capitalization of the world.

After a certain point in history, however, the expressed universality of the UDHR began to be contradicted by the change in rights demanded by the evolution of capital. Global corporate right requires regionally or globally asserted civil or economic rights, and those rights in turn need to be guaranteed by national states that not only suppress social rights but also admit political rights only to the degree necessary to allow citizens to choose the political colour of their oppression.

CHAPTER III

The Contradictions

All human communities are defined by the structure of their rights, which find expression as uncodified customs, traditions, norms and values, as formal codified laws or as a hybrid. Here, following an accepted definition, I take rights to mean entitlements or claims to do something, to use or dispose of goods and services. As entitlements, by definition rights are the embodiment of forms of socially legitimated power, whether in the form of custom or law. Although threats and the use of coercion have always been important sources of power, the main immediate source in all social formations rests in rights.

These rights and the associated powers, moreover, may belong or extend to different groupings. A collectivity embracing a whole population may possess rights communally, that is, as an aggregate unit. Other rights may extend to narrower social units such as a band, a clan, or family, or to social categories such as children or the disabled or the elderly. They can be possessed even more narrowly, as private property – that is, as exclusive individual rights (including corporations as fictitious individuals), the dominant form of property relation in a capitalist mode of production.

Although the concept of property can refer to a thing, its use here refers to a *relationship* to a thing; in this sense property refers to a right or claim or entitlement to the use and disposal of goods and services. This meaning of property, then, becomes synonymous with the meaning of right. That is why, for instance, with the advent of the welfare state after World War II legal circles engaged in discussions about the "new property," which was a reference to newly legislated entitlements to government goods and services, in the form of housing, pensions, medicare, social assistance, and so on.

The set of rights or property relations that characterize a social formation find their source in the social division of labour. They reflect the ways in which people produce and distribute the means of their subsistence. The inequalities inherent in a social formation and the social conflict that arises from the division of labour, as well as the attendant power relations, are reflected in the nature and structure of the system of rights. Inasmuch as these inequalities reflect the relative balance of power, so too is that balance reflected in the shape of the formal or defined rights of that social formation. Historically, formal or codified rights were always explicitly unequal until the bourgeois revolutions of the eighteenth and nineteenth centuries, when the claim of equality of rights for all first appeared.

In proclaiming equal rights for all as individuals, the UDHR gave voice to a vision of the world in which there were no inequalities of right. On the one hand, then, the UDHR and subsequent related documents encouraged humans to think of themselves as equals, if only in the possession of abstract rights. As a result, these declarations have been the grounds for great hopes for colonial nations, working classes, indigenous peoples, and women, among others. On the other hand, the growing social and economic inequalities associated with capitalism are perpetuated through the exercise of private rights, of civil and political rights. The belief of equality of rights, then, has gone a long way towards obscuring the pervasive and real inequalities that are intrinsic to the capitalist mode of production because the equality of rights is strictly abstract.

Human rights, then, throw a shroud over the cause of the inequalities of the system because it is in the exercise of these civil and political rights that inequalities are realized, while, at the same time, human rights in the abstract are the declared paragon of human equality. The inequalities and inconsistencies in human rights themselves *and* the contradiction between these abstract rights and the inequalities of real life are all veiled by the widely held belief in the inherent equality and universality of human rights. The analysis of some of the key inconsistencies in human rights reveals their relative nature and ideological function more clearly.

IN PRINCIPLE

The Contradiction in Private Property

The American Convention on Human Rights (1969) is perhaps the only official human rights document that includes a statement explicitly acknowledging this contradiction. Article 32 (2) states: "The rights of each person are limited by the rights of others, by the security of all, and by the just demands of the general welfare, in a democratic society."[1] To be sure, the rights referred to here are civil rights: in particular, the right to private property, the most fundamental of human rights. The clause points out that the exercise of exclusive individual civil rights finds barriers in the exercise of the same rights by others or in the protection of general interests. Indeed, the principle and practice of private property represent the right "to exclude others" from the enjoyment of personal possessions. The freedom of one individual to exercise the rights of private property ends when it comes up against the freedom of another. It is a self-contradictory notion of liberty in which each person's freedom negates that of every other person and the general welfare – or the more freedom (rights) possessed by one, the less by others.

The freedom of the individual as possessor of private property is only fully realizable when no other right confronts that freedom, or when all other rights are subordinated to it. This is the reason why private property rights lead its possessors to see in all other individuals the limits to their freedom, the limits to the exercise of their individual rights. The very nature of a system of private property leads each person to exclude all others from the enjoyment of privately owned goods and services, except through mutual exchange; it also reproduces its possessors as solitary individuals and stands opposed to all relations implying unity, communality, or social bonds of any sort, except those based on contract or material self-interest.

This contradiction rests at the heart of the system of private property. Given that exclusive rights are also competing rights, the system necessarily results in the expansion of some individuals' rights at the expense or subordination or usurpation of others' rights. Competition cannot form the basis of an equality of material well-being; it can only produce a social formation of social and material inequalities. The inevitable outcome of a system of exclusive rights is always a structure of unequal wealth and power, resting on the legally defined abstract equality of private, individual, competing rights.

The Corporation and the Individual

Within civil society, this contradiction within private rights is most obvious in the conflict between corporate and individual civil rights. In the struggle against feudal obligations, the rights of individuals to work for themselves and to benefit from the product of their own labour were very significant factors because they constituted a legal guarantee for the existence of free farmers, artisans, and other holders of private property in the means of production. As the decay of feudalism accelerated so too did the accumulation of private, moveable capital, which, when invested in the means of production (including land) and distribution, gradually deprived self-employed artisans of their independent means, dispossessed farmers of their holdings, and bankrupted small merchants. The process of dispossessing the labour force of its independent means of production was the making of the working class; and at the same time it transformed the civil rights of the individual as self-reliant and self-supporting. Given the necessity of finding employment in order to survive, the actual producers had to relinquish the right to control the use or disposal of their own labour-power, and the right to the product of that labour. These rights were transferred to the employer, and later to the corporation, the purchaser of the labour-power. The rights that initially belonged to independent commodity producers became for them largely abstract with their transformation into workers, while for the corporations those rights became in practice their privileges.[2]

The history of the legal incorporation of aggregated capital is different in different countries, but the end result everywhere is by and large the same. Governments have granted the corporate form the fictional legal status of an individual, conferring certain civil rights of the individual on the corporation. Incorporation grants what were initially the civil rights of independent, individual capitals to the embodiment of collective capital, the corporation. But this bestowal is not simply the extension of the legal definition of "person" to the corporation; when corporate capital arises it does so in opposition to individual capital. If all capital remained divided in small, independent forms, there would be no corporate form, because the corporation is formed and grows in part through the concentration and centralization of small capitals, as it does in part through the purchase of labour-power. Corporations can only exist by usurping these independent self-supporting forms and "freeing" the labour force tied to them. A petty-commodity mode of production is marked by *individual* private rights to the product and means of production, while a capitalist mode of production is characterized by *corporate* or aggregated private property. The success of incorporated collective, rather than individual, capital becomes the modus vivendi of the system. On the surface, then, while the employment contract in a capitalist system appears as a contract between two equal possessors of civil rights, there is in fact a contradiction in that one is buying the rights of the other, and this other has no choice but to sell – to one or another employer.

The contradiction arises from the act of incorporation, with its granting of individual private property rights to the corporation as if it were an individual. But the corporation is an individual only in a juridic fictional sense; in reality, it is a joint entity that represents forms of organized, collective capital, in contrast to the individual commodity producer (artisan, farmer, merchant), who represents individual ownership over the means of production (which has always implied strict limitations to the development of industry, trade, or commerce). Armed with civil rights, the corporation, as a form of the accumulated wealth of the community or communities in private hands, receives the right to employ this pooled capital for the benefit of a small number of owner-investors and managers without regard to the fate of employees or the community. It can do whatever it wants to do with the capital, within the confines of state regulations. In the name of the rights of private property, then, corporations can bankrupt small businesses and destroy communities (by closing factories, mines, or mills, moving equipment, or investing elsewhere). They can damage the health of workers and communities by polluting the environment, and they can even impoverish whole countries.

Capitalism is not a system of small, disparate individual capitals; it is a system of organized collective capital. Although in principle it rests on private rights belonging to all as individuals, in practice these rights are also embodied in the corporation, which usurps many of the rights of the non-incorporated. The rights belonging to the incorporated form of capital constitute the raison d'être of the system; and modern liberal democracy protects the rights of corporations as individual rights in the very constitution of the state, through the courts, and in the institution of the rule of law; and the operation of the economy provides for the ascendancy of incorporated capital over other forms of capital. The constitutional guarantee of individual rights originally reflected a system of independent commodity producers, but in a capitalist system it translates into protection of the largest embodiment of such rights – the corporation.

This protection is not merely constitutional. It also comes in the form of extensive legislative protection for corporations against themselves (for example, the regulation of competition, and bankruptcy) and against trade unions, consumers as individuals, or groups, investors, and other victims of corporate mismanagement or criminal actions. As well, governments provide massive subsidies, both direct and indirect, to promote corporate growth, which amount to a redistribution of public monies from one class to another; and they also establish and maintain police and military forces to secure the pre-eminence of corporate rights.

Because of the centrality of the principle of private property to the system, its embodiment in incorporated capital, and its consequent importance in law and politics, any criticism of the harmful effects of the more or less unrestrained movement or operation of corporate capital becomes something akin to sacrilege. Workers' strikes, even for living wages or health and safety regulations, can be seen to be dangerous to the system, and a threat to private property in general, because they challenge the viability of the corporation. The danger is magnified when workers combine their labour-power into a collective form to confront collective capital in the workplace, or when they combine their political voices in the form of a party that advocates state-owned corporations or facilitates the collective activity of workers to confront corporate right and its constitutional basis. The exercise of civil, political, and social rights by workers and other elements of the non-corporate sectors becomes largely secondary to, or even subversive of, the private rights of the corporation. Using constitutionally based civil rights, the corporation has by and large legalized its authoritarian role in the workplace and its right to take the wealth of a community, region, or country (in the shape of resources or value-added goods and services) and invest where it pleases and distribute profits to a small number of owner-investors.

In contemporary capitalist social formations, control over the realization of most civil rights has passed into corporate hands. Private rights over individual possessions now extend by and large only to consumer goods, given that the value of most means of production has long been well beyond the reach of working people, making an independent means of existence unlikely except for a few. Even the most expensive consumer goods and services – houses, cars, holidays, education – are more often than not purchased on credit.[3] The right to security is by and large the right to security of possessions; and this again concerns mainly the rich and the corporate sector. The role of the police in the defence of corporate private property during workers' strikes or in the dispatch of their duties in well-to-do residential areas, compared to their role in working-class or poor neighbourhoods, reflects this right. The right to justice is profoundly circumscribed by the cost of lawyers and the courts. Freedom of speech has been all but appropriated by corporate control and the self-serving use of the media in film, radio, television, and book, newspaper, and magazine publishing. Freedom of assembly is increasingly constrained by the enclosure of "public" functions in private spaces, such as shopping malls, private highways, land, and buildings.

This growing usurpation by corporations of the possibility of realizing individual civil rights is advancing more or less rapidly everywhere. As a consequence of globalization and associated neo-liberal policies, there are, in all but a tiny number of nations, attempts to make all aspects of the social allocation of goods and services dependent on so-called market principles. In effect this means that the production and distribution of all goods and services not already in private corporate hands are being shifted from the public to the private sector, the realm of exclusive corporate accumulation. With this transfer, the possibilities for exercising civil (and social) rights pass increasingly into the hands of the corporation. As the global means of production and distribution become controlled by fewer and fewer corporations, the possibility of realizing civil rights by anyone anywhere becomes dependent on corporations. As a result, the institution of private property that frames the constitution of the liberal-democratic state increasingly represents in practice only the civil rights of the corporate sector; and the exercise of individual civil rights is progressively at variance with the expansion of the corporation.[4]

The essence of the modern capitalist nation-state has always been the defence and advancement of corporate rights; and these rights in their most sizable and collective form usually define the very character of the nation. In the United States it was said, "What is good for General Motors is good for America." In Canada a well-known book about the building of the privately owned Canadian Pacific Railway was entitled *The National Dream*. The witticism that Canada was a railway (a private corporation) in search of a nation lost its meaning only after World War II, with the diversification of resource industries and the construction of new means of distribution. Inasmuch as corporate rights have a shared prominence with social rights, embodied in the form of state-owned public goods and services, the character of the nation may well possess a corresponding sense of state-sponsored social responsibility alongside the private corporate interests that dominate.

Because corporate rights are the dominant interests, the security of the nation or the protection of the national interest is really nothing more than the security or protection of the rights of the major corporations, framed by the composite national property relations. The state, then, defends corporate rights against the conflicting domestic demands of subordinate corporations and, more particularly, of subordinate classes or peoples arguing for non-corporate civil, social, and collective rights. As for the national interest abroad, corporate rights must be defended against foreign demands for protected or socialist development. To defend corporate rights, military expenditures at home and abroad become a political priority in government spending, undermining other expenditures. Spending on the military and police has always had as its hidden rationale unequal civil rights and, as their consequence, the truncated provision of social rights.[5]

In the United States corporate right corresponds to an assumed particular right of the sovereign individual in at least one issue. The corporate right to produce and distribute small arms coincides with the individual's presumed "right to bear arms" in Article II of the amendments to the U.S. Constitution.[6] This relationship helps to perpetuate the continuing structure of civil society: the persisting dominance of the organized corporate sector is in part dependent on the maintenance of the fractured and divisive relations among the non-corporate sectors of civil society. The interpretation of Article II as the "right to bear arms" for individuals is one guarantee of the disjunctive existence of the non-corporate sectors. It is a "right" that hinders the building of organized, co-operative bodies with common interests, in the form of trade unions or social movements, to confront the prevailing organized sector of civil society, corporate capital, and its organized representative in the form of the state. This "right" confirms a system in which each citizen sees in every other citizen a possible enemy, in which fear and distrust and mere self-interest are taken as natural, and common interests are obscured.

The proliferation of small arms around the world in part performs the same function. The industrial countries help create and maintain civil societies everywhere as disintegrated, fragmented arenas of competition between and amongst corporate and non-corporate sectors.[7] In this context, corporations can extract resources and exploit labour-power while minimizing costs, and the non-corporate sectors are incapacitated by the weight of the wide distribution of small arms, the promotion of the "right" or need to possess them, and paramilitary or mercenary units as corporate/state proxies hired to protect corporate interests and sow terror.[8]

Civil Rights and Social Rights

Although civil and social rights are both components of the UDHR and co-exist in the rights regimes of the industrial world, in theory and practice they contradict one another. Civil rights are in principle exclusive while social rights are inclusive; civil rights imply individual rights to the social product, while social rights imply generalized rights to the social product – rights resting on a degree of socialization of the social product but still within a system of private property. The underlying principles for one are private and individual, and for the other public and universal. Although the two may co-exist with social rights as concessions, the contradiction lies in the logic that the complete realization of one side would preclude the existence of the other.

Civil rights reflect the premises of the system; they constitute a guide to making law and to "justice" and to the administration of government. The role of the state is to legislate, maintain, and enforce the property relations of civil society; and civil rights are the measure or standard against which the activities of the capitalist state are assessed. Social rights, on the contrary, reflect the contradictions within the system; they are attempts to address vagaries in the ability of the market to reproduce the system. Inasmuch as goods and services in a system of private property – including essentials such as food, clothing, housing, education, and health care – are primarily produced and supplied as commodities, via the marketplace, their enjoyment is necessarily restricted by the price mechanism. Access to these goods and services can be minimized or even denied by the intrinsic inequalities of the system. Social rights attempt to redress this "shortcoming" in the market; posed as rights, they contradict the normal outcome of the exercise of civil rights.[9]

If the market fails to provide for social reproduction, or if popular forces in civil society, particularly class-conscious working classes, become sufficiently organized to demand countervailing rights that threaten the prevailing corporate rights, then the state will act to make concessions or to suppress social, political, and non-corporate civil rights. Military dictatorships, or short-term emergency laws in capitalist countries, suppress the rights of the working and other classes and groups while leaving corporate rights intact. There are numerous examples, particularly in Third World countries, of how governments defend and advance corporate rights at the expense of all other rights. When the powers in place have contained social unrest and/or maximized the exploitation of resources, elements of liberal democracy and rule of law may be re-established. Despite appearances, however, those political structures merely allow for alternating caretakers of a framework of prevailing corporate rights – within which certain concessions are made for the sake of social stability.[10]

At the heart of this contradiction is the fact that the corporation is collective capital. As such, it is the driving force of growth and the main embodiment of private property, the principle of civil society. Accorded the status of an individual, albeit a fictitious individual, the corporation gains constitutional guarantees of civil rights. Other collectivities do not possess such guarantees because they are not aggregations of private capital and so are not granted that same status. What rights they may acquire always take the form of countervailing rights, as in the case of trade unions and their rights, employees and employment standards, and a long list of groupings and their corresponding entitlements, including consumer rights, children's rights, women's rights, and the rights to primary and secondary education and to medical treatment. All of these countervailing rights conflict with the exercise of corporate right. In principle corporate right stands at odds with the rights of almost every other component of civil society.

Corporate Right and Civil Society

That corporate right stands at odds with the rights of almost every other component of civil society is a point grasped by Adam Smith at the beginning of the industrial era. He stated: "The interest of the dealers [capitalists] ... in any particular branch of trade or manufactures, is *always* in some respects different from, and even opposite to, that of the public." And their "interest is *never* exactly the same with that of the public, [they] have generally an interest to deceive and even to oppress the public, and [they] accordingly have, upon many occasions, both deceived and oppressed it."

In 2001, thirty-nine pharmaceutical companies took the South African government to court to challenge legislation allowing the importation of cheaper generic drugs, especially for the treatment of AIDS, and to license the manufacturing of patented medicines at lower prices. This legislation, they argued, violated their international patent protection agreements. In effect, they were demanding that corporate rights over production, distribution, pricing, and the profits derived from this business came before the well-being of the millions of sufferers impoverished with HIV/AIDS who could not afford the cost of name-brand drugs. The suit was abandoned when it engendered worldwide disapproval, and when the legal case promised to force the companies to reveal certain "business secrets, including pricing policies, profit levels, and the source of funding for research into key anti-AIDS drugs."

In this exposé of corporate rights, the role of the U.S. state as global protector of TNC interests was also unveiled. "The Clinton administration backed the drug companies and put South Africa on a 'watch list' of nations declared patent pirates." South Africa was later dropped from the list when it convinced the U.S. government that its law did not violate the patent rights of these corporations.

• A. Smith, *Wealth of Nations*, p.203, emphasis added; *The Guardian*, April 19, 2001; *The Financial Times*, April 19, 2001; *The Guardian*, March 14, 2001.

Political Rights and Corporate Civil Rights

Another contradiction exists between the rights of an individual to vote, stand for election, and petition the government *and* the property relations that form the basis of the constitution. The prevailing property relations in a liberal democracy – those that inform the rule of law – are most importantly civil rights; but the majority of the population, as employees, are not able to exercise, as civil rights, their essential interests regarding the disposition or product of their labour; these are rights that the corporation has purchased in the employment contract. Unless there are political parties that advocate an end to corporate private property, this state of affairs means that the majority must always vote or stand for a party that necessarily acts against its own interests, or at best provides concessions to those interests. In a class system, universal enfranchisement and the principle of "one person one vote" obscure the difference in meaning that the same right holds for persons of one class (those who live from the revenue of capital and/or manage capital) and those of another class (the broad working classes, whose livelihoods are subordinate to capital). A populist argument to circumvent this contradiction is to reconstruct a society of small, self-employed producers; but with the establishment of industrial capitalism, the rights of corporate capital cannot be dissolved into the dispersed precapitalist individual rights of ownership without destroying the achievements of that industrialism. The demand today for rights of ownership by workers over their labour and product of labour necessarily translates into demands to socialize the already collectivized, albeit private, assets of the corporation.

A political party genuinely representing the interests of the working-class majority would have to follow policies that run contrary to the prevailing rights. It would face the dilemma of seeking electoral success within the framework of the system that it would be seeking to overturn. In other words, the possibility of popular sovereignty in a liberal democracy is countermanded by a property framework that embodies the sovereignty of corporate private property. At the heart of this contradiction is the question: popular sovereignty or corporate sovereignty? In principle, the two cannot co-exist; in practice, working people can attempt only to exact concessions within the highly restrictive framework defined by the interests of the corporate sector.

The expansion of corporate civil rights also contradicts the existence of political rights. Given the concerted pursuit of neo-liberal policies from about 1980, the public sectors in all countries – state-supported education, medical care, pensions, insurance, transportation, highways, electrical power – have been moved systematically and progressively towards privatization and deregulation. The state intervention in civil society that reached its high point in the late 1960s in the Keynesian welfare state has been consciously undermined and gradually dismantled. The more that the public sector is placed into the private sector, the more that these public goods and services, which were once the subject of government policy, are removed from the possibility of political control. Public access to information about the public sector, moreover, even though always restricted, does not apply to the private sector; through privatization and deregulation, then, citizens are increasingly deprived of knowledge about important economic and social matters. Decision-making power over these formerly public goods and services has been passed to the corporate sector. It is not the public interest but the private interests of the few that underlie the policies of corporate ownership and determine the direction and form of economic expansion.

This contradiction between political rights and corporate civil rights is exacerbated by the regional and global operations of the most significant corporations, which take place within the confines and with the support of semi-sovereign quasi-state agencies at those levels to demand and promulgate the policies they want. What they achieve is at the expense of the power of the national state and whatever limited expression of the "will of the people" that may be found there.

In the North American Free Trade Agreement (NAFTA) of 1994, for instance, Chapter 11 gives a corporation the right to challenge a host of national, provincial/state, and municipal laws and policies. A "regulatory takings" clause allows a corporation to claim that its potential future earnings were damaged by a law or regulation and to sue the government for compensation. Chapter 11, moreover, provides for a treaty-based dispute mechanism, a special tribunal, to hear complaints and decide on compensation. This "investor-to-state" dispute panel is not accountable to duly elected governments, and yet it can determine the amount of compensation and award what may be huge sums of public money to corporations that successfully make their cases.[11]

The case of Hong Kong also provides an example of how these issues work in practice. Until 1997 and its return to the People's Republic of China (PRC), Hong Kong was a city state governed by a colonial administration appointed from London. Beginning in 1950, Hong Kong rose to become a major manufacturing centre, particularly in the production of clothing and textiles and later plastics and electronics. Complementing this export-based production, the city also became a significant world financial centre. A growth in tourism completed the picture of a dynamic economic centre. But economic power and the accompanying civil rights were concentrated mainly in the hands of a few British corporations and large local interests. The British government granted no political rights of any consequence, at least until the end of the colonial regime in the 1980s, when London began to encourage the democratic aspirations of the people, both to create difficulties for the PRC and to suggest that the British government itself was interested in democracy for its colony. The very limited political rights of people in the colony made it a corporate nirvana for a handful of businesses; as an outpost of corporate rights with a voiceless and compliant labour force, it was declared a near realization of the ideal of "economic freedom." As *The Economist* reported:

> The Heritage Foundation, an American think-tank, crowned Hong Kong "the world's freest economy" for the seventh year in a row. Yet this followed a report a week earlier from the European Parliament, which declared that Hong Kong was anything but economically free. The parliament's concern was that a few local business tycoons are powerful enough to keep new entrants at bay, by fair means or foul.[12]

The ideal of Hong Kong came at the expense not only of the civil rights of corporations outside the inner circle but also of the political and civil rights of its population – facts that invariably went unmentioned by corporate-financed think-tanks and business magazines.

Human Rights and Institutionalized Religion

The human rights of the UDHR, and its two covenants and associated declarations, represent the evolving, summary, abstract affirmation of the outcome of several centuries of struggle by various classes, strata, groups, and peoples, first against privilege and arbitrariness in precapitalist systems and then against inequalities within a system of private property. As such, they stand as the clearest embodiment of the ethics of contemporary capitalism. These ethics, specific principles of conduct, make the standards of the marketplace the core of civil rights, and offer the right of political participation – but only to the solitary, atomized individual of civil society, and only as a choice between policies of private accumulation within a framework of private property. A set of concessionary social and environmental rights completes this ethical system, providing the means of tempering the social instability and human and ecological degradation resulting from the principles and operation of market relations and from the vacillating ability of the market to provide for the social reproduction of various sections of the population.

Despite the estranged nature of the ethics of capitalism, what marks it as historically progressive is the extension of these civil, political, and social rights in the UDHR to all adults as abstract equals. This extension implies the equal worth of all individuals, which is precisely the point that makes human rights contradictory to all the major institutionalized religions – Islam, Hinduism, Christianity, Buddhism, Confucianism, and Judaism. All of these belief systems are similarly the product of evolution over many centuries, and their creeds or articles of faith continue to be revised today; but none of them has yet managed to embrace the abstract equality underlying the ethics of modern capitalism.

This failure is most evident in their treatment of women. Not a single major religion professes a creed in which women are portrayed as the abstract equals of men. To the contrary, all of the prevailing doctrines depict women as inferior or subordinate to men, sometimes in very demeaning language.[13] Women are denied equal rights in religious practices; their subservient social roles are rationalized in religious dogma; and in their communities they suffer a variety of acts of violence, humiliation, and inequity justified by religious teachings. For the most part, the history of the major contemporary religions contains long sagas of brutality towards women. Such views and practice are the obverse of the perception and role of the male, who is either the dominant or the only *subject* in these religions. Given the religious indoctrination of most of the world's peoples, these institutions stand as perhaps the pre-eminent ideological forces in the perpetuation of the presumption of the dominance of male right.

Although the teachings and practices of the major religions contradict the equality of rights for women in the UDHR, the subordination of women in capitalism (and in the state capitalism that passes for socialism) is of such significance in maintaining unequal relations of power that enormous amounts of time and money are spent on keeping women subordinate. In the ideological reinforcement of this subordination, religious doctrines on women serve an important function. Equality of rights may be a central aspect of the formal ethics of capitalism, but the practice for women is anything but equal. Precapitalist or medieval ideas about the nature of women in modern religious guise serve to justify the economic extra-exploitation of women, in employment and in the home, as employees and as mothers and wives and prostitutes and mistresses.

The postwar social transformations spawned by capitalism – which have forced the employment of women and children, undermined the family, and given rise to a secularized society – have to a certain extent among the major religions encouraged ecumenism, liberalization, and changing views on women. But religious ethics change slowly and invariably lag behind demands by subordinate groups for social justice; and with respect to women, all of the major religions remain patently conservative forces that contradict women's rights as human rights. In preserving the dominance of the male they reaffirm the subordination of women and help provide the justification for women's unequal exploitation.

If for the most part the major religions do not wholly acknowledge the equality of women, they are at least showing movement in that direction. That is not the case with respect to the rights of the child. In the 1989 UN Convention on the Rights of the Child, Article 13 states, "The child shall have the right to freedom of expression." Article 14 reads, "State Parties [the signatory governments] shall respect the rights of the child to freedom of thought, conscience and religion." The practice of institutionalized religions has not generally shown respect for these rights; the religious indoctrination of children well before the age of majority is common practice and indeed of central importance to the continuation of organized religion. Religion is a belief system dependent on faith, the "assent of the mind to the truth of what is declared"; it is not grounded in reasoned argument or empirical evidence. The indoctrination of young minds with religious teachings reflecting the ideologies of the iniquitous systems that gave rise to them violates the innocence of children and undermines their ability to develop free of intolerance and open to reason.

These violations in effect produce beliefs that are simply inculcated in the young mind as dogma; and, learned during the formative years as attitudes, ideas, and feelings, these beliefs become one of the most difficult things from which to free oneself. Assumptions of male dominance and female subordination, obedience to authority, and an acceptance of fate are among the most common features. A belief in the "ordained" nature of the social order, the idea of justice and plenty in another life, conditional on certain conduct in this life, and love in the abstract but intolerance in real life are others. Indoctrinated children become proponents of a set of religious beliefs and learn to see themselves apart from people of other religions, even though the only difference is a difference in religious indoctrination.

Institutionalized religions also show a disrespect for human immaturity or vulnerability in other ways. Physical abuse of the innocent in the context of formal religions has a long history and remains endemic.[14] Examples abound within the Christian churches, particularly in their historical treatment of institutionalized indigenous children, and in the abuse perpetuated by individual priests, nuns, and ministers who by virtue of their position and its ordained qualities were endowed with a trust and have possessed powers over the indoctrinated far beyond positions of authority in the secular world. In Canada alone, thousands of children in church-run orphanages and schools suffered enormous injustices through abuse by religious authorities. Pedophile priests have long been a serious problem for the Roman Catholic Church. After an investigation of the issue in Britain, a report by Lord Nolan "made 50 recommendations for preventing a repeat of the child abuse scandals that have tarnished the image of the Church."[15] In the United States, as elsewhere, the Catholic Church has only very begrudgingly admitted to the problem of child abuse by its priests, but the enormity of the issue may become part of its undoing.[16]

Religious intolerance derives its content from religion itself. In the first place, all religious sects see all others as apostatical, as heretics or lost sheep. Because the chief characteristic of all religious sects is that each one sees itself as the only bearer of the truth, all sects by their very nature stand in contradiction to all others. To admit to the truth of another is to do damage to the sanctity of one's own religion. This belief in an exclusive truth has also given rise to internal religious intolerance. All religions are also characterized by bigotry towards their own denominations – as the historical relations between Protestants and Catholics, Shiites and Sunnis, and the various sects of Protestantism, Judaism, and Hinduism reveal.

In the second place, inasmuch as religions of whatever creed embody the formal or informal ethics of a given social system, they constitute a significant bulwark for that system. The aspirations of modern states and their dominant corporations often assume, and can even request, religious justification. In the United States, the Catholic hierarchy, along with many Protestant fundamentalist sects, rationalized the war in Vietnam. In Latin America this same hierarchy worked against the socially conscious "liberation theology," consistently supporting the status quo no matter how ruthless and repressive. No small part of the crisis in Judaism rests on the decades of blatant violations of a host of international laws, conventions, and customs committed by the state of Israel as the Jewish state.[17]

The Bearers of Truth

The characteristic belief of a religious sect to see itself as the sole bearer of truth has led to a series of infamous historical acts in which dominant religions have sought to eradicate the physical and spiritual presence of others. There is no shortage of examples. The Catholics, among many notorious acts, have the ill-famed "auto-da-fe" of Fray Diego de Landa, who commanded the many hundreds of books of the Mayans to be burned in 1562 as "superstition and lies of the devil." Even within Catholicism, the Great Schism of 1054 continues to be a matter of intolerant feelings between Roman Catholics and the Greek Orthodox, as witnessed in the Pope's visit to Greece in 2001. In the same year, the Taliban in Afghanistan destroyed numerous ancient statues of Buddha as being "offensive to Islam." Not to be outdone for intolerance, "one of Israel's most senior rabbis" and founder of Shas, "the third largest party in the Israeli parliament," gave a sermon "calling on God to annihilate the Arabs."

In 1992 a certain sect of Hindus in India destroyed a sixteenth-century Muslim mosque for religious reasons. In 2002 "communal violence" between Muslims and Hindus in the Indian state of Gujarat climaxed with the massacre of over 2,000 Muslims. This list could be vastly longer.

• "Greece Fills with Protest over Pope," *The Guardian*, April 27, 2001; *The Daily Telegraph*, April 10, 2001; Human Rights Watch, "We Have No Orders to Save You: State Complicity and Participation in Communal Violence in Gujarat," April 2002.

IN PRACTICE

The Unequal Rights of Men and Women

The most obvious and widespread contradiction in human rights is the inequality between men and women in law and in everyday life. Surprisingly, however, this contradiction has not been so obvious for the overwhelming majority of writers on human rights – unless they are women. Even the most critical and aware of male writers on rights rarely make any mention of women's rights as human rights. Indeed, most writing on human rights is silent on the question of women. Nevertheless, nowhere in the world today in any domain do women share with men equal rights in practice – even though in some jurisdictions they may be more or less equal in law. In all contemporary nation-states, regardless of the mode of production, the lack of equal rights for women in theory and practice is ubiquitous, and violations of human rights for women are everywhere commonplace.

Numerous national and international government institutions and non-governmental organizations and agencies have presented catalogues of the unequal laws and practices that continue to exist almost half a century after the UDHR. The legal systems around the world, for instance, remain highly prejudicial to women; in no country is the behaviour of the police, judges, or lawyers, or the content of legislation, free of negative bias towards women. Equal political rights for women in liberal democracies are relatively recent – in most of Europe, North America, and the former USSR, these rights were in place shortly after World War I, but in most of the rest of the world they arrived only after World War II. Everywhere, however, the practice of politics remains strikingly male-dominated.[18] In custom or in law in many parts of the world, women are still the property of men. Marriage and family laws in much of the world still mean more or less a "civil death" for women. Numerous countries tolerate widespread cultural practices prejudicial to women: female infanticide, the abortion of female fetuses, prenatal scans for "unwanted daughters," the prohibition of or restraints on birth control, genital mutilation, child betrothal, the selling of female children, denial or restriction of education, forms of purdah, and the normalization of pornography.[19] Other forms of violence are explicitly aimed at women, and considered culturally acceptable: the practice of suttee, "honour" killings, dowry assaults and murders, acid attacks, the traffic in women, sex tourism, domestic violence, and, more generally, sexual harassment. All the major religions characterize women as inferior or subordinate beings, denying them equal rights in religious practices. The objectification of women by the mass media is universal; and their demeaning presentation is widespread. Women's contribution to history, politics, science, and the arts has been by and large unrecognized; in the recorded history of human development, women appear hardly to have existed.[20] The UN Population Fund 2000 Report on the condition of women spoke of "a massive global violation of human rights."[21]

Women: Culturally Accepted Violence and Killing

According to Amnesty International (May 2001), "The torture of women and girls persists on a daily basis across the globe .... It is fed by a global culture which denies women equal rights with men, and which legitimizes violence against women." In another report (Sept. 21, 1999), Amnesty charged that "several hundred women" were being "killed each year for suspected affairs, for seeking divorce, and for being raped. The death of these women and girls typically comes at the hands of male family members who have virtual immunity due to legal bias and judicial practices."

It would seem that Amnesty International is erring on the side of caution with these numbers. The UN Population Fund estimates "that as many as 5000 women and girls are murdered by family members each year in so-called 'honour killings' around the world." According to the Human Rights Commission of Pakistan, "More than 1000 women were victims of these crimes" in 1999 in that country alone.

According to UNICEF, in India in 1997 more than six thousand "bride burnings" or other dowry deaths occurred because the dowries were "considered insufficient." The U.S. State Department found that about ten thousand incidents of female infanticide took place in India in 2000.

The U.S. State Department also found that an estimated one to two million girls and young women were being "trafficked around the world for forced labour, domestic servitude or sexual exploitation."

• Amnesty International, "Broken Bodies, Shattered Minds"; S. Nebehay, "Honor Killings of Women Said on Rise Worldwide," Reuters, April 7, 2000; S. Goldenberg, "A Question of Honour," *The Guardian*, May 27, 1999; Gendercide Watch <www. gendercide.org>; B. Crossette, "Unicef Opens Global Drive to Halt Killings of Women," *The New York Times*, March 9, 2000; <www.peace.ca/unicef.>; U.S. Department of State, "Trafficking in Women and Girls: An International Human Rights Violation," 1998.

Despite the UDHR and other documents espousing women's rights, then, an enormous gulf exists between the declared universal equality of men and women and the reality of the legal status and condition of women around the world. Although that reality is marked by a continuing persistent, pervasive, and systemic discrimination, the UN documents serve at least as a relative measure of the degree of women's equality in rights, and progress towards it, and as mileposts in consciousness about the nature of humanity.

The persistent violations of equal rights and remaining widespread formal inequalities in many nation-states do call for some sort of explanation; and for that we can begin with two United Nations reports. In 1980 the UN Conference on Women presented statistics showing that "women do between two-thirds and three-quarters of the work in the world" and "produce 45% of the world's food." But, the report continued, "They are still granted only 10% of the world's income and 1% of the world's property."[22] In 1995 the UN *Human Development Report* declared itself to be "a major indictment of the continuing discrimination against women in most societies." It stated, "In no society do women fare as well as men," and concluded that "men receive the lion's share of income and recognition for their economic contribution, while most of women's work remains unpaid, unrecognized, and undervalued."[23] These statements point to the continuing rationale for discrimination against women – a rationale resting in the significance of the large percentage of women's work that is unpaid or underpaid in relation to the production of the total social product. Only when and because women were declared to be in theory equal to men did it become possible to grasp the nature and extent of this inequality.

Even under different industrial modes of production, the importance of women's unpaid or underpaid labour was understood, at least implicitly. Decades before equal rights were formally declared universal in the UDHR, women had achieved equality in law in the Soviet Union. As a product of the first socialist revolution in 1917, women's rights were advanced in Russia more than anywhere ever before. The revolution was, after all, made in the name of the oppressed; and government control over the means of production and provision of necessities allowed, at least initially, for public policies that began to socialize domestic or private life and opened political life to the participation of women. Despite this formal legal equality for women (unique in the world at the time) and considerable progress in their condition and status, the advancement of women was stalled by the late 1920s in the face of the drive for accumulation in the industrial sector.

With the ascendancy of Stalin and the emergence of bureaucratic control over the socialized property, the promising though limited accomplishments of women, and the progress made in confronting the dominance of male right, found their limits.[24] The emphasis on industrial capital accumulation meant that sacrifices in public spending had to be made in other sectors. The sacrifices included the experiments to socialize domestic life and efforts to bring women into the political arena. These shifts in priorities were confirmed in giving constitutional protection to the nuclear family and the state idealization of motherhood, marriage, and family. (Still, unlike elsewhere, spouses in the USSR continued to be equal in law; divorce was easier and legally less prejudicial to women than before; child care remained highly socialized; and women had more control over reproduction.) The curb on the further socialization of domestic functions – or the re-institutionalization of the family – checked the declining extra-exploitation of women as the rate of increase of their paid work in relation to their unpaid domestic and volunteer labour slowed, stopped, or began to reverse.

All the socialist revolutions that followed brought rapid and significant advances for women's rights and status, above all putting an end to the widespread treatment of women as the property of men. In every case, however, the early achievements met their limits before critical elements of male dominance could be surmounted.[25] Socialized property did allow for public policy restricting gender discrimination and for the socialization of many domestic functions, but in no case was there enough democratic access to public policy to advance women's equality, to address, beyond a certain degree, the so-called "woman question."[26] The dominance of male right or the discrimination against women was never fully confronted. For the most part, these regimes were state capitalist systems, not experiments in workers' control, and so the undervaluing of women's paid labour and the ratio of paid to unpaid labour were always a factor in calculations – by politically dominant men – over the direction of economic development.

After World War II, when the demands for national self-determination from the anti-colonial movements and for equal rights for all humans could no longer be ignored or resisted, the United Nations, in its Charter and the UDHR, sought to contain those demands by defining them within the confines of capitalist liberal democracy. New conditions for capital accumulation on the global level had to be established; the social reforms of the Soviet Union were well known; workers' disaffection with the capitalism of the 1930s was no distant memory; and the extreme intolerance and inhumanity shown by the leaders of Germany and Japan stood as a mirror to the conscience of the capitalist world.

With these UN documents, women's rights in the liberal-democratic nations began to improve, along with, ipso facto, a concomitant albeit slow decline in male privilege in law.[27] But the idea of gender equality, even in principle, let alone in practice, met with resistance and assumptions of dominant male right at every step.[28] The very language of the Charter had to be challenged in order to include the phrase "equal rights for men and women," so that human rights would be seen to encompass women's rights. Similarly, there was debate over the language of the UDHR. Ultimately the words "all

men" and "brothers" were dropped in favour of "everyone" and "human beings,"[29] although several masculine pronouns and possessive adjectives, not to
mention a reference in Article 1 to "a spirit of brotherhood," remained. That
article entreats human beings to look upon and behave towards each other as
equals, but women cannot be brothers. If the phrase had read, "in a spirit of
sisterhood," the predominantly male framers[30] of the UDHR might have understood the issue more clearly.

The problem of language merely reflected how women's rights were still
being ignored or subordinated to human rights as male rights. To this day, then,
a long struggle continues to reassert over and over again within the United Nations that human rights must also include women's rights. Since 1945 the UN
has promulgated over twenty different instruments that specifically concern
women. Those efforts represent both the continuing inequality of women and
the difficulty of realizing women's rights as human rights. Each attempt points
to key areas of discrimination against women and stands as a measure of, for
the most part, unrealized national implementation.[31]

In 1946, within a year of the creation of the Charter, for instance, the UN
adopted a declaration to promote women's participation in the work of the UN
– reflecting the obvious shortage of women in official posts. In the same year
women argued for and succeeded in having created a subcommission of the
Commission on Human Rights. The new body, the Commission on the Status
of Women (CSW), would deal with women's rights as human rights. In 1947 the
CSW was obliged to intervene to have the UDHR drafted in gender-neutral language, and by and large succeeded; and in 1951 it pushed the International Labour Organization (ILO) to adopt a convention "Concerning Equal Remuneration for Men and Women for Work of Equal Value." In 1952 the CSW spurred
the UN to adopt the Convention on the Political Rights of Women and, in 1957,
the Convention on the Nationality of Married Women. During the 1960s the
CSW continued to promote and sponsor more resolutions on women's rights
and, more broadly, social rights. The 1970s saw the beginning of the world con-
ferences of women under the auspices of the United Nations, and the decade
ended with adoption of the Convention on the Elimination of All Forms of
Discrimination against Women in 1979. By the early 1980s this Convention had
given rise to a committee (CEDAW) established to monitor compliance by national governments. By the late 1980s an NGO was formed to press further the
demands of the Convention and oversee its implementation – the International
Women's Rights Action Watch (IWRAW). As late as 1993 the Vienna World
Conference on Human Rights was pushed to affirm that "the human rights of
women and the girl-child are an inalienable, integral and indivisible part of universal human rights."[32] It would be difficult to imagine more convincing testimony to the inequality of women than these persistent and apparently necessary
efforts by women to affirm their abstract equality and to attempt to realize it.[33]

But even the promises made at the 1995 Beijing Conference on Women to have universal ratification of the Convention by 2000 have not come to fruition. The United States, among several other countries, has not ratified the Convention, and many of those governments that did ratify it did so only with numerous written reservations. Even the abstract equality of the Convention remains an unrealized goal for women. On the twentieth anniversary of the Convention, in what was an obvious understatement, Amnesty International stated, "Millions of women still have no right to live in safety, to think and express themselves freely and without fear, and to participate in the public life in their own countries."[34]

These examples – of the need for special UN conventions and committees, not to mention NGOs, to advocate for and protect women's rights – point to certain contradictions in the human rights of the UN Charter and UDHR with respect to the rights of men and women. One contradiction is between human rights as abstract rights and a component of international law *and* particular national laws, customs, and religious canons; in other words, the majority of national legal systems, numerous customary practices, and all the major religions violate equal rights for women as defined in the UDHR. Another contradiction arises between formal human rights *and* everyday empirical reality, even where national laws and policies declare universality of equal rights. Unofficial discrimination, even where official equality exists, means that everywhere in the world the daily lives of women bear little resemblance to the lives of men.

Whatever progress has been made since 1948 in achieving equal rights in law, in practice, and in consciousness, it is clear that enormous inequalities remain. Developments in women's equal rights, moreover, have not been all in one direction; since the 1980s many changes have brought greater inequality – especially with the coming of neo-liberal policies around the world and the consequent dismantling of social reforms. In the Third World and the formally "socialist" countries,[35] in particular, economic, cultural, and social reforms had previously benefited women more than elsewhere; but that is no longer the case.

Whether women's rights are being advanced or retrenched, the struggles to include women's rights in human rights are in effect struggles for equal rights within the liberal-democratic framework. To argue that women's rights are human rights is merely to say that men and women should be equal as individuals possessing individual private rights – in particular the civil and political rights of the UDHR. Defined in this way, the struggle for women's equal rights can be fought for, abstractly considered, without challenging capitalism or its system of liberal democracy – just as Afro-Americans in the 1960s fought for their civil and political rights without presenting a threat to the nature of the system itself.[36] Although this goal of equality frames much of women's struggles and will remain the goal within liberal democracy, it is not to be confused with emancipation from exploitation. The struggle for equal rights does not encompass the structural and institutional reasons for the continuing subordination of women. The practice and possibility of equal civil and political rights for women in capitalist societies are constantly thwarted, circumvented, or circumscribed by certain socio-economic realities and social structures that the demand for equal rights does not address.

The resistance to human rights for women in the liberal democracies arises for substantially the same reason that equality was limited in the "socialist" states. That is, women's unpaid labour in domestic life and undervalued labour in employment represent net gains to those who dominate, whether as fathers, brothers, sons, husbands, or as corporate capital in the form of business enterprises and governments. As the UN reports show, women produce a significant portion of the total social product of all nations and yet receive a fraction of the value of their labour as remuneration.

This condition is of enormous significance to the structure of ruling relations and the foundation of those relations in economic structures.[37] The chief defining characteristics of capitalism, and its driving motive, are the production of surplus value (the difference between the value of what is produced and the value of the components of production – an important part of which is labour-power) and the accumulation of that surplus value in private individual and corporate hands. If the value of the labour-power hired can be kept below the average value of labour-power for similar work, then, the more surplus extracted and the greater the increase in accumulated capital. Given the significance of undervalued labour[38] in the production of surplus value, the prospect of pay equity would reduce the amount of surplus that can be extracted from women's labour; it would produce a rough equation between the surplus value drawn from male and female labour. The obvious potential negative effect of such equality on profits goes a long way towards explaining corporate and government resistance to paying women as equals of men.[39] Undervalued women's labour, moreover, tends also to make women see themselves as inferior and submit to dependent relationships. It also causes a general downward pressure on wages, which allows for the increased extraction of surplus value in general.

Given that nothing inherent in women accounts for this inequality in the value of labour-power, its source must rest in the structure of society. As a system of accumulation of wealth in the form of commodities possessed by individuals (and corporations as fictitious individuals), capitalism must socially reproduce itself in a manner that allows for the continuation of individual property rights; social reproduction must take place in an institutional form that produces the members of society as individual owners. It is for this reason that the nuclear family, rather than some socialized form of social reproduction, is the form of family that comes to prevail in a capitalist mode of production.[40] Under capitalism (including state capitalism), the nuclear family is defined as the initial site of social reproduction. It is a sphere outside the economy strictly speaking, and therefore is without paid labour or an independent source of revenue. With the divide between the economic and the domestic, the nuclear family arises as a dependent institution and as the preserve of women because their biological role makes them central in social reproduction, a process that, at least here, begins in the family. So structured, the family creates a dependence on a male earner, and gives rise to the commensurate institutions of legalized marriage, motherhood, the private household, the assumption of the pre-eminence of male right, and children as possessions of parents.

The importance of the nuclear family to the system rests in its fundamental functions. First, it constitutes the venue for an essential part of social reproduction within the framework of private property relations. As such, it is the initial institutional means of reproducing members of society as private individuals, as the embodiment of private property rights (if only over their labour-power). Here humans are reproduced as capital in the form of labour-power, as producers of surplus value in the form of workers, and as consumers of commodities. The household, or the beginning site of social reproduction, moreover, is defined as a private domain (and until recently, more or less outside the purview of the law), yet is dependent on an external source of revenue; and children are defined as the private property of parents – previously, of the male, as were (and in many countries still are) dependent women.

Second, because domestic labour generally falls by and large to women, the nuclear family is the main site of the extra-economic exploitation of women, whether they remain in the household, dependent on the income of the male, or work in paid employment. The unpaid domestic labour – child care, food preparation, and cleaning, for example – is *necessary* to economic reproduction; but it is performed in the nuclear family outside the marketplace and is therefore not directly productive of surplus value. If the woman is not employed, the value of her domestic labour is included in the wage or salary of the "breadwinner," or in state subsidies in the case of unmarried women with children, or in part in various forms of state-provided children's allowance. If she is employed, the value of her domestic labour is included in her wage, or in the case of joint family incomes, in the wages of both partners. If we were to take account of unpaid labour in the domestic sphere, we would have to amortize the hourly rate of wages and salaries over the whole period – of both domestic labour and paid labour. By accounting for the value of domestic labour in this way, we can see that when wages and salaries fall below the ability of one income to maintain women as unemployed, dependent domestic "homemakers," women, by necessity, have to enter the paid labour force.

Domestic labour is devalued to the lowest possible level by the structure of the family itself because women who are not employed are subordinated to the main revenue earner, usually the male (father, husband, son), who supplies the household expenses. This inequality makes possible male domination and undermines the possibility of love and mutual respect. The inequality, moreover, runs through the domestic realm; until relatively recently in most of the world, household goods (even the home itself) and wives and children were considered the property of men. Only in the last few decades in most of the industrial countries has the state legislated protection for dependants in the home, and equal rights for married couples over household goods and children. But in much of the world there is still no equal right to household property and no legal recourse for wives or children if neglected or abused by male earners. Here is the institution within capitalism (and other systems) that serves as the first site of exploitation of the labour of women. The "remuneration" for labour in the household comes only indirectly as part of the wage or salary of the employed partner, usually the male, and is "paid" in the form of household expenses and on the sufferance of the waged member of the family.

Third, the very existence of the institution of the nuclear family provides the abiding ideological rationale for women's exploitation in the workforce. The family is the site of women's socially defined role as wife and mother and therefore as economically dependent and as unpaid producer. The occupational streaming and pay discrimination of women in employment rest on the implicit assumptions that women are ultimately dependants, their earnings are supplementary, and they are best suited for domestic duties – child care, food preparation, cleaning, and other services. These assumptions are affirmed in the structure of the nuclear family; and as long as female subordination persists in this form of family, so too will the attendant ideological views of the "natural" roles of women.

Fourth, the family has functioned as a mechanism to obscure the role of women as a significant part of the "reserve army of labour." It has allowed for the movement of women in and out of the labour force as supply and demand for workers wax and wane, obscuring many of the problems associated with unemployment. It allows women to enter the labour force at different points in their lives, when economically necessary, and to "retire" from paid work for varying periods in order to raise families or when employment is not possible. As an institution, the family does not function this way for men; it enables women to be unseen and uncounted as unemployed, to have a role and status outside the economy proper, but it does not do so for men. It makes women into non-subjects in civil society as long as they remain economically dependent, a state of being that contributes to their inferior status; and it makes them into compromised subjects when they are employed.

The inequality of women and the institution of the nuclear family, then, go hand in hand. By dint of its nature, its social functions in relation to the system as a whole, the institution of the nuclear family lies at the heart of the subordination of women, with all the economic benefits for the production of capital that flow from this subordination.

Given this argument, the UDHR contains yet another contradiction with respect to women's equality. On the one hand, the declaration of human rights includes and implies women's rights, but on the other hand it makes the family essential to the existence of society. Article 16 (3) states, "The family is the natural and fundamental group unit of society and is entitled to protection by society and the State." Many types of family have existed throughout history, and all of them represent the initial site of social reproduction in which members are moulded as embodiments of the prevailing property relations. But the one type that is most appropriate to the capitalist mode of production is the nuclear family, which reproduces society in the form of private owners. The reference to family in the UDHR can only be to that same type of family, which it takes as essential and defines as basic to modern society and deserving of defence by the state. Because of its functions – to reproduce members of society as commodities and as producers and consumers of commodities[41] – the family is to be defended by the state. A social unit outside of economic relations but dependent on those relations – the site of the exploitation of unpaid labour and of women's dependence on men, and the source of the rationale for unequal pay and treatment in the workforce – is deemed natural and to be protected. It is an institution that embodies and advances the prevailing property relations through which the benefits of women's subordination are channelled into male, corporate, and government hands. The UDHR's proclamation of the equality of women is not consistent with this definition of the nuclear family as natural and entitled to defence by the state.[42]

Women's equality with men varies inversely with the vitality of the nuclear family as a dependent social unit. At certain times in the history of capitalism, when the viability of the family was undermined – due to, for instance, mass mobilization of men for the armed forces – women experienced degrees of increased freedom. Since the late 1960s, however, the demand for women's equality has taken on a more permanent significance because of unfolding contradictions between the economy and the nuclear family.

Because the family is economically dependent on paid labour, it is only as viable as the economy is able to provide support for it. Periods of economic recession or depression, with high rates of unemployment or underemployment and lower wages or no wages, inhibit the reproduction of the family as a dependent social institution. The long secular decline in male wages/salaries from the 1970s on in the industrial countries has undermined the feasibility of a social unit structured as dependent on a wage/salary that must provide for household costs, which include the unpaid labour of a wife and mother. The consequent growing necessity of women's employment is inconsistent with the persistence of the traditional nuclear family. As economic dependence on the male wage-earner is undermined, the principal site of male dominance or women's inequality begins to break down with a corresponding growth in demands by women for equality in the workplace and in the home, and for pre-eminent rights over birth control and abortion. General challenges to the assumption of male dominance, and the structure and view of the world based on this assumption, also arise.

As more women of the working classes move into the labour market, there is a concomitant rise in the demand for equality with men because once in receipt of a wage or salary women are less economically dependent and therefore less materially and socially subordinate to men. In turn, the demand for more equal rights at work is accompanied by the demand for more state policies that socialize domestic functions. The pressures for public policies on such matters as child care, school meals, broader public education, family planning, medical programs for women, and maternity/parental leave are all products of the economically necessary shift of women into the labour force. For the most part, these are demands for the socialization of domestic life, for the transfer of the functions of the nuclear family from the private to the public domain.

While the vagaries of the business cycle and the long-term secular trends of capital accumulation have always incapacitated the functions of the nuclear family for certain strata and classes, so too does the accumulation of capital itself impair the viability of the family for all; the growth of capital contradicts one of its own premises. Capital strives to commodify all aspects of life, and the functions of the family are no exception. Child care, food preparation, clothes-making, education, socialization, cleaning, and laundry are all subjected to the process of commodification or transformed with labour-saving devices. Indeed, many of the traditional family functions have long been capitalized. The domestic sphere of social reproduction is in this way socialized, albeit in the process of its capitalization. Just as the labour of the independent commodity producer was socialized by the penetration of capital into production, so too is the family socialized through the capitalization of its functions, that is, the encroachment of capital into the household. Although, arguably, all aspects of social reproduction could be commodified, it is not easy to make commodified social reproduction cheaper than domestic social reproduction carried out by unpaid women's (and men's) labour. The complete commodification of domestic functions constantly rubs against this limit.

The more forced by economic necessity into the labour market, the more women have made demands for equal rights in practice and for new social rights, that is, for state socialization of many key domestic functions. These demands have two implications that subvert the structure of women's subordination. The pressure to realize equal rights threatens the economic benefits that accrue from keeping women subordinate; and the growing state socialization of domestic functions endangers the persistence of the family as the basic institution for social reproduction of human beings as embodiments of the relations of private property.

As a reaction to these implications, at least two significant broad policy shifts can be identified in the neo-liberal agenda that informs state actions. One shift is to privatize or dismantle government programs that have socialized domestic functions – to promote the capitalization of these functions or force them back into the nuclear family. Care for the very young, the elderly, the ill, and the handicapped are all being shifted as much as possible back into the home or into commercial or charitable care facilities. The other reaction is to encourage and reinforce the nuclear family despite its declining economic viability. This is done by publicly sanctioning the nuclear family as a good in itself, promoting "motherhood" and publicizing the alleged unhappy consequences of "maternal neglect," further restricting or abolishing rights to abortion or birth control,[43] limiting access to welfare for single mothers, and prosecuting delinquent fathers. Given that these policies retrench public entitlement to socialized domestic or reproductive functions, they exacerbate and expand the unpaid labour of women, increase the possibilities for the continued assertion of male dominance, and countenance the ideological subordination of women.

Because these policies form part of the terms of World Bank and IMF loans or credit facilities, as structural adjustment policies, they have another, albeit indirect, consequence. The resulting spoliation of local or regional economies, collapse of currencies, and accompanying rapid decline in living standards have created the conditions for organized sex trafficking in women and children. This illicit trade has for some time been particularly widespread in Asia and now increasingly occurs in Eastern Europe. It involves hundreds of thousands of women and children traded across international borders every year, and has become a multibillion-dollar business.[44]

All forms of inequality meet with opposition of some sort; and the various historical forms of subordination of women are no different. Throughout recorded history women have actively and passively resisted their inequality; and they have chronicled their bitterness, anger, and frustration and registered their defiance over male usurpation of their freedom.[45] Even today the efforts to realize the rights of women as human rights have powerful detractors that include the organized major religions, corporations, and national states.[46] The resistance will cease only when equality has been realized.

The Rights of Children

On the surface it is an anomaly of the UDHR that human rights do not extend to children, except in certain vaguely worded articles – 22, 25, and 26 – that do not define children's rights as such. In other words, all those who have not reached the age of majority, which is eighteen for the United Nations, are not specifically declared to have all the rights in that document. All human rights extend only to those who are defined as "persons" in law in a capitalist society; and a "person" is defined as someone over the age of majority, as a rational, autonomous possessor of private property rights, if only over one's own labour-power. Children are not persons in this sense; their principal legal status consists of being possessions of their parents or guardians or wards of the state until the age of majority.

This omission points to the nature of the premise of the UDHR: human rights reflect the principles of a system of private property that needs to define a certain age at which someone can assume legal responsibility for holding rights as a self-sufficient, autonomous being. Children, in this system, are necessarily dependent on a wage-earner (or the state), and they are therefore defined as wards of those they are dependent on. It follows that they are excluded from formal political rights and certain civil rights that accrue to "persons," although they are the beneficiaries of state protection and of certain social rights – that is, the state provision of certain goods and services that are specific to children or are not entirely restricted to the legally defined person.

The UDHR and particularly the UN Convention on the Rights of the Child (1989) envisage no social institution other than the nuclear family as a means of raising children and show no sense of children being raised in ways other than to create autonomous individuals.[47] The underlying assumption of human rights and children's rights is a system of private property that has no place either for family forms that do not imply the inheritance of private property or for the socialization of children as altruistic social beings. For hundreds of millions of people, then, and especially for tribal or Aboriginal peoples who possess their land and resources in some common way and do not define the family as nuclear, these rights do not have a lot of meaning.

The UN Convention on the Rights of the Child assumes that, as dependants, children are born into nuclear families and that parents have pre-eminent rights over them (Article 5) – the only caveats being that if the declared "rights of the child" or national laws concerning dependants are violated, the state may intervene (Articles 9, 19), and that the views of the child must be weighed in some way (Articles 12, 13, 14). The Convention does not address just how and when this should happen or at what age, among other questions. Nonetheless, the document unwittingly poses a contradiction between parental rights and declared children's rights. Early in the history of capitalism the rights of parents were absolute, but since then they have been successively, albeit cautiously, conceded or compromised by the assertion of children's rights by national states and the United Nations intended to protect children from exploitation and to ensure the provision of certain elementary needs.[48] This shift from absolute parental authority to increasing rights for children and more state responsibilities requires some explanation.

Parental right and the nuclear family go hand in hand, for it is in the family that children are defined as the possessions of their parents. The structure of the family itself, however, makes it an institution that is not necessarily benign, and indeed it can potentially be a dangerous place for children.[49] The family is characterized by unequal power relations, in which the children, if not also one parent, are dependent on a wage-earner and on the nature and socio-economic position of the parents. (The family is also the location in which the legal "person" as parent must abandon the individualistic principles of marketplace society and exercise responsibility for another, albeit a dependant. Here is yet another contradiction between the principles of capitalist society and humanity.) These structural elements of inequality between earners and non-earners and between parents and children make the family in principle, if not in fact, the site of subordination of the dependants. Here they are inferior in power, status, dignity, and rights.

As a social unit conditional on the structure and viability of the economy, moreover, the family is only as sound as is the assurance and size of the revenue used to support it; and these factors are determined by position in the class structure and the rise and fall of the business cycle. Unemployment, underemployment, or well-paid employment all have an impact on the integrity of the family. The consequent degree of structural completeness and relative financial security of the family, in turn, profoundly influence the fate of the children. The relation between economic cycles and inequality and the degree of integrity of the family is especially marked for certain strata of the working class, although less so for those classes with the means of withstanding economic change.

In many parts of the world industrial capitalism has destroyed, and in other parts continues to destroy, the economic foundations of non-capitalist family forms, and in their place offers, if anything, the nuclear family. At the same time, with its cyclical growth capitalism creates the conditions for the continual breakdown and renewal of the family in the working classes, as well as the conditions for chronic dissipation of the family in the lowest strata. Except for those who can afford to maintain the integrity of the family, and thus the semblance of mutual interest and concern grounded in inheritance law, the nuclear family as a dependent social unit can only be a dysfunctional institution. It remains, however, the only location for the social reproduction of society and the site of the pre-eminence of parental right. Parental power over children and key factors in their development resides, then, in a social institution that has inherent structural inequalities and whose integrity, for the working classes at least, varies with the business cycle, the structure of the economy, and rates of unemployment and underemployment.

Parental authority means that parents have the right to determine (albeit now usually in circumscribed ways) the fate of their children to a certain age, but the dependency of the family on the vicissitudes of the economy also means that due to economic hardship parents may not be able to provide for their children, or have few choices but to force their children into wage-labour or to sell them as little more than slaves. It is for this reason that the need to proclaim the rights of children arises. That necessity began with the coming of industrial capital-ism[50] and continues today wherever capitalism penetrates and dissolves precapitalist or traditional social formations, or destroys communities and various working-class strata through chronic unemployment. In effect, children's rights ensue from the need to protect children from parental, criminal, and corporate abuse when no form of family exists with sufficient integrity or social and economic means to provide them with the care, protection, and education needed for their development.[51] The exercise of parental authority against the interests of the child arises not from some malevolence on the part of the parents, but from the structural inequality of power in the nuclear family and the relation of this institution to the inconstancy of the market economy.

The rapid expansion of the market economy in the 1980s and 1990s – its demand for a cheap labour supply and destruction of non-capitalist modes of production and family forms – produced a great rise in the exploitation of children. The basic cause of child labour is always economic necessity. Even though the preamble to the 1999 ILO Convention on Child Labour suggests that other causes may exist, it offers no explanation other than "child labour is to a great extent caused by poverty."[52] Indeed, in a marketplace society there can be no reason other than economic demands to put children out to work. This economic imperative has increased since 1980, with the continuing destruction of non-capitalist and traditional social formations and growing impoverishment everywhere – two conditions that have accompanied the globalization of capital and the application of neo-liberal policies.

Increasing impoverishment means that the nuclear family, an economically dependent structure, can no longer be maintained in its defined ideal form – with one parent, usually the woman, outside the labour market and dedicated to home care. As wage-labour increasingly becomes the only form of labour, and as the value of wages and salaries declines, dependent family members become less and less sustainable as dependants and must increasingly become a source of additional revenue. This was the most likely cause of the rise in the participation rate of women in the labour force in many industrial countries beginning in the 1970s; and it would appear to be the cause of the rapid rise of child labour beginning in the 1980s. A great deal of domestic labour within the family has shifted to children as parents strive to augment or simply maintain their level of paid labour.

The main concern of organizations and agencies that try to address child labour has been the growing role of children at work outside the domestic sphere. As with undervalued women's labour, and all forms of coerced labour – prison, slave, military, bonded, and indebted labour – child labour provides enormous economic benefits. Although child labour is often unseen (partly because children are not legal "persons"), its use brings significant gains to those who exploit it directly or indirectly. It also creates a downward pressure on wages in general. Children are in a sense ideal manual workers: their education is limited, and they are unworldly, malleable, and often functionally illiterate; perhaps most importantly, they are more or less without civil or political rights or the support and protection of social rights.[53]

A relatively straightforward relationship exists between the destruction of non-capitalist modes of production and the ensuing poverty, the breakdown of the existing family structure, and child labour: the more advanced the destruction the worse the poverty, the less functional the family, and the more child labour there is. This is the case both within nation-states and for nation-states as a whole. The region of the world with the largest amount of child labour by far is Asia (excluding Japan), with about 60 per cent of the total, followed by Africa with about 32 per cent, and Latin America and the Caribbean with about 7 per cent.[54] The industrial countries have a growing amount of child labour, but because of their relatively high per capita wealth, the level is still only a fraction of the other regions. About 95 per cent of all child labour is found in Third World countries. Yet these figures are only estimates because there are no national or international studies on child labour that can claim a relatively accurate count. The illegal or amoral nature of much child labour, moreover, as well as its existence, for the most part, in the "informal economy,"[55] makes an assessment of its extent difficult.

The estimates of child labourers vary at between 200 million and 500 million. The ILO, which has collected data and done some of its own studies, has sought a certain credibility by presenting only conservative estimates. In the late 1990s, its studies show, about 250 million children between the ages of five and fourteen could be defined as working, although it cautions that this figure is an "underestimate." It did not consider the data on children under ten to be reliable, but deemed the number of working children in this category to be "significant." The ILO does not include in its calculations the number of working children between fifteen and eighteen, moreover, because it accepts fifteen as the "internationally recommended minimum age for work," even though the definition of child for the United Nations extends to eighteen, as it does in the ILO Convention on Child Labour. The underestimate, then, does not even include age categories usually included in the definition of the child. About a half of working children between five and fourteen, the ILO believes, work full-time; but the data does not include domestic labour in the child's own home. Gender discrimination in child labour, moreover, is obvious from the data; it is mainly female children who are sold into slave-like conditions as domestics in the homes of the well-to-do or as prostitutes. Most, if not all, child workers, furthermore, are paid less than the national minimum wage (if such exists), and many are not paid at all, particularly those who have been sold, those who are bonded or indentured, or those who work in family enterprises. Above all, the figures show that the trends of all forms of child labour are on the increase.[56]

The response to the rapid rise in child labour in the 1980s was not to address underlying causes but to draw up declarations of children's rights. The earlier UN Declaration on the Rights of the Child in 1959 spelled out basic civil and social rights for children, but stayed largely clear of challenging parental rights. It carefully stated that "wherever possible" a child should be raised by parents ("for love and understanding," and "the atmosphere of affection and moral and material security"). Even a Soviet proposal to protect children against corporal punishment "met considerable opposition."[57] Twenty years later, in 1979, the evidence of child labour and exploitation was not yet sufficiently obvious to convince rights advocates that they had to do anything beyond the 1959 Declaration; and the UN International Year of the Child even saw a "protracted debate on whether or not there should be a convention [that is, practical measures] and what it should contain."[58] But in the 1980s, with the rapid advance of neo-liberal policies in every industrial nation and structural adjustment policies demanded throughout most of the Third World, came the undermining of the economic feasibility of the family and the rise of child abuse and homeless children.[59] And so there arose the need for a convention – something more than a mere declaration – a call to action, of sorts, by signatory states.

When the United Nations adopted the Convention on the Rights of the Child in 1989, the rights spelled out did not engage all those who fell within the definition of a child. Underlying the text is a particular vision of childhood; it concerns children who live under some sort of familial or state authority; it does not address the question of children who have been abandoned, orphaned by a disease such as AIDS, sold by parents, victimized by war or natural disasters, or have escaped authority and live on streets – except to see them reunited with their families, adopted, or placed in an institution. If children's rights were written for the many tens of millions of children abandoned, disowned, orphaned, sold, prostituted, or forced to work or take up arms, they would very likely appear rather different than those of the Convention.[60]

Increasingly large numbers of children live outside families, or in chronically dysfunctional ones, and have little or no hope of ever living in a family that can provide the "atmosphere of happiness, love and understanding" envisioned in the Convention. Such words constitute a mockery of the conditions of many tens of millions of children; and the several articles of the Convention that call for reuniting children with their families or for placing them in an institution or for adoption are similarly quite out of touch with the reality of very large and growing numbers. The assumption of the Convention is that the nuclear family as a private sphere is the normal place for childhood development; there is no institution imagined outside the family or the temporary guardianship of the state-sanctioned agency or organization. That is because the fundamental premise of the Convention, like the UDHR, is the social reproduction of the human being as the embodiment of private property.

The Convention also contains contradictions that reflect other changing realities. Parental responsibility for raising children, for example, is held to be "primary" (Article 18), but in the same clause this responsibility is qualified by an externally defined condition – "the best interests of the child" – which is to be the parents' "basic concern." The statement provides no clarification on the dividing line between the "best interests" – the asserted independent right of the child – and the rights of the parent.

Those "best interests" are clearly intended to mean actions of benefit to children. But in a free-enterprise society, where the economic foundation of the nuclear family continues to erode, that goal is increasingly difficult to achieve. Even if the state removes a child from an abusive family/parent or non-family situation (on the street), the alternative is often no better. State or church-run institutions (orphanages, reformatories, prisons, residential schools, quasi-military camps for delinquents) are staffed by bureaucratic officials whose role in child care is first of all a job and source of revenue or act of charity and perhaps second a matter of human concern. Such institutions have little room for the "happiness, love and understanding" thought to exist in families. Even foster care confronts the same dilemma: the ostensible purpose of child care is subordinated by the primary considerations of the caregivers: money, employment, religious teaching, correction, charity.

The introduction of the rights of the child "to participate" (Articles 12-15) also contradicts, in principle, the role of parental authority and responsibility. In acknowledging a qualified notion of self-determination for children and intimating that children can make judgments about their own interests, those rights directly conflict with parental rights. There is another issue here. To define children as thinking and feeling human beings is a positive step because it begins to acknowledge them as more than merely dependants; but in the context of capitalist society it is also a potentially dangerous development because it also begins to define them as autonomous beings, as self-determining atoms. It begins to treat children as "persons" and so shifts their legal status in the direction of the sovereign owner of one's own labour-power, able to make independent decisions about what they do, implicitly able to enter into contracts.

Contracts or not, children continued to enter the labour force in increasing numbers throughout the 1980s and 1990s. Following the principle of better late than never, the ILO passed a resolution in 1996 "concerning the elimination of child labour," but as the evidence of more and more child labour continued to mount, it finally moved in 1999 to adopt a convention "for the Elimination of the Worst Forms of Child Labour." In doing this, however, the ILO was not calling for the elimination of child labour; it was only issuing a summons "to prohibit and eliminate the worst forms" of it.[61] Moreover, the Convention does not set objective standards to be achieved or establish mechanisms for its implementation or monitoring; indeed, it calls for the very organizations that most profit from child labour to be party to the establishment of such mechanisms. Article 5 states, "Each member shall, after consultation with employers' and workers' organizations, establish or designate appropriate mechanisms to monitor the implementation of the provision giving effect to this Convention." Rather than directly protecting children from exploitation, then, the approach provides their employers with a key role in overseeing protection. If nothing else, the lame nature of the Convention implicitly recognizes the significant economic benefits of child labour and the need to ensure its continuation by assuaging its critics, whose best case against child labour rests on these "worst forms."[62] The capitalized sweat and blood of children continue to form an increasing part of the value of the world's consumer goods, with the implicit concurrence of the ILO Convention on Child Labour.

So economically significant is the use of coerced and child labour around the world that the World Trade Organization "procurement rules forbid the consideration of non-commercial factors, such as human rights, in government purchasing decisions." This restriction includes, as a violation of GATT rules, attempts to ban imports of goods made with child labour.[63]

Neither the UN Convention on the Rights of the Child nor the ILO Convention on the Elimination of the Worst Forms of Child Labour includes time frames or defined objectives or assessable goals for implementation. Not all governments, moreover, have signed these treaties, and, if they have, the fulfilment of the terms of the conventions rests on the policy priorities of the signatory governments. In a capitalist system, in which the principal role of government is to ensure the reproduction of capital and the reproduction of the social basis of capital accumulation (the initial stage of which, for now, is the nuclear family) the allocation of resources for ensuring children's rights and protecting children from exploitation is not among the highest priorities. This is because children are still seen as the responsibility of the family; and when children are outside the family, governments have no reason to address issues of labour unless and until they are obliged to confront those issues and put resources into supporting the family or getting the child back into a family or surrogate institution.

These conventions contain another, overriding contradiction. With the family increasingly breaking down, often dysfunctional, or non-existent, the conventions grant the national state the responsibility for monitoring the implementation of their provisions. Yet it is precisely the state that is in question with respect to its treatment of children. Most governing authorities have adopted a neo-liberal philosophy that has a "minimal state," a decreasing degree of state intervention in civil society, as its objective. That philosophical view suggests a declining acceptance of the responsibilities laid out for the state in the UN Convention on Children. Children also cannot assume the state to be a benevolent surrogate parent. The UN Committee on the Rights of the Child has had several sessions since the early 1990s to examine the issue of "state violence suffered by children." As part of these meetings, the Committee has held discussions on a number of issues: the state use of "children in armed conflict," state tolerance of and even collaboration in the "economic exploitation of children," "state violence suffered by children living in institutions managed, licensed or supervised by the state," state "administration of juvenile justice," and state violence in the form of "extra-judicial or summary execution" of homeless children.[64] In a report on child torture and ill treatment, Amnesty International stated that the abuse of children by state agencies "continues to be the world's secret shame, a daily reality ignored by governments everywhere."[65] State-supported abuse, the report revealed, can be found in all countries regardless of the level of development. Children outside the family, then, have no reason to assume that the state will protect them or that their treatment by the state will be benign. For the state, children are a political, military, or economic issue, not a human or social question.

Rights for children arise only because of the poverty and attendant social dislocation that come with the economic cycles of capitalism and the political policies intended to advance the rights of corporations in opposition to those of working people, indigenous groups, and the environment.[66] These rights are a product of a system of private property relations and therefore conform to and reflect the interests of the system; they do not contradict the system, but rather attempt to reinforce the nuclear family as the institution ultimately responsible for children or to protect them from the worst effects of economic exploitation. In an imagined system of socialized property, democratically administered, the issue of rights for children would not arise because children would not be the bearers of private property in labour-power or through inheritance. Instead children would be considered to be part of the whole, a system without exploitation, and be seen as the embodiment of the future to be cared for and loved by all.

The Right of Self-Determination of Peoples

Implicit in the UN Charter and UDHR is a world made up of self-determining nation-states and international relations in which the nation-state is taken as the fundamental political and economic unit, with a sovereignty that cannot be transgressed except under narrow and specific circumstances.[67] In the aftermath of World War II, however, this perception of the world did not correspond to the reality experienced by most of the world's peoples. Far from being self-determining, the vast majority of people lived as members of colonial empires, of mandated territories,[68] protectorates, occupied lands, or under other forms of political and economic subordination. The outcome of World War I had left the world substantially as it was before the war – divided into territories under the relatively exclusive domain of European nations and the United States – except for the regions included in the USSR.

After World War II, the situation changed. Capital could no longer expand within this international structure of exclusive regions because to do so would only lead to further clashes as nationally defined capital. The postwar reconstruction of capitalist Europe and the United States required new conditions for accumulation, and principal among these was the opening of the colonial empires to access by all capital, particularly from the United States. There was, moreover, in the aftermath of the war numerous civil wars and wars of liberation in the colonies and quasi-colonies throughout Asia, Africa, and the Middle East. Together these conflicts constituted the beginning of a historical juncture in the struggle for self-determination as capitalist or socialist. For the United States and the victorious colonial powers of Europe, the postwar era required continuous efforts to resist the appeal of socialism as a form of liberation from decades of colonial oppression. The movements for change had to be embraced or contained within the framework of liberal democracy and national/international capitalist development. For the most part, however, the necessary economic conditions for liberal democracy were not present in these subject nations, and puppet regimes of various sorts with national figureheads had to be installed as counters to the broad support for socialism or independent national development.

In this struggle for self-determination by colonial peoples, the United Nations was employed primarily in the form of peacekeeping operations[69] to achieve the U.S. objective of defeating or preventing any move to self-determination that would take the form of socialism. Even as many of these struggles continued, the United Nations adopted in 1960 the Declaration on the Granting of Independence to Colonial Countries and Peoples, which defined the "right of self-determination" as a right to be exercised "in conformity with the provisions of the UN Charter"[70] – "provisions" that were and remain fundamentally the principles of liberal democracy and private rights.

The dilemma of the *direction* of self-determination is in part hidden in the words "colonial countries and peoples," which the UN document does not define. Those words would appear to refer to the peoples of the colonial territories conceived as an integral unit, but rarely in practice was there such integrity. The colonial peoples were divided along numerous lines – class, caste, clan, "tribe," ethnicity, religion, language, mode of production – which usually precluded an easy consensus over the postcolonial future. The question of self-determination implies the "will of the people" and so devolves upon what constitutes the "people." In effect, the "people" are for the most part defined everywhere as those who reflect the interests of the most powerful sector of society; and the determination of the most powerful sector usually becomes a contest between the capitalist and labouring classes, broadly defined, or between those classes and institutionalized religion or some other social force, including puppets promoted by the Western imperial powers. Whichever organized social force could manage to gain sufficient power to presume to speak in the name of the "people," to assume the mantle of the "nation," would become the embodiment of the right of self-determination.

The prevailing assertions of national self-determination in the nineteenth century amounted to the declaration of the interests of capital over a certain territory; and national self-determination was only as strong and successful as the strength and character of the national capitalist class. Where other factors, such as language, religion, and ethnicity, are pre-eminent in defining the people or nation (for example, the Québécois, Scots, Welsh, Basques, Kurds, Palestinians) but not associated with the unified interests of capital or labour, self-determination either does not succeed or becomes a compromised version of nationhood (Quebec, Scotland, Wales). When the interests of capital and the strategic interests of some group coincide, as with the Zionist goal of a Jewish home in Palestine, political, economic, and military aid is provided to achieve the goal, despite unprincipled actions in its realization, and continuous violations of human rights.[71]

By the early twentieth century the struggles of the working classes had gained enough understanding and experience to mount socialist or working-class demands for national status. The Russian Revolution of 1917 was made in the name of a people's right to self-determination, in which the people were the working classes. Unfortunately, the main principle of the Revolution – to bring an end to all forms of discrimination based on private property within the nation – came up against the reality of a substantial percentage of people working as owners of private property in land. Later, after the principles underlying socialized property as the form of national self-determination had been largely abandoned, the system itself began to lose legitimacy under the weight of cynicism, disillusionment, and the coercion necessary to keep alive the idea of the people's self-determination as a deceit. By the end of the twentieth century, the same loss of belief in the "people's will" was taking place in the liberal democracies.

After World War II, the idea of self-determination in the form of socialism had not yet lost its sense of promise; and the demands for socialism persisted or grew in the former colonial nations. Countries in Asia, Africa,[72] the Middle East, and then in Latin America saw many attempts to assert the self-determination of a people employing the principles of socialized property rather than of corporate capital. As the inequities of capitalist penetration throughout the Third World increased in the following decades, so too did the interest in socialism. Although that interest was eventually compromised and frustrated, nevertheless it did indicate that the self-determination of nations does find expression by and large as a class interest. The whole postwar era to the early 1990s was marked, with minor variations, by two dominant forms of self-determination defined by class interests – capitalist and socialist – which engaged in a continuous contestation, variously covert or openly aggressive.

In the Cold War era, lasting almost to the end of the twentieth century, the world's two dominant nations, the United States and the USSR, interfered continuously in the affairs of foreign states in order to influence the class direction of the right of self-determination. Over several decades, the growing class inequities and corruption within the "socialist" states and the sheer weight of the economic, military, and ideological power of the West, led by the United States, sanctioned the interests of capital in the form of liberal democracy or dictatorship as the voice of the "people" almost everywhere in the world. But for these interests to prevail, the United States had to intervene around the world to prevent the right of self-determination of nations – a point made clear by U.S. statesman Henry Kissinger in his well-known, infamous remark about Chile in the early 1970s: "I don't see why we need to stand by and watch a country go communist because of the irresponsibility of its own people." It is difficult to name a country that has not experienced unsolicited U.S. intervention in its internal affairs in some form or other since 1945. Indeed, any discussion of the right of self-determination in the absence of an analysis of U.S. subversion around the world takes on the appearance of otherworldliness.[73]

Although national capital usurps the voice of the majority, or the voice of national capital becomes the voice of the nation, capital does not remain national. Part of the reason for the success of capitalist nations in this contest with socialism lay in the postwar creation of "global enabling frameworks" for capital – sets of oversight mechanisms for capital at the transnational level, initially comprising the IMF, World Bank, and GATT[74] – that allowed for and encouraged the accumulation of capital on a global level, greatly increasing its drive for more expanding markets and ever higher levels of technology. The more that capital expanded and became global in its operations, the more it lost its national character and became capital *sans* nationality, the transnational corporation. Its voice at the regional and global levels became embodied as the policies of the enabling frameworks, along with regional agreements and multilateral monetary and military pacts. Since the 1970s, these frameworks have placed strict limits on the ability of all nations to determine national priorities. The right of self-determination as national capital or working-class interests is now a diminished right, to say the least; and the right of self-determination of the nation-state in the twenty-first century is no longer a right with any future. The illusions are left in place – as a basis of the continuing legitimacy of political structures – but any goals of national self-determination are now highly and increasingly and irretrievably circumscribed by global or regional mechanisms for the expansion of capital.

* * *

As defined and applied since their inception, human rights are relative to present and past historical conditions. The contradictions implicit in these rights reflect the contradictions in the mode of production and corresponding division of labour, class structure, and political forms that they produce. This is why human rights have been and are the subject of intense contestation and continue to be the form in which demands for change are expressed under capitalism. They are not absolute in any way; and they reflect the struggles and changing status and consciousness of subordinate and dominant classes, peoples, strata, and groups in a certain era. They are the abstract statement of the human condition at a stage in human development and self-recognition.

The contradictions also make it clear that human rights are not, as they are often treated, homogeneous. The rubric of human rights covers many different and incompatible rights, the most overarching of which is the logic of corporate civil rights that contradict all other rights. In general civil rights, moreover, are inconsistent with social rights; and collective or co-operative rights stand opposed to private property rights. What are called human rights, then, are composed of a heterogeneous amalgam of opposing claims with antithetical premises.

These contradictions reflect the interests at stake struggling for resolution – for a result in which the inequality of power is taken to an extreme or brought to a close. Relations of unequal power can never be stable; although there can be respite from conflict for periods of time, that respite is not to be confused with resolution or reconciliation. The status and structure of human rights can be seen as the expression of the state of social and political conflict, and just as these conflicts evolve so too does the definition of human rights.

These contradictions point as well to a paradox. While human rights are an expression of a stage of human development, their core elements are taken as absolute. By asserting the principles of evolving contemporary circumstances as if they were the essence of humanity, human rights perform an ideological function. Understood as "human" and therefore as essential, they become the absolute measure of human relations and so preclude consideration of other forms of right, other definitions of humanity, and a critique of liberal democracy. The demands and rights, the meaning of humanity, and forms of governance that exist outside the framework of human rights are, from this perspective, variously dismissed, criticized, rejected, ridiculed, or simply not comprehended because of the ideological function of the UDHR and associated covenants and conventions. As such, human rights can and have become a weapon in theory and practice for upholding and advancing the prevailing relations of unequal power.

At the same time, the use of the UDHR as a measure of the theory and practice of liberal-democratic states cannot simply be dismissed. It has been employed by many, but none so well as Noam Chomsky, to expose the extensive and horrific violations of human rights by the industrial states, particularly the U.S. government. That exposure amounts to unveiling the hypocrisy of American foreign policy, and to some degree of its domestic policy. But taking the accusation of these violations no further than pointing to hypocrisy reveals an understanding of the UDHR that accepts the underlying premises of the human as mere individual and possessor of exclusive rights. It is to miss the point that hypocrisy in foreign and domestic policy is a manifestation of the contradictions within and between the three main components of human rights. As long as the exposure of the violations remains on the level of citing hypocrisy and evincing moral outrage, and as long as human rights are taken as legitimate final goals, we will not understand why the violations persist and the struggle continues. [75]

If the coming of the UDHR in the middle of the twentieth century represents a significant turning point in the development of human consciousness, at the beginning of the twenty-first century it has come to the end of its life as a set of theoretical and practical goals. The arrival of a global capitalism of highly concentrated and centralized transnational corporations has exacerbated a contradiction that has existed all along, between the rights of corporations and all other rights. The regional and global enabling frameworks that represent the interests of TNCs have little reason to respect the rights of non-corporate interests. Defending those rights that remain, and demanding their extension, is to use the principles of competitive capitalist nation-states against an emerging transnational system of cartelized and oligopolistic TNCs. The continuing struggle for these rights, then, remains progressive only because they conflict with TNC rights and the agencies of the transnational quasi-states that violate them. Indeed, the preconditions that obliged national capital to accept by and large the broad range of human rights have more or less passed away. The struggle to maintain these rights in a transnational political economy, then, exposes not only the limits of these rights but also the necessity of the TNCs of the post-Cold War world to ignore the principles that capitalism once purportedly rested on – unless pressured by threats from subordinate classes or peoples, or by the need to maintain a degree of legitimacy. Human rights necessarily begin to take on new meaning.

CHAPTER IV

Rights Outside Capitalist Relations

All the human rights as found in the UDHR reflect the character of civil society and its relation to the state in a capitalist social formation. The respective importance of these rights in a given nation reflects that state's history of class struggle. This condition means that at certain times all but the prevailing corporate rights can be suppressed if these rights are seriously threatened by the advance of the political, civil, or countervailing rights of non-corporate sectors. In countries with other modes of production or in those with hybrid or articulated modes, these so-called human rights can appear in some cases as only partially valid; in others they appear as simply alien, as demands from another world.

"SOCIALIST" COUNTRIES

Although the leading example of "actually existing socialism," the USSR, has now passed into history as a "socialist" state, and the main remaining disparate examples (for instance, China, Vietnam, and Cuba) are in different ways transforming themselves, a brief note on what has passed for "socialism" will, perhaps, help to cast light on the nature of human rights. The socialism referred to here is defined as a mode of production in which state rights over the land and water and most of the means of production prevails; and the workers remain employees, but of the state. A single political party purports to represent the interests of the majority, the working people, and determines the policies and priorities of economic (and political and cultural) activity. To the extent that private ownership rights exist, they are limited mainly to housing, small landholdings, and consumables, but do not, with minor exceptions, extend to resources or the means of production. Given that the essential relations of capital remain in this model, although the possessor of capital in the means of production has changed, a more appropriate label might be state capitalism.[1]

This generalized state ownership means that the state assumes the direction and management of production and distribution of the social product, the central activity in civil society in a capitalist society. If the capitalist state embodies, protects, and promotes the abstracted property relations of civil society, allowing for the relative autonomy of multiple private corporations in the capitalist economy, the "socialist" state assumes ownership and direction and so subsumes the economy, which only appears as such, as a separate sphere, in a capitalist mode of production. State or collective ownership of the means of economic and social reproduction, then, precludes the attachment of civil rights, that is, private individual or corporate rights, to these means. It follows that civil rights, inasmuch as they exist in a "socialist" system, do not have the significance that they hold under capitalism, where they underlie and define the very basis of economic power and social reproduction based on private ownership of the means of production.

In these "socialist" states, with a single political party purportedly representing the common interests of the proletarian and peasant majority as the "dictatorship of the proletariat," and other class interests excluded from political expression, the main political rights allowed are those *within* the single governing party. There is no need, therefore, for political rights that imply a choice of class-based parties or policies.[2] Political rights exist in capitalist societies because the various conflicting private interests of civil society require mechanisms to determine which faction of capital will dominate state policy and control the public purse within the general framework of corporate private property. Political rights and structures allow for alternating parties that offer more or less reform to a constitutionally protected framework of private rights. Parties whose programs promise to overturn this framework (such as the early socialist or communist parties) are generally outlawed, just as parties representing the interests of private capital are outlawed in "socialist" states. Each system obliges political rights to be exercised within a particular property framework.

When the state and single party presume to embody the main components of civil society – ownership of the means of production and safeguarding the interests of the working class – civil and political rights, which exist because civil society exists separately from the state, diminish or disappear.[3] At the same time, the presumption of embodying the interests of the people emphasizes the question of social rights, which are developed in the direction of universal inclusion. The striving to provide social goods and services for all becomes a hallmark of "socialist" countries. For this reason, historically, the standards of public health, education, and culture have been highly developed (and they remain relatively so today in Cuba) compared to nations of similar industrial development.

The Rise and Fall of Social Rights

Even at the height of the Cold War a writer of a widely used text in the West could state, perhaps with some exaggeration: "By 1960, the Soviet Union had achieved 100 per cent literacy. [In that decade] the Soviet Union [had] four times as many students in higher education as Great Britain, France, Italy, and West Germany *combined* ... and annually graduate[d] more than three times as many engineers as the United States." Similar achievements were made in medical care, culture, the emancipation of women, child care, eradication of diseases, and average life expectancy. Similar cases may be made for China and Cuba in the first decade or so after their revolutions.

With the introduction of capitalist reforms in Russia in the 1990s, social reproduction became secondary to the so-called economic reforms that brought widespread corruption and the plunder of the vast state sector. The most cynical of economists referred to this colossal swindle of the people, deemed necessary for the assertion of civil rights for corporations, as "shock therapy." The collapse of the USSR as socialized capital meant the decline of its social security system and resulted in "the steepest plunge [in life expectancy] yet recorded in an industrialized country in peacetime .... The growth of AIDS and HIV infection is already the fastest in the world. Drug use ... has risen sharply. Tuberculosis has reached epidemic proportions."

Other reports make similar assessments: According to a statement from the head of the Russian Academy of Medical Sciences in 2000, "Russia is on the verge of a demographic crisis." A report from the State Statistics Committee noted: "Deaths outnumbered births in 1999 by 788,000. In the past 8 years, Russia's population has shrunk by 2.8 million, or more than 2%, and now stands at 145.6 million people .... The life expectancy of a Russian is 56 years – lower than most 'official' Third World nations."

With adoption of the so-called market reforms, state responsibility for human health and well-being has been increasingly abandoned in the scramble for private ownership over the vast state sector and in the pursuit of the private accumulation of capital.

• Aspaturian, "Soviet Union," pp.402-3; *The Globe and Mail*, Dec. 2, 2000; *CovertAction Quarterly*, no. 69 (Spring/Summer, 2000), p.17.

With the collapse of the "socialist" regimes in the USSR and Eastern Europe, and their progressive transformation in China, Vietnam, and Cuba, the role of corporate private property is being reinstated. With some exceptions, the state-owned means of production are being more or less rapidly privatized, social rights are being progressively dismantled and deregulated, and the constitution and legal system are being changed to protect private property. As a result, civil society has to be reclaimed or reinvented – it has to be reconstructed formally as the arena of division and inequality that it remained all along in truncated form, but with its institutional expression suppressed. The presumption that the state and party had precluded the existence of a civil society through a near monopoly of ownership and political right could not be true as long as control over the state and party remained in bureaucratic hands – that is, as long as the "actually existing" working classes were prevented by these structures and institutions from direct control over their own social and material reproduction. The size of the ministry of police gave the lie to this presumption. As long as the state and party remained institutions separate and different from the people themselves, the existence of a vestigial civil society could only be suppressed or usurped and in those ways minimized. Implicitly, it was always there but never allowed to find expression as such because formally the state and party always presumed to embody the interests of the majority of the people.

This discrepancy in state-controlled capitalism parading as a form of people's control was exploited by the West through the question of human rights. In 1973 in Helsinki, the Conference on Security and Co-operation in Europe was convened with representatives from all of Eastern Europe (except Albania) and Western Europe, along with Canada and the United States. It concluded in 1975 with an agreement and a "declaration of intentions." Aside from questions of European security and co-operation across a wide field, the accord included significant statements about respect for "human rights," and it expressed "intentions" to "promote" and "encourage" these rights as found in the UDHR and its associated covenants. The so-called Helsinki Accord soon found a ready audience in the Eastern bloc countries because of the restrictive nature of the Soviet system. The stated agreement to promote a freer flow of information and a range of other liberal-democratic rights generated new activity in intellectual circles. It encouraged human rights activists by giving them a certain protection from the state through attention in the Western media and support from Western leaders. The Charter 77 group in Czechoslovakia, a direct consequence of the Helsinki Accord, was one of the best-known of such groups; but throughout the Eastern bloc and the USSR human rights committees were set up in support of the Accord, and certain individuals were raised to celebrity status.[4] It is difficult to say how significant these movements were in the ultimate demise of state capitalism in Eastern Europe and the USSR, but that they played an important role is beyond doubt.

The regimes dominated by corporate ownership and those dominated by state ownership of the means of production clearly show significant differences in the theory and practice of human rights. Corporate ownership places an emphasis on civil and political rights (which give freedom to capital to act within the framework of corporate private property), and a resistance to or minimization of social rights because in general they serve to decommodify labour-power, restrict the sphere of private accumulation, or contradict corporate rights in other ways. State ownership of the means of production places an emphasis on social rights (which follows from the presumption of a workers' state) and a dismissal or downgrading not only of civil rights because of state ownership of the means of production, but also of political rights because the party presumes to be the voice of the people.

In the so-called socialist regimes, the state and party remained separate from the people and ultimately became controlled by members of a privileged elite. This structure not only gave the lie to any assertions about being a workers' state but also created an abiding rationale for demands for certain civil and political rights. If the people have no access to public policy decision-making or ownership of the means of production, they will make demands for one or the other and struggle to achieve some sort of access, or descend into cynicism and apathy. Such demands were inevitable, but were treated as aberrations or as external attempts to undermine the system.[5] The inherent foundations of the demands and their persistence led to chronic, though usually low-level, political and economic unrest and the consequent need for a pervasive and coercive security system in support of the "existing untruth."

In capitalist regimes the state embodies the prevailing corporate property relations, and, bounded by a constitutional framework that reflects them, political parties give voice to certain class and strata interests in civil society. The declared equality and universality of civil and political rights and their abstract existence in the form of law obscure the reality of the restrictive nature of the framework and the financial prerequisites necessary for their realization. The regulated assertion of corporate rights impinges on or denies the civil rights of non-owners of the means of production. The subordination and circumscription of the civil rights of working people lead to social unrest and the demand for compensatory social rights. Corporate rights and social rights, however, are contradictory in principle and often openly so in practice, and so the more unmitigated the corporate rights the greater the need for an increasing police and/or military presence to suppress or contain countervailing demands.

In capitalist regimes, for all practical purposes, civil rights for the majority are restricted to claims for consumable goods and services realized through purchase. Political rights, although instrumental in achieving social rights, are highly circumscribed within a certain property framework. Social rights stand as real and positive achievements for the majority, attained in a system that in principle contradicts such rights and constantly seeks to minimize or dismiss them. In "socialist" regimes, with civil rights largely subsumed in state ownership of the means of production, those rights are also restricted to claims for consumable goods; and political rights are highly circumscribed within a single political party. Here too, social rights represent the real gain for the working classes but are usually more extensive than in capitalist systems. Both types of regime give names to the illusions of popular control – the "will of the people" and the "dictatorship of the proletariat" – but the significant rights and real gains for working people rest in whatever *social rights* they achieve or are granted to facilitate their social reproduction. In both systems these social rights are always administered by agencies of the state; they are never endowed with the power that the rights of ownership confer; they are never administered by the people themselves.

With the demise of the "socialist" states in Eastern Europe came the need to reinvent or reformulate their civil societies and corresponding administrative agencies of the state. New constitutions were introduced to guarantee civil and political rights; state assets were privatized, in many cases, particularly in the former Soviet Union, amounting to the massive theft of what was supposed to be public property. But before the institutions of civil society and the agencies of a liberal-democratic state could be constructed, rapid changes at the global level undermined any possibility of building modern capitalist nation-states. Global corporations and criminal organizations often gained dominant ownership rights in the production and supply of essential goods and services; and the coming of multiple political parties meant little for political rights given the constitutional protection for transnational corporations and the neo-liberal policies demanded by the IMF and World Bank and Western states. Within a decade, the former "socialist" countries of Eastern Europe were left with declining social rights and with civil and political rights for the majority no more meaningful than in the liberal democracies of the West. If the "dictatorship of the proletariat" proved illusory, the coming of the civil and political rights of a capitalist civil society amounted to new illusions. The working people of Eastern Europe now experience the same illusions as their counterparts in the West, but with fewer of the social rights they once had.

HUMAN RIGHTS AND THE THIRD WORLD

It is usually outside the liberal democracies of the industrial nations that the question of the relativity of human rights becomes an issue. The challenge to the idea of the universality of human rights comes, for the most part, from the Third World, from those nations that in attempting to "modernize" might have been expected to make the strongest case for fullest application of these rights.

As a category the Third World is less than exact; it is a loosely used term, and usually includes a host of nations that are vastly different in significant ways.

As used here, the term refers to nation-states that have at least one of two dominant characteristics.[6] One is the existence of sizable percentages of the population remaining outside full-time contractual or wage-labour – that is, large numbers still existing within precapitalist modes of production. In such countries the formation of modern civil society remains incomplete. The other characteristic is a high degree of economic dependence on one or more industrial nations or transnational corporations, implying political policies that reflect the demands of those nations or particular TNCs and not broad domestic interests. The relative significance of these two factors lies at the heart of the debate on cultural relativity and human rights.

Where the development of civil society (most importantly, the relations between capital and labour) is incomplete or remains profoundly heterogeneous, the development of social rights is obviated by the existence of non-capitalist (traditional) or petty commodity systems of production and distribution that provide necessities more or less inclusively for their respective social units. Even in the industrial nations up to the 1930s, the existence of a sizable percentage of the labour force on the land, largely in precapitalist petty commodity production (the "family-farm"), or self-employed, lessened the need for social reforms. Only after the Great Depression and World War II – and therefore the near completion of the making of the working class or the all but destruction of pre-capitalist strata or groups – were social reforms developed to become the relatively comprehensive "welfare state" of the postwar era. In many Third World countries the making of the working class remains incomplete, although that formation continues to be pressed through the destruction of the environment, civil wars, the "war on drugs," the usurpation of land rights, "development" projects, and the privatization of land.[7] Still, the working class generally far from includes the whole of the adult working population; and as long as the population is structurally divided by ethnicity, religion, language, and so long as substantial numbers of people continue to live outside wage-labour, the need for social reform (of the relations of capital) and the demand for it will remain limited.

Civil rights, furthermore, are highly restricted. Although a state exists in all Third World countries, an incomplete development of civil society means that the foundation of the state is correspondingly limited. If the state is defined as the embodiment of the abstracted prevailing property relations in civil society, the practical manifestation of these relations in civil society today comprises, for the most part, TNCs, certain powerful local interests, and the policy priorities of the IMF, World Bank, and WTO among other global or regional agencies. The property framework that those forces demand is maintained by the state and does not normally include the property relations of those sections of the nation that have not been incorporated into the relations of corporate capital. The civil rights of a capitalist mode of production have little meaning to those living outside or marginal to a market system – except as destructive, or even alien, claims enforced by the weight of state coercion.

Political rights are similarly limited when part of the population remains outside civil society, or is perhaps only tangentially related; in those positions political rights are of little significance. Citizenship may be denied to those who live in the non-capitalized side of articulated modes of production, or indeed it may not appear to the people as a necessary status or desired objective. Moreover, the political rights that do exist for those who are part of civil society are circumscribed; the property relations that inform civil society and that the state embodies are usually determined by forces outside the nation. If the state is accountable to external forces that control the economy, then political rights for the populace, even if they exist, are largely illusions.

That situation would appear to be the case in South Africa with the beginning of the end of apartheid in 1990. During the apartheid years, the struggle led by the African National Congress focused the political aspirations of the Black majority of South Africans on the achievement of liberal democracy and associated civil and political rights.[8] The agreement to end apartheid and introduce liberal democracy circumvented, at least in the short term, the possibility of a struggle for socialism and at the same time preserved the same property relations that had existed under apartheid while opening South Africa even more to the demands of global capital. Change in the 1990s brought increased global corporate access to the economy, a new framework for its development, and new possibilities for a few Black South Africans – Black businesses, some access to the corporate managerial strata, and significant entry to the bureaucratic strata of government[9] – but very little changed for the majority.

In general in Third World nations, the practice of human rights is limited by the distorted development and divisive nature of the civil society and by the continuing political, economic, and military interference by former colonial powers and the U.S. government. While numerous large-scale violations of human rights have taken place in newly independent countries in Africa and Asia, for the most part these have been the consequences of the colonial rule of the immediate past – a product of corrupted domestic elites, the arbitrary drawing of national borders, and the continuing postcolonial interference by industrial nations. The U.S. state in particular has been in the forefront of violations of human rights and the establishment of authoritarian regimes throughout the Third World since the 1950s in order to guarantee and protect the world operations of capital against the possibility of socialism or national development.[10]

An African Concept of Human Rights

Given that almost every country of Africa is characterized by relatively high degrees of foreign economic dependency and the incomplete development of a modern civil society (and so the truncated reality of human rights), many writers have focused considerable attention on the difference between Africa and the West, and have argued for the existence of an African concept of human rights.[11]

The specificity of African rights in these arguments rests on examples from persisting non-capitalist or precolonial modes of production that stand outside or are articulated within the dominant capitalist mode. Large segments of the populations have continued to live outside or are tangentially related to the modernized sector. As a result many features of the non-capitalist ways of life, though by and large now fractured and dissipated in some way, remain operative as customs and practices, or at least remain alive as ideals. At the heart of most of these now-fragmented modes of production was the reality of a communalism of various sorts and degrees. The foundation of these co-operative social units rested in enduring collective forms of land ownership or nomadic ways of life; and it was expressed in consensual forms of decision-making and in views of "personhood" as part of a contiguous whole. For very large numbers of Africans, a person is not defined as an autonomous solitary being but as a relationship to a community. To be human is not to be the possessor of private rights or the exclusive owner of material goods but to have roles and obligations in a larger social unit, to be an integral part of a whole. Freedom is not a matter of the autonomy of the relation-less individual but of the acknowledged necessity and reciprocity of social relations.

As long as facets of these non-capitalist or precolonial ways of life have continued, analysts could make the case for the cultural relativity of rights, because where these different modes of production exist they carry with them concepts and practices of rights that are qualitatively different than those defined as human rights in the UDHR. Given that Africa has had many different types of modes of production,[12] however, the case for a single African concept of rights is less than solid; there are as many concepts of rights as there are modes of production and stages of development. There is, then, an argument for cultural relativity of rights based on different cultures as viable social communities, but not for the idea or reality of a unique pan-African set of rights. As the capitalist mode of production comes to prevail in Africa and imposes its own ethics, so too the voices arguing for an African concept of rights based on traditional communities decline.

Under colonial regimes, indigenous non-capitalist rights for specific tribes or ethnic groups were also often left in place while civil and political rights were selectively imposed for the colonizer or certain civil rights were granted solely to investors or corporations, foreign and domestic. The resulting hybrid or articulated system of rights is probably best understood as a transitional form, a stage in the breakdown of precapitalist rights, and not as a distinctly African form. Furthermore, when certain rights of non-capitalist social formations, those of a clan or tribe or chiefdom, for instance, are transferred to a capitalist social formation, they often simply constitute the instrumental use of cultural differences, and amount to arbitrary rule by hereditary or other rulers.

Another hybrid form came in the experiments of non-traditional African methods of nation-building after colonialism. The most widely known example was Nkrumah's attempt to overcome the colonial legacy in Ghana, to build the economy and address the problems of many ethnic groups, little infrastructure, limited technology and capital, and few educated nationals through a mix of domestic and foreign, private and public capital. His use of economic planning and state funds and corporations to modernize, to build a new nation, and create an accompanying political stance of Third World non-alignment had limited success, in large part because of the opposition it encountered in the industrial countries. Although widely maligned by the West, Nkrumah's policies found their principal motivation in the utter failure of mainstream Western economic policies – formulas employed in colonial and postcolonial regimes to modernize or Africanize the newly independent nations – to prevent the continuous draining of the surplus generated back to the former colonial metropolitan interests.[13] In the end, the United States and the former colonial powers saw the attempt at indigenous national development by means of a mixed economy and the politics of non-alignment as socialist and/or nationalist and, therefore, as taking these countries entirely or partially outside the orbit of global capital.

The idea of a distinct African concept of human rights based on certain kinds of communalism is not plausible, then, given a number of factors: there has been no one indigenous African mode of production; most of the non-capitalist ways of life in Africa have been or are being destroyed, and those that remain are usually dissipated or purposively articulated with the prevailing capitalist mode of production; the attempted experiments by Nkrumah (and Nyerere, Cabral, and others) wrongly assumed fair trade relations and good faith from the industrial nations in building independent postcolonial nations; and those experiments were in any event sabotaged and are no longer. For many of the same reasons, it is not plausible to imagine the viability of the human rights of the UDHR in most of Africa. As long as TNCs and the industrial states conspire to forge and support authoritarian governments,[14] as long as the World Bank and IMF demand crippling structural adjustment policies that exacerbate poverty and foreign dependency and usurp political independence, and as long as civil society is left fractured along religious, ethnic, and linguistic lines, the possibilities for human rights and liberal democracy remain mere illusions.

The future of Africa is further darkened by the prospects entailed in U.S. plans for the continent put forth in the 1990s. The African Growth and Opportunity Act made its way through the U.S. legislative process in 2000 and promises to be a NAFTA for Africa, a U.S.-led reconstruction of the continent based on the establishment of market conditions for the receipt of U.S. aid and foreign direct investment. In the words of a briefing paper:

At the core of the Act is another attempt to force African governments to prioritize a series of free market principles, including cuts in government expenditures, privatization of government corporations, new rights for foreign investors to buy African natural resources and state firms without limits, deep cuts in tariffs, and membership in the World Trade Organization.[15]

In June 2002, a much-promoted initiative said to be African in origin, the New Partnership for Africa's Development (NEPAD), was released, co-terminus with the G8 meeting in Canada. NEPAD promised all the elements of the failed model of the West: liberal democracy with civil and political rights, market capitalism, and integration into the global economy. It made no mention of social rights or economic development in any way other than through subordination to market forces. NEPAD appeared to be exactly what Washington wanted for Africa.[16]

The breakdown of communal rights and the failure of the process of capitalist modernization have left the most vulnerable people exposed to pervasive abuse in Africa. Women and children have suffered disproportionately in the last several decades, particularly in sub-Saharan Africa. The conflict has seen a pervasive denial of property rights to women,[17] extensive sexual abuse, and the widespread use of children in war.

Still, the attempts to formulate the idea of an African concept of human rights do indicate the existence of different rights and ways to be human relative to different modes of production – a point that, again, illustrates the relativity of the human rights of the UDHR,[18] and the difficulty of applying those principles when the conditions of a capitalist mode of production are not present. The attempts indicate the possibility of asserting rights for peoples, and not merely individuals, and of asserting the right of peoples to determine their own fate free from the dominance of corporate civil rights and the global regulatory agencies.

After more than three decades of destructive and often fomented civil wars, genocide, brutal dictatorships, and foreign interference and intervention, the communal or co-operative foundation for a distinctive African notion of rights has all but disappeared; but at the same time an African human rights more or less like the UDHR has been asserted. With the near-destruction of non-capitalist modes of production and experiments in a mixed economy, Africa was ready for a declaration of human rights similar to the West, where a comparable destruction had taken place earlier over several centuries. The African Charter on Human and Peoples' Rights was adopted in 1981 and came into force in 1986, and a related African Commission on Human and Peoples' Rights was established in 1987. Like the UN Charter and the UN Commission on Human Rights, those efforts contained a similar definition of human rights and were intended to promote and ensure the protection of "human and peoples' rights." They provide the same emphasis on individual rights, private property, and the nuclear family as the "basis of society" – and this in a continent in which private rights have meant little for the overwhelming majority and polygamy remains common. The African Commission, like the UN body, possesses no judicial powers and was made subordinate to the Organization of African Unity (OAU), to which it submitted reports.[19]

Established in 1963, the OAU was transformed into the African Union (AU) in May 2001, following an earlier attempt in 1994, in the form of the African Economic Community (AEC), to create an African common market similar to the European Common Market. The AU was to be an organization "aimed at economic integration and social development [of Africa] which should lead to political unity."[20] The goal of the Union is to "ensure speedy establishment of all the institutions [of the AEC] such as the African Central Bank, the African Monetary Union, the African Court of Justice, and in particular, the Pan-African Parliament." Modelling itself after the European Union, the AU is intended to create a single continental capitalist market accompanied by a pan-African political structure. There is mention of compliance with the UDHR and the African Charter, but no suggestion of an African concept of human rights.

Islamization and Human Rights

The resurgence of Islam since the 1970s has given rise to Islamization, or the establishment of Islamic republics and the accompanying promulgation of Sharia, the divine law of Islam said to derive from the Koran and other sources. Many countries in the Middle East, Africa, and Asia "have proclaimed Islam to be the state religion and/or Sharia to be the principle source of law."[21] Given the incompatibility of the human rights of the UDHR and theocratic rule, these developments have engendered many debates on the cultural relativity of human rights in the Islamic world.[22]

Many aspects of the ethical codes of Islam would appear to be inconsistent with the underlying tenets of human rights. The prescribed roles and position of women under Sharia are the most obvious examples. Such incongruities, however, are found more or less in all institutionalized religions; there are no formalized religious teachings or practices that are completely consistent with the principles of human rights – especially on the question of women. In a secular liberal-democratic state, these inconsistencies are confined to aspects of private life, along with religion itself, and do not then in principle affect the prevailing political and economic relations and the legal promotion of human rights. When a particular religion is proclaimed to be the religion of the state, however, the principles of human rights are invariably compromised or applied only expediently by the state.

The case of Israel provides a good example. To define the nation of Israel as a Jewish state means that its establishment could only come about through the violation of the human rights of non-Jews, in particular Palestinians – violations that have been continuous and egregious and well documented by every major human rights organization, among others, throughout the history of Israel.[23] The creation of a religiously defined state in Israel is no different than the creation of states in countries that have defined themselves as Islamic republics. In neither case is the issue one of cultural relativity, but rather the use of religion to define certain matters of state. The central question is why the formation of an Islamic theocracy takes place in some nations and not in others in which Islam is the prevailing religion.

Our definition of Third World nations pointed to two key defining characteristics: an incomplete development of civil society and/or overweening foreign economic and political intervention. Such "underdevelopment" rarely provides the conditions necessary for the establishment of either national capitalism or socialism. Continuing foreign economic intervention hinders or distorts the growth of domestic capital and therefore the establishment of a sizable and relatively coherent domestic bourgeoisie; and the continuing divisions and fractures in the non-corporate side of civil society – along lines of class, caste, ethnicity, tribe, gender, language, mode of production – mitigate the development of a relatively coherent working-class majority. Even the territorial boundaries of these nations in many cases came into being through the arbitrary assertion of colonial power. Because of the nature of colonial or quasi-colonial exploitation, only with difficulty have these countries produced an indigenous, organized group, sector, class, or strata that could, on its own, plausibly represent the "nation."

Islamic States

An enormous lack of clarity exists around what constitutes an Islamic state, and many contentious issues surround the definition. What constitutes Islam – which sect possesses the truth and which is apostate? Is a Muslim majority sufficient? Must all the laws be derived from religious teachings? Or are co-existing forms of rule, Sharian and secular, possible? Do mullahs in government make for an Islamic state? Is there only one valid interpretation of Sharia? Can an Islamic state be defended by a non-Islamic state?

None of these unresolved questions have prevented the proclamation of Islamic rule in numerous states, but the problems they raise have also allowed some Muslims to argue that no states in the Muslim world are Islamic states. If we replace the word Islam with Judaism, we can also ask the same questions about Israel.

In almost all postcolonial states, the central problem has been to locate an organized component that could credibly embody, or act in the name of, the "nation" – which is in effect a political framework for a set of prevailing property relations. Only a few possibilities exist for galvanizing these usually socially fractured entities. One is the military as an organized coercive force unifying the country through conscription, the imposition of uniform laws, and the principle of might is right. The modern history of Turkey in part serves as an example. Another possibility is a social class or ethnic or tribal group that commands enough resources and organized strength to assume the mantle of the "nation." A coalition of classes and groups united around the prospects of postcolonial nation-building could also provide the means. Yet another possibility is an imposed puppet monarchy; and still another is the assumption of power by a prevailing institutionalized religion. Since independence, some postcolonial countries have experienced several different combinations of these ruling structures, in each case representing the "nation" in different ways.

After World War II, former colonized or subject peoples made many attempts to build modern nation-states and fulfil aspirations of self-determination by means of coalition movements of nationalists that advocated a national property framework including forms of state capitalism in a mixed economy. These regimes were generally popular because the state corporations opened up for the new citizens opportunities that were not possible under colonial rule, and because the governments allowed for the co-existence of other forms of property, including communal and small capitalist holdings. The legal system and the nature of rights adopted reflected this hybrid economic structure.

In the eyes of the former colonial powers, however, independent national development – even to the modest degree that it was attempted after World War II in Nasser's Egypt and the Iran of Mosaddeq, for example – was seen as a threat or even as socialistic because of the use of state capital, the nationalization of some foreign corporations, and a certain policy resistance to continued foreign control and private investment. The same questions had arisen earlier, after World War I, with the Bolshevik revolution and the collapse of the Ottoman Empire, when considerable interest in socialism and national development grew throughout the Middle East. As a consequence, these postcolonial attempts at nation-building suffered continuous subversive activity from the industrial countries, particularly the United States, Britain, and France, aimed at undermining the possibilities of national or state capitalist growth. If independent national development in the former colonies meant domestic control over the direction of economic development and restrictions to foreign investment, then, it was in the interests of the industrial nations to establish puppet monarchies or military cliques that could pretend to embody the "nation" while remaining subordinate to the industrial powers, leaving the development of the country to the interests of private, foreign investors.[24]

Throughout the Middle East and North Africa such regimes benefited, for the most part, only small domestic ruling elites and foreign corporations; and they often lacked broad national legitimacy because they excluded the majority from the benefits of national wealth and the domestic social and political opportunities that went with independent national development. The police or military trained and armed by industrial nations, generally subverted human rights, with the exception of corporate rights. When the right of national self-determination is thwarted, when other human rights are denied, and when privileges are granted to foreign interests, the state requires a continuous coercive presence and activity.[25]

In the absence of a puppet monarchy or military junta or representative political movement with a sufficient degree of legitimacy, institutionalized religion was the only other organized sector of society that could presume to embody the "nation." In this sense, Islamization becomes a means of imposing a form of unity where other means have failed, or where there is little cohesiveness if ethnicity or class or tribe have proved insufficient to tie the "nation" together. As with all religious authority, Islamic rule is decreed from above; it is not the result of the exercise of democracy of any sort and is not necessarily supported by the majority. Sometimes it has been imposed in the face of great resistance from various sectors in civil society, although at the same time it can have significant support from deprived classes, sectors, and strata.[26] The imposition of Islamic rule, then, has mostly to do with the powers that be, national or global.

Without exception, the declaration of an Islamic republic has been a means of maintaining arbitrary control of some sort. It does not represent the rule of law – that is, of secular law passed by a legislature – but the rule of religious law, of Sharia. It does not represent the sovereignty of the people but that of a hierarchy or group of priests, of the mullahs, of those who interpret the religious teachings,[27] often in league with secular corporate powers. It stands as the antithesis of forms of governance that are democratic or that may undermine the private accumulation of capital. Whether Islamization supports ownership by national or foreign interests, it does not oppose the process of capital accumulation.[28] Everywhere, it has served to maintain the powers and wealth of undemocratic rulers in the name of the "nation." It has served to prevent aspirations from below for democratic reforms and fundamental social change, and even to permit foreign domination over economic and military policies.[29]

Despite numerous instances of Islamization, the ideas accompanying the proclamation are by no means settled issues. There is little agreement on fundamental questions such as property forms, sovereignty, or even the interpretation of Sharia. As with all religions, Islamic creeds have evolved over time and in different places, and the entire range of its tenets is subject to many interpretations – which explains why religion is amenable as an instrument of social control and manipulation. There is no one Islam, just as there is no one Christian or Jewish or Hindu faith; there are only sects and scholars and schools that vie with one another in their claims to possess the true rendering of the sacred texts.

Not surprisingly, then, attempts to map out an Islamic human rights have produced nothing to compare in coherence to the human rights of the UDHR.[30] However much two statements on Islamic rights – the Universal Islamic Declaration of Human Rights (1981) and the Cairo Declaration on Human Rights in Islam (1990) – attempt to emulate the UDHR, both invoke Sharia as the framework for these rights. The Arab League's Arab Charter on Human Rights (1994), moreover, does not contain many of the key rights and guarantees provided in the UDHR.[31] Wherever Sharia is invoked, furthermore, its interpretation follows the different sects, the struggles of their priests, and national differences, making it far more open to arbitrary variations than is the interpretation of the human rights of the UDHR, which generally follows the changing structure of capital and associated struggles.

The application of Sharia provides a public form of repressive social control over various strata of working people. In general, wherever it is practised it is an important means of upholding relations of dominance, in particular of autocratic rulers over subordinate classes and of men over women. Aside from benefiting the clergy and most established property owners, Islamization and Sharia have consistently had a dramatic effect on females: restricting to varying degrees dress codes, education limits, legal status, employment possibilities, equality in marriage and divorce, and in child custody; and imposing a variety of other discriminatory laws and regulations.[32]

Like other religions, Islam has played different and even contradictory roles in different societies; and like other religions it has been employed as an instrument for gaining the upward mobility of certain strata, for establishing clerical autocracy, for achieving mass mobilization or mass discipline, for countering secular left or liberal nationalist movements, and for guaranteeing control by domestic and even foreign commercial interests. After 1970 the U.S. government made increasing use of Islam in the pursuit of its foreign policy interests in the Middle East. In particular, Islamic fundamentalism was used to undermine all ideas, political parties, and movements in the region that might contribute to secular modernization that was nationalist or socialist, and it was used to combat the Soviet influence. To this end, Washington helped to create and maintain dictatorial regimes that proclaimed themselves Islamic republics (Saudi Arabia, Sudan, Pakistan, Afghanistan, for example), and trained and armed Islamic militias for use in Central Asia and elsewhere.[33]

The chief problem for Islamization, as with all forms of theocracy, is that the capitalist social formation ultimately demands the separation of church and state; in other words, a marketplace civil society calls for a secular state, whose principle is the rule of law, that is, subordination to the prevailing property relations of civil society. State religion can be useful for governing in certain instances and for certain periods of time. State Shinto in Imperial Japan, for example, was employed to unify the "nation" for purposes of war; it was, however, disestablished in postwar Japan to facilitate the country's reconstruction using U.S. capital. Short of disestablishment, the church in unity with the state can also be relegated to a nominal existence without real powers while providing ideological support to the status quo – which is the role of the Anglican Church in Britain. Although politics and religion complement each other – in fact, they require each other – they cannot be the other. The sacred and the profane do not mix well; they make demands on each other that in principle cannot be fulfilled if each is to remain what it is. The religious state denies the self-determination of a people; and it contradicts the full range of the ethics of capitalism and associated ideas of human rights, liberalism, secularism, individualism – and their extensions in the forms of socialism, trade unionism, feminism, and atheism or agnosticism.[34] The contradictions of global capitalism bring their own ethics and political forms of rule, and can tolerate theocracy only as a temporary instrument.

Just as there is no Christian, Buddhist, Hindu, or Jewish way of producing agricultural products or manufacturing goods or building factories, airports, and modern cities, or of managing finance, there is no Islamic way. The rule of the mullahs is nothing more than a reflection of the postcolonial condition and the continuing Western interference in the affairs of countries with Muslim majorities. Islamic rule is always bound up with many entrenched conservative class interests, and for this reason it necessarily rubs against the demands for the full range of human rights or for socialism that accompany the growth of capital and the working classes. Ironically, Muslim clerics face a dilemma, in part of their own making, when they demand Islamization yet simultaneously encourage the accumulation of capital – capital ultimately insists on its own secular ethics.

HUMAN RIGHTS AND THE FOURTH WORLD

The new-found consciousness about human beings that arose from World War II and was ensconced in the UN Charter and UDHR spurred changes in the attitudes of the governments of industrial nations towards Aboriginal peoples. Almost from the beginning of European expansion, non-European peoples were subjected to systematic oppression that included policies to enslave, assimilate, dispossess, isolate, or annihilate. Only gradually and usually after 1945 did the white settler states, colonial administrations, and "new world" governments begin to acknowledge the nature of their actions against indigenous peoples.

The question of Aboriginal rights has direct implications for an estimated 300 to 600 million indigenous people around the world – people who continue to live in defined territories and within social formations with significant non-contractual relations and non-commodified goods and services in their social reproduction.[35] The questions raised by the demands for these rights have implications for the rest of humanity.

The relativity of human rights as defined in the UDHR becomes obvious amidst the arguments for and declarations of the rights of indigenous and tribal peoples. There is a stark contrast between the civil, political, and social rights of a system of private property *and* the customary rights exercised by and belonging to Aboriginal peoples.[36] One set of rights is based on a form of property that is formally defined, alienable, and exclusive to the individual, while the other set is based on forms of property that are generally informally defined, not alienable, and exclusive to a collective. Although these property forms may overlap in practice and pretend a certain harmony,[37] they are not in principle compatible.

Aboriginal peoples have put forward demands for collective forms of land tenure, control over fisheries and subsurface resources, and forms of nationhood that do not necessarily include a state or strictly defined borders – demands that contradict the nature of the modern state and its premise of the system of private accumulation of capital. The demand for self-determination based on collective property implies forms of governance that run counter to the rule of private property implicit in liberal democracy. Demands for collective intellectual and cultural rights are an impediment to the advance of commodified culture and the commodification of indigenous knowledge.[38]

Indigenous rights reflect property systems that existed in much of the world prior to European contact. These systems had not, except in some limited cases, developed forms of individually exclusive rights. While a wide variety of forms of indigenous rights have existed, they have generally been exclusive to families or kinship groups, clans, or larger units, or have taken the form of usufruct. Private individual rights to the products of production were developed only where the practice of producing for exchange was well established, but commodity production in precolonial Aboriginal social formations was for the most part limited. The initial contact of Aboriginal peoples with Europeans marked the confrontation between two contradictory forms of property.

In this confrontation of incompatibles, one side or the other had to be subordinated or destroyed. The nature of the initial contact varied, but invariably the final outcome of the contradiction was resolved in favour of the right of might – the power of superior armed forces, accompanied by genocide, disease, and generations of unscrupulous actions. Over several centuries of European expansion in North and South America, Africa, Asia, and the Pacific, the rights of most of the original inhabitants to the use of land and water were purportedly "ceded" to Europeans through conquest, treaties, purchase, annihilation, decree, or mere assumption. Still, given the failure of the Europeans to honour contracts and treaties and their arbitrary usurpation of indigenous territory, among other questionable actions, many of these Aboriginal rights were never actually extinguished in favour of private property rights.

As more and more of the world's wealth is accumulated in the form of capital, and as capital in the form of the corporation has become transnational and vastly more concentrated than ever before, the pressure to develop the world's resources as capital has grown. To be exploited as corporate capital, resources by definition must be open to private ownership, and here is the rub. The scramble for the world's resources raises the question of just who actually owns them. Nowhere in the world has this question found any adequate resolution because property relations remain relative to a mode of production and the nature of the social struggles within it. Ownership remains an open question despite the assertion of state and corporate rights on one side. Aboriginal rights or indigenous claims that were not extinguished now present certain barriers to the further exploitation of resources by corporations around the world; and they provide significant legal and ethical challenges to Europeans, who simply assumed the legitimacy of their private ownership.[39] Even where indigenous rights were thought to be extinguished, given the questionable legalities surrounding the event, that extinguishment is no longer clear or certain.

In most cases around the world, the conflict between corporate private rights and indigenous rights continues by and large to be addressed, as it was in the past, by various forms of violence. Many methods are employed – direct police/military intervention, genocide, externally financed and fomented civil wars, structural adjustment policies, mercenary armies and paramilitary forces, forced transmigration, the use of legal systems grounded in private property, the banning of language and culture – in the effort to disassociate indigenous peoples from their property relations and to assert private property rights over resources. Few countries in the world are free of the implications of this conflict, past and/or present.[40]

The forcible assertion of private rights over communal or indigenous rights marks the history of almost all nation-states. From the peasant wars in Germany to the highland clearances in Scotland, from the wars of conquest and the enslavement of the "new worlds" by European mercantile powers to the slave trade in Africa, no continent is free of this violent transformation. In fact, in this conflict between private exclusive rights and collective rights is contained the whole modern history of humankind – that is, the history of the expansion of capital and the resistance to it by those dispossessed and/or those obliged to be part of it as slaves, coerced labourers, or wage-workers. The growing capitalization of the world represents at the same time the gradual usurpation of all other forms of wealth and the transformation of all other property relations into private corporate relations. By their nature the relations of capital have led to the concentration of wealth in the form of private property and power at one end, and the growth of wage-labourers and the dispossessed at the other.[41]

An analysis of this continuing conflict, as old as capital itself, sheds light on several issues. The expansion of a system of private property in the form of nation-building, for instance, is always accompanied by some form of violence. Historically and today, when private property succeeds in this conflict the violence always results in dispossession, impoverishment and/or wage-labour, or forms of forced labour as the means of subsistence. While often justified on spurious ethical, racial, religious, or national grounds, the ultimate justification is that might is right. The privatization of the world's commons, in the final analysis, rests on this foundation.

Justification on this basis is necessarily contradictory. A system of private property always develops in the direction of increasing inequalities and therefore always at the expense of some, and ultimately the majority; its expansion and maintenance, then, are necessarily accompanied by forms of coercion and ideological obfuscation. It follows that private property can never be a stable or enduring form of right; such ownership exists as a violation of the rights of the original inhabitants, or usurpation of the rights of others, and can only be perpetuated by continuing forms of deceit, violence, or coercion.

The three groups of contradictory human rights – civil, political, and social – remain largely alien to tens of millions of indigenous peoples and are in part antithetical to their interests. The much-vaunted liberal democracy has rarely provided even a forum for the expression of indigenous rights, let alone self-determination over the use and disposal of ancestral lands and resources. To be consistent with the precepts of liberal democracy, all forms of property must be transformed into private property; everyone must be rendered a private individual. Because the prevailing forms of Aboriginal rights do not take the form of private property, the world's indigenous peoples and their rights go unmentioned in the UDHR and are largely unrepresented in the United Nations.

Reflecting the principles of private property, the UN was slow, to say the least, to acknowledge the existence of Aboriginal rights and to provide a modicum of representation. In the 1970s the UN Subcommittee on the Protection of Minorities and Prevention of Discrimination commissioned a study on discrimination against Aboriginal peoples. The resulting reports led to the creation of the UN Working Group on Indigenous Populations (WGIP) in 1982. Over the next decade the WGIP produced more studies that consistently revealed similar patterns of treatment the world over: widespread discrimination, marginalization, usurpation of land, and planned destruction of languages and cultures. Yet the WGIP meetings clearly stated that there was little agreement on what "indigenous" meant, let alone what should be done or declared.[42] At the 1993 Vienna meeting of the UN, all the conference could produce on indigenous affairs was a Declaration and Programme of Action calling for an International Decade of the World's Indigenous Peoples to begin in 1995 and a proposal to establish a permanent forum for indigenous peoples in the UN. After six more years of meetings and discussions, in July 2000 the UN adopted a resolution to establish a "Permanent Forum on Indigenous Issues as a subsidiary organ of the Economic and Social Council (ECOSOC), consisting of 16 members equally divided between governments and indigenous representatives."

Aboriginal Conventions

In the postwar era, the main UN-related document on Aboriginal peoples was the 1957 International Labour Organization's Indigenous and Tribal Populations Convention (no.157), which had as its main objective the "progressive integration" of Aboriginal peoples "into the life of their respective countries." In 1989 the ILO replaced that document with the Convention concerning Indigenous and Tribal Peoples in Independent Countries (no.169), which altered the explicit intention of the 1957 Convention to enhance integration and assimilation. The concept of "peoples," however, was explicitly defined in the 1989 Convention as not having any meaning in international law, thus precluding their representation as coherent "nations" in international organizations.

The 1989 Convention, moreover, states: "These people shall have the right to retain their own customs and institutions, where these are not incompatible with fundamental rights, defined by the national legal system and internationally recognized human rights." The subordination of collective rights to the "fundamental rights" of the UDHR is explicit. It is this assertion of the primacy of human rights over collective Aboriginal rights and the assumption of the authority to determine what violates human rights that give the state the power to override any Aboriginal rights impinging on private property or prevailing religion. Here lies part of the rationalization of governments to take what measures they do to circumscribe or usurp indigenous rights.

• See Speed and Collier, "Limiting Indigenous Autonomy in Chiapas, Mexico."

Almost thirty years after the UN acknowledged the question of Aboriginal rights and over fifty years after the adoption of the UDHR, indigenous peoples had achieved only a very compromised form of representation. The Permanent Forum was merely a subordinate organ of a rather weak UN council; it was not even given observer status in other UN venues – a status granted to many NGOs and other representative agencies of certain populations. Even the representation that indigenous peoples received was only partly chosen by their own groups; and the permanent aspect of the forum amounted to ten-day annual sessions. It is, moreover, a forum *on indigenous issues* and not the forum *for indigenous peoples* called for by the Vienna Declaration. The Permanent Forum may be a step forward, at least going beyond the practice of calling Aboriginal people "guests" at the WGIP meetings in Geneva. But because it provides no venue for sustained debate, critical analysis, the formulation of demands, or the protection and advancement of their rights, it may be more of a mechanism to deflect attention from real issues and to absorb the energies of Aboriginal representatives.

Although indigenous peoples asked the League of Nations in 1919 for representation, there has been until now no mechanism for the international representation of the world's millions of indigenous peoples. But what they now have is little other than a powerless forum that will engage the activities of some of their leaders and representatives, create the illusion that their issues are being heard, and give the impression that they have an identity at the United Nations.

* * *

If a consciousness of Aboriginal rights calls into question the circumscribed nature of human rights, it also, albeit tragically, reveals a positive aspect to the declarations of human rights. It was the violent processes of the assertion of private property, continuing today, that brought the destruction of Aboriginal rights and gave rise to the levelling effect of modern civil and political rights through which humans began to see and understand themselves everywhere as human, albeit as atomized individuals. The human rights of the UDHR represent a historic step in the development of human self-consciousness, but it is only a step in a longer series; it represents a stage in which all humans, because defined simply as possessors of individual rights, are seen as the abstract equal of all others – a necessary presupposition to the understanding that we are not exclusive entities but rather our relationships.

The existence of different forms of right – including the right to self-determination through means other than liberal democracy and the "right to development"[43] in ways other than in a "rights-based" manner that allows for the pre-eminence of corporate capital – are not compatible with the human rights of the UDHR as premised on the exclusive individual. Indeed, the attempts to pursue other forms of self-determination and other roads of national development have met a variety of fates, from ridicule and criticism to sabotage, armed intervention, and military coups d'état.

Even attempts by Third World nations at the United Nations in the 1970s and 1980s to negotiate changes to the structures of world trade allowing for more national independence and a more equitable distribution of the wealth of the world met with resistance and ultimately failure.[44] By the late 1970s, after the initial proposals for a New International Economic Order and the effect of global recessions on commodity prices, the increasing influence of the World Bank and IMF and the imposition of authoritarian and dictatorial governments in Latin America, Africa, and Asia all put paid to the idea of a new order that might benefit the Third World. Since the 1980s three forces – regional and global enabling frameworks, the TNCs, and the governments of the industrial states – have made any renewal of such an overture next to impossible through tied aid, indebtedness, economic dependence, blackmail, corruption, dictatorship, militarization, and unequal treaties.

At same time, these same three forces, in their normal activities, have become the worst violators of human rights. National political rights are usurped by the policies imposed by external agencies; social rights succumb to structural adjustment policies; and the civil rights of domestic interests are subordinated to those of the TNC. A world made over in the interests of the TNC can only come at the expense of all rights other than corporate civil rights.

CHAPTER V

The Curious Unanimity

In a world of such stark contrasts and contradictions, it is curious that in many conflicts all sides seem to be in favour of human rights. Socialists and conservatives, trade unions and corporations, indigenous groups and capitalist states, movements on the left and right all seem to be advocates for human rights. It would be strange if they were all advocates for the same thing.

Part of this enigma may be explained by differences in the meaning attached to the concept of human in human rights. Those who emphasize and promote civil and political rights see the human as "economic man," the solitary pursuer of self-interest. Those who focus on social rights see the human as a social being with responsibilities beyond the self. Both see their respective views as capturing the essential nature of the human being. The human as "economic man" is indeed the human of human rights; but, as we have argued, it is neither universal nor essential. The human as social being captures part of the definition of human essence, but then it is not the human in human rights.

Part of the oddity may also be because the UDHR itself embodies a contradiction between the form of property underlying civil and political rights (namely, private property) and the property that informs "economic, social and cultural" rights (state regulation and redistribution of socialized capital). Within the framework of liberal democracy, an emphasis on one side or the other places the advocates of human rights in a similar contradiction. Moreover, calls for human rights may refer only to civil rights for corporations in, for instance, a newly opened market economy; it could refer to demands for more political rights in the form of a liberal democracy that reflects different coalitions of capital in civil society; or it could refer to demands for social, environmental, or Aboriginal rights. Given the internal differences and contradictions of the UDHR, the many calls for human rights can produce strange bedfellows.

CONTRADICTORY DEMANDS

Within liberal democracies, the different demands for human rights are an expression of conflict between various classes and strata; the demands from Aboriginal peoples represent the contradictions between systems of individual and collective property; environmentalists argue for a defence of the world's commons in the face of abuse by corporate and state private property; and the distinct character of the so-called socialist and some Third World countries rests on the development of social rights. These differences indicate that the meanings of right and human are far from settled. They remain contested terrain.

Support from the Right

By the "right" of the political spectrum within liberal democracy we refer to those groups, individuals, parties, and movements that promote and advance corporate private rights as pre-eminent in the property framework that defines the political system. The question of the "far right" takes us beyond this framework, into the realm of political dictatorship and therefore the negation of the rule of law and of civil and political rights. Of the many positions on the right, here we only consider what is common to the positions that attempt to operate more or less within the confines of liberal democracy.

For the right in general, human rights comprise civil and political rights and not social rights. These advocates argue, and correctly, that social rights broadly speaking are of a different order of right; they are for the most part countervailing rights, entitlements or claims that contradict the unmitigated exercise of civil rights, especially in their dominant form as corporate rights. The rights that define the system – civil and political rights grounded in exclusive individual entitlement – are the only ones, in their view, that merit defence. Social rights, for the most part, impinge on the operation of corporations, whereas civil and political rights are the means by which corporate interests are advanced.

The right makes a defence of civil and political rights for this reason alone. The existence and maintenance of civil rights reflect and ensure the relations of capital; these rights are the rationale of corporate domination over other sections of civil society. Political rights allow for the alternation of parties in government, representing moderate shifts in corporate power within a broad private property framework, while allowing a modest choice of more or less reform within the system – an important part of the illusion of popular sovereignty and legitimacy for the system.

Here lies a partial explanation for why the U.S. government has long been an advocate for human rights in its foreign policy.[1] While this advocacy has lent a humanitarian appearance to U.S. activities abroad, the meaning given to human rights is limited to civil and political rights; and the reality of U.S. actions is another matter altogether. If there is a social side it is restricted to programs that are best defined as forms of charity; they do not take the form of the establishment of actual entitlements to education, health, and social security because that step would constitute the creation of countervailing rights.

The recruitment of U.S. youth in the Peace Corps and other state-sponsored programs for overseas social work stand as examples of forms of charity. "Volunteer" workers are even sent to countries where the United States has been responsible for widespread torture and the death of tens of thousands of people – as in Guatemala, where some U.S. NGOs and charity groups now ply their trade as gifts for a people whose human rights (and indigenous rights) were for decades violated by U.S. government agencies in the most brutal ways.[2] In general, moreover, in the industrial nations the growing social needs that accompany the progressive dismantling of the welfare state, of social rights, are addressed increasingly with forms of charity.

Until the late 1970s and early 1980s the platforms of many parties on the right possessed an element of noblesse oblige; within strict limits a paternalistic sense of social responsibility came into play, the source of which was probably little more than the pricked conscience of the privileged. In Britain and some Commonwealth countries this phenomenon became known as Red Toryism – that is, the advocacy of corporate right with a limited admission of social right. In the United States a similar political position carries the label of liberalism. By 1980, in particular with the coming of Thatcher in Britain and Reagan in the United States, conservative parties began to purge members with a social conscience and create parties that were singular in their approach to public policy. Thatcherism, Reaganism, neo-liberalism, and neo-conservatism became the new labels for the policies that openly favoured private corporate rights above all else and pushed for the corresponding dismantling of social rights, promotion of charity, deregulating state oversight powers, and privatizing state-owned corporations. Despite all this, the new right can still profess support for human rights – defined emphatically, however, as simply civil and political rights.

Support from the Reformist Left

Within liberal democracy, the reformist left of the political spectrum refers to all those groups or individuals, parties, and movements that want to mitigate but not transform private corporate rights as pre-eminent in the mainstream property framework with the establishment of countervailing social rights. Those who want to eliminate corporate rights take us beyond the boundaries of liberal democracy into forms of collective property and therefore the negation of the rule of corporate-dominated law and of civil and political rights as attached to private property.

The reformist left premises its defence of human rights on an acceptance of the precepts of the capitalist mode of production – in particular, the assumption that liberal democracy permits the genuine expression of political will and provides the basis for mitigating the operation of capitalism. Given this, the advocates see human rights as social rights as a means of ameliorating the worst effects of the system; as reforms within the system, social rights put a "human face" on the labour market, corporate authority, and the state. They amount to the partial decommodification of labour-power, to a certain respite from the terror or insecurity of the labour market and dictatorship in the workplace. They are, however, countervailing rights, and therefore exist usually at the expense of corporate rights in some way. Given its acceptance of liberalism, the reformist left does not grasp that social rights are tolerated as concessions only as long as the economic and political conditions demand and/or allow such compromises.

The left may also defend or demand human rights as civil and political rights in the face of dictatorship, authoritarian rule, or corporate arbitrariness. In other words, the demand for these rights comes to the fore when they are absent for the population at large or in certain subsections, in those countries or regions in which few rights except rights for corporations are recognized.[3] Where the demand for these rights is achieved – where an authoritarian government of one sort or another is defeated or reformed – the establishment of civil and political rights merely provides the people with civil rights subordinate to those of the corporation, and with political rights that provide limited policy alternatives within a framework of corporate private property. This is the meaning of the return of "democracy" to many Latin American countries in the late 1980s and 1990s after years of military dictatorship.

In both of these cases, the reformist left plays the role of mediator between the powers that be and other classes, strata, and groups. It is able to play this role only as long as the conditions obtain that allow for social and economic compromise. Once these conditions have dissipated – and the viability of a broad range of social rights has been undermined – the reformist left fractures into apologists for the growing inequalities, or more radicalized opposition, or stalwart believers in political doctrines whose time has passed.

The reformist left and the right of the political spectrum support or demand different aspects of human rights for different reasons. And as long as human rights are defined as they are in the UDHR, these demands will not step outside what is or was possible within a capitalist social formation and its political form, liberal democracy. The relative weight and respect given to different aspects of human rights merely reflect the relative balance of power, or the nature of the struggles within the system, and the particular historical conditions that obtain at a given time.

THE MEETING GROUND OF LEFT AND RIGHT: NON-GOVERNMENTAL ORGANIZATIONS

For the most part, the social function of non-governmental organizations (NGOs) straddles the line between the reformist left and the principled right. For the left, they are organizations with a heightened social or political conscience that are not a formal part of the mainstream; their extra-parliamentary status provides a cachet of political independence and critical distance. For the right, the principles they advocate and the practical activity they perform bolster the sense that capitalism does work; and their presence indicates that where capitalism falters, there is accommodation.

Most countries are home to hundreds of NGOs, attempting to address a wide variety of issues. Well over a thousand NGOs have consultative status at the UN, but an estimated 26,000 or more "internationally recognized" NGOs operate at the global level.[4] NGOs have existed for decades, but the enormous expansion of their numbers in the 1980s and 1990s most likely had much to do with the pervasive adoption of neo-liberal policies. By and large, NGOs have occupied themselves with one or another of the entire range of social rights – the very rights that neo-liberal policies have been designed to undermine or eliminate. As public policies and programs in education, health, social insurance, and child care, among others, have been reduced or dismantled, NGOs have been provided with financing and their raison d'être has been confirmed.

Their apparently benign and apolitical nature belies the consequences of their programs and activities. Many NGOs presume to speak on behalf or in the name of a certain group or strata or, indeed, assume proprietorship of an issue; yet few are democratic in operation. For the most part just how representative their views are and how they determine their positions remain unclear. Most of these organizations are formed or directed from outside the constituency or communities within which they work. They absorb, moreover, the energies of individuals, groups, sectors, and classes that might otherwise have presented a challenge to state policies; and they dampen a possible critical awareness about the link between the problems they are supposedly addressing and the nature of the economic and political system itself. Instead they concentrate on finding local, individual, or community solutions.[5] Their very existence, then, detracts from the exercise of political rights or the demand for the extension of such rights to the global level.

The term non-government organization itself is somewhat deceptive. Many NGOs are funded by governments or state aid agencies, and/or by philanthropic foundations such as the Ford or Carnegie foundations and the Soros Open Society Institute. In these cases the agendas and operations of the NGOs almost certainly conform at least implicitly to the foreign policy goals of the sponsoring governments or foundations. Defined by such aims, these NGOs may well act as the "forward agents" of states or other sponsoring groups, much as certain religious organizations did in the past and still do. The non-official status provides NGO members with access to and influence over organizations, activists, officials, and movements – access and influence that they would not otherwise have. On the whole, they serve to maintain the system as it is; if they are critical, their fault-finding tends to remain at the level of pointing to state or corporate corruption, unfair trade policies, or human rights violations. NGOs are unlikely to be more critical because they are part of the system itself; adopting the idea that the relations of capital may be the source of the problems would be little short of biting the hand that feeds them.

On the National Level

Although most NGOs deal with aspects of human rights in one way or another, only a few actually make the defence of human rights the central point of their existence.[6] The most obvious examples at the national level are the civil liberty associations found in some liberal democracies. These organizations exist to promote and expand existing civil and political rights and to fight against their violation; and their existence and perspective rest on the same premise as that of civil rights: that civil society is first and foremost a world of competing, atomized individuals with exclusive private rights. This presupposition places them at one with the system. It does not allow them to step outside the social complex they work within, and as a result whatever criticisms they have are necessarily limited to objections to violations or abrogations of civil or political rights and not to the system itself.

For the same reason their perspective has no room for class interests or collective rights, which means that they rarely if ever defend the broad range of social, environmental, or Aboriginal rights because, in general, such rights are not within their purview. The narrowness in their self-proclaimed mandates means that their activities do not embrace some of the most important rights for subordinate sectors of civil society. As a consequence, they are restricted to the defence of abstract equal individual rights for all, but this in a world that is in practice not at all equal and, indeed, is increasingly unequal.

From the point of view of subordinate sectors of civil society, civil liberty associations can be important when they defend civil or political rights in the face of corporate or state arbitrariness. The right to assemble or demonstrate or petition and the civil rights of women, workers, renters, and minorities have all been defended by these associations, and defended they must be in a society defined by class, ethnic, gender, and other inequalities. If it appears that these associations are defending these rights against the state, it is only because the state, through its legislative and executive powers, necessarily favours the interests of the dominant sectors of civil society.

At the same time these associations play a significant role as a bulwark for mainstream ideology. Their defence of rights, as if civil and political rights were the only rights to be defended, hinders a clear understanding of the inequalities and iniquities in liberal democracies. It constructs the problem of violated rights as strictly an issue of rights and not an issue of the system itself. Moreover, the defence of certain rights, such as freedom of speech, as strict absolutes allows the owners of the mass media not only the right to promote certain ideas but also the opportunity to prevent counterpositions, because the defence of freedom of speech as an absolute or abstraction ignores the question of ownership. Private property in the media contradicts freedom of speech; it turns a right into a privilege and precludes the rights of non-owners. By defending the abstract right and ignoring the reality of ownership and control, they appear to fulfil their mandate to defend freedom of speech, even in the face of the pervasive and growing real unfreedom.

In this way, civil liberty associations become by and large defenders of the status quo – a system of individual rights – without reference to the class iniquities of the system or other forms of right. Theirs is the perspective of the defender of the abstract ideal of marketplace society. But most civil liberty associations are poorly funded and thus limited in their staffing and ultimately in their effect. In defending the principles of the system, they become gadflies to the forces that abuse these rights, a nuisance to the prevailing powers. Far from being a serious challenge to the structure of power, they are in the final analysis an important ideological buttress.

State-supported national, provincial/state, and even municipal human rights commissions exist throughout the industrial world, and the same criticisms apply to them. But in those cases, governments can control the mandates, budgets, and key appointments, rendering the commissions limited in independence and ability to act. Integral to the adoption of neo-liberal policies, moreover, many governments have systematically restricted the powers and budgets of these human rights commissions in order to undermine their already limited resistance to prevailing corporate rights.

NGOs on the Global Level

The NGOs that occupy themselves with human rights issues on the global level tend to ignore the issue of economic, social, and cultural rights, or at least carefully select some of those issues for attention. Most of them prefer to focus their efforts almost exclusively on certain civil and political rights. This is particularly true of the NGOs based in the United States. Human Rights Watch (HRW), for example, appears to follow the lead of Washington in omitting references to the International Covenant on Economic, Social and Cultural Rights, ignoring violations of broad social rights, or employing arguments similar to those of representatives of the U.S. government, stating that social rights are questions of policy whereas civil and political rights are issues of principle.[7]

For organizations, parties, movements, or peoples that reject capitalism and its politics and strive to create a different way of life, these human rights NGOs not only are of little help, but also can be part of the problem, even if they are free of state sponsorship. Some are not so free and yet pretend as much and provide an avenue for political interference without the appearance of direct state involvement.

Human Rights Watch

Human Rights Watch (HRW) – an umbrella organization that includes a number of subgroups focusing on specific areas of the world (Americas Watch, Africa Watch, Helsinki Watch, Asia Watch, Middle East Watch) – is an American child of the last stages of the Cold War. According to the organization, it began "in 1978 as Helsinki Watch, to monitor the compliance of Soviet bloc countries with human rights provisions of the landmark Helsinki Accords." The U.S.-based agency was originally created to use human rights as a means of helping to destabilize state-capitalist regimes in Eastern Europe, including the USSR itself, whose ruling elites had already lost much of their governing legitimacy. According to one account, the Helsinki Final Act "encouraged the mobilization of independent groups, justified transnational networks with sympathetic activists and sub-state actors in the West, and thereby enabled societal forces in the East to mount unprecedented challenges to regimes which had long monopolized social and political space."[8]

But Eastern Europe was not the only place in those years that human rights could be used to support or advance U.S., or more generally Western, interests. In Central America in the 1980s the issue of human rights was employed to discredit and malign the armed resistance to U.S.-supported dictatorships in the region. HRW describes the role of a predecessor organization: "In the 1980s, Americas Watch was set up to counter the notion that human rights abuses by one side in the war in Central America were somehow more tolerable than abuses by the other side." Given Central American politics of the time, that was clearly a position aimed at undermining resistance to U.S.-sponsored oppression and atrocities.[9] The success of these two Watch organizations encouraged the same interests to create other Watch committees to cover the rest of the world. In 1988 these groups were consolidated under the rubric of Human Rights Watch.

The organization claims to be independent in that it refuses to accept government financing of any sort. Its funding, however, comes from individuals, as well as foundations, which have policy agendas. The names on the board of directors and advisory committees of HRW, moreover, read like a "Who's Who" of past and present high officials in government, significant business figures, foundation people, and members of the U.S. academic elite, often based in so-called think tanks. The interests at stake are more or less self-evident in the lists of these directors; it is difficult to consider the organization as being politically neutral. At best, it might be seen as the expression of the truncated social conscience, couched in a philosophy of instrumentalism, of a largely American elite strata wedded to the status quo.

Still, over the years HRW has taken principled and critical positions on issues that are not central to the interests of TNCs. It worked, for example, to set in place treaties to ban the use of child soldiers and land mines; it also claimed to have participated in "the legal action" taken against Chile's former dictator Augusto Pinochet in London and worked "to buttress the important principle that even former heads of state can be held accountable." It has, moreover, criticized aspects of the U.S. intervention in Afghanistan and the treatment of captured combatants. The apparent conflict between its willingness to be put to political use and these principled positions is a paradox that reflects the contradiction in its purpose, which is, in part, to defend certain principles and therefore the credibility of a system that, dominated by global corporate rights, increasingly and blatantly cannot honour them.

Human Rights Watch reports fall into roughly three categories. What might be called "red flag" reports call attention to egregious violations of human rights or aspects of international law by U.S.-supported regimes, violations that could reflect poorly on the legitimacy of the U.S. role. Rarely, however, do the reports link the violations to Washington. Instead they foster the sense that these regimes are somehow beyond the pale and their transgressions of human rights reflect merely internal shortcomings. Other reports call attention to regimes outside complete subordination to global capital or in conflict with the United States, or perhaps signal and justify soon-to-be targets of U.S. foreign or military policy. In effect they pave the way for U.S. intervention or Western aggression. A third set rebukes Washington for actions that violate aspects of domestic or international law. That set is perhaps the weakest area of HRW reporting, although it could easily be the most extensive.

HRW on Cuba

In a widely used compilation of human rights documents, the preface to the section on Latin American instruments states:

> There is abundant evidence that the concept of human rights in Latin America has been employed as a weapon against revolutionary regimes, particularly Cuba. Regimes which threaten the system of private property and foreign private investment are likely to be denounced by the O.A.S. [Organization of American States] organs as "threats to regional security" and as inimical to human rights, whilst military regimes which accept the economic *status quo* will remain free from condemnation. The paradox is thus the likely use of machinery for the protection of human rights to justify intervention in the name of the regional organ, the O.A.S., with the purpose of conserving a system which tolerates appalling social injustice.[10]

This passage raises the question of the instrumental use of charges of human rights violations. Although the commentary was written several decades ago, the biased handling of such accusations is no less an issue today; and Cuba still figures prominently as the object of these charges. Our interest, however, is not to expose the political use of human rights (which is more or less obvious) or to defend Cuba (it can defend itself), but to analyze what is problematic about using the human rights of the UDHR as a measure for countries such as Cuba.

Among the many activities and reports of Human Rights Watch, its 1999 report on Cuba illustrates the problems inherent in assuming that human rights transcend different economic systems and that to be human is to be the "economic man" of capitalist market society. The most obvious problem is the HRW itself – a U.S.-based organization largely directed by U.S. elites and staffed mainly by U.S. citizens, criticizing the policies and practices of a small island nation that has refused to bow to the will of the U.S. government and to succumb to the U.S. military and economic intervention that has characterized the history of all of Latin America, including Cuba.[11]

The report, entitled "Cuba's Repressive Machinery," begins:

> Over the past forty years, Cuba has developed a highly efficient machinery of repression. The denial of basic civil and political rights is written into Cuban law. In the name of legality, armed security forces, aided by state-controlled mass organizations, silence dissent with heavy prison terms, threats of prosecution, harassment, or exile. Cuba uses these tools to restrict severely the exercise of fundamental human rights of expression, association, and assembly.[12]

Much of the report carries on in the same vein, documenting the means by which Cuba silences political opposition and the lack of political and civil institutions that characterize capitalist political systems.

After making the case that Cuba is not a liberal-democratic state, the report examines efforts taken to change the situation. It points out that with the "demise of the Soviet Union," Cuba's main trading partner and economic support, the island nation had to search for new trade relations, a situation that, according to HRW, gave the "international community ... new opportunities to press for human rights reforms." It adds, with a tone of lament, "Unfortunately, the huge divide between US policy and that of Cuba's major trading and investment partners has prevented the development of an effective, unified policy that could bring about change in Cuba." It continues: "The embargo [the U.S. policy] has not only failed to bring about human rights improvements in Cuba but has become counterproductive, providing a pretext for Castro's repression while alienating Washington's erstwhile allies." The underlying sense is that the U.S. embargo, while widely criticized outside the United States as itself a violation of human rights and international law, was well intentioned but ineffective. In these statements, HRW appears less the objective critic of injustice everywhere than the active advocate for change in certain quarters, especially in countries with policies opposed by the U.S. government.

In the concluding section of the report, the authors take a more critical stance on U.S. policy and describe the embargo differently: "The embargo is not a calibrated policy intended to produce human rights reforms, but a sledgehammer approach aimed at nothing short of overthrowing the government." Although this is a more accurate assessment of U.S. policy, the writers do not analyze or make any further comment on this patent violation of the right of self-determination of a nation or the effect of that violation on the people of Cuba. The reason may well lie in the recommendations that the HRW makes "To the Cuban Government." Ironically, while not openly advocating a political transformation, HRW proposes significant changes to the Cuban constitution, criminal code, structure of the courts and legal procedures, labour laws, civil and political rights, and prison system. Indeed, if the Cuban government followed through with these recommendations, the intention of the embargo would be more or less realized, and Cuba would no longer have the government it has or be the country that it is.

Conspicuously absent from the report is any mention of the whole range of social rights. Yet economic, social, and cultural rights are as much a part of the definition of human rights in the UDHR as are civil and political rights. And few countries in Latin America have matched Cuba's achievement in this area of rights. For that matter, even the United States has not matched Cuba's achievement on most measures of universal public health, literacy, housing, or basic education; but HRW, like most human rights advocacy groups, completely ignores this issue.

The report is steadfastly critical only of what the organization perceives to be violations of civil and political rights; and it does this without discussion of the context, of the consequences for Cuba of the U.S. attempts to sabotage its economy, assassinate its leaders, mount a military invasion, engage in continuous espionage and political interference, and impose an economic blockade. Any objective appraisal would have to take these factors into account. The report mentions the embargo, but only to say that it has been unsuccessful and that it violates certain civil rights. Even here HRW is circumspect in not fully examining the degree to which the U.S. embargo violates international law and national sovereignty.[13] The report, then, does not acknowledge that Cuba has been under constant siege since shortly after the 1959 revolution, and that this siege has undoubtedly had an impact on the direction of its many changes.

A central part of the context of U.S. violations of Cuban sovereignty is Cuba's attempt to create a socialist society, and Cuba's role in assisting attempts in other countries in the struggle for socialism. Indeed, the Cuban revolution was spawned by the corrupting influence of capital and the dictatorial government under Batista (and that regime's disregard for human rights). The revolution was made in the name of justice, human dignity, equality, people's control over their own lives, and freedom from arbitrary police and military actions and the impoverishing effects of corporate control over production. Some of these goals would appear to be similar to the purported goals of the human rights NGOs. But an NGO such as HRW sees in socialism only the repression of the civil and political rights that it assumes to be somehow fundamental to all of humanity but that belong in principle solely to capitalist civil society and political systems. In this way, it becomes an advocate, perhaps unwittingly, of a particular mode of production and its political structures. Because, like other NGOs, it operates mainly on the level of the political and civil and is a product of this particular system, which it understands as the very embodiment of the meaning of democracy and freedom, it can see no further.

If human rights provide a theoretical measure of the policies and practice of a capitalist system, they are not the measure of a socialist system. With respect to Cuba, the problem is not whether civil and political rights exist or are violated, but it is how to judge or measure a system that is not capitalist, in which the state, by subsuming control over the economy, performs a different role and civil society, as in a capitalist social formation, does not exist. Within socialism, with its state ownership of the means of production rather than private ownership, the provision of public goods and services for the people becomes the goal of production, replacing the goal of private accumulation of capital within a system of civil and political rights. An appropriate critique of Cuba would begin by assessing it in terms of what it purports to be, namely, a socialist system, and by taking into account what it has had to do to defend itself against the United States. It is contradictory to judge it in relation to the principles of what it clearly is not, a capitalist state.[14] The principles of one system cannot be the measure of another.

If Human Rights Watch wanted to evaluate Cuba's success as a socialist system, the most telling of standards, among other criteria, would be the degree of popular control over the process of planning and production, the equality of women in all realms, the social condition of children, the degree of socialization of domestic functions, the degree of access to education at all levels, and the possibility of free and critical development of the cultural realm. These touchstones provide the main elements for measuring the achievements of a system that purports to be socialist. Cuba might not do so well in an assessment of these areas, but regardless HRW, which sees no other ideal political form than liberal democracy, would never undertake an evaluation of Cuba on these grounds.

Clearly, the various organizations that "watch" over the fate of human rights in regions around the world, although apparently working at arm's length from the states that oversee the regional and global enabling frameworks, share with those states the same acceptance of capitalism and its political forms. But with the expansion of capital, accompanied by demands to dismantle social rights and to override national political and civil rights, the critical reporting of human rights abuses by the HRW organizations only serves to obfuscate the main source of abuses around the world.

In March 2003, when the United States attacked Iraq, HRW busied itself with reports on allegations of Iraqi human rights transgressions; and it left more or less unmentioned the violations of the UN Charter and many UN conventions by the U.S. and U.K. forces. It stated that it would not comment on the war's legal status. Here, then, were the two faces of HRW: it presumed to report on allegations of misconduct, mainly by one side, while refusing to question the legality of the war. HRW either ignored or barely mentioned reported allegations of the U.S./U.K. destruction of civilian water supplies, electrical power, and food depots; the random bombing of civilian residential areas and some hospitals; enormous civilian casualties; the mistreatment of captives by U.K. and U.S. forces; the firing on and killing of journalists; and the bombing of public communication systems in Baghdad. While raising the matter of past Iraqi violations, it did not address the bombing of Iraq by the United States and United Kingdom over many years and the threats of aggression, the effect of the UN sanctions on civilians, and the U.S. use of depleted uranium and cluster bombs, among other travesties of international law.

It may be that HRW avoids examining the enormity and pervasiveness of U.S. violations of human rights over many years around the world because of the potentially profound challenge that such an examination would bring to the legitimacy of capitalism and liberal democracy. But if an organization such as HRW were to focus its attention exclusively on the violations of human rights committed by the U.S. government at home and abroad over the years, it would have little time or energy to examine or report on violations anywhere else. Just to review the existing official documents detailing the U.S. government's contempt for human rights since the 1948 UDHR would be an exhausting task.[15]

The Problem of Amnesty International

Since its beginning in 1961, Amnesty International (AI) has become a global organization with an annual international budget in 2002 of over £20 million, a membership of over one million, and many thousands of registered activist groups located in almost every country of the world. The main focus of its work has been to campaign against "detention without charge or trial, unfair trials, torture or ill-treatment, the death penalty, 'disappearances,' and extra-judicial executions."[16] While it continues to do this work, in August 2003 Amnesty International formally adopted a broader "mission" statement to include many activities that it had been carrying on for some time: research and reports on specific rights violations and on certain countries, as well as public demonstrations, educational projects, and the lobbying of governments, agencies, and organisations. The size of its staff and budget is similar, it says, to the "level of resources that the UN devotes to human rights issues as a whole." Its rapid and continuing growth is impressive testimony to the concern that humans feel for the arbitrary fate suffered by many thousands of people at the hands of official-dom. It is also testimony to the limited existence of effective international authoritative mechanisms for addressing these transgressions.

The picture of what appears at first sight to be an organization standing on high, unassailable moral grounds fades on closer examination. The problem begins with the very mandate that AI has assigned itself. Its 1997 "Statute" proclaimed its overarching goal: "To promote awareness of and adherence to the Universal Declaration of Human Rights and other internationally recognized human rights instruments, the values enshrined in them, and the indivisibility and interdependence of all human rights and freedoms." Following this statement, the organization outlined what it attempts to do in practice, which is to focus on individuals who have suffered abuses at the hand of the state and its machinery, to document the violations of political and civil rights, and to assist in the restitution of those rights. In 2003 the organization became a little more circumspect and declared as its vision: "a world in which every person enjoys all of the human rights enshrined in the Universal Declaration of Human Rights and other international human rights standards." Here lies the first problem: while AI purports to promote awareness and adherence to the UDHR – which includes civil, political, *and* a wide range of "economic, social and cultural" rights – the most significant thrust of its practice is the focus on specific civil and political rights, and mainly of certain individuals. Despite lip service paid to the "indivisibility and interdependence of all human rights," AI makes only limited effort to advance economic, social, and cultural rights or what we have elided into the rubric of social rights. At some point, AI decided that human rights were divisible, and that some are much more important than others.

Given that AI is staffed, funded, and based in the West, this position should not be surprising. Like other human rights organizations, AI takes capitalism and its political form, liberal democracy, as unquestioned norms. Implicit in its "object and mandate" (in 2003, "vision and mission") AI assumes the separation of civil society and the state and the corresponding civil and political rights to be inherent, equal, and inalienable, as the UDHR and other declarations assert. The organization has no vision beyond this; the only democracy is liberal democracy, and the only society is the civil society comprising individual (and corporate) contractual relations. In this system, as we have argued, social rights are not fundamental; indeed, they are contradictory to the civil rights of corporations, and therefore can appear as subversive to the system. For AI, social rights as a whole have never been a significant issue.

Given these unexamined economic and political assumptions, AI similarly has no position on the rights of indigenous peoples as indigenous peoples. It is, indeed, silent on the systematic usurpation of non-capitalistic property rights by governments and corporations and the attendant destruction of the means of subsistence of non-commodity producers and the massacres of peasants, pastoralists, and other tribal or Aboriginal peoples. As with social rights, these issues are largely beyond the mandate and purview of AI. The reason for this omission most likely flows from the definition of human rights in the UDHR, as sets of individual rights that do not extend to indigenous peoples claiming sovereignty as a collective right, within or beyond the legal boundaries of a capitalist state. Much of the widespread destruction of human life and habitat taking place around the world is happening to people who for the most part have not fully entered a mainstream civil society and so often lack material assets in the form of private property and the inculcated discipline and subservience necessary for wage-labour. For them, the violations of human rights amount to, at most, the right to life, freedom from slavery, and prohibition of cruel or degrading treatment. While some AI reports point to these issues the organization does not define as pertinent to human rights issues much of what is happening to indigenous peoples.

The organization concentrates its activities in campaigns "against violations of *certain* civil and political rights,"[17] which include fair trials for all prisoners, the end to torture and executions, and the release of "prisoners of conscience." More specifically, it emphasizes support through educational programs, letter writing, demonstrations, and legal aid. It defines "prisoners of conscience" as people imprisoned or detained solely because of their political or religious beliefs, or by reason of gender, national or ethnic origin, language, or colour. But there is an important caveat: an individual can only be so defined "providing that he or she has not used or advocated violence."[18] At first sight, the purpose of these efforts seems beyond reproach: it is an act of humanity to dedicate time and energy to support other people beyond one's own interests, to securing justice for those unfairly imprisoned or tortured. But what seems to be is not always what is.

In choosing its "prisoners of conscience," AI makes an effort to separate the violation of the individual's rights from the context that gave rise to the violation. As one Amnesty spokesperson wrote: "We attempt to separate the events from the political relationships that create the environment that spawns and nurtures oppression."[19] This strict focus on the violation of an individual's right, this separation of the victim from the circumstances of oppression, decontextualizes and so depoliticizes the act of oppression. In doing this, AI creates the impression that political repression of many thousands of people each year is merely a question of individual violations multiplied many times over. It obscures the nature of the repression, indeed trivializing it by making it appear as a matter of just so many individual tragedies – which, of course, is not what repression is. The focus on the violation rather than the context allows AI to ignore the conditions that produce and foster oppression: "To members of Amnesty International, the individual prisoners are important; they [the members] do not work to change systems of government."[20] This approach addresses a symptom while ignoring the cause. But it is more than this: it is to obscure the cause by making the symptom everything. AI becomes part of the problem.

The separation also means that AI does not take into account the systemic oppression that produces, for example, chronic unemployment, illiteracy, homelessness, and poverty for many tens of millions – all of which are violations of social rights as defined in the UDHR. Oppression for AI is narrowly defined as that which is associated with the denial to individuals of certain civil and political rights, as defined in liberal democracy, through unlawful acts, violence and/or imprisonment.

Similarly, this separation also obscures the negative impact of international economic relations on human rights as defined in the UDHR in Third World countries. For AI, the effects of unequal trade relations, of national indebtedness, of structural adjustment policies on human rights are all non-issues. And yet all of these relations between the First and Third worlds have been well documented as the main reasons behind the destruction of the entire range of human rights in the so-called developing nations. To facilitate the operations of foreign corporations and benefit domestic elites, civil, political, and social rights have all been contemptuously dismissed in many economically dependent countries. Numerous governments have been deposed and replaced with brutal dictatorships at the instigation of the industrial nations for the same reason.[21] But for AI these massive violations stemming from the policies of Western governments – the consequence of unequal global trade relations and the agencies that regulate them – are precluded from consideration by its self-imposed mandate.

If the separation of the victim from the circumstances of detention depoliticizes the act of oppression, it also means that "prisoners of conscience" are depoliticized – that is, disconnected from the reasons for their arrests. AI does not confer with prisoners about their desire to be "adopted," to use the organization's own patronizing language. The assumption is that all who are imprisoned want to be free regardless of the political significance of their imprisonment. A trade unionist, an environmentalist, a political opponent, among others, may well have principled reasons for going to prison, and, just possibly, remaining there becomes a statement of those principles. For people who take on a cause that goes far beyond their own individual interests, imprisonment may well advance that cause or reveal the injustice of the regime that made the arrest. If freedom, moreover, becomes contingent on repudiating the cause and/or facing exile, as is often the case, the choice to remain in prison may be the only option. In these circumstances, the intervention of AI, its "investigation" to see if the prisoner qualifies, and the "adoption" may well appear presumptuous, to say the least. From the perspective of AI, the human goal does not go beyond the self. The genuine human empathy of AI members for those suffering injustice is unwittingly degraded to a single, narrow issue, the violation of an individual's civil or political rights.

There also can be more in this adoption process than meets the eye. The act of choosing a "prisoner of conscience" can itself be political; it can undermine imprisonment as a statement of political conscience by focusing on the violation of civil or political liberties and detracting from the cause. The imprisonment or assassination of a trade unionist for organizing, for instance, has nothing to do with the individual but with the principle of union rights.

Because the "prisoner of conscience" is always an individual and the violation always the violation of certain civil or political rights, AI has paid less attention to repression against whole groups. For AI, the widespread practice of state persecution and repression – of trade unions, political movements, indigenous peoples, ethnic groups, Roma, for example – has been far less important than the persecution of particular individuals.

AI's focus on the violation and not the context implies an indifferent or impartial approach to human rights violations. The approach presents the appearance of political neutrality, but this is not quite the case. The separation holds an inherent bias, which is that repression is defined ipso facto as the violation of certain civil and political rights and not as a violation of rights of much broader significance: forms of repression, such as an attempted eradication of a way of life, of a people's habitat, even of a people, of a town or village, of ideas, of political opposition, of trade unions, of the fulfilment of women's rights as human rights, are not treated by AI as subjects for its active work. The separation allows AI to define repression as something that it actually cannot be: simply the violation of an individual's civil or political rights. There are, of course, cases of sheer arbitrariness in which people are arrested or tortured for no specific reason (to induce terror, for example), but these acts never occur outside of a context. The bias lies in the failure to call into question the reason or context or system that gave rise to the violation. In this way, the very fact of repression is depoliticized.

Repression, the main object of AI's activities, is very narrowly defined, but it is also saddled with a significant proviso: the detained individual must not have "used or advocated violence." Critics of AI have referred to this stipulation as the "Mandela Clause," because when Nelson Mandela was first imprisoned in South Africa AI adopted him and lobbied for his release. While in prison in 1964 he was convicted of earlier conspiring to bomb government buildings, and because of that conviction AI rescinded his "adoption" as a "prisoner of conscience" and confined its lobbying efforts to issues of the fairness of the trial and the prison conditions. The organization argued that it could not hold "a double standard" by insisting that authorities refrain from violence and violation of rights while at the same time supporting prisoners who committed or advocated the same.

This apparently balanced approach is not quite what it appears to be. First, the state authority and the prisoner are not two equal sides to a dispute. On the one hand, the machinery of the state – the police, military, legal system, state budgets, and public policies – all constitute an organized system for the maintenance of unequal property relations. On the other hand, the non-corporate sector – the broad working classes – remain by and large unarmed and unorganized, and the poorer they are the fewer the material assets or means they have to realize their abstract civil rights or even to demand political and social rights. Given this difference of power and financial wherewithal, the state can oppress more or less indefinitely as long as the people remain unorganized and do not resist by force of arms. No amount of letter writing has ever changed a regime. Violent resistance, moreover, usually comes when all other avenues of change and discussion have been exhausted. As Nelson Mandela wrote in 1961: "The people's patience is not endless. The time comes in the life of any nation when there remain only two choices: submit or fight. That time has come in South Africa. The time has come for the people to meet the violence of the racist state – the police and its army – with armed resistance."[22] The failure of AI to ask why people advocate violence and take up arms against oppression means that its pretended balanced opposition to violence by either the state or the prisoner instead constitutes a bias in favour of the state.

The alleged balance is also problematic given the failure of AI to condemn the full range of state violence, which can come in a wide variety of forms. State violence and violation of rights can even be systemic: for example, in the form of apartheid or in the religious definition of citizenship, as in Israel and in states defined as Islamic or, indeed, as Catholic. AI's practical activities are restricted to a narrow range of violations of certain civil and political rights of individuals. While it refuses to support prisoners who advocate or use violence, AI does not condemn many of the state's wide-ranging forms of violence. While prisoners can be abandoned for advocating violence, the state suffers at worst only limited censure. This double standard implicitly favours the established regime, no matter how dictatorial or violent.

The ostensible balance appears even more curious given the preamble to the UDHR, which implies the right of a people to resist and seek to overthrow a regime that does not protect the civil and political rights of its citizens. Admittedly the passage in the UDHR is rather mealy-mouthed, but its intent is clear: "Whereas it is essential, if man is not to be compelled to have recourse, as a last resort, to rebellion against tyranny and oppression, that human rights should be protected by the rule of law."[23] The UDHR does allow, then, for the possibility that the people may have to take up arms against an unjust regime; yet AI, whose self-appointed mandate is "to promote awareness of ... the UDHR," refuses to support those who advocate violence or the use of arms to resist regimes that respect few rights except for those pertaining to corporations.

The problem of Amnesty International is that it has itself become one of the difficulties surrounding the curtailing of human rights abuses. Its focus is on the symptoms of a contradictory system and not the causes; and, moreover, it concentrates only on certain symptoms, not all. The causes that it ignores are inherent in the socio-economic system that AI takes as the norm: capitalism and the liberal-democratic state. The focus on symptoms gives the illusion of preventing or ameliorating the abuses without questioning their source; and this is the reason why, for all its sizable membership, large budget, and weighty reputation, it achieves very little in alleviating human rights abuses, while it continues to play a significant role in obscuring the extent, and the causes, of repression.

That human rights advocacy can become part of the problem is not merely an indirect consequence of the organization's assumptions and attempts to be politically neutral. AI has allowed itself to be used politically. In 1986 AI released a report on human rights abuses in Nicaragua just before the U.S. Congress was to vote on funding for the infamous Contras. The U.S. support for the Contras was a clear violation of international laws and human rights. But the violations implicit in the U.S. funding of the Contras and their crimes, or the U.S. blockade of Nicaraguan harbours, were not made the subject of an AI report. In the same year another AI report on human rights within the USSR was released prior to disarmament talks between the United States and the Soviet Union. AI also became a signatory to the United Nations' controversial Global Compact. And it was, moreover, only in 1998 that AI made its first report on the domestic policies of the United States; given the extent of published data on violations by the U.S. government at home and abroad, the AI report was very limited, restricting itself to charges of hypocrisy, of violations of civil rights by state officials, and of the continuing use of the death penalty. The report made no mention of the corrupted political system, violations of political and civil liberties by the FBI or CIA, limited social rights, and documented abuses of human rights by the U.S. government abroad.[24]

Because human rights reports can be used politically to advance foreign and domestic policies or to blunt criticism, control over human rights organizations is not a matter of indifference. AI and its many national and regional sections can be dominated by groups that ostensibly support human rights but do so in ways that are less than impartial (such as in the case of pro-Israel or pro-U.S. factions) or that are instrumental in forestalling social change or popular resistance to the status quo.

In most of its reports, AI finds fault with the immediate perpetrators of human rights violations. At the same time, wittingly or unwittingly, it deflects attention away from the fundamental but not so proximate cause – global corporate demands and the role of the industrial nations, in particular the U.S. government and its agencies. AI has repeatedly shown itself to be not quite what it purports to be.[25]

THE MEANING OF SOCIAL RIGHTS

The whole range of social rights is more or less beyond the defined mandate and purview of AI and most human rights organizations, despite their acceptance of the proclaimed indivisibility and interdependence of the human rights of the UDHR. Such rights, then, are not only by and large ignored but also not seen as rights to be defended in the way that civil and political rights are. Yet for the overwhelming majority of people it is social rights that matter most.

For working people, the real achievements with respect to human rights lie in the realm of social rights. Rights to education, health care, and social security, to food, clothing, and shelter, to cultural development, to employment standards, and to organize unions and to strike all represent advances for working people when and wherever achieved. These are the rights that provide certain, albeit limited, opportunities for working people to realize their potential, that allow them to become more than just wage-labourers, that modestly decommodify labour-power and free workers from abject dependence on the necessities and dictates of employment. These rights represent claims to that part of the social surplus that is collected from wages and salaries in the form of taxes, premiums, and deferred income; they constitute entitlements to benefit from a redistributed part of personal income. But they are countervailing rights – rights that in principle contradict the pre-eminence of corporate rights and give respite from the discipline and arbitrariness of the labour market and place of employment. In this sense, their very existence, though always limited, represents class victories in a class-divided system.

The relative balance of social rights for working people and civil rights for corporations is determined by and large in the struggle between working classes and the managers of capital. The extent of the social rights associated with the Keynesian welfare state represents the varying degrees of class success or compromise, measured by the scale of comprehensiveness and universality of these rights. The struggle for social rights has always been, moreover, conditional on the circumstances of the time; in other words, the KWS has been nothing other than a set of time-bound, fluctuating compromises in social systems characterized by chronic social conflicts. When the conditions that allowed the realization of these always contested compromises began to erode, the systematic retrenchment of the KWS commenced.

Civil and political rights are important to the working classes, but as means to an end, as instruments in a system of corporate private property that institutes social reform only under the dual pressures of maintaining the system's own viability and legitimacy and of threats from the organized sector of the working classes. In liberal democracies, in which non-corporate sectors do have these rights to varying degrees, the exercise of those rights is always within the confines of the system, that is, framed by prevailing private rights and ipso facto dominated by corporate private rights. Although civil and political rights can be a rallying cry against a despotic government, their attainment is paradoxical because they appear in the form of a constitution framed by the principles of private property disguised as the will of the people. While civil and political rights can be employed to change so-called public policy, to shift state priorities in order to win social reforms within this framework, those same rights can also be employed (and have been, especially since the 1980s) to let the people "do it to themselves" – to deny themselves the very reforms that provide respite from the exercise of corporate right, because elected governments in capitalist countries now have few choices but to favour corporate rights.

Recent examples of "returns" to "democracy" illustrate the point. When the generals in Chile and Argentina stepped away from absolute power in the late 1980s and 1990s, the change for the working classes amounted merely to the possible restitution of a small number of limited social rights through electoral means; a coherent network of restrictions grounded in national constitutions, trade relations, state indebtedness, IMF and World Bank agreements, foreign corporate ownership, and often special constitutional rights of political status and intervention for the military severely constrained that possibility. Much the same happened in Indonesia, Nigeria, and South Africa. Liberal democracy was restored with much ceremony, corresponding political institutions were put into place, and human rights organizations were confronted with fewer instances of violations of civil and political rights. Attention then shifted, in some cases, to national "reconciliation"[26] – to attempts to heal the wounds of outrageous crimes, without regard to the causes of the crimes. The object of the day became forgiveness, exoneration, reconciliation, amnesty, even martyrdom, and then attention moved to a new day that would ostensibly hold civil and political rights for all. The work of human rights organizations turned to reconciling past conflicts and watching for new violations of the newly cast civil and political rights.

In all these instances, social rights were consciously and firmly held to a minimum. In these countries the poverty remains unremitting, unemployment or underemployment are high, public education and medical care are consciously underfunded, and culture is increasingly commodified. Homelessness or shantytowns become normal conditions, few if any labour standards are enforced or even legislated, and trade unions and strikes are circumscribed. The restitution of liberal democracy brings a certain legitimacy to the system; it promotes abstract civil and political rights and thereby justifies the dominance of corporate private property and the exploitation of labour. It obscures the reasons for the fate of working people with the notion of a sovereign people and equality of civil and political rights. Social rights are what matter most to working classes in a capitalist mode of production; but they matter not as ends in themselves, rather as rights that mitigate economic inequality. Civil and political rights are increasingly mere abstractions and illusions for all but the corporations and the well-to-do. Moreover, TNC civil rights strive to usurp all other rights, to put an end to social, co-operative or communal rights as anomalies to the system; and these efforts are particularly obvious in relation to indigenous rights around the world. These two kinds of rights, corporate and social, can co-exist only in a form of compromise. Otherwise, there is no meeting ground; in principle, one right precludes the other.

If human rights organizations worked to advance human rights as social rights, instead of focusing almost exclusively on certain political and civil rights, they would as a matter of course raise questions about the intrinsic social and economic inequalities of the system, about how and why these inequalities can only continue to grow, and about the relation between liberal democracy and class property. In raising these questions, they would come to understand the significance of their selective promotion of certain rights as part of the ideological bulwark of capitalism.

To disabuse ourselves of the notion that human rights are absolute is extremely difficult, but the contradictions of the system itself are showing the way. The abrogation and continuous violations of the entire range of human rights for the majority by the very authorities and prevailing powers that are supposed to embody and protect those rights make obvious the need for a reconsideration of the belief in their absolute nature.

CHAPTER VI

The Future of Human Rights

If human rights at the national level are a product of social conflict and evolve in relation to the nature of these national conflicts, the postwar changes that blossomed in the 1970s into a distinctly new transnational level of economic activity brought a new dynamic of conflict that created complications for the persistence, defence, and advance of human rights. The future of human rights will be determined by the nature of social conflict as it unfolds at both the national and supranational levels.

GLOBALIZATION AND HUMAN RIGHTS

Early in the 1970s the globalization of capital began to undermine the foundations of the KWS. The very existence of the nation-state with its nationally bounded labour and capital markets was gradually transformed by trade agreements, common markets, and the rapid growth in the 1960s of the so-called Eurodollar. The Fordist mode of production succumbed to a revolution in technology, spawned in large measure by computers, which transformed production, distribution, and communication, further undermining the national markets and changing the structure of the working classes. In most nations union membership declined, and increasing government restrictions on their rights weakened the union movements. Wage levels began slowly levelling within and across nations; and with this the social wage, the fiscal foundation of the welfare state, also began to decline. By the end of the 1980s, "actually existing socialism" had been exposed for its injustice and corruption. The theory and practice of "socialism" lost their appeal as an alternative to capitalism for working people, and their indirect role as a rationale for the welfare state disintegrated. For all these reasons, the decline of social rights in the West began to be obvious in the 1980s. By the end of that decade, the peoples of Eastern Europe began to exchange the illusions of the "dictatorship of the proletariat" for the illusions of equal civil and political rights, and in the process lost many of their social rights. Most of the postwar conditions underlying the KWS were unravelling.

Globalization undermines all nationally based rights because it implies the shift of the locus of capital accumulation from the national to the global level; a result of this shift is that few mechanisms remain for non-corporate interests to exercise their civil and political rights to mitigate the effects of the pre-eminence of corporate rights.

Integral to globalization is the formation of regional and global enabling frameworks consisting of organizations and agencies making rules and regulations for transnational economic relations that embrace directly or indirectly every country of the world. The frameworks actively promote, regulate, and defend regulatory systems and development strategies for corporations at the transnational level.[1] The system also includes dispute resolution mechanisms for national differences, state-corporate conflicts, and intercorporate civil disputes.[2] The institutions of liberal democracy all come into question in the context of these supranational agencies and quasi-states. The non-corporate sectors of the nation-state have no access, democratic or otherwise, to these structures. Working people and indigenous nations have little or no representation at the transnational level, although some NGOs and IGOs (international government organizations) – hardly democratic institutions – do purport to speak on their behalf in global forums.

If political rights are circumscribed by these enabling frameworks, so too are civil rights. On the supranational level these structures define private rights for corporations alone, without establishing any similar rights or any means for giving a voice to or providing powers for non-corporate sectors. The regulatory regime defined by the WTO, IMF, and World Bank and regional markets such as the FTA, NAFTA, and EU have granted corporations legal rights that are greater than domestic corporations and even national and local governments. Corporations can pursue their own interests at the expense of national sovereignty and of the services and programs that benefit working people and protect the environment.[3]

With the existing rights for non-corporate sectors facing systematic suppression in a number of ways, including the use of neo-liberal policies in the industrial nations and structural adjustment policies elsewhere, struggles to defend these rights in the face of various forms of repression will necessarily continue. In a transitional world order with an unaccountable global dimension, no obvious alternative to such struggles exists. The demands that arise from these struggles will be as varied as the interests behind them. In liberal democracies the main contradiction between labour and capital will take the form of the struggle for the defence of social, political, and civil rights, on one side, and more exclusive transnational corporate civil rights, on the other. Working people will necessarily strive to protect trade union rights and rights to public education, health care, and social security. Corporations will strive to diminish political rights and to expand their exclusive rights to every arena available for the private accumulation of capital. In client dictatorships and other authoritarian regimes, the struggle of working people will focus more on winning civil and political rights – the abstract possibility of having a voice in determining public policy. Indigenous peoples will necessarily fight against the usurpation of Aboriginal rights and the state's insistence that they accept the civil and political rights of a capitalist social formation.

Non-Corporate Rights at the Global Level?

If, beyond the jurisdiction of nation-states, a relatively coherent and efficacious system of supranational rights exists for corporations, there is no similar system of agencies, mechanisms, or quasi-states that provide a viable, active, defence of the rights of working people, among other non-corporate entities, at that level. The ILO conventions, the so-called "core" conventions, include the rights to organize, to bargain collectively, to equal pay for equal work, and to be protected from discrimination and forced labour, among many others. But all of these rights are left to national governments to ratify, legislate, implement, and enforce. The ILO does periodically review the compliance by national states with these conventions, but it can do little other than publicize the infractions as a kind of leverage to shame governments into adherence.

Other attempts have been made to define and protect workers' civil and social rights. There is a long history of the assertion of international standards with respect to slavery, forced labour, child labour, hours of work, health and safety, and wages, but such efforts were always confounded by problems such as securing national agreement and compliance, enforcement, and adjudication. For almost as long, there have been attempts to establish conventions and standards for social insurance and social security at the international level. In 1952, for instance, the ILO adopted a Social Security (Minimum Standards) Convention, which was gradually ratified by most of the industrial states. But the Convention does not apply to countries that have not ratified it; and even those that have ratified it are able, with conditions, to limit their participation to just three of the nine listed standards. Moreover, a host of problems remain in measuring and ensuring compliance. More recent endeavours to set forth standards for workers come in the form of the "social clause," which lists standards to be inserted into international agreements of various sorts. National and international forums have tried to introduce the "social clause," but to date its use remains limited.[4]

Unlike corporations or states – which at the global level are collective entities yet defined as fictitious individuals – no similar definition exists for indigenous and tribal peoples, trade unions, social classes, women, and children.

Trade union rights – indeed, the rights of all non-corporate sectors – are defined, by and large, as national countervailing rights. To the degree that these rights for working people and their organizations are defined at the transnational level, there are no supranational oversight agencies with the authority to enforce them. Some regulatory mechanisms deal only with specific rights, some are limited geographically, and all are limited in accessibility. United Nations commissions and monitoring agencies for human rights have little if any effect on the compliance record of member states.[5] The enforcement of human rights practices is selective, if it takes place at all, and the mechanisms that do exist for monitoring human rights accords and the hearing of complaints are complicated in procedure. These mechanisms are also time-consuming, and often follow arbitrary judicial procedures. They exist, moreover, under the jurisdiction of executive bodies and have no independent source of finance. Financial cutbacks to the United Nations and national human rights commissions have led to the circumscription or even prevention of their operations, and to the manipulation or skewing of the emphases of their work.[6]

There is a viable global structure, then, solely for the advancement of corporate private rights, making them pre-eminent at the global level and subordinating national configurations of all other rights. With relative impunity, the representatives of TNCs, national states, and global agencies for capital make policies and take actions that negatively affect non-corporate interests and result in injurious and destructive activities across borders. Because national states must act more or less in the interests of capital, the people of the world are increasingly left voiceless (with the decline of governing power in liberal democracies) and defenceless (with the decline of social rights and with little legitimate recourse to the assertion of global corporate rights). With no political rights to speak of at the global level, non-corporate sectors in the emerging global civil society have few means of countervailing leverage. It is difficult for these same sectors to exercise national rights, such as they are, in response to the decisions at the global level. When political activity cannot find a legitimate outlet, however, it becomes extra-parliamentary or extra-legal. Given the growing nature of this predicament everywhere, resistance outside legitimate institutions can only continue to increase.[7]

The many thousands of existing NGOs and IGOs and voluntary agencies, as well as the UN Human Rights Commission, do not, however, constitute any kind of coherent and authoritative framework for the advancement or protection of the interests of non-corporate collective entities. Although certain UN agencies, numerous NGOs and churches, and occasionally other organizations are allowed various forms of observer, advisory, or consultative status at the UN and in other transnational policy and executive forums, they have few if any rights as active participants. Few of them, moreover, can claim to have their

The Future of Human Rights • 123

own participatory democratic mechanisms or means of accountability to their constituencies, let alone to the people of the world. The non-corporate sector of the world remains without representation in the decision-making and administrative forums of the regional and global quasi-states.[8]

The situation in the early twenty-first century has a certain historical parallel with the coming into being of the modern nation-state. The rising ascendancy of capital from the sixteenth to the nineteenth centuries saw the concomitant growth of a governing structure and legal system reflecting almost exclusively the demands of local/national corporations. Only when the nation as a whole was defined by the relations of capital, and the working class had come into its own, were the governing structures and legal systems changed to reflect broader social conflicts and countervailing powers. Modern capitalist democracy, with universal suffrage and its limited concessions to the working classes, emerged only in the twentieth century. For a long time prior to this, the national capitalist state was a state for capital only, just as now at the global level the emerging and coalescing set of agencies and organizations that oversee international relations recognizes only the rights of capital.

The persistence of the national state becomes a problem, then, for the achievement of popular representation at supranational levels because it assumes the mantle of national representative. As the embodiment of the prevailing relations in a national civil society, however, it necessarily represents primarily the general interests of corporations, both at the national and transnational levels. Because of its very nature it prevents the rights of citizens from moving to the global level to confront and therefore mitigate corporate private rights at that level. The argument that a national state "with a social conscience" might make a difference for its citizens is difficult to make when state sovereignty means less and less in the face of TNCs and the supranational frameworks.

The idea of a liberal-democratic state at the regional or global level, as the formation of the European Union implies, includes the establishment of all the associated rights at these levels – without the national state as mediator. The idea requires building a more or less coherent regional or global civil society – resembling the civil society of nation-states, including corporations, trade unions, churches, other groups, and citizens as citizens of the region or world – with civil, political, and social rights in relation to a transnational state. It means establishing the rule of law at these levels so that TNCs and regional or global agencies and organizations could to some degree be held accountable. This could not, then, be a structure of rights that presupposes a permanent role for the national state, or that defines humans as "nationals."

While the structure of regional and world governance today is a long way from resembling a liberal-democratic state, movement in that direction is not completely implausible, as the existence of the EU suggests.[9] It is an unlikely path for history to take, however. Establishing the modern liberal-democratic state at these levels would produce the same now obvious limitations seen at the national level. The same critique of national liberal democracy could be levelled at regional or global liberal democracy. While the structure would in theory allow for countervailing forces to exact concessions from TNCs and mitigate the worst effects of capital accumulation, important civil rights could no more be realized for the majority than at the national level because of the requirement of having the financial means to do so and the vast oligopolies and monopolies held by TNCs over the world's means of production, distribution, and communication. Political rights would similarly be framed by a constitution and rule of law informed by the primacy of corporate private right. Social rights would remain countervailing rights, always in the form of compromises and for the most part consisting of a state-directed redistribution of the social wage. Humans would remain defined as isolated individuals separated from genuine social links by contractual relations. There would be at best limited admission of rights based on collective or co-operative claims, such as Aboriginal rights, or other demands for socialized capital. All the contradictions in human rights found in the nation-state would be replicated at the transnational level.

In the transition to a global social formation, human development has arrived at an interregnum that includes two main levels of jurisdiction: the national and the global. The national framework, on the one hand, encompasses and contains for the most part the struggles between various non-corporate sectors and the large corporations, in particular between the working classes and corporate management. The regional and global frameworks, the quasi-sovereign groups of institutions and agencies, on the other hand, have been designed for and operate by and large in the interests of capital alone. Here, national state representatives promote national corporate interests *and* the interests of capital in general – there is only limited formal representation of the interests of the non-corporate sectors. The structure of rights in the world, then, consists of increasingly dominant regional and global civil rights for corporations and subordinate national or limited regional rights (civil, political, social) for the non-corporate sectors. Unless the non-corporate sectors create regional and global organizations and demands to match the structure of transnational corporate rights, there can only be further retrenchment of non-corporate rights at the national level.

RECENT GLOBAL MECHANISMS FOR ENFORCEMENT

The first modern international instruments to address the violation of what was to become human rights came after World War II were the ad hoc military tribunals in Nuremberg (1946) and Tokyo (1948). So widespread, systematic, and conscious were the atrocities committed against civilian populations by the governments and armed forces of Germany and Japan that the Allied nations could not allow a general amnesty and believed they had to establish responsibility for the crimes and punish some of the key perpetrators. The tribunals, however, were circumscribed and limited by many conditions – among other reasons,[10] none of the main Allied governments could be said to have a clear conscience in their prewar treatment of colonial and subject peoples or in their wartime acts (in Hamburg, Dresden, Hiroshima, Nagasaki) or in their postwar treatment of prisoners of war. Still, the trials marked a turning point in the growth of human self-reflection. Here, Allied representatives defined new crimes at the international level (genocide, crimes against humanity, against peace, additional war crimes, and complicity in these crimes); and the tribunals levied these charges against officials of the defeated nations. Significantly, the tribunals also affirmed that anyone, including heads of state, who commits an international crime can be held responsible under international law.[11]

The supranational nature of these tribunals – international prosecution of crimes against international law in an international court – became an early preoccupation of the United Nations; and by 1953 the UN had prepared a draft proposal for a permanent international criminal court. By that time, however, the Cold War had begun, and from 1945 through the next few decades, wars of national liberation continued or opened on every continent. In China, Indo-China, Greece, Korea, Malaysia, Indonesia, the Philippines, the Middle East, and then throughout Africa and Latin America, the former colonizing nations and particularly the United States became engaged in wars to retain colonial or other subordinate nations within the new international framework for capital. For the Western powers fighting these wars, it was not a time to have an international criminal court, however circumscribed, as a standing reminder of the meaning of genocide, of crimes against humanity and against peace, and of war crimes, let alone as a means of allowing the possible prosecution of guilty parties.

By the 1990s the need to maintain the legitimacy of capitalism and its governments in the face of a growing world consciousness of human rights and their violation began to make it necessary to resurrect the postwar tribunals and investigations. In the long and violent efforts throughout the postwar decades to resolve the question of sovereignty in favour of capital, gross violations of human rights were committed in Africa, Asia, and Latin America. Whole nations were divided, usually along class or racial lines, and in the end left embittered, disjointed – rent by fear, guilt, and an abiding sense of injustice. In many of these countries, when the war had purportedly ended, the violations continued but on a more modest level to ensure that capital could prevail, that demands for social justice, along with national aspirations of independence, could be minimized, and that organized protest could be kept under control.

So extensive and horrific were these crimes against unarmed civilian populations by government armed forces and death squads – such a travesty of every aspect of human rights except corporate civil rights – that the crimes and the question of culpability had to be addressed and veiled or deflected to ensure that some national cohesion could be restored and a degree of political legitimacy provided to the new post-conflict governments. To create the grounds for national reconciliation in order to re-establish the *status quo ante* once the threat to it had been removed by these crimes, an authoritative acknowledgement of crimes had to be delivered and a resolution for the victims had to be at least attempted. For these tasks, two mechanisms have been employed – truth and reconciliation commissions and UN-sponsored ad hoc tribunals – and a third came into being in 2003 – the International Criminal Court. While promising to address the violations and enforce human rights, these mechanisms have done more to obscure the underlying causes of the crimes than anything else.

Truth and Reconciliation Commissions

About twenty truth and reconciliation commissions had been set in place by the mid-1990s in countries in Latin America, Africa, and Asia; and they continue to be proposed in various countries as a means of addressing the trauma of extensive crimes committed by state agencies over many years, crimes often encouraged through foreign interference. But, as their mandates and limitations reveal, their alleged purpose is not possible to realize.

While their characteristics vary considerably, none of the commissions are free of significant shortcomings. Some, for example, have been set up not through any independent public process but by an existing government that was party to the planning and execution of the crimes. Their mandates have always been predetermined and carefully restricted to the investigation of certain types of violations and not others; and their powers have often been circumscribed to include no more than the gathering of evidence, identifying the victims, granting reparations, and proposing preventive measures for the future. Some were not mandated to identify the people who were culpable; and restrictions have always been placed on the contents of the final reports. In some cases the final reports have not been released. Very few of the commissions have been granted any powers of prosecution or other judicial functions; often the existing judicial systems and police forces involved in the crimes were left in place with minor changes. Some commissions were set up after amnesty laws were promulgated to ensure that possible prosecutions would be blocked. Many were given relatively short time constraints of six to eight months, and very few more than a year, to complete their work. The question of staffing usually raised problems of principle, and bias, and the size of budgets placed invisible limits on their work. Few of them were mandated to explore the involvement of foreign governments in the planning and execution of the crimes. Very few were granted the authority to examine the role of public or private organizations in the crimes. Given these limitations and constraints, it is no wonder that, aside from helping to re-establish the *status quo ante*, most of these truth commissions have provided at best a measured catharsis for a few victimized sections of society.[12]

Because of the calculated use of these limitations and constraints, moreover, the truth commissions have functioned to obscure the real issues. They leave largely unexamined, as if they were non-issues, the reasons for the atrocities – their political and economic rationale and the nature and degree of foreign involvement. Instead they shift the focus away from these underlying issues to the moral domain or individual suffering and/or responsibility. Just as they leave unexplored the reasons for the crimes, so too do they often deny or excuse, as not conducive to reconciliation, the prosecution of those responsible, which means that the victims are left to deal with an unresolved injustice.

The commissions became exercises to put the past to rest; they have offered a means of burying past injustices and obscuring present ones, of adding legitimacy to new regimes after the purported threat was removed. They were never intended to change the conditions that gave rise to the crimes or to uncover how and why they took place.[13] All truth commissions have been instruments of compromise designed to maintain the fundamentals of the status quo; and as a result the "truth" of their findings reflects the necessities of the continuation of systems of inequality.[14]

Not only could truth commissions not resolve the social dislocation caused by massive human rights violations, but they also often did not even fulfil the terms of their existence. Almost ten years after the Truth and Reconciliation Commission in South Africa was established in 1994, Human Rights Watch and Amnesty International jointly called upon the South African government to complete the implementation of the recommendations, which were to provide "restitution, compensation, and rehabilitation" to the victims, to bring more violators to justice, and to release the remaining reports.[15] Many of the underlying issues and contradictions that gave rise to the atrocities of the apartheid era remain not just unresolved, but also irresolvable by means of such commissions.

UN Ad Hoc Tribunals

The other means of addressing widespread human rights violations has been the use of United Nations ad hoc tribunals – the most prominent and expensive so far being the 1993 International Criminal Tribunal for the Former Yugoslavia (ICTFY) and the 1994 International Criminal Tribunal for Rwanda (ICTR).[16] Until 1999 the record for both of these bodies was revealing. By that time the ICTFY had indicted somewhat over eighty people (most of them Serbs), but had only twenty-six of them in custody and a mere five convictions, including the most important one, "the deputy commander of a prison." The ICTR had indicted only thirty-five alleged transgressors of human rights, with almost as many in custody and a small number of convictions. From the beginning it has been plagued by staff corruption and incompetence.[17] Almost a quarter of the lawyers for the prosecution were dismissed in 2000 for being "absorbed in their own narrow self-interest."

The situation began to change in June 2001 when the former president of Yugoslavia, Slobodan Milosevic, was delivered into ICTFY custody at The Hague. The attention paid to his arrest made the ICTFY appear less than even-handed as prosecutors of the criminals in a war with atrocities on all sides. In an apparent act of judicial arbitrariness, perhaps to counter the appearance of anti-Serb bias, the chief prosecutor of the Tribunal pressed for more indicted officials to be arrested and sent from Croatia. Many of the actions of the Tribunal, however, have brought forth questions of serious legal irregularities.

Yugoslavia's newly installed president considered Milosevic's abduction to be constitutionally illegal; and many commentators have suggested that the arbitrary action was a product of pressure placed on the Yugoslav government by the United States, which, according to the argument, made financial aid for reconstruction dependent on the surrender of the former president to the Tribunal. If this were the rationale, those responsible for spiriting him out of the country did not simply give up their former leader in a questionable manner to a tribunal with questionable legitimacy, but they also compromised the sovereignty of their country in at least two ways. The act subordinated the government's right to prosecute Milosevic in Yugoslavia to the right of the Tribunal; and the acceptance of aid for reconstruction with the usual linkages of free trade, deficit reduction, and public-sector retrenchment would allow broad national policies to be determined by the loan agencies and the powers behind them.

The restricted mandates of the two tribunals guarantee that they will never shed light on reasons for the conflicts. There are questions around due process and double standards or victor's justice, and there are other fundamental shortcomings. First of all, they are ad hoc tribunals, specific to particular events. They are designed only for certain circumstances and enjoined to address only specific aspects of the events under investigation. This specificity means that they are tailored to address certain aspects of certain situations while excluding other situations and aspects that the presiding powers do not want investigated or adjudicated. This specificity in itself is an obvious violation of certain principles of the rule of law and contrary to judicial practice and principle in most countries. It follows that the key difference between a Slobodan Milosevic and a Henry Kissinger, for instance, lies in the power and authority behind them and not in the nature or extent of their crimes. Among key figures responsible for human death and suffering since World War II, Kissinger, the U.S. Secretary of State under President Nixon, is arguably one of the leading contenders – as has been pointed out in two articles that make the case against him for war crimes and crimes against humanity.[18] The crimes of Milosevic, alleged or proven, however unjustifiable and inexcusable, make for a poor comparison.[19] Indeed, the actions of many postwar U.S. governments could easily be the subject of many international criminal tribunals – and probably would be if it were not for U.S. dominance in the UN and the Security Council, and its consequent power to authorize and initiate or veto these tribunals.[20] Moreover, many human rights watchers, Amnesty International among them, believe that the very actions of the NATO powers that bombed Yugoslavia include indictable war crimes.[21]

Also largely unexamined are the questions of the independence of the tribunals from NATO country financing (NATO countries constituted one side of the military activity in Yugoslavia, and some of these same countries had a certain involvement in Rwanda), and the determination of the rules of procedure. Both issues point in the direction of political trials,[22] or at least leave open the question of trials for purposes other than bringing about some form of legal justice.

Another problem has to do with the source of their authority, which is the UN Security Council. It is a body that is only in part elected by the UN General Assembly; and it is not, according to the Charter, accountable to the Assembly or to the world's citizenry. Its five permanent members are the only members with veto powers; the privilege and rationale for permanent status have always been controversial and are no less so today. This established structure, and the Council's indirect domination by the United States, make it an undemocratic and arbitrary executive organ.[23] The institution that created the tribunals and defined their mandates, then, rests on dubious authority – an authority that has nothing to do with democracy or popular representation, and everything to do with degrees of power and a political structure that largely reflects the world situation of the immediate postwar years. If the legitimacy of the Security Council is in question, so too is its decision to create ad hoc rather than permanent tribunals for these crimes. Given the apparent need for increasing numbers of war crime tribunals, a permanent independent international court, with financing separate from the parties involved, would at least give the appearance of justice being done. If the principles of liberal democracy comprise the spirit of the United Nations, the structure and practice of the Security Council stand in stark opposition.[24]

Yet another problem for these tribunals is their focus on individual responsibility. Both of them have concentrated almost exclusively on individual criminal acts and on the prosecution of individuals thought to be responsible. Their indictments, moreover, have included only some of those thought to be responsible – by and large those who countered the strategic interests of the foreign governments and global agencies involved. The tribunals have made no attempt to uncover the political and economic causes of the events in the two countries; and they have spent little effort on inquiring into the role of foreign states or international institutions or agencies, including those of the UN, and even the Security Council, whose role in Rwanda and the former Yugoslavia remains unclear if not questionable.[25] Structural adjustment policies also played a significant role in both cases, but the tribunals are not mandated to assess the implications of IMF and World Bank policies and practices.[26] They have similarly ignored the question of the role of the churches in the Rwandan genocide. They were not, in general, given the mandate to establish the broad facts of the conflicts over which they were to adjudicate.[27]

The singular focus on the individuals alleged to be responsible is a central part of the obfuscation; it fails to take into account the systemic and institutional or organizational violations of human rights and helps to disguise the reasons underlying those violations. Even if, for instance, the arrest of the former Chilean dictator General Pinochet in London in October 1998 had led to a trial and conviction in a court of law in Spain (or in Chile), this procedure would not necessarily have exposed the reasons behind the Chilean coup d'état of 1973, or the intimate involvement in it of the CIA, as revealed finally by the U.S. government itself.[28] It would not bring to light the society-wide experiment in neo-liberalism in Chile under the junta, or the subsequent introduction of a highly restricted political system that passes for liberal democracy, or the continuing poverty of a large portion of the population in the midst of high rates of capital accumulation.[29] The possible exposure of years of systematic violations of human rights by global institutions and agencies, TNCs, and foreign governments, and rationalized by the media and government spokespeople, can be obscured by the prosecution of a single person or a few individuals, as leaders and/or symbols.

This is not to say that individuals involved in these violations are without responsibility, but individuals always act within a systemic framework. They are motivated by social, political, and material interests, and outside of those interests their acts have no meaning. In the cases of the crimes committed in the former Yugoslavia and in Rwanda, much of the responsibility lies beyond these countries, with the governments and agencies of the intervening industrial nations.[30] The same criticism also applies to the truth and reconciliation commissions.

The Nuremberg Judgment, while also giving primacy to individual responsibility, did recognize that an organization could be defined as criminal if it had conspired to commit unlawful acts. The judgment found that several Nazi corporate bodies or groups, such as the Leadership Corps, the Gestapo, and the SS, were indeed criminal and that voluntary membership and knowledge of their crimes constituted a crime in itself.[31] This principle could be extended to business corporations, as the Nuremberg trials did in indicting Alfried Krupp, among other German officials of corporations that participated in the Nazi crimes.[32] The principle could also be extended to other organizations or agencies implicated in violating human rights or other international laws. Personnel aside, a case could be made that the operating principles and "mission" or purpose of a state, its agencies, other organizations, and corporations may well constitute contradictions of a range of human rights.[33]

In the end, given that the focus on individual responsibility in both the commissions and tribunals covers up the real causes of the crimes, or the interests behind them, the nation fails to achieve reconciliation over what was done in its name or on its territory. When only individuals are indicted, convicted, and punished, the causes of their actions are taken to be individual; and the underlying interests and causes not only remain unexposed but also continue to be present, albeit often in different forms. Important aspects of the truth are never revealed; instead, what passes for truth amounts to a partial admission of individual crimes, and reconciliation at best can only be the acceptance of injustice and possible reparations for the victims.[34]

Compromised Commissions and Tribunals

Neither the truth and reconciliation commissions nor the ad hoc tribunals have had as their objective the impartial adjudication of human rights violations, the pursuit of criminal justice, or disclosure of the political and economic rationale of the crimes. The dilemma for their framers was how to address the deep social divisions caused by violations without questioning the responsibility that lies within the system itself – while also providing the appearance of authoritative resolution. The results so far suggest that these bodies have served to ensure the continuity of the global system by appearing to speak to the crimes and to allow for admissions of guilt, a measure of atonement, limited penalties, reconciliation with injustice, and gestures of forgiveness. But the political and economic structures that gave rise to the violations continue, though somewhat changed to be sure – apartheid laws have been removed, dictatorships "democratized," civil wars brought to truce. In every case, however, conditions for capital investment have been given a new lease. A system of private property continues to prevail, and the economy is opened to or prepared for international investment. The political form of liberal democracy is resurrected or constructed (often with political/constitutional guarantees or privileges for the military), and the WTO, IMF, and World Bank determine broad economic policy. Global corporate civil right comes to predominate; political rights are circumscribed by the property framework, other constitutional restrictions, and global demands; and social rights are moved into the domain of charities.

Japan: Postwar
Treaties and Trials

Unlike West Germany, which found many thousands of Germans guilty of war crimes after the Nuremberg trials, Japan has not prosecuted any Japanese war criminals after the Tokyo trials. Many crimes, and the political, economic, and institutional causes of them, have never been addressed. For the victims and the citizens of Japan, then, there has been no admission, let alone resolution, of the effects of these war crimes. The problem was dramatically illustrated in the 1999 decision of the UN Subcommission on Human Rights, which found that Japan owed compensation to more than 200,000 wartime "sex slaves," to whom Japan begrudgingly and belatedly acknowledged "moral responsibility."

The Japanese Imperial Army is estimated to have enslaved no less than 200,000 women from the mid-1930s to 1945 – and perhaps as many as 400,000 – for sexual services for Japanese troops. These women were "recruited" in all the countries occupied by the Japanese and were systematically interned in "comfort stations" in which rape, torture, trafficking, and other sexual crimes were committed.

In 2000 a Peoples' Tribunal was established in Tokyo to determine responsibility, to demand compensation, and to publicize the extent and horror of these crimes. The Women's International War Crimes Tribunal on Japan's Military Sexual Slavery met in December 2000. The Tribunal found "Emperor Hirohito and other high-ranking Japanese military and political officials" to be responsible for "crimes against humanity in approving, condoning, and failing to prevent the rape and sexual slavery of women" in the Japanese occupied territories. It also found the Japanese state responsible, and demanded apologies and reparations.

The Women's Tribunal also underscored the point that its very existence was due to the failure of the postwar Tokyo Trials to prosecute more than a few thousand Japanese officials for a narrow range of crimes – completely ignoring the systematic "military sexual slavery." Gender bias was obvious not only in this omission, but also in the very peace treaties that closed the war. The Women's Tribunal pointed out that because of gender bias the treaties left unaddressed crimes specifically aimed at women, providing the Japanese state with the argument that the treaties and trials had addressed responsibility for its wartime actions without any mention of these specific crimes against women.

However important this Women's Tribunal was in drawing attention to Japan's unaddressed war crimes against women, it also pointed to a lost opportunity for the women themselves. Probably for the sake of credibility, the Tribunal carried out the trial by remaining as much as possible within the confines of existing international law. The trial, then, was limited to raising only certain questions – mainly, the culpability for the crimes. But establishing culpability does not reveal the root of the problem, even though it may find those immediately and ultimately responsible. The question of the source of gender bias and the horrific consequences in war and peace remain unanswered. The real reasons for sexual crimes by the military, and the postwar implications of those crimes, are not to be found in determining who were the specific perpetrators. It is the nature of the social formation that condones, allows, ignores, and perpetuates unequal gender relations that is ultimately responsible; and this cannot be grasped by pursuing a trial within the confines of existing law.

Among other things, this Women's Tribunal should have led to other investigations of similar crimes in the postwar era by the military – in particular, the U.S. armed forces. There is certainly enough material to indict U.S. officials for the systematic use of "Rest and Recreation" sites in the Korean and Vietnam wars. During these wars, through agreements or treaties with the Philippine and Thai governments, Washington established designated sites or urban areas where large numbers of women were procured as prostitutes for U.S. servicemen. These are not only crimes of the past but are also ongoing. The fate of many thousands of women in the former Yugoslavia is also now not dissimilar, given the presence of thousands of NATO troops.

• Fielding, "Japan's Sex Slaves"; Women's International War Crimes Tribunal, "Japan's Military Sexual Slavery"; Brock and Thistlethwaite, *Casting Stones*; Turshen and Holcomb, eds., *Women's Lives and Public Policy*; Moon, *Sex among Allies*.

As it turns out, then, those individuals, agencies, and governments that have aided the expansion of the conditions of capital accumulation and in the process perpetrated violations of human rights, even to the point of massive loss of life and extensive destruction of the environment, are rarely if ever called to account or even thought of as violators. For their role in conspiring to commit acts that necessarily violate human rights there is probably sufficient evidence to indict successive government leaders of the United States, United Kingdom, France, Belgium, Israel, and the former Soviet Union, as well as the officials and operatives of foreign secret services (CIA, Mossad, MI-6, KGB, French secret service), the administrators of NATO, the World Trade Organization, IMF, and World Bank, the corporate officials of many TNCs, and these organizations themselves. At first glance, even the idea that these officials and bodies are indictable within the existing framework of human rights seems absurd. What before was unthinkable, however, is no longer.

Old charges once dismissed are beginning to be heard, and new charges are being made. In 1998 Bishop Desmond Tutu, chair of the South African Truth and Reconciliation Commission, visited the United States and suggested that the country was in need of its own similar commission – an idea perhaps not well understood by his hosts but one that is unfolding in a number of many-sided ways. A UN-sponsored truth and reconciliation commission in Guatemala in 1999 openly laid responsibility for the deaths of tens of thousands of people at the feet of the U.S. government and military forces, forcing President Clinton to apologize.[35] Similar evidence of U.S. involvement exists for the civil war in El Salvador, and Nicaragua, among other Central and South American states.[36] Between 1984 and 1986, the International Court of Justice summoned the courage to challenge the legality of U.S. action against Nicaragua.[37] Just as Americans have learned about the crimes of Henry Kissinger, some U.S. citizens have discovered the nature of the crimes of the U.S. Department of Defense at its School of the Americas, and have begun to hold their own "truth commission" into its purpose and history.[38] Another "peoples' tribunal," the Korea International War Crimes Tribunal, has exposed the massive crimes committed by U.S. military forces against civilians and war prisoners.[39]

The actions of other countries and organizations have similarly come under close scrutiny – a situation that was more or less inconceivable not long ago. The Israeli government and certain Jewish organizations have increasing difficulties in using the Holocaust to justify, even to themselves and Jews around the world, the formation of their state through violations of the rights of Palestinians, as well as other continuous and widely condemned violations.[40] Even the institutional manifestations of the world's dominant powers, the G7 and IMF and World Bank, became the subject of an "international peoples' tribunal" in 1993 in which those bodies were "indicted" for the effects of their polices in violating human rights.[41] In regular sessions held by the Permanent Peoples' Tribunal, TNCs, among other organizations, have been exposed for their violations of human rights and environmental regulations.

Guatemala:
Atrocities and the United States

In 1999 the United Nations released its Historical Clarification Commission report *Guatemala: Memory of Silence*. This nine-volume report was the result of the 1996 peace accord that brought an end to the war in Guatemala; and in it the UN commission "concluded that for decades the United States knowingly gave money, training, and other vital support to a military regime that committed atrocities as a matter of policy and even 'acts of genocide' against the Maya people." Tens of thousands of people were tortured; more than a million were displaced from their land; and an estimated 200,000 people were killed. The responsibility for over 90 per cent of all the torture, executions, systematic rape, and massacres was laid at the feet of the U.S.-supported and trained paramilitary forces and the CIA.

The worst of the atrocities has now stopped, but the repression continues. In 1999, when Bishop Juan José Gerardi released a church report listing names of those responsible (the UN Commission report did not give names) he was bludgeoned with a concrete block. In May 2001 Sister Barbara Ann Ford, an American nun who worked with the Catholic Church and other rights groups, was killed in Guatemala City. Since the peace accord of 1996, many assassinations of rights workers have taken place and numerous judges have been forced into exile. In May 2001 a UN human rights verification mission to Guatemala reported that, since 2000, the police have become "the principal responsible parties for the gravest human rights violations." Americans, in particular, have been involved in the training of these police. In 2002 Amnesty International reported that the country was experiencing a "human rights meltdown."

• United Nations, Historical Clarification Commission, *Guatemala: Memory of Silence*; see also Jonas, "Dangerous Liaisons: The U.S. in Guatemala"; Amnesty International, "Guatemala's Legal Legacy."

This raised consciousness about the violation of human rights is also seen in the use of national laws to prosecute foreign officials accused of international crimes. The attempted extradition of General Pinochet in 1998 by the Spanish judge, Baltasar Garzon, to be tried in Spain for torture and crimes against humanity, is amongst the most prominent examples.[42] Although that extradition did not succeed, in June 2003 the Mexican government sent the former Argentine military officer, Ricardo Cavallo, to Spain to be tried by Garzon for crimes committed during the so-called "dirty war" in Argentina between 1976 and 1984. Another notable example is the 1993 Belgian law of universal competence, which allowed Belgian courts to have jurisdiction over international crimes, regardless of the nationality of the accused or the country where the alleged offence occurred. Among the most prominent of those indicted was Ariel Sharon, the prime minister of Israel, for his role in the massacres of Palestinians in the refugee camps of Sabra and Shatila. Over the years, about thirty foreign heads of state or former leaders became the subject of official complaints under this law. In recent years charges were extended to former and current U.S. officials – President Bush I (George H.W.), Vice-President Dick Cheney, Secretary of State Colin Powell for the 1991 bombing of Baghdad, and General Tommy Franks for events during the U.S. invasion of Iraq in 2003. President Bush II (George W.) and Prime Minister Tony Blair were added in June 2003 to the list of those charged. By this time, Belgium had come under significant pressure, in particular by the Israeli and U.S. governments and certain "business circles," to amend the law. Members of the Bush II cabinet made it clear to the Belgian government that this law and the headquarters of NATO and other international organizations, as well as many large corporations and foreign investors, in Brussels were incompatible.[43] In response, in April 2003 the Belgian legislature amended the law; but in June 2003 it revised the clauses that allowed for universal competence, "days after Donald Rumsfeld, the U.S. Secretary of Defense, ordered a freeze on $350 million funding for NATO buildings in Belgium and threatened to pull the alliance headquarters out of the country unless the 'absurd' law was scrapped."[44]

The growing consciousness of human rights also brings to the fore unresolved guilt over past crimes – a guilt manifested in the main through apologies, that is, the acknowledgement of responsibility for wrongdoing. Over the decades since World War II, many governments have made apologies for past offences within their countries for wartime internment and expropriations, among other things. The Roman Catholic Church also felt compelled to admit "the past and present sins" of the church in order to liberate its "communal conscience."[45] Although the crimes committed by the U.S. government in the war against Vietnam have not been admitted or addressed, they continue to trouble the conscience of many Americans who were party to them.[46] Many millions of Americans protested their government's war in Vietnam and came to understand the nature of their government, but for many who served in the war there are often bitter unresolved memories.

These and many other examples suggest that the step forward in human self-consciousness represented by the UDHR can never be reversed,[47] even though such consciousness now more than ever is confronted with the growing dominance of global corporate civil rights and its effects.

On the surface, it would appear that the truth commissions and the ad hoc tribunals, as the mechanisms for the highly circumscribed and controlled prosecution or mere acknowledgement of human rights violations, have served as instruments for obscuring the underlying causes of gross violations of human rights and the responsibility of governments and organizations. They illustrate the degree to which officialdom in the industrial nations is willing to abandon the standards of judicial procedure and principles of the rule of law in the pursuit of political and economic ends. The commissions and tribunals have served as the means for pretending to reconcile the irreconcilable – that is, the divided societies in which different social sectors have vied for different forms of sovereignty – national rule versus global, or people's rule versus a ruling framework for capital. In the process, they have vindicated an economic system that allows for increasing disparities in wealth and provides few and decreasing political options for change through formal and legally legitimate means.

The School of the Americas

The School of the Americas, renamed in 2001, is now called Western Hemisphere Institute for Security Cooperation. According to SOA Watch, "The former Congressperson Joseph Kennedy stated, 'The U.S. Army School of the Americas ... is a school that has [produced] more dictators than any other school in the history of the world.' In total the school has produced at least eleven Latin American dictators." This count does not include at least two of the military officers who took part in the attempted coup against Chavez in Venezuela in May 2002. U.S. military training throughout the Third World has brought similar tragic results.

• SOA Watch, April 13, 2002; on U.S. military training for the Third World, see Hartung and Moix, "Deadly Legacy."

Although the commissions and tribunals have been valuable instruments in the foreign policy of the industrial nations, in particular the United States, they have been addressing internationally defined criminal acts – violations of human rights, genocide, war crimes, and crimes against humanity – and in this way constitute forms of international adjudication of international crimes, producing a certain international jurisprudence regarding the prosecution of individuals for the violation of international law. In so doing, the ad hoc tribunals and reconciliation commissions imply in principle what Nuremberg and Tokyo also implied: the creation of a permanent international criminal court that in theory could eliminate the political and judicial bias inherent in transitory, ad hoc structures (though without eliminating the biases of a system of private property). In practice, however, this was not to be; the U.S. government was not about to subordinate itself to any independent, international, court.

The International Criminal Court

After World War II the possibility of a UN-sponsored international criminal court was actively pursued but did not come to fruition. More than fifty years later, in July 1998, its founding statute was adopted at a conference in Rome, with 120 nations voting for the treaty, 21 abstaining, and 7 voting against. By December 31, 2000, 139 states had signed the treaty, and by April 2002 more than 60 countries had ratified it, allowing the Court's jurisdiction to be established in July of the same year. In September 2002 the first Assembly of States Parties (ASP) met at the UN in New York to work out the administrative structure for the Court's inauguration in 2003. In February 2003, the ASP elected the first eighteen judges to the Court – seven women and eleven men representing most of the regions of the world.

The Rome Statute was the beginning of the creation of the International Criminal Court (ICC). The document outlined the nature of the crimes that the Court could address, its jurisdiction and relation to national states, and some of its operational procedures.[48] In principle, by creating a permanent international criminal court, the Statute challenged the structure of international criminal adjudication as controlled in large measure by the UN Security Council and the U.S. government. If it were possible for it to become a genuinely independent court, it would transcend important elements of national sovereignty, undermining the pursuit of domestic and foreign policies and superseding national laws in prosecuting and sentencing persons charged with violations defined as genocide, war crimes, and crimes against humanity. It would also stand as a reminder to officials of all nations that they could be charged as international criminals if they were party to such crimes – and these officials might include state representatives and administrators at all levels, military personnel, and even corporate executives.

The idea of an ICC free of entrenched and controlling interests and universal in its jurisdiction will probably remain hypothetical. Even at the national level in capitalist countries, where nominally independent courts have prosecuted corporations and the rich and powerful, such prosecution, relative to "street crime," is infrequent and conviction even more so. And this in a system that, although designed for capital accumulation, still finds corporate and political crime to be little short of pervasive. At the global level, then, in a world made in the image of TNCs, the ideal of an independent, neutral, objective judicial system is unlikely to be established when the economic order rests on the perpetuation of growing inequalities and is widely complemented by corporate illegal activities and state suppression of dissent.

With good reason to fear an ICC,[49] the United States was one of the seven nations that initially voted against the Statute, along with China, Iraq, Yemen, Qatar, and Israel – all countries with poor human rights records, and all with good reason to fear an international jurisdiction within which their officials could be prosecuted and, by implication, their foreign policies judged to be in violation of international law. After a book-length case had been made for his indictment, Kissinger was himself quite clear about the dangers of such a court for U.S. personnel.[50] His concern was probably heightened by President Clinton's signature on the Statute "only hours ... before the cutoff date" on December 31, 2000. A senior official under George W. Bush confirmed such fears. Undersecretary of State John Bolton pointedly stated: "Our concern goes beyond the possibility that the prosecutor will target for indictment the isolated U.S. soldier.... Our principal concern is for our country's top civilian and military leaders, those responsible for our defence and foreign policy." He added: "No U.S. presidents or their advisors could be assured that they would be unequivocally safe from politicized charges of criminal liability."[51] Far from being "politicized charges," the existing evidence and allegations of U.S. crimes gathered by numerous organizations and agencies, from the UN to Human Rights Watch to Amnesty International, following the new Statute of the ICC, clearly establish a record of actions that can be defined as genocide, war crimes, and crimes against humanity, among other violations of human rights.[52]

Clinton's signature came only after rigorous diplomatic efforts to ensure that the mandate and operation of the Court would not impair, diminish, or threaten the ability of the U.S. government to pursue its foreign policy.[53] Even then Washington was aware of the potential danger of ICC exposure of U.S. actions, and Clinton refused to submit the treaty for ratification or recommend further action until it was changed.[54] In pursuing its goal of minimizing the possibility of prosecution of its citizens and state organizations by refusing to ratify the treaty, the U.S. government effectively eliminated the prospect of a court operating with equanimity under an international rule of law.

Following the U.S. interventions, the very mandate and jurisdiction of the proposed court as laid out in the Rome Statute were highly circumscribed. Its procedures were similarly hobbled: the ICC will only be able to pursue criminal investigations referred to it by the UN Security Council, individual nations, or an ICC prosecutor with the concurrence of the state in question. Among other limitations, it can only deal with "serious" war crimes that entail a "policy or plan" in their execution; charges can proceed to investigation only after a pre-trial approval; the Security Council can vote to postpone investigations for as long as twelve months, "on a renewable basis"; only individuals can be prosecuted and not governments or their agencies or national or transnational corporations; and only crimes committed after July 1, 2002, can be prosecuted.[55] After pointing to some of these limitations when the Rome Statute was released, Amnesty International suggested that the ICC was "crippled at birth."[56]

The International Criminal Court, even if disabled from the outset, has become a reality. Although, like all courts of law, it can and will be used by the powers that be to advance their interests, the friction between its statutory limitations and what it purports to be will undermine its ability to function and possibly make it an object of censure and provoke demands for reform. In the meantime, it stands mainly as a symbolic alternative to the ad hoc nature of current tribunals (and their questionable mandates and prosecutions), and as a permanently established court that could act as a deterrent to certain international criminal acts. As a symbol, it could act as a potential, albeit modest, obstacle to a range of extra-legal practices by the U.S. and other governments and to unilateral military interventions, covert operations, and extra-territorial abductions of alleged criminals.[57]

However compromised, the ICC remains at least a symbolic challenge to the pre-eminence of U.S. policy around the world. Washington has argued that the existence of the Court opens its own military and government officials to "frivolous or politically motivated investigators and prosecutions." Unwilling to subordinate its personnel to international rule of law, it has continued to subvert the principles and practices of the Court. On May 6, 2002, in an unprecedented move, the Bush administration "renounced" the U.S. signature on the treaty and then went on to seek a Security Council resolution that would exempt U.S. service personnel on UN peacekeeping operations. It managed to receive this exemption for a one-year period – an exception that can be renewed annually. At the same time, the Bush government began to pressure signatory nations to sign bilateral accords agreeing not to surrender U.S. citizens to the ICC. Among other things, the pressure included threats to curtail U.S. military aid.

If these efforts were not enough, the U.S. Congress passed the American Service Members Protection Act (ASPA). Made law in August 2002, the Act prohibits U.S. involvement with the ICC, allows for punitive actions to states that join the ICC, and refuses U.S. participation in peacekeeping unless U.S.

personnel are granted immunity from prosecution. Most striking of all, the Act authorizes the president to "use all means necessary and appropriate" to extract U.S. personnel apprehended by the ICC. This provision, dubbed the "Hague invasion clause," indicates the distance that the U.S. government is willing to go to ensure the immunity of its officials and agents in the pursuit of its foreign policy.

The countries of the European Union were the main force behind the formation of the ICC, and so Washington expanded its pressure on these nations. In August 2002 it increased its efforts to undermine the treaty by pressing for bilateral agreements with the EU states and by warning that the U.S. role in NATO would be threatened if U.S. citizens were not granted impunity by the NATO signatories to the ICC.[58] By the end of September 2002, the EU had by and large capitulated to U.S. demands by laying out "a set of vague benchmarks" guiding bilateral arrangements with the United States. Instead of insisting on the universality of the jurisdiction of the ICC, the EU was to allow its member states to sign bilateral accords with the United States to grant immunity from prosecution.[59]

An ICC without universal jurisdiction cannot have the credibility needed to oversee the consolidation of international rule of law. Washington had succeeded in undermining the power and jurisdiction of the newly minted international court. It could now continue to press for the extension of U.S. law and courts, and national commissions and ad hoc tribunals, as its answers to international crimes of genocide, war crimes, and crimes against humanity. In doing this it would avoid independent mechanisms able to indict and prosecute U.S. personnel and by extension reveal the intent and effects of U.S. foreign policy.

Here, then, was the world's strongest military and economic power actively working to abort an attempt to expand the international rule of law. Its extensive efforts to undermine the ICC were an open statement that the United States would not subordinate itself to any higher authority on criminal matters. No international tribunal would be allowed to investigate or prosecute a U.S. citizen; Americans were to be granted legal impunity for crimes under the jurisdiction of the ICC on the pain of economic sanctions and/or military action. The world's pre-eminent power had refused to acknowledge the will of the overwhelming majority of the world's nations. It had unilaterally created a de facto "two-tiered rule of law" – one jurisdiction for U.S. citizens and another for other citizens. It would do as it pleased without concern for international efforts to bring certain crimes within a global rule of law.

The national reconciliation commissions and the international ad hoc tribunals, by contrast to the ICC, can be valuable instruments for the foreign policy of the world's industrial powers because they can be designed to fit particular issues without raising broader questions of responsibility for genocide, war crimes, and crimes against humanity, and without subjecting agents of these powers to criminal investigation or prosecution. The ICTFY fits this pattern, given that there is prima facie evidence of war crimes by NATO officials.[60] The contradiction between Washington's pressure to use the two ad hoc tribunals and its subversion of the authority of the ICC also points to the instrumentality of these mechanisms. As the executive director of Human Rights Watch, Kenneth Roth, stated: "This stunning hypocrisy sends a signal that the rule of law is only for other people, not for U.S. nationals. It cannot be in America's long-term interest to undermine the rule of law in this way."[61] On the contrary, the sabotage of the ICC is in U.S. interests, as Roth himself pointed out in an earlier article in which he concluded: "The real reason behind Washington's blackmail is the most troubling. An increasingly influential faction in the Bush administration believes that the U.S. military and economic power is so dominant that the United States is no longer served by international law."[62]

The possibility of creating an independent international court that would operate within the confines of the UN Charter and the UDHR, above national jurisdiction, has been seriously undermined. The subversion of the development of such a mechanism, however, opened the door to the realization that international laws have no independent and impartial mechanisms for their enforcement. It revealed a world with the formal trappings of international law but with very limited possibilities for enforcement – a world characterized by the right of might and dominated by a nation with the morality that accompanies capital accumulation.

A genuinely independent and impartial international criminal court within the existing system of international law would have a much different structure. The very nature of its legal purview would have to change; its mandate would have to encompass violations of all three categories of human rights, as well as Aboriginal and environmental rights. It would have to be financially independent, have democratic mechanisms for the appointment and oversight of judges and juries, and possess viable means of enforcing and appealing decisions. Its accessibility would have to be open to all; it would have to make available free legal counsel; and it would have to be given the power to try governments, corporations, agencies, and organizations, as well as individuals. If these characteristics, among others, were in place, there would be a semblance of equitable, disinterested, and non-partisan adjudication of international crimes, instead of the validation of the outcome of economic and military superiority that now passes for justice. These characteristics have never existed at the national level because, once in place, they would make it possible to challenge the very nature of the system. For the same reason, they will probably never be allowed at the global level.

Indeed, these characteristics could never comprise the structure of an international court because a world framed by corporate civil rights cannot furnish a judicial mechanism that would consider as legitimate countervailing rights or other rights outside the prevailing framework – and because in a world of privileged rights and power differentials those who hold power are not likely to give it up, or have their actions fairly adjudicated. More broadly considered, a world of contradictory interests simply cannot provide justice for all. In a world of profound differences between the rights of classes, strata, groups, and peoples, the success of one party to a dispute is measured by the subordination or defeat of the other. With contradictory rights there can only be winners and losers – until the logical end point of such a system is reached when there is nothing more to win and nothing more to lose.

* * *

The future of human rights, indeed of all rights, will be determined in the same way that rights have always been shaped, and that is by the struggles that give rise to them. At present, of the two broad arenas of struggle, one embraces all the contradictions of rights at the national level that reflect the inherent conflicts of national civil society; the other concerns the contradiction between the emergence of corporate rights at the supranational level, replete with agencies and mechanisms and military might to enforce them, and the gradual usurpation or subordination of all other rights at the national level. Now established at the regional and global levels, capital can with impunity ignore, undermine, or override all rights that do not advance its interests, while national governments and their military and police must cope with the resulting social unrest.

Despite the historical significance of human rights in the development of the self-consciousness of humanity, the future of these rights is tied to the future of the forces that brought them into being. Their pervasive violation is testimony to the coming of a new era of struggle for rights, ushered in by the changing structure of capital and the working classes, that can no longer pretend to have the character of the human rights of the Universal Declaration of Human Rights.

CHAPTER VII
Principles for the Future?

A social formation with irreconcilable divisions cannot be the final goal of the struggle of subordinate classes, strata, and peoples. Although civil, political, and social rights were fought for over many decades by subordinate groups within the confines of capitalist social formations, the resulting victories merely "completed" the formation of modern liberal democracy. The achievement of universal suffrage has simply allowed non-corporate sectors of civil society the possibility of exacting concessions via legitimate means. The most important of these concessions were rights based on collective or co-operative claims, including trade union rights, and rights based on socialized capital, such as entitlements to medical care, unemployment and accident insurance, social security, and pensions. These rights have always taken the form of compromises, but the struggles that gave rise to them always had as their goal something grander than the results that were achieved.

The outcome of these struggles, then, did not reflect their implicit aim, as women discovered in their campaign for suffrage. In winning political rights, and then more civil rights by challenging the legal definition of "person," women achieved the right to be equal to men merely in the possession of abstract rights; their actual conditions of life changed very little after winning the right to vote. Inequality in the possession of rights was the immediate problem that they confronted – a problem that had to be challenged given that inequality can only be suffered, never enjoyed. By winning formal political equality, women freed men from holding political rights as privileges over women, which in turn set the stage for a realization by both that what they had achieved was less than what they intended, and that the accomplishment of equal possession of political and civil rights did not alter the fundamentally iniquitous nature of a system of private property.

Given that all rights remain relative to a mode of production, the human rights of the UDHR are no different in this regard than the medieval divine right of kings, the rights of slave owners in ante-bellum United States, or the rights of feudal seigneurs in pre-revolutionary France. Even within the history of capitalism, the role of civil, political, and social rights has gone through numerous changes over time; their evolving characteristics have reflected the strengths of social forces and material interests. Rights stand as the formalization of power relations only as long as the relations that they embody persist.

Despite the historical importance of an ideal of universal equality, the fact that it is only an abstract equality goes far to disguise real material inequality. The abstract possession of equal human rights also masks the reality of inequality in a way that earlier forms of rights did not.[1] The slave, the serf, and the colonial subject had no illusions about the equality of rights; inequality was acknowledged in the form of the rights themselves. With human rights, the loudly proclaimed abstract equality of right veils and confounds the nature of the increasingly obvious and growing inequality of wealth and power.

Just as slave-owners, feudal seigneurs, and monarchs of the mercantilist era defended their rights by all means at their disposal and believed in their absolute nature, so too do those who benefit from today's economic inequality – which flows from the pre-eminence of corporate rights – defend the human rights of the UDHR as being complete and ideal. It follows that these same beneficiaries also accept liberal democracy as the "end of history"[2] and see human rights as ends in themselves, as sacrosanct. That is why there are such adamant assertions about the universality and absolute nature of human rights. The Vienna Declaration, for example, repeatedly proclaimed the absolute nature of these rights and insisted that "Human rights and fundamental freedoms are the birthright of all human beings."[3] It was the representatives of the industrial nations, in particular the United States, who were most insistent about the inclusion of these and many other similar phrases. Yet, however much these rights are proclaimed to be god-given, or eternal and universal, or a birthright, they become a matter for history books when the mode of production that they rest on changes or is transformed.

RESPECT FOR HUMAN RIGHTS

Despite frequent and solemn declarations from the United Nations and representatives of the major industrial powers, the respect of these same organizations and governments for the majority of the human rights of the UDHR has become increasingly open to question. The evidence regarding political rights is everywhere. The role of liberal-democratic governments in the formation of client dictatorships around the world, past and present, has become more and more obvious and exposed. The corruption of governments by large corporations is a matter of daily press reports; it is no longer only an issue in the Third World but also occurs in most of the industrial nations – with Italy and Japan leading the way, perhaps, but the rest not far behind.[4] The corporate control of the political agenda in the United States has become a matter of much analysis in the media since the presidential election of 2000.[5] At the WTO meetings, TNCs can actually purchase the privilege of access, not just to the meetings but also to the government ministers attending. Representatives of the WTO, the

World Bank, the IMF, and certain countries are now openly acknowledging the lack of public representation in global regulatory agencies. It is becoming obvious that the demands of TNCs and the global agencies that represent them are increasingly tying the hands of capitalist democracies.

The evidence is just as pervasive with respect to civil rights. The extent of torture around the world, according to Amnesty International in 2002, is "widespread and practiced systematically," and on the increase, spawning continuing international legal efforts to ban or control such practices. Article 5 of the UDHR is specifically aimed at the prohibition of torture and "other cruel, inhuman, or degrading treatment or punishment." This ban was reaffirmed in Article 7 of the International Covenant on Civil and Political Rights (1976), and re-emphasized in the UN Convention Against Torture (1987) and again in the Optional Protocol to the Convention in 2002.

The legalization, legitimization, or acceptance of torture or cruel mistreatment is a mark of dehumanization in a government and/or society. When official agencies condone or carry out these practices they stamp the system they represent as having lost sight of a fundamental principle of international law that embodies a human universal – our social nature is violated when conscious harm to another is systematically perpetrated. For this reason the Convention Against Torture makes the proscription of these practices into a form of *jus cogens*, a principle "from which no derogation is permitted."[6] The use of torture damages the humanity of all concerned – the victims, the torturers, and the system that tolerates it. Directly or indirectly, it carries anti-social implications for all. Such a conclusion is not always easily grasped, however. To define humans as self-sufficient individuals is to deny these implications because the corresponding view of society is but the sum of the parts and human interest is merely self-interest. Torture in this context becomes just another means of accomplishing the goals of the system.

In polite circles, the U.S. government is not usually associated with the teaching of torture, the spread of the weapons of torture, and their use. Yet, even before September 11, 2001, the extent of physical abuse of prisoners in the United States was enough to elicit expressions of "concern" by the UN Committee Against Torture, as well as Amnesty International and Human Rights Watch.[7] After September 11 the Bush administration was accused of using torture at its bases in Bagram in Afghanistan, Guantanamo Bay in Cuba, Diego Garcia in the Indian Ocean, and in "secret detention centers overseas," and of sending many suspects to "foreign intelligence services whose practice of torture has been documented by the US government and human rights organizations."[8] Weeks after this *Washington Post* report, HRW lamented, "No U.S. official has disavowed its assertions or announced any corrective measures."[9] There were also "credible reports" that the practice of torture received the "approval of high-ranking officials," and "to the amazement of the international community, the U.S. government has openly admitted that it is now using certain 'stress and duress techniques.'"[10]

The mass media in the United States received these charges and admissions, as with earlier allegations, with discussions about the need to use torture – using "September 11" or the "war on terrorism" or national security as the rationale for legitimizing its use.[11] The very limited condemnation of the idea probably reflected the already existing widespread public and official acceptance of forms of torture and of torturers in the United States.[12] Certainly, the pervasive portrayal of violence, misogyny, mistreatment, and murder in popular culture in the United States has done much to desensitize the public. But the social acceptance of cruel treatment for whatever reason opens the door to an ever greater dehumanization of society[13] – which is entirely consistent with the commodification of every aspect of life, and of the accompanying disparities of wealth and sense of worth and worthlessness of human beings as commodities.

The widespread acceptance of cruel treatment in the United States made for a similarly limited negative reaction to the Bush administration's opposition to a new UN treaty to strengthen the Convention Against Torture. In July 2002, over the objections of the United States, the UN adopted an Optional Protocol to the Convention, establishing a mechanism of international inspections of detention centres in those states ratifying the treaty.[14]

Civil liberties are suppressed in other ways. The trade in new devices and equipment for social control and torture continues to expand, with the United States as the largest exporter of "high-tech restraint devices."[15] An ever-expanding arms trade has as its rationale more or less one objective – the suppression of the political and civil rights of subordinate classes and peoples.[16] State-sanctioned repression and terror continue to be major issues for human rights groups and political opposition. It is well documented that the U.S. government was responsible for torture in numerous dictatorships that it sponsored after World War II.[17] The training of military and police forces of the underdeveloped world by the industrial powers is pervasive; and the violation of human rights is a central part of these programs.[18] Unfair trials, arbitrary imprisonment, capital punishment, prison labour, and abuse of prisoners occur throughout the world, the liberal democracies included.[19] Forced labour, child labour, bonded labour, slavery, and prostitution are all apparently on the rise.[20] Corporate crime on an enormous scale is a matter of frequent reporting in the business news; and direct corporate violations of human rights have been widely documented.[21] For women, civil rights, in practice, remain more or less unequal everywhere; and there is considerable evidence that the violation of the rights of women is increasing, in especially violent forms. So-called "honour killings," in particular, are rising in some countries and are often committed with complete impunity.[22]

Because social rights are usually countervailing rights, they are not seen as being fundamental to the system and so are often ignored by international organizations. Yet given that "economic, social, and cultural rights" are included in the definition of human rights in the UDHR, their violation must count as a violation of human rights. While the UN Commission on Human Rights, Amnesty International, and Human Rights Watch do raise questions periodically about their violation, that is not the central focus of these organizations, despite their assertions about the "indivisibility" of human rights. Social rights, where they exist, are also faced with constant pressure from the agencies of the "global enabling framework" to be entrenched or dismantled. The consequences are visible everywhere. The decline of available and good-quality public education creates growing levels of functional illiteracy, making independent national economic growth more difficult; the cutbacks to public health-care facilities bring a decline in public health; the denial of funding for public or subsidized housing brings more homelessness; the restrictions to unemployment and industrial accident insurance produce more poverty and despair; small and unindexed old age pensions produce poverty in old age (particularly for women); the lack or shortage of child-care facilities exacerbates child abuse or neglect. Everywhere, the increasing privatization of government-provided goods and services is undermining social rights and transforming them into matters of charity; and everywhere the disparities in wealth grow.[23]

If the lack of respect by liberal-democratic governments for the civil, political, and social rights of the UDHR is growing, it might be said that rarely was there ever any respect for Aboriginal rights. Most capitalist states with Aboriginal populations have long taken the position that Aboriginal rights should be extinguished and Native cultures assimilated or exterminated. The very first modern liberal democracy provides perhaps the clearest example: from the time of the American Revolution, successive U.S. governments have attempted to extirpate or assimilate indigenous peoples by every possible means, from the Indian Wars to the continuing contempt for lands claimed by indigenous people by allowing destructive corporate or state use.[24] The contradiction at play here is the same today around the world; the rights of private individual and corporate ownership are incompatible with the collective rights of Aboriginal peoples. Millions of indigenous peoples in several thousand tribal nations around the world are confronted with this contradiction, and many of them have been forced to take up arms to defend themselves from physical annihilation, let alone the violations of their Aboriginal rights.[25]

Similarly, respect of environmental rights by governments is at best limited because such rights hinder the exercise of corporate civil rights. Environmental rights are asserted in two fundamental directions: against the destruction or degradation of land, water, and air (making them unusable or dangerous as habitat), and against the commodification of the environment (privatizing the use of land, water, airwaves, knowledge, and forms of life), making them inaccessible except for corporate use or by means of contract).[26] These rights are, for the most part, the result of efforts by NGOs, people's movements, and green political policies, but they are outside the range of rights of the UDHR. Internationally, they appear in the form of multilateral agreements, treaties, conventions, and protocols; nationally, they are embodied in oversight agencies, laws, regulations, and standards.[27] Although they sometimes pertain to specific groups, in general they are a set of rights that implicitly benefit everyone. Nonetheless, they circumscribe corporate attempts to expand the "externalities" of the processes of production and distribution – that is, to shift responsibility for as many before-and-after production costs as possible to society, individuals, or future generations.[28] The costs of pollution and waste disposal come in the form of publicly funded environmental clean-ups, poor health, increases in healthcare expenditures, loss of plant and animal species, and global warming, among other results, and are borne in one way or another by society at large and not directly by the beneficiaries of corporate ownership. Environmental rights diminish the range and types of "externalities" for which a corporation can evade responsibility and so lower the profit derived by the owners/investors. For this reason, such rights are ignored, resisted, minimized, and denied.[29]

On the violations of human rights, there is now an enormous catalogue of reports by such NGOs as Amnesty International and Human Rights Watch, Statewatch, International Women's Rights Action Watch, and Children's Watch, among many others, and quasi-government bodies such as the UN Human Rights Commission. The evidence is massive and indisputable and from every corner of the globe – even though the agencies often omit the violations of collective rights such as social rights, Aboriginal rights, and environmental rights.

Externalities

"Externalities" are accounted for more or less indirectly through environmental destruction and the death or degradation of the health of all living things. The significance of this indirect form of accounting is that the costs associated are placed upon society as a whole or on the individuals directly harmed, rather than on those who benefit from the increased profits of industries that do not account for these negative costs of production and consumption.

Externalities are in effect a hidden way of redistributing wealth. In this sense, environmentally induced ill health in all classes, for example, must be seen as the consequence of the shifting of costs from one class to another.

Although the almost exclusive focus on specific violations and the individual victims and perpetrators obscures the nature of the problem, increasing numbers of people have a growing understanding of the causes. Throughout the literature and even within UN organizations, there is an expanding awareness that chief amongst the causes is the very nature of economic development in the form of commodity trade and corporate capital accumulation, aided by international agencies and the governments of the world.[30] The national framework for capital accumulation that gave rise to the civil, political, and social rights of the UDHR has been subordinated to an accumulation process at the regional and global levels, and here global mechanisms for the advancement and enforcement of human rights are limited in number and circumscribed in mandate.[31] Corporate right at the transnational level is pre-eminent and overrides all other rights; indeed, to the TNCs, and the WTO, IMF, and World Bank, all other rights appear as nothing but impediments to capital accumulation. Their ideal is a world that approximates a marketplace society in which the right of private property prevails.

Accumulation at the regional and global levels differs from the declining accumulation process at the national level in two main ways. The dominant transnational corporations are now many times larger in their assets and revenues than the Gross Domestic Product of most countries. One study pointed out that "of the largest [100] economies in the world, 51 are corporations; only 49 are countries," as measured by corporate sales and national GDPs. It also found that the combined sales of the top two hundred corporations are greater than the combined economies of all countries minus the biggest ten.[32] The concentration of ownership, continuously increasing, is also vastly greater than ever before, which means that fewer companies control much more through vast systems of interlocking corporate interests. These two characteristics of the global economy – the enormous size of TNCs in relation to GDPs and the growing rate of concentration – make the corporate right of ownership at the global level far more powerful and centralized than it ever was, in general, at the national level.

In turn, the size and concentration provide corporations with enormous powers over governments through a variety of means: the national debt, investment blackmail, and bribery and corruption. Moreover, global agencies pressure governments into changing policies that bring national programs and goals into line with the interests of TNCs; this is the meaning of the adoption of neo-liberalism and structural adjustment policies. National armed forces have increased links with a small number of large corporations that manufacture arms and consequently have an interest in maintaining tensions and/or armed conflict.[33] The global media are dominated by a similarly small number of global companies, thereby limiting the possibilities for political expression and narrowing cultural forms and restricting the means of dissemination.[34] Transnational control over production and distribution of cultural products and food completes the picture of growing global domination by TNCs.[35] Liberal democracy as an avenue for the expression of national corporate and subordinate interests becomes more and more restricted.

Liberal democracy and its associated rights have as their premise a civil society characterized by class conflict and competing corporations with relatively dispersed ownership. It is an arena that requires a mechanism to allow competing policies within a general framework – hence the system of political party alternations representing different factions of capital and certain subordinate interests within a constitution framed by private property. Liberal democracy and its contradictions framed as compromises were realized as the Keynesian welfare states; such systems reached their high points in the 1950s and 1960s when corporations grew in number and embraced new opportunities for accumulation on the domestic and international levels. Since the 1970s, as the large corporations have increasingly moved to the global level and there intensified their concentration of power, the premise of liberal democracy has begun to fall away; and national governments have progressively appeared as shells of past national economic relations, now with a new role as national regulatory umbrellas for global corporations. With the development of the global and regional quasi-states, simultaneously with the rise of the TNCs, liberal democracy seems increasingly powerless in the face of the policy demands made from the transnational level.

If the liberal-democratic state is losing its former function with the erosion of its competitive premise in a national civil society, it is doubtful that without a similar premise liberal-democratic rights will ever be established at the global level. The increasingly limited competition between ever larger conglomerates, oligopolies, and cartels of transnational corporations and the absence of subordinate class representation at that level mean that a global civil society similar to what once existed at the national level does not exist and will not evolve. Relatively non-competitive monopolistic, oligopolistic, or cartelized TNCs have little need at the global level for a political structure and mechanisms or a system of rights that allows different factions to compete for alternating control over public policy and the public purse. The premises for a transnational liberal democracy and associated rights are not there. As global corporations develop a supranational regulatory structure for themselves, they have ever fewer contradictory interests and face fewer contending organized counterforces at that level – other than recalcitrant national interests and poorly organized people's resistance.

This two-tiered structure of rights allows the civil rights of TNCs embodied in and promoted and defended by a global enabling framework to stand opposed to the civil, political, and social rights of working peoples, as well as Aboriginal, environmental, and other collective rights, at the national level. With limited political, economic, or legal leverage against the pre-eminence of global corporate rights, the non-corporate sectors do not have the same means of exacting countervailing social rights or civil and political rights that they have at the national level. And there is no other reason why TNCs, with assets and revenues many times greater than most of the world's national states, would agree to share power and the global social product via a politically determined means that would include representation of the interests of subordinate groups.

This same two-tiered structure of rights underlies the widespread violations of human rights recorded by many NGOs and the dismantling of social security programs throughout the world via neo-liberal and structural adjustment policies. To promote access to material and labour resources for TNCs in the non-industrial world, national states dismantle or retrench social rights, and they dismiss, abrogate, and usurp Aboriginal rights, creating mass migrations and forced transmigrations – many millions of displaced and dispossessed, which at once "frees" the land for commercial exploitation and creates a capitalist labour force. Fomented civil wars produce the same effects. The exploitation of the resources without regulation leaves the global environment dissipated and polluted, violating the right to life of all. Corporate rights override all other rights unless those other rights are defended or fought for.

THE "CORPORATIZATION" OF THE UNITED NATIONS – "THE GLOBAL COMPACT"

The United Nations has long been a friend of the corporate sector, but now more than ever it offers its services for the establishment of a global market, and its once apparently neutral role has seemingly succumbed to the pre-eminence of global corporate rights. In the reconstruction of capitalism after World War II, the UN was central in providing the liberal-democratic rationale for the "new world order"; and as the promulgator of the UDHR and other human rights declarations and conventions, it helped furnish the "human" and democratic face for the expansion of capital and domestic and foreign markets. But by the end of the twentieth century, when capital had become global, the role of the United Nations had begun to reflect this change.

In the early 1970s, in response to the aspirations for independence by many Third World nations, the UN created the Centre on Transnational Corporations (CTC) to help poor countries monitor the activities of TNCs and to produce a code of conduct for regulating and assessing the impact of TNCs on those countries.[36] After years of negotiations over the content, the last draft of the code was simply shelved in 1992 when the CTC was in effect dismantled and moved to another agency of the UN. In the same year, global corporations and one of their principal organizations, the International Chamber of Commerce, played a large role in the planning and outcome of the UN Earth Summit in Rio de Janeiro. Not only did they insist on eliminating the use of the term "transnational corporation," but they also brought to the fore the notion of corporate self-regulation.[37] In the final document of this conference, on sustainable development, corporations were given no prescriptive guidelines and government representatives signed protocols that were by and large mere promises.

Since the early 1990s corporations and/or their organizations have played an increasing role in the activities of the United Nations and all of its agencies, from UNESCO to UNCTAD to WHO to UNCHR. But the person who was to consolidate this relationship was Washington's choice for the new UN Secretary General, Kofi Annan. Soon after he was appointed in January 1997, Annan appeared at the World Economic Forum, a private venue for private interests, and said: "Today, market capitalism has no rival.... The private sector is the dominant engine of growth, the principal creator of value and wealth.... This is why I call today for a new partnership among governments, the private sector and the international community."[38] This was Annan's affirmation that he was the right man to remodel the United Nations for a world dominated by transnational corporations, and this was the immediate background for the latest subordination of the UN to the interests of the TNCs: the Global Compact.

At the World Economic Forum in January 1999, Kofi Annan proposed "a creative partnership between the United Nations and the private sector." In his preamble, he said that "the everyday work of the United Nations ... helps to expand opportunities for business around the world." He insisted that "the goals of the United Nations and those of business can, indeed, be mutually supportive." And then came the plan: "I propose that you, the business leaders gathered in Davos, and we, the United Nations, initiate a global compact of shared values and principles, which will give a human face to the global market." In practice, it was to be the UN and corporations working together to promote the "values" of three "areas" – "human rights, labour standards, and environmental practices."[39]

In this speech the Global Compact was compared to the post-World War II development of social safety nets and other measures intended "to restore social harmony and political stability" after the "bitter" lessons of the Great Depression. While suggesting that the Compact was to be a kind of global New Deal, Kofi Annan was proposing something quite different. It was an agreement, he stated, to counterbalance the "enormous pressure from various interest groups to load the trade regime and investment agreements with restrictions aimed at reaching adequate standards in the three areas." It was to offset a possible "threat to the open market, and especially to the multilateral trade regime." To do this, he suggested that the corporate side of the Compact should uphold labour and environmental standards and human rights through their own self-regulated conduct. As for the UN side, he said: "The United Nations High

Commissioner for Human Rights, the International Labour Organization (ILO), the United Nations Environment Programme (UNEP) – all stand ready to assist you … in incorporating these agreed values and principles into your mission statements and corporate practices." Moreover, "in the political arena" the UN would "help make the case for and maintain an environment which favours trade and open markets."[40]

The intent of the Global Compact, then, is to provide a means for corporations through association with the United Nations to effect "a reduction of damaging criticism" of business practices and to resist the imposition of forms of independent regulation and monitoring for compliance that are implicit in third-party codes of conduct by encouraging them to regulate themselves in the three areas mentioned. In doing this, it was argued that "an important governance gap" that underlay "much of the unrest seen in Seattle during the WTO conference" in 1999 would be filled – as if corporate self-regulation could take the place of democracy. Even the UN High Commission for Human Rights was put at the service of the TNCs.[41] As for the rest of the UN, its agencies were pledged to assist the corporations in meeting the goals of respecting and practising the nine principles comprising the Compact.[42]

The dubious nature of the corporate commitment to the nine principles covering the three areas is self-evident in the partnerships undertaken and in the corporations that have endorsed the Global Compact. The UN Development Programme tried to establish a Global Sustainable Development Facility and invited several large corporations to contribute, including Shell Oil, Dow, and Rio Tinto – all of them among the worst violators of human rights and environmental regulations in the world. The proposal was cancelled after extensive criticism from NGOs around the world. UNESCO, however, has "partnered" with the U.S. fast-food chain McDonald's and Disney, one of the great purveyors of commodified American culture, to give out a kind of youth award at Disney World. The UN High Commissioner on Refugees, moreover, "co-chaired the Business Humanitarian Forum with UNOCAL, an oil company notorious for complicity in creating thousands of refugees, along with many other human rights violations in Burma." The World Health Organization "allows secondments of staff from the private sector," even from pharmaceutical companies.[43] Numerous oil and gas companies, pharmaceutical and chemical firms, mining corporations, and Nike have signed on. Many of them are well-known as violators of the rights listed in the Compact, and yet the UN agencies agree to "partner" with them. No evidence exists that the records of these corporations in the three areas of rights have changed in any way; the Compact is not designed even to monitor their activities, let alone provide a way of confirming corporate claims.

The Compact has moved a few companies to adopt their own codes of conduct and instigated some business associations to create their own projects or partnerships to monitor and implement the rights that they feel need to be addressed, and in some cases even to report and verify compliance.[44] Nevertheless, not many corporations have submitted their activities to any sort of monitoring, even by business-friendly groups. If the interest in complying with the rights listed in the Global Compact were genuine, the need for company- or industry-specific codes of conduct and business-based monitoring groups would not be there; a certifiably independent and accountable third-party organization would be the only appropriate and legitimate means of carrying out these functions.

The reasons as to why these particular corporations are interested in wrapping themselves in the flag of the United Nations, or why certain business associations – such as the International Chamber of Commerce, International Organization for Employers, and World Business Council on Sustainable Development – are instrumental in promoting the Compact are clear enough. But what is curious are the endorsements by the International Confederation of Free Trade Unions (ICFTU), Amnesty International, Lawyers Committee for Human Rights, and Human Rights Watch, among others. Their presence on this list, at the very least, indicates their concurrence with the premises, objectives, and methods of the Global Compact – which in turn raises numerous serious questions about their role in defining, protesting, and monitoring human rights violations. It places them in a global structure that has nothing to do with democracy and everything to do with promoting the idea of a world run by self-regulating corporations. In their endorsements, then, these organizations have implicitly compromised their own principles.

Critics have also argued that by initiating the Compact the UN not only declares its support in principle for corporate-driven economic development, but also is actively working to advance that agenda. By implication the UN therefore places itself beyond the possibility of taking either an independent or a critical position on the activities of TNCs. The Compact, moreover, appears to preclude the prospects of other forms of economic growth that might include cooperatives or collectives, Aboriginal ways of life, nationally distinct directions, or the use of socialized capital.

In addition the Global Compact has no monitoring or enforcement mechanisms, which is a major deficiency for any agreement concerning the conduct of TNCs. But this omission is the *sine qua non* for the participation of corporations and their organizations: the lack of both an independent process of accountability and a means of determining responsibility for TNC actions is part of the design. Compliance with the rights listed in the Compact has been left to corporate self-regulation.

Some commentators have noted that TNCs were getting a "blue wash" – a laundered image – by associating themselves with the UN's blue flag. In exchange for merely promising to self-regulate in certain areas of human rights and labour and environmental standards, the TNCs that sign on receive the co-operation of UN agencies and the UN commitment to promote world development in the form of so-called free trade and the commodification of the means of existence. Yet the contradiction in this partnership is obvious: a quasi-public body, which presumes to be the voice of "We the Peoples of the United Nations" and whose raison d'être is purportedly the common good of the people of the world as outlined in the Charter and UDHR, has subordinated itself to the use of private corporations, whose interests are not those of the people of the world and whose sole responsibility is to their shareholders. The rights of corporate interests stand opposed to those of all others, and the only global organization that purports to speak for the rights of all has aligned itself with one side.

Criticism has also taken the form of a counterdocument, the "Citizens Compact," composed by a group of NGOs one year after the Global Compact.[45] Among other things, the Citizens Compact calls for two main objectives: first, to reject the notion of the self-regulation of corporations and to develop "a legal framework" that includes monitoring to oversee the conduct of TNCs; second, to maintain what it considers the independence of the UN as the embodiment and promoter of "universal values" and the institutional home of instruments and mechanisms for the protection of the rights of nations, peoples, and individuals, particularly in opposition to the predominance of corporate rights. Although it takes a modest critical stand, the Citizens Compact is little more than a call for the status quo ante with an appeal for some global corporate regulation, an arm's length relation between the UN and TNCs, and some "transparency" in UN "dealings with the private sector."

The criticisms go no further, even though the nature of the Global Compact raises many fundamental questions. Among other things, the Global Compact reveals the undemocratic nature of the United Nations – its lack of accountability to the world's peoples, despite its pretence of speaking on their behalf. The organization provides no means for the people of the world to make their voices heard or to level criticism in any significant or effective way. The Compact also points to the ideological nature of the UN commitment to individual (corporate) rights and private property in its policies and operations. It points to the subservience of the UN to the TNCs in principle and practice and to their efforts to create a global trading regime based on corporate private property. The Global Compact precludes the possibility of a citizenry choosing state capitalism or socialism; it makes no mention of Aboriginal rights or any kind of cooperative or collective entitlement. It is an arrangement made in the interests of a privileged minority without debate or discussion.

Despite the suggestion by the UN Secretary General that the Global Compact is similar to the attempt to provide the "social safety nets and other measures" created in the industrial nations, the parallels between the Compact and the postwar creation of national welfare states are not there. The electorate in the industrial countries always held a degree of political leverage in the form of political rights and a modicum of government accountability, but the transnational level provides no political rights or mechanisms of accountability. The agencies of global or regional enabling frameworks are only indirectly responsible to the government representatives of the industrial nations and to the TNCs. The national welfare state, moreover, was premised on several factors: relatively closed national markets in labour and capital, the expansion of socialism, rising real wages and salaries that could in part be redistributed, competitive national corporate sectors, alternative political choices, and rival strategies for national capital accumulation. But none of these phenomena exist in any meaningful way anymore. The national welfare state also involved massive use of socialized capital in the form of public corporations, education, medical care, pensions, and more. By contrast the Global Compact, in its promotion of the world market, presumes the privatization of this social capital as an integral part of global restructuring. Central to the "great compromise" at the national level was the abiding class conflict that needed to be mollified; the compromise was not the product of a voluntary agreement by the corporate sector. Now class conflict has been largely restricted to the national level, and the UN has defined the Global Compact as a voluntary agreement on the part of TNCs to self-regulate.

The Compact could be characterized as a concordat amongst the global ruling elites of business, governments, the United Nations, and certain NGOs, with no reference to the people of the world. It is an implicit acknowledgement that the citizens of global civil society are the TNCs, some NGOs, and national states, and that the world's peoples are merely the increasingly disenfranchised citizens of their respective countries. At best, the role of the people of the world in the agreement is to serve as a labour supply, and the purpose of the Compact is, in the interests of social stability, to encourage corporations to treat workers in accordance with the rights itemized in vague general terms as "the nine principles."

This attempt to put a human face on globalization may temporarily forestall popular demands for respect for the full range of human, labour, and environmental rights and for corporate social responsibility and accountability. But it does not address the decline of the relative efficacy of liberal democracy in the nation-state, or the lack of democracy at the global level, or the preclusion of alternative forms of development. It also raises the question of how to adjudicate the violation of human and other rights in an impartial way when the UN has "teamed up" with one side. In the absence of any form of democracy and alternatives to private corporate accumulation, widespread demands for something other than what is offered – other than the global pre-eminence of the private rights of self-regulating corporations – will only continue.

The pre-eminence of private rights means the subordination of all other rights, which is what the United Nations has accepted and promotes with its Global Compact. If in 1945 the role of the United Nations was cast as the political manager for the postwar reconstruction and expansion of capital, its seemingly relatively autonomous position has now shifted to active support for the continued development of the global marketplace. It is a kind of acknowledgement of the passing of the age of the human rights of the UDHR – an age that at least provided the possibility of countervailing rights within a system of private property. Now only one set of rights matters. The UN has become a "key business partner," in the words of Mary Robinson, the former UN High Commissioner of Human Rights.[46] The unfolding of this partisan role helps us both to interpret the past actions of the UN and to illuminate the nature of the growing dichotomy of interests at the global level.

THE MEANINGS IMPLICIT IN HUMAN RIGHTS

At the beginning of the twenty-first century the status of human rights is perhaps clearer than at any other time in the roughly fifty years of existence of the UDHR. The United Nations has openly declared its willingness to support the expansion of corporate civil rights across the globe, couching its support with nothing more than moral entreaties to TNCs to regulate themselves over a narrow range of specified non-corporate rights. The growing dominance of corporate civil rights proceeds more or less rapidly with the centralization and concentration of TNCs over all aspects of production and distribution around the world. The formalization of these corporate civil rights within global or regional frameworks means the systematic and progressive usurpation of the powers of national government and, where it exists, liberal democracy.

The same process demands the retrenchment or transformation of all forms of property not already in the form of corporate private property – hence the neo-liberal policies imposed around the world to abridge or eliminate the social and civil rights of the non-corporate sector and, by implication, the right of self-determination of nations. By dint of these developments, global corporations confront no formal, organized, authoritative, or official opposition; violations of all human rights, except global corporate civil rights, necessarily increase; and the possibilities for compromise only grow narrower.

These changes have provided the context, the end of an era, that allows us to understand the meaning of human rights in a way that was very difficult to do in earlier stages of their development. The now clear contradiction between human rights at the global and national levels *and* the assertion of transnational corporate rights makes explicit the contradictory foundations on which human rights have always rested. Because the overwhelmingly dominant TNCs and their oversight agencies no longer need to compromise with or make concessions to the non-corporate sectors, we can now clearly see that the demands for human rights never were fulfilled, and cannot be.

This realization contains the answer to the riddle of human rights. How could a set of rights be proclaimed to be universal, absolute, inherent, indivisible, and equal but never find universal acceptance, enforcement, or realization, and always be contentious, and everywhere be violated to varying degrees? The answer is that these rights are not what they are claimed to be; like all sets of rights, they are historically specific and reflective of the contradictions of the period; and therefore they are always a matter of contestation. They are called "human" because the same abstract rights are declared to belong to all humans, albeit as solitary, competing individuals whose interrelations are based on contract – the only form of human existence recognized in marketplace societies. This answer can only be fully appreciated at the end of the era in which human rights were given their fullest expression, the era of the development of capital in its national forms.

Paradoxically, the continuing defence of human rights becomes an important means of protecting subordinate classes and peoples in the face of the expansion of global corporate rights. Yet, at the same time, human rights in themselves cannot be the real goal of these struggles. Implied in human rights is something much different from what lies on the surface.

Social Production

"Social production" refers to the nature of production under capitalism in which large numbers of people in many stages are involved in the production and distribution of any given product. While production and distribution here are social, always consisting of numerous workers and operations, the ownership of the process is in private, corporate hands. Because of this form of ownership workers are denied civil rights over their labour and the product of their labour, albeit as social labour and social product. In short, if civil rights for workers over the means of production and distribution, given their social nature, were to be realized they would have to be as social or collective rights.

The demand, for instance, for the fullest extension of civil rights for all implicitly embodies the means of realizing those rights. In an earlier age of petty commodity production, the realization of civil rights by individuals took the form of the self-employment of farmers, fishers, artisans, and small shopkeepers grounded in individual ownership of the means of production. But in an age of mass production and global productive capacity, with individual production rare and social production of goods and services the norm, the means of realizing the rights to one's labour-power and product of labour necessarily translate into some form of collective ownership of the means of production. In other words, with the coming of industrial capitalism, private property in the means of production and distribution has become a form of social capital – that is, the corporation *is* organized and collectivized capital as material means and labour power. As such, it usurps the role of the individual producer and denies the possibility of realizing these rights to those without the financial means of owning the corporation or, more usually, even part of it. In the present era, those who are without can only realize their civil rights over the means of production through a transformation of private, albeit collective, ownership into the social ownership of collectivized capital.

Similarly, the demand for the fullest extension of political rights implies more than popular representation in the legislature (the institution that makes, amends, and debates the merits of law) and access to the executive branch (that exercises power). The whole of the political process in a market-based political system takes place within the confines of a constitution and the rule of law that together amount to a fixed framework of prevailing property relations that implicitly give primacy to corporate private rights defining the nation's "general affairs." The "will of the people" has no practical meaning here; and this condition is particularly obvious when the framework of corporate rights shifts to the global level, exposing the limits of national liberal democracy in demands for national conformity with globally defined corporate rights. Implicit in the demand for full political representation and participation in the legislative and executive branches, then, is the control by the people over the "general affairs," not as a legal framework of prevailing private property relations, but as the actual, direct, practical affairs of the people.

The demand for social rights at the national level in the industrial nations has been met with begrudging concessions that amount to a certain regulatory protection for working people and the redistribution of a portion of wages and salaries with the effect of modestly decommodifying labour-power and its production and maintenance. With globalization, these rights have been progressively retrenched, and some even eliminated, over about two decades, creating a world of increasing hardships and stark material inequalities.[47] The global labour market, moreover, is unable to provide more employment for a growing labour force. Already global unemployment and underemployment stand at about a third of the total global labour force, and while populations grow the relative demand for labour declines.[48] Given constant and rapid changes in technology, there are few prospects that this trend will be reversed. The demand for the fullest extension of social rights therefore implies the demand for the decommodification of labour-power, freedom from the vagaries of labour market, freedom from dictatorship in the workplace, social security for those who are not able-bodied, the promotion of health as public health, and equal access to individual development through education and the arts. The fullest extension of social rights would mean the end of marketplace society and of the treatment of humans as atomic individuals acting through "rational choice" to maximize self-interest. It would mean the end of social rights as countervailing rights, making their content instead the objective of production and distribution.

The demand for the fullest extension of Aboriginal rights implies forms of collective ownership over the world's resources. Prior to the coming of modern commodity production and corporate private property, most of the world's resources and means of production were defined as "commons" of one sort or another. They were largely collectively "owned" – that is, they were used or employed in ways that did not entitle individuals (or corporations) to exclusive and self-interested rights over their disposal. It is true that the commons were restricted to certain social units such as clans, tribes, villages, and nations, but the collective rights were also generally limited to subsistence, to simple reproduction, not to private accumulation of wealth at the expense of nature and other social units.[49] The fullest extension of civil, political, and social rights would coincide with the fullest extension of Aboriginal rights and entail the collective ownership of all resources and means of production by all. It would amount to the assertion of a global commons as the prevailing principle for the use of nature.

Environmental rights have always constituted some form of restriction on the assumed right of corporations to produce and distribute without concern for the destructive effects of their operations on humans and the world around them. Every stage in the production, distribution, and consumption of commodities includes "externalities" of private enterprise – all of those unaccounted costs, external to the price of the commodity in its production and consumption, that nature, governments, and individuals must bear in a system of production for private profit. The fullest extension of environment rights would oblige all aspects of social and capital reproduction to be sustainable in the sense that production and consumption would have to account for all externalities and be respectful and protective of the integrity of all the elements of life on the planet.

With the fullest extension of all of these rights, all rights themselves will have been transformed. At present, the private, albeit collective or corporate, ownership of capital precludes giving practical meaning to most individual civil rights for the majority. In the future, for everyone to have civil rights in practice, private ownership of the means of production would necessarily have to be transformed into a form of collective ownership that obviates the meaning and practice of exclusively individual civil rights. Although all citizens have political rights, those rights can be exercised only within a particular property framework, ensconced in a constitution that precludes the political choice of alternative forms of property, and that is meaningless at the global level. For the "will of the people" to be genuinely exercised, the people themselves would have to control directly their social and material reproduction. The social rights that exist invariably take the form of countervailing rights in a marketplace, dispensed by reluctant governments, and always open to manipulation and retrenchment. For there to be genuine social rights for all, the content of those rights will have to become the very objective of production and distribution instead of being the reluctant concession from the main objective, the private accumulation of capital.

Implicit in the human rights, then, are goals qualitatively different from what has actually been achieved or could be achieved within a capitalist social formation. In the present era and economic system, these goals have been cast in the only way they could have been, as human rights reflecting the contradictory nature of a capitalist mode of production. But the logic of the demand for their fullest extension in an age of global corporations would put an end to these rights as rights – that is, as claims or entitlements exclusive to certain groups or nations, which are privileged in their ability to realize these claims or entitlements. If all rights were possessed by all, and able to be realized by all, and became the active principle of social life and the object of social and material production, not merely the reflection of unequal property relations, they could no longer be the expression of any sort of exclusive claim or entitlement or of a materially restricted ability to realize them.

When the means of production and distribution for global necessities become so highly productive that they can provide for all in abundance,[50] the material basis of the division of labour declines; and with little or no division of labour, the rationale for the unequal distribution of products of labour erodes, as does the basis of private property relations. Where there is no basis for exclusive claims, there are no rights. In theory, human rights disappear with the attainment of the material and technological basis that minimizes or eliminates the division of labour. The immediate future, however, is more likely to see the enforced dominance of the rights of private corporate capital, of corporations as fictitious individuals, over all other rights, rather than a transformation of the rights of all individuals into co-operative and collective forms of social reproduction. Nevertheless, the growing resolution of all rights into the pre-eminence of the rights of transnational corporate capital, on one side, and the subordination of the rights of all other sectors of the global economy, on the other, will bring the next step into a sharper focus for both sides.

On the surface, it is a great historical irony that the very system that brought into being the first claimed universal set of rights can honour them increasingly only in the breach. Indeed, the contradictions of the system have simply evolved, making the uneasy tensions in human rights that could formerly be managed and expressed for several decades as compromises at the national level now no longer containable.

The Irrepressible Spread of Resistance

In all social formations throughout history, the rights of some have been subordinate, in practice if not in theory, to the rights of others; and for this reason there has always also been resistance. Whether suppressed or compromised, or unconscious, passive, or dormant, resistance will always be present whenever there are unequal power relations.

At the beginning of the twenty-first century there is open resistance everywhere at every level. Since the 1980s no part of the world has been free of significant manifestations of counterreaction to the assertion of global corporate rights and the corresponding neo-liberal policies.[51] There are as many demands and protests as there are transgressions and negations of rights. Although they are met variously with armed force, political and legal repression, or ideological censure, both the resistance and the consciousness of unrealized human rights that it spawns continue to expand.

Because the source of the conflicts lies in contradictory rights, there can be no genuine resolution anywhere without the end of these contradictions. There can only be the domination of some by others, with the possibility of time-limited concessions. The Keynesian welfare state, or the "grand compromise," of the postwar period, for example, was predicated on the conditions of the postwar era that made such a rapprochement possible. But the achievement of the welfare state only represented a passing historical appeasement in the contest between conflicting rights. In the industrial states, these preconditions have been in decline for some decades; and as they change and mutate, so too do the possibilities alter for exacting concessions. Contradictory rights the world over are becoming more obvious and more acutely experienced.

The objective of the regional and global enabling frameworks for corporate rights is to transform as many property relations as possible into a single form, private property. The objective is to subordinate all the rights that comprise human rights to the single right of corporate private property. Its express intent is to make all civil, political, and social rights, and Aboriginal and environmental rights, contingent on private property relations, whose exercise is supposedly determined impersonally in exchange, in what is euphemistically called the market, as if it resembled the free exchange of goods and services produced by independent individual entrepreneurs. There is, of course, no market in this sense; there are only varying degrees of monopoly over production and distribution by large global corporations, whose numbers are in constant decline through mergers and acquisitions and whose control over world resources continuously expands and concentrates. This concentration of transnational economic power is antithetical to the idea and reality of a market and of human rights. Given these developments, governments, corporations, and international institutions have little need to accommodate the demands for human rights and the challenges to their transgressions. Indeed, the WTO, IMF, World Bank, and the U.S. state have implacably opposed concessions in the form of social rights at the national and global levels.

In resisting this transformation, the non-corporate sectors of the world economy have been handicapped by the uneven development of a consciousness about neo-liberalism and the lack of enduring representative organizations, making the possibility of co-ordinated opposition difficult. Still, there has been no shortage of manifestations of opposition to these policies for as long as they have been promulgated. In the early years of the twenty-first century, the continuous and unrelenting usurpation by corporate property rights of all others and, most dramatically, the U.S. invasion of Iraq in 2003 and what that violation of international law signals have served to raise the consciousness of all the world's non-corporate sectors and to increase the understanding that meaningful civil, political, and social rights for the people of the world are increasingly a matter of history.

For over two decades, the imposition of neo-liberal policies around the world has been rationalized as inevitable – it was said that "there is no alternative." The truth of that assertion lay in the imperatives of capital accumulation, the growth of TNCs, the consolidation of transnational frameworks for capital accumulation, and the absence of a significant organized counterforce. Over time, the arbitrary assertion of global corporate rights has spawned a growing reaction: the world's subordinate classes and peoples have increasingly been driven to resist. They too have no alternative.

CHAPTER VIII
September 11 and the New Behemoth

Although the rights of the UDHR mark a watershed in the development of human consciousness, like all rights they are historically relative. They reflect the fullest development of the contradictions of capital in its national form, but they do not represent the contradictions of global capital. Indeed, by the end of the twentieth century they appeared increasingly as anomalies. The events of September 11, 2001, and the aftermath constitute another historical turning point – they comprise the dramatic declaration that the rights of the UDHR cannot be realized within the framework of global capitalism. The conditions of their existence have changed; the inherent contradictions in human rights need not be realized any longer as compromises. In the near absence of organized demands for global countervailing rights, regional and global frameworks for capital are able to assert the pre-eminence of corporate civil rights over all other rights.

The passenger planes that crashed into the Pentagon, the World Trade Towers, and a field in Pennsylvania on September 11 presented Americans and the rest of the world with a catastrophic act of terror that immediately became the rationale for a U.S. presidential declaration of a "war on terrorism," an openended war against an ill-defined, illusive, and potentially pervasive enemy. Because this was not a declaration of war with defined goals or a clear-cut enemy, it was for all intents and purposes a declaration of a continuous state of war.

With a declaration of war the state usually assumes a range of supreme powers, the authority do to whatever is necessary to advance and protect the prevailing interests of the nation. It arrogates to itself powers superior to the constitution to which it is normally subordinate; it can act as if the rule of law and the entire range of civil, political, and social rights persist not by established right, but by permission. In the absence of specific enemies or objectives, moreover, a declared state of war can only be a pretext for arbitrary actions for the foreseeable future. When the declaration is open-ended, constitutional rights and the rule of law can also remain arbitrarily and indefinitely subordinated to the executive branch of government.

In the days that followed September 11 the Bush administration did not seek a formal declaration of war from Congress, but rather confined its declaration to assertions that war had been declared by the terrorists and that the United States had to respond. Using the shock and urgency of the terror and an appeal to patriotism, the administration presented Congress with an important piece of legislation, the U.S. Patriot Act, much of it drafted before September 11. With hardly a critical word, Congress passed all the legislation and the military budget increases needed to give the executive branch most of the powers that it would have received had there truly been a war and a constitutionally valid declaration made by Congress.

These dramatic changes continued to unfold even though more than two years later the parties responsible for the events of September 11 had not been conclusively identified. U.S. officials did not at any time build a formal case against those they held accountable – al-Qaeda, its leader, Osama bin Laden, and the Taliban regime that seemingly allowed their training in Afghanistan. No persuasive factual evidence had been offered for their culpability in the attacks, and no attempt at a legal case had been made. In fact, rather than promote investigations into the cause of the events, the Bush administration continued to make efforts to thwart inquiries by Congress into the apparent failure of U.S. intelligence agencies to prevent the attacks.[1]

A spectacular act of terror, without a proven culpable party, and a presidential declaration of a "war on terrorism," without Congressional approval, provided the Bush administration with the exceptional powers befitting a nation at war. The use of those powers allowed Washington to broach a new era of class relations. It would now have the rationalization and the formal authority for new assertions of power on two fronts: the domestic and the global. It would have the excuse for the indeterminate and arbitrary abrogation of the entire range of established national rights and the violation of international laws in the pursuit of a world subordinate to global capital.

Such is our contention. These developments, we suggest, are what had to happen in one way or another; they had to happen sooner rather than later; and they had been planned at least since the end of the Cold War.

PEACE AS A PROBLEM

The end of the Cold War meant that by 1991 the threat of "communism" or "socialism" had lost its significance. The threat had been the ready rationale for Western, particularly U.S., dominance throughout the world and had justified the massive public investment in the military-industrial corporations through military and secret service budgets. It had excused political and military interventions, vindicated the undermining of expressions of national independence from or defiance to U.S. hegemony, and mitigated opposition to the repression of domestic dissent.[2]

By the late 1980s the impending transformation of the Soviet Union and the end of the rationale for the Cold War were already engendering considerable discussion on the possibility of a "peace dividend"[3] – that is, the redirection of much of the military and secret service budgets to civilian purposes. In theory at least, peace would allow for the global shift of hundreds of billions of dollars annually from producing and maintaining the means of repression to, in part, the fulfilment of the social needs of the people of the world. The idea of peace, however, could not be allowed to spread or raise hopes or gain credibility because of the consequences for the existing structure of capitalist relations.

The idea that peace is a problem for capitalist relations deserves some clarification. There are two integrally related factors that, given the status quo, make the possibility of peace impossible. One is the practical necessity to defend the iniquitous and oppressive relations at home and around the world that underlie global capitalism and its advance. The other is the political economy of military spending, or the mechanisms by which the global coercive force is maintained and massive profits are acquired without relying on the market. A world that needs military force for its maintenance is a world that needs a large arms industry.

The Need to Defend Global Class Relations

Transnational capitalism is not free of the contradictions inherent in a national system of corporate private property. It remains a system of production whose defining characteristic is the drive to accumulate capital in ever more concentrated and centralized forms. It reproduces itself as a class system that benefits one class at the expense of all other classes, peoples, and nature. As a global system it increasingly exercises power over national states without popular legitimacy or democratic access.

Its limits, however, lie in these same characteristics. As transnational capital continues to consolidate its control, the question of the viability of global capitalism grows. A system is only as viable as its ability to provide the material means and environment for the social reproduction of its members, its provision of hope for a better future, and its possession of at least the illusion of democracy. It is not that the present global system of production and distribution does not have the capacity to provide sufficient means for the healthy reproduction of all.[4] It is that a system of private property prevents the production and distribution for social need and has as its *modus vivendi* the sole motive of maximizing wealth and power for some at the expense of others. For this reason, hope for a future increasingly seems to lie outside this system, and existing political processes everywhere are characterized by growing cynical disbelief.

This is also the reason that entire regions of the world have been pillaged and continue to be. The nature of the Third World economies has been skewed by structurally unequal trade agreements that have inhibited industrialization and discouraged the growth of value-added exports, thereby lowering national revenues and standards of living, and encouraging corruption. Substantial foreign loans have been extended to facilitate commodity exports, frequently given to non-representative governments and corrupt officials. The loans become part of the national debt of these countries whose economies have been rendered dependent and unable to generate sufficient revenues to repay the loans. Their citizens are saddled with the obligation to repay by means of a relatively standard set of policies that include the devaluation of the currency, the removal of protection for national enterprises from foreign investment and trade, the elimination of exchange controls on the "repatriation" of profits, and encouragement of foreign ownership and use of land. The policies also include the dismantling of the public sector (curbs on state expenditures, privatization, and deregulation) leading to the disintegration not only of public education and health services but also of the physical infrastructure except that which benefits corporations.[5]

The structure of these relations leaves few alternatives for the dependent countries; almost without exception they have faced a spiral of growing indebtedness and a future of perpetual underdevelopment. There is no possibility of escape from this predicament while they remain within these relations, which allow the industrial countries to maintain their agricultural and manufacturing subsidies and protection from imports and extraction of profits. Through these unequal trade relations and the "odious debts"[6] that complement them, the dependent countries and their populations are locked into subordination to the demands of the IMF, World Bank, WTO, and TNCs.[7] Their economies have been more or less reduced to serving the global commodity and labour markets.

The disparities of wealth and income grow not only between the peoples of the so-called Third World and the First World, but also between classes in all countries. In contrast to the general increase in living standards in the industrial countries between 1945 and the late 1970s, poverty is now growing everywhere;[8] and given the nature and tendency of the system – to reproduce and advance the unequal distribution of wealth and power – there is little prospect, while within it, for reversing this trend.

While global capitalism is not free of the business cycle and other effects of accumulation and centralization of capital, the deregulation and privatization that accompany globalization have set the stage for the exacerbation of these problems. Periods of recession and economic stagnation continue to recur globally and regionally. Massive corporate bankruptcies continue to take place. In 2001 the number of publicly traded companies that filed for bankruptcy broke all previous records; the assets they held were also the largest in history; and at least forty-five corporations with more than a billion dollars in assets went bankrupt in that year alone.[9] The implications of continuing large corporate bankruptcies for banks, other corporations, and states and their citizens will take years to unfold. A high rate of unemployment and its continuing secular rise persist throughout the world – a trend not likely to change given increasing bankruptcies and the continuous advance of ever more productive technology. The 2003 International Labour Organization report *Global Employment Trends* estimated that "the number of unemployed worldwide grew by 20 million [after] the year 2000, to reach a total of 180 million" in 2002. It also stated that the number of workers earning $1 a day had increased to 550 million, the level of 1998. Youth unemployment, informal employment, child labour, increased gender inequality, and poor working conditions had all increased throughout most of the world.[10] Economic growth rates are everywhere stagnant or down over the last two decades, and the rate of profit has closely followed.[11] An advisory panel to the U.S. Congress reported in 2000: "The International Monetary Fund and the World Bank have largely failed to bring financial stability to the developing world."[12]

While state indebtedness has created serious social problems, political crises, and economic stagnation in much of the Third World, private and public debt in Japan, the European Union, and the United States is greater than ever before in history. The implications of this debt load suggest that in the foreseeable future the majority of people will not be able to expect anything like a period of rising living standards, a reduction of poverty, or an increase in the quality of health services and education. The World Bank itself admitted that the poor nations that borrowed the most had in recent years become more impoverished.[13]

A system that is based on unequal economic relations and expands by exacerbating inequalities cannot in the long run remain stable. Even when there is periodic stability, that stability is always threatened by the corruption that characterizes the corporate sector. Whatever morality capitalism has, it has been forced on it; and even though the rules and regulations legislated by the state are designed fundamentally to facilitate the accumulation of capital, a constant feature of the corporate sector has always been corruption. There is no country that is free of extensive corporate corruption, although some national business sectors are more dishonest than others;[14] and there is no political system in the world that has not become profoundly mercenary,[15] tying legislative members and senior bureaucrats into varying levels of venality. It is probably not possible to determine if the levels of corporate and state corruption are greater now than in the past, but the declining role of government oversight, decreasing regulation, and the process of privatization have opened the door to more opportunities for corruption, both at the national and global levels.[16]

These obvious consequences of global capitalism – increasing Third World debt, persisting unfair trade relations, embedded corruption of government and corporations, growing wealth and income disparities, the impoverishment of whole classes and countries, and the destruction of the environment – require ever greater efforts to mask or deny because everywhere the very viability of the system is coming into question. Increasingly, it is understood that the system is patently without a morality of its own, that it cannot provide material necessities for its populations, that it is impoverishing a sizable part of humanity, and that in the future it will provide at best the pretence of democracy.

Wherever there is injustice, there is resistance; and this is as true now as in past ages. But the nature and extent of the injustice, the jurisdiction within which it is perpetrated, the degree of understanding of the injustice, and the character of the resistance that follows all change over time. Since about 1980, however, the progressive imposition of neo-liberal policies by global and national institutions has produced a common cause, that is, an injustice that is universal, within a framework that is in part global. In short, the neo-liberal or structural adjustment policies – overriding constitutional government, usurping civil rights, undermining environmental protection, and dismantling legislated protection for workers from the vagaries of the market and terror of the workplace – give pre-eminence to a particular property form, global private corporate rights, and so generalize or globalize injustice. These policies progressively appropriate from the people of the world their remaining limited and bounded political, civil, and social rights.

This is no abstract or philosophical notion of injustice. It is injustice as defined by the system itself – it is the violation of the principles of the UDHR and associated conventions and declarations. It is an injustice imposed by global corporations and the state machinery that acts on their behalf; they violate the very principles on national and global levels that they once called their own. In the course of their expansion, TNCs require the subordination of national and subnational rights, and the evasion or violation of international agreements, treaties, and laws. The neo-liberal policies imposed to facilitate their activities embody global class injustice; they impose the pre-eminence of global corporate right over all other rights and so benefit a class of owners and managers at the expense of all other classes and categories of people, as well as of the environment. The result is necessarily a resistance that becomes global.

In the 1980s demonstrations against the global agencies of the TNCs usually maintained a focus on national and local issues, but in the 1990s protest movements increasingly acquired a global consciousness. The resistance that was everywhere – from armed insurrection to NGO activities to spontaneous protests to trade union strikes to general political rallies – reflected an understanding that each struggle against particular neo-liberal policies was part of a bigger conflict. These demonstrations attracted tens of thousands of people, and in some cases hundreds of thousands; they have taken place in every region of the world; and they represent a growing understanding of the global class war that is underway.[17]

Numerous demonstrations and meetings with a global perception occurred throughout the 1990s: Lyon in 1996, Amsterdam in 1997, the opposition to the Multilateral Agreement on Investment (MAI) in 1998, Cologne in 1999. But the actions in Seattle in 1999 that disrupted the WTO ministerial conference are now often given as marking the arrival of a genuinely global consciousness of the worldwide impact of the neo-liberal policies that comprise the Washington Consensus and ignore the lack of democracy at the global level. The large demonstrations that followed in Prague and Okinawa in 2000, Quebec City and Genoa in 2001, and Washington in 2002, among others, all reflected the clear sense of a global struggle against undemocratic policies and processes. The success of the demonstrations – in forcing the meetings of the G8, WTO, World Bank, and the IMF wherever they took place to require massive security measures, and to be held behind fences, police lines, or in isolated venues – increased global awareness of the lack of popular legitimacy of these bodies and at the same time pointed to the worldwide understanding of these organizations as problems. The injustice of neo-liberal policies was compounded by the arbitrary military action taken against Iraq in the spring of 2003 by the United States and Britain; in February of that year, in anticipation of this invasion, demonstrations took place around the world in what is considered to be the largest global manifestations of popular protest in history.

The continuing growth of this consciousness led to the need to go beyond demonstrations and teach-ins to consider more broadly what was happening. In January 2001 a forum outside the confines of national governments and existing transnational agencies was established: the World Social Forum in Porto Alegre, Brazil, became the venue for annual discussions and planning for a world not dominated by TNCs and their global agencies. The Forum has now branched to other cities and regions beyond Brazil,[18] implying that the organized non-corporate sectors of civil society in many parts of the world have begun to plan for a future world without corporate domination.

This spread of awareness of alternative visions for development, the continuing opposition to neo-liberalism and the agencies that promote it, the refusal of several normally compliant governments to support U.S. efforts at the UN to gain approval for the invasion of Iraq, and the enormity of the demonstrations against the war all constitute clear signs of the growing global understanding of and opposition to the role that the United States has assumed for itself in the post-Cold War era.

The events at the September 2003 ministerial meetings of the WTO in Cancun, Mexico, represent another important marker in the expansion of this opposition. At these meetings it became clear that the pledges made by the United States and the European Union at Doha in 2001 to phase out their national subsidies to agriculture and lower tariffs on Third World imports were not going to be honoured. Before the scheduled conclusion, the talks were halted and the meetings adjourned; the majority of the Third World delegates rejected the proposals on offer. This stand may be seen as one of the first concerted actions by the Third World in opposition to U.S. and EU trade policies since the failed attempt to realize the demands formulated in the early 1970s as the New International Economic Order (NIEO).[19] All the major Third World countries were aligned in the Cancun rebuff; but a number of the largest – the Group of 22, spearheaded by Brazil and India and supported by China, South Africa, and Egypt, among others – led the opposition.

Most directly, the inconclusive ending to the meetings pointed to the unwillingness of the Third World to continue to accept the detrimental trade practices of the United States and European Union, in particular their agricultural dumping and subsidies and import tariffs, resistance to "fair trade," environmental destruction, and promotion of intellectual property rights and monopoly ownership of water supply. The conclusion also signalled the probable end of business as usual at the WTO: the United States and European Union would no longer be able to make and impose trade agreements via the organization without moderating their own practices. Recognizing the nature of the outcome, the U.S. representative acknowledged that Washington's goal of "global trade liberalization through the WTO" was for the present not going to be achieved, and after scolding the delegates for "some pretty negative speeches," he suggested that the United States would spend more time pursuing its strategy through bilateral and regional agreements.[20]

This "empty-handed" ending also pointed to the limits of the destructive effects of neo-liberalism: increasingly, the governments of the Third World find it difficult to ignore the negative political, social, economic, and environmental consequences of neo-liberalism or structural adjustment policies. The precipitant closing of the meeting also marked a step in the growth of understanding of the role of the global enabling framework in imposing unequal trade relations, and thereby assisting in the destabilization of the social fabric of whole nations, the impoverishment of millions, and the destruction of the environment, provoking a recognition of the need to change the nature and direction of development. The premature ending may also be seen as the implicit acknowledgement of a link between non-corporate groups in civil society and Third World governments. But in the final analysis, the Cancun meetings represent, by and large, a dispute between sectors of capital over the distribution of global resources.

All of these developments over the last two decades of the twentieth century and continuing in the early years of the twenty-first century have made it clearer than ever before that a rationale was needed for "containment" and for obfuscation of the unequal relations of the global economy. These pervasive national and global class and other antagonisms are not reconcilable within the present world system. The inequity of the relations of globalized private property inexorably produces greater attendant injustices, and it is these in turn that produce new demands for an expanded role for the military.

The Political Economy of Military Spending

Washington dominates the global enabling framework that defines and oversees these structured unequal relations. On the basis of its economic and military might, Washington in effect determines the terms of global trade and guarantees the security of those relations to the benefit of TNCs, the U.S. economy, and the rest of the industrial world. The global reach of the U.S. military, the systematic programs to make interdependent most of the other national military forces, and a covert surveillance system approaching total administration over the world cannot be otherwise. A world of unrelieved global grievances requires a global means of control.[21] There can be no peace in an unjust world; there can be only constant conflict.

A brief survey of the reach of the U.S. military makes the case for its centrality in maintaining relations of global dominance. Throughout much of the 1990s, the United States maintained "more than 200,000 troops on foreign soil and more than 50,000 personnel" on ships in foreign seas. In 2001 it had "more than 800 foreign military installations including 60 major ones," a "military presence in 140 countries including significant deployments in 25 countries," defence treaties with 31 states, and "defense cooperation commitments with another 29 nations"; and it conducted "more than 170 overseas" joint combined exercises a year.[22] The United States runs a vast military training program that touches about 180 nations, almost every country in the world, and that produces about one hundred thousand U.S. trained armed forces personnel annually worldwide.[23] According to the researchers, "Despite its absolute reduction in military spending" throughout much of the 1990s, the "U.S. share of worldwide military spending" increased to almost one-third in that decade.[24] Its share of the world arms market grew to almost one-half during the same period.[25] In 1999 the U.S. Defense Secretary declared, "We have an overwhelming advantage over any potential adversary.... We like that and want to keep it."[26] The statistics, however, tell only part of the story; with rapidly changing military technology, the Pentagon maintains powerful oversight and intervention capabilities without the actual presence of U.S. personnel.

Although world expenditures on military goods and services saw a relatively steady decline during the 1990s, they remained well above $700 billion annually.[27] With the increase in regional disputes in Africa, Asia, and Latin America, these expenditures began to rise by 1998; in 1999 world military spending in general had begun to increase, and all aspects of the U.S. military presence overseas began to grow significantly.[28] In the United States, public investment in the military has been substantially larger than anywhere else in the world. In 2002 the U.S. military budget request for 2003 was "six times larger than that of Russia, the second largest spender." It was "26 times as large as the combined spending of the seven countries traditionally identified by the Pentagon as [its] most likely adversaries (Cuba, Iran, Iraq, North Korea, Sudan and Syria)." It was "more than the combined [military] spending of the next 25 nations," including all the industrial states.[29] In the early years of this new century the military budgets of the world's governments exceeded $800 billion annually.

If the military spending and arms exports of NATO countries are added to those of the United States, the conclusion is obvious: with the demise of the Soviet Union and the embrace of its former republics and associated states into the relations of global capital, there is no nation or group of nations outside the United States and its allies that could conceivably present a significant military threat to these powers. With the United States leading, the Western industrial nations overwhelmingly dominate the production and proliferation of the military goods and services that serve to defend the global economic system – a system that has to be defended because it is iniquitous.

Although the end of the Cold War brought an end to the main rationale for continuing large military budgets, the subsequent decline in spending did not last long. Despite election promises to "reduce the proliferation of weapons," U.S. President Clinton continued the policies of his predecessor to promote arms sales around the world. In its first year, his administration "more than doubled" arms sales; and during his first term, 1993-96, "the U.S. government sold, approved, or gave away $190 billion in weapons" to many countries. The Clinton administration also made it "U.S. policy to deploy a National Missile Defense (NMD) system" – carrying forward a policy similar to that of the Reagan government in the 1980s.[30] In his second term Clinton requested substantial increases to future military budgets from 1999 to 2005. At the end of his presidency, the U.S. administration called for staged increases amounting to $1.6 trillion for the military for the fiscal years 2001 to 2005.[31] During the presidential election campaign of 2000, the Democratic Party candidate, Al Gore, pledged more funding for the Pentagon than did George Bush. And all this took place at a time when there was no notable threat to the security of the United States.[32]

The rationale for increases in military spending that the Clinton government lacked came on September 11, 2001. In the aftermath of these attacks, the Bush administration called for about $38 billion for "homeland defence" separate from another increase of $48 billion for the Department of Defense. In the budget request for 2003, the new government asked for over $396 billion for "defence," including $16.8 billion for nuclear weapons development in the Department of Energy. These were the largest increases in military expenditures in about twenty years and signified a "return to deficit spending" to accommodate new military spending. Outstripping the Clinton request, the new Bush regime submitted "plans to spend $2.1 trillion on the military over the next 5 years."[33]

The relative size of this budget indicates its significance. The figures represent the Bush administration's requested "budget authority" to spend on the military in 2003 and in subsequent years. The $396 billion amounts to almost 50 per cent of the "discretionary" part of the U.S. budget for 2003 – that is, the part that is not "mandatory" and on which Congress can change priorities through ordinary legislative procedures. To view U.S. military spending in this way reveals its size in relation to all new spending, but it does not tell the whole story. It does not include military spending in departments other than the Department of Defense (such as nuclear weapons in the Department of Energy, the military aspects of NASA, activities of the Coast Guard, veteran's benefits, foreign military aid, as well as various functions of the FBI and CIA, among other agencies and departments). Because the amount defined in the "budget authority" designates new money, moreover, it does not include spending for past military ventures (that part of the national debt incurred for military purposes). Estimating the portion of these expenditures for military purposes can never be exact, but the point to be made is that considerably more of the total budget than the "budgeted authority" for the Department of Defense is dedicated to military purposes.[34] This has been the case throughout most of the Cold War period.[35] Depending on how the total military expenditures are calculated, the annual total may be more than $200 billion over the annual budgetary request for "defence."[36]

As military spending is made a key priority and increased, it has impacts on other aspects of the discretionary part of the total annual U.S. budget. Since at least 1998 almost every part of Congressional discretional spending – other than military spending – had suffered funding cuts on an annual basis: infrastructure (roads, bridges, sewers, water systems), public education, transport, hospitals, health and treatment programs, housing, food aid, environmental protection, foreign aid, disaster relief, health and safety, and more. Expenditures by the Bush administration in 2003, moreover, required more state borrowing, resulting in an increased national debt that would have to be serviced, potentially drawing funds from the discretionary side of the budget.

This brief survey suggests that a change of the political party in power does not significantly alter U.S. military policies. While political change in the White House can mean more or less spending on the military, it has not recently brought a qualitative change in policy. Indeed, no government of any capitalist nation has ever argued for world peace through disarmament and arms control or ever called for the vast expenditures on the military and police to be spent instead on civilian social needs, environmental cleanups, or conversion of the military machine. The Clinton administration by and large promoted for the Pentagon the same policies adopted by the Bush I and Bush II administrations. Even without the drama of September 11, increases in military spending were requested and cutbacks to social programs were instituted. Threat or no threat, the same spending priorities were being followed; the difference was mainly one of degree.

Since World War II the political coloration of capitalist governments has varied, but the military policies have remained much the same. There are two main reasons for this. One, to use the words of Clinton's defense secretary, William Cohen, is that "U.S. economic power is still dependent on military strength and a strong defense industry,"[37] or, to cite the more general and aphoristic phrasing of the journalist Thomas Friedman, "The hidden hand of the market will never work without a hidden fist – McDonald's cannot flourish without McDonnell Douglas, the designer of the F-15."[38] In other words, because global economic relations are anything but equal or permissive of genuinely democratic determination, military coercion in the form of national or multinational armed forces is required to expand, protect, and police them. There was and is no alternative to these means of maintaining the economic status quo; the consolidation of world economic power – that is, the securing of unequal access to world resources and the policing of that access – demands a global military presence.

In tacit acknowledgement of this point, global agencies and organizations, and most trade agreements, consider that state subsidies to military production – tax concessions, assisted sales promotion of weaponry, and various forms of protection for military industries – are necessary for "national security" and are therefore different from similar "barriers to trade" for non-military goods and services. Structural adjustment and neo-liberal policies, moreover, have meant dramatic reductions in public investment, but the same polices have not been equally applied to the reduction of military expenditures. Global agencies and the U.S. government have, then, made a concerted effort to promote a "free market" in civilian goods and services while at the same time maintaining policies of state intervention in support of the military. In the name of security, they advocate a welfare state for the military-industrial complex while demanding a "free market" for the civilian sector.[39] The unfreedom of the "free market" requires for its maintenance a state-supported military presence.

That military budgets and policies persist in a relatively stable manner and depend on state welfare, despite the election of governments of different political persuasions, is in part due to the structure of influence in capitalist states. In other words, to understand some of the reasons why military policies, and not peace plans, in the post-Cold War period have prevailed in government agendas is to understand how certain corporate sectors have actively influenced government in their own interests. Most of these mechanisms of political influence are employed in all the industrial nations, but among these countries the United States is by far the largest producer of military goods and services.

The most obvious means of influencing government policy is the lobbying of officials and legislative members by corporate representatives. In the United

States lobbying is a massive multimillion-dollar undertaking pursued both by scores of companies specializing in that activity and directly by corporations themselves. The "political contributions" from military industries are significant; millions of dollars are directed to presidential campaigns, political parties, members of Congress, and members of specific committees in legislatures that approve budgets.[40]

Another mechanism is the close interrelationship between executive positions in government and private corporations. Intimate links exist between appointments to the cabinet and to the executive branches of the civil service and the military *and* similar positions in large corporations. In the United States, as in most industrial countries, there has been a long-standing tradition of movement of senior executives between these arenas, including former CIA and FBI officials sitting as directors on the boards of major military corporations. In this regard no U.S. administration is any different from its predecessor.[41]

Another device for manipulating support for the military budget in the United States has been an activity referred to as "front-loading," which is "the practice of planting seed money for new programmes while downplaying their future obligations."[42] Programs that begin with a certain expectation of total costs come to require much more investment to complete – extra monies known to be needed from the beginning but not disclosed by the corporation and others involved in promotion of the project.

Yet another practice to ensure the compliance of the U.S. Congress in maintaining or increasing military spending has been labelled "political engineering," that is, "the strategy of spreading dollars, jobs, and profits to as many important congressional districts as possible."[43] This is the process of tying votes to the flow of government money; when jobs and local or state economic development depend on military spending, members of Congress find that votes are similarly tied. It is a means whereby "political engineers" can pressure members of Congress both to vote for front-loaded programs after the real costs are revealed and to maintain military spending, regardless of other considerations.

The Search for a Threat

The dilemma in the early 1990s was that military spending could not be drastically reduced, and certainly not converted to civilian purposes, for fear of upsetting the relations of national and global power, even though there were no identifiable serious external threats to U.S. pre-eminence to justify the continued spending. The need for an external threat arises because the unresolvable global iniquities among classes, nations, and peoples cannot be the official or stated reason for U.S. dominance over integrated global military forces. No system can admit that it is inherently unjust; indeed, it must maintain the opposite position – that it is an inherently just system that is threatened by irrational forces, demagogic leaders, incompatible ideas, or hostile systems. To justify the buildup and geographic expansion of coercive force, a state needs to locate a credible threat, without which the real reasons for the need for coercion become apparent.

Although transnational corporations require a global military presence to defend iniquitous relations, oversee the privatizing and deregulating of the state sector, and to suppress dissent, at the same time this extension of military reach needs a military-industrial complex to produce the goods and services necessary for the task of global policing. The expansion of the industrial production of military goods also needs an excuse that detracts from the nature of the system itself. Although armed forces and the industries that produce military goods and services exist for the same reason, each develops its own dynamic for expansion within this world of conflict: one rests on the principles of bureaucracy (particularly in government and the military); the other rests on the search for ensured levels of profit.

For several reasons, then, a threat had to be established that was at least comparable to the "evil empire" of the 1980s – to rationalize the perpetuation of national military and "security" budgets, to keep all forms of resistance and criticism in check, to justify the evident decline in the powers of national liberal democracy, to maintain oppressive relations around the world, and to veil the assertion of arbitrary global power. The vilification of the Soviet Union by the Reagan administration served to justify increased military spending even though the only peace overtures made during the entire Cold War came from the USSR and Mikhail Gorbachev, the last leader of the Soviet Union, was instrumental in ending the Cold War.[44] After 1991 the whole global system of inequality and its need for repression required another "evil" to replace the one that had disappeared. There had to be a threat that was abiding, demonizable, and antipathetic to the principles of capitalism or, better, a negation of "civilization" itself. To find a credible threat became one of the defining aspects of the 1990s in the United States.

Even before the demise of the Soviet Union, U.S. strategists and military analysts realized that the transformation of the Soviet Bloc would also bring the collapse of the main rationale for U.S. military and secret service spending. Anticipating these changes, foreign policy experts at the Rand Corporation began to shift the focus of fear from the Soviet Union to the problem of "uncertainty."[45] Unfortunately, because uncertainty is a condition of nature and has always existed in a multitude of forms and always will, it does not provide a compelling basis on which to rest demands for increased military spending, continued international intervention, or the suppression of dissent. But it was the best object of alarm or fear that the Pentagon and associated think-tanks could proffer as an alternative to the socialism of the Soviet Union at that time.

The problem was put clearly in a candid moment in 1991 when Colin Powell, then the chairman of the Joint Chiefs of Staff, said in a report to the U.S. Congress: "I'm running out of demons. I'm down to Kim Il Sung and Castro." This was a remarkable admission; the absurdity of casting the leaders of North Korea and Cuba as serious and plausible threats is not worthy of comment, but what is notable is the response to the demise of the supposed main threat to the United States. For Powell and the Pentagon, the demise of the USSR did not represent the opportunity to decrease military and intelligence spending and to realize the so-called peace dividend and convert state expenditures on armaments to address global problems of health care, education, and poverty – in short, to build a better world for all now that the main "evil" had disappeared. His response embodied the concern to find a new object of fear. Socialism certainly was and is a threat to capitalism, but the substance of Powell's comment was an admission that the socialist threat implied in the Soviet Union was not the only reason for maintaining the huge defence budgets. With the USSR gone, another threat had to be found. If there were no threat, there would be questions about the legitimacy of continued military spending and the real reasons behind it. State support of the massive U.S. military-industrial complex could not be left without a rationale because it was central to the existing structure of the U.S. economy and the maintenance of the global relations of power.

The maintenance of a massive U.S. presence around the world and the reversal of planned defence budget cuts had to have a convincing rationale. Throughout the 1990s, the threat of "uncertainty" was constantly referred to, but that threat was clearly insufficient to justify the extent of U.S. military control, let alone its expansion and the new strategies being developed. In 1993 the U.S. secretary of defense tried to address this issue in his "Bottom-Up Review" of the post-Cold War prospects of the U.S. military. "The Cold War is behind us," the document began. "The Soviet Union is no longer the threat that drove our defence decision-making for four and half decades – that determined our strategy and tactics, our doctrine, the size and shape of our forces, the design of our weapons, and the size of our defense budgets – [it] is gone." The paper went on to define the "new dangers" and "new opportunities" of the "new era."[46]

The "new dangers" included the "spread of nuclear, biological and chemical weapons," the growth of regional rivals or "ethnic and religious conflict," the potential resurrection of the Soviet Union, and the possible "failure to build a strong and growing U.S. economy." The first danger, the spread of weapons of mass destruction, is generally considered to be a plausible regional threat, but it lacks credibility as a threat to U.S. global military dominance. The overwhelming U.S. superiority in military technological, influence, and information makes the use of such weapons unlikely, except as desperate last measures or pretexts for intervention. As a threat to the United States, "rogue states" are more a rhetorical ruse than a reality. The danger of the rise of regional rivals is also unlikely, given the state of Russia's military and economy and the integration of China into the WTO. Given the extent of U.S. military and economic penetration in the rest of the world, there are simply no other credible potential rivals.

The possibility of the resuscitation of the Soviet Union is now nothing but far-fetched. "Democracy" and the "free market" there have brought widespread corruption and crime, the economy and military are in difficulty, and its people have been degraded and demoralized.

The last perceived danger is the most interesting; here we see the association of U.S. military strategy and economic growth. The use of the military to defend and expand global economic relations, however, clearly could not be used as a plausible public rationale because it would expose the nature of those relations as requiring coercive force to maintain them.

No credible fear appeared in the 1990s that could replace the Soviet Union. In the absence of believable threats, the military analysts began to imagine an array of hypothetical wars or crises that might arise or could be instigated. Dubbed "wild card scenarios," these imagined threats included many different justifications for a continued global military presence around the world. They covered various forms of armed conflict – civil wars, regional disputes, border issues, rebellions – all of them containable as local or regional. Although these scenarios were limited and temporary, they could be profitable for arms sales and would provide ongoing excuses for military preparedness.

In this vein, through much of the 1990s the Pentagon employed the "two-war concept" – that is, the need to be able to fight two simultaneous regional wars. Despite much use of this rationale, in 1994 the secretary of defense said, "I think that it is an entirely implausible scenario that we would ever have to fight two wars."[47] In the absence of something better, the excuse continued to be used even after the 1997 National Defense Panel reported that the two-war hypothesis "may have become a force-protection mechanism – a means of justifying the current force structure."[48]

Even different branches of the U.S. armed forces bemoaned the disappearance of the key danger that had vindicated large military budgets. In 1995 the USAF, still uncertain about its role in the new world order, revealed its dilemma in a study of what the future held. Entitled "New World Vistas," the document began by stating the problem: "The Air Force and the Nation are at the brink of a new era. Our Cold War adversary no longer exists, and we now face threats which are not precisely defined. The situation is further complicated … by the absence of well known adversaries." For the past fifty years, it stated, the country's strategy and development of technology had been defined by "the Soviet threat. Now that threat has disappeared." With what seemed a tone of lament, it stressed, "Now … no well defined enemy exists."[49] Once again the end of the so-called Soviet threat did not result in an argument for the downsizing of the USAF, but rather engendered the search for a new threat or threats to justify the existence of the air force and the persistence of U.S. global dominance – which the USAF itself had begun to discuss in 1990 in its white paper "Global Reach – Global Power."

Even mainstream political scientists got in on the search. This problem of the post-Cold War era was the context for a 1993 article, "The Clash of Civilizations?" by Samuel Huntington.[50] If socialism were for now a spent force, the next "dominating source of conflict will be cultural," he mused, making many sweeping assertions about the meaning of culture and ignoring the role of the United States and other states in the promotion of Islamic fundamentalism for their own political ends.[51] "The paramount axis of world politics will be the relations between 'the West and the Rest,'" he continued, and "a central focus of conflict for the immediate future will be between the West and several Islamic-Confucian states." These "non-Western modern civilizations," he opined, will increase their "economic and military strength relative to the West," and "this will require the West to maintain the economic and military power necessary to protect its interests in relation to these civilizations." The article was notable for its tendentious portrayal of world affairs, its questionable use of the term "civilization," its apparent lack of awareness of U. S. military might, and its obvious straining to identify a credible enemy to replace the eclipsed American phobia of "communism."

By 1997 Huntington had revised his thesis – perhaps because there were too many examples of Islamic fundamentalists being used by the United States for its foreign policy goals in the Balkans, Afghanistan, Chechnya, and Palestine; perhaps because the United States has had some rather fundamentalist "friends" such as the dictatorships in Saudi Arabia and Pakistan, and the Taliban; and perhaps because China, the "Confucian state," was rapidly becoming more capitalist than socialist. The enemy as "Islamic-Confucian states," a thinly veiled race-based invented threat, was clearly not going to work. Later in the same year, Huntington had to admit that the United States was "in a position where, unlike in the cold war, when our major problem [was] to develop the power to support our purposes in the world, *now our major problem is to develop the purpose to guide our power.*" The statement put the current problem very well. In the mid-1990s the United States was in need of an excuse to maintain or build up its military spending and to take on the role of guarantor of the interests of global capital. Without a credible threat at this time the Pentagon could only manufacture imaginary dangers.

A STRATEGY LONG IN THE PLANNING

With the demise of the Soviet Union, it was not difficult to understand the necessity of establishing a single global authority with a comprehensive strategy for maintaining the transnational relations of power. This decisive event obliged the United States to change its military strategy; no longer could Washington focus on the containment of and opposition to socialism; now it had to integrate the Soviet Bloc countries into the relations of global capital and assert a single dominant enforcement authority over the world. Other reasons for a worldwide strategy and set of policies included the need to control dissent and popular resistance, to limit the full range of established and expected rights that might challenge corporate right, to contest the defence or continuing existence of forms of socialized capital, to threaten defiant nations or peoples or movements, and to preclude defection from a global system of subordination to transnational capital. These were the objectives that had to be worked out in the 1990s.

Global Ascendancy and "Full Spectrum Dominance"

Throughout the 1990s the U.S. military made numerous attempts to define for itself the new roles that it would have to undertake in the aftermath of the Cold War. One of the earliest and most comprehensive documents came to light in the form of a "leak" to *The New York Times* in 1992. A revised draft of what the Defense Department called a "Defense Planning Guidance" was released two months later, but it made substantially the same points.[52] Without much doubt, these documents provided the blueprint that has formed the basis of U.S. foreign policy ever since.

A key objective in both documents was the prevention of "the re-emergence of a new rival." No other power would be allowed to dominate a region with sufficient resources to challenge U.S. ascendancy. Another objective was "to show the leadership necessary to establish and protect a new world order" that would satisfy "the interests of the advanced industrial nations" and so "discourage them from challenging our leadership or seeking to overturn the established political and economic order." To achieve these goals, ad hoc military arrangements would be encouraged, facilitating consent to U.S. leadership, and multilateral defence agreements would be developed to promote co-operative action and deter "the renationalization [sic] of security policies." Preventing Russia from reuniting the members of the Warsaw Pact or the former Soviet Union was another key objective. In both documents, U.S. dominance in the Middle East figured strongly in order "to safeguard our access to international air and seaways and to the region's oil." Central to achieving this continued supremacy in the region was the defence of Israel and the ensuring of its "qualitative edge," meaning the maintenance of its military superiority and provocative policies.[53] What is striking in all this is the significant political role that the Pentagon had defined for itself.

Many other Pentagon policy papers dealing with more strictly military matters were published over the next few years. These "strategic vision documents" culminated in 1996 in the report *Joint Vision 2010*: "the vision set forth by the Chairman of the Joint Chiefs of Staff for military operations of the future." Central to this conception of the role of the U.S. military was the notion of "full spectrum dominance." The doctrine amounted to little less than a "revolution in military affairs." It was a "vision of a twenty-first century military" defined by four main components. The first, "information superiority," was "the key to achieving full spectrum dominance" and involved major new surveillance and intelligence-gathering systems. Next was perpetual "technological innovation," intended to keep the upper hand in all aspects of future war-making. Included here was the militarization of space, now considered "the fourth medium of warfare – along with land, sea and air." The third element, "operational changes," took into account the massive new and constantly changing technologies making their way into military programs.

The fourth component was the "integration of coalition partners." Here was one of the most significant breaks with the past; from now on the United States would seek to develop its military strategy by integrating the armed forces of other nations. Prior to 1996, this approach had already become an aspect of U.S. military practice, at the very least taking the form of training of foreign military and police forces, which expanded enormously in the 1990s.[54] The strategy involved the inclusion of foreign military personnel in the command structure and planning process, and included the policy of "interoperability" – the standardization of equipment, training, doctrines, and even language. Indeed, *Joint Vision 2010* called for "full spectrum multi-national planning and training; proactive coalition building; and international involvement in all phases of JV2010 concept development, assessment and integration."[55]

"Global leadership" was the phrase the Pentagon used throughout the 1990s, but not until 1997 did it spell out the full significance of this redefined role. In its *Quadrennial Defense Review* of that year, it spoke of the need for permanent global "military superiority."[56] This predominance was seen as synonymous with "leadership," and it was proposed that, as the leader, the government use the armed forces in three ways: to "respond to crises, shape the strategic environment in ways favorable to U.S. interests, and prepare now for possible future threats."[57] While the *Review* reiterated many of the new strategic roles laid out in earlier Pentagon plans, one important new aspect had been added: the idea of "environmental shaping." Here again is the assertion of a much more political role for the Pentagon – the idea that the U.S. military would be involved in establishing and securing the restructured geopolitics of the new world order.

Further proposals for military change culminated in another report, *Joint Vision 2020,* released in the year 2000. It encapsulated the decade-long process of redefining the role of the U.S. military in a world without the threat to the dominion of private property implied in a socialist China or USSR, and in an age of permanent technological change. This context obliged the redefinition of the scope and nature of military control over the global domain of capital. It is in this document that the concept of "full spectrum dominance" is placed at the forefront of the new military doctrine of the United States.[58]

This new canon of U.S. military strategy was clearly spelled out: "The joint force of 2020 must be prepared to 'win' across the full range of military operations in any part of the world, to operate with multinational forces, and to coordinate military operations, as necessary, with government agencies and international organizations." The two main principles were "total force" and "fully joint." The former referred to the integration of all possible elements of military, police, and civilian forces into a single force and command structure. The latter was the notion that every aspect of the "total force" should be "intellectually, operationally, organizationally, doctrinally, and technically" within a common framework – a state that the Joint Chiefs of Staff called "jointness." Included in this concept was the integration of multinational military forces and "interagency partners," and the "interoperability" of all U.S. and partnered military processes.

Although the rationale of this new doctrine of "full spectrum dominance" was posed as "the global interests of the United States and the continuing existence of a wide range of potential threats to those interests," the Pentagon had overlooked the much broader nature of its new role. By including the integration of multinational forces and international agencies, both government and non-government, it was asserting U.S. leadership over a global military strategy and structure. *Joint Vision 2020* simply spelled out what a global economy – with one prevailing property form defined and regulated by a set of agencies at the global level and with unequal class, national, and regional relations – required in an age of permanent technological change.

The Militarization of Space

One of the earliest conceptions of the U.S. military as *the* global power, not just the pre-eminent capitalist state, came in 1990 with the publication of the U.S. Air Force white paper "Global Reach – Global Power." The thrust of the paper was contained in the title: henceforth, the USAF would plan and operate as if the world were its domain. Part of this new definition included the assumption that space would be part of the operational base of the Air Force. "The United States has become an aerospace nation," the document declared, and "The Air force is inextricably intertwined with the aerospace industry." An updated version of the paper in 1992, after the Gulf War, emphasized the same themes.[59]

Pursuing these ideas, students and faculty at the USAF Air University in 1994 produced a multi-volume study of the possibilities "to exploit the space high ground in pursuit of national security objectives." The study, *SpaceCast 2020*, stated the issue clearly: "If the United States seeks to continue to be a great power, let alone the world's only superpower, it must maintain a dominant presence and capability in space."[60] The authors were also clear about the significance of space: the "two paramount military advantages of space – unparalleled perspective and very rapid access to the Earth's surface." And "the single most important reason to be in space is to acquire a 'Global View.'" Such a view, they asserted, was the means to achieve the global reach and power mentioned in the preceding document. Using space to acquire a "global view," the study went on, the new Air Force would be "instantly aware ... globally dominant ... selectively lethal ... and virtually present."[61]

Following *Joint Vision 2010* in 1996, the USAF continued to develop its strategic mission statements. It produced a further refinement of "Global Reach – Global Power" in a new document, *Global Engagement: A Vision for the Twenty-First Century Air Force*. Here was outlined a strategy to maintain "asymmetric force," allowing the U.S. military to dominate in any instance of hostilities. Central to maintaining the ascendancy was the prescription: "The Air Force must plan to prevail in the use of space."

Within two years of this "vision" document, the U.S. Space Command unveiled its "Long Range Plan" in 1998. Its main point was straightforward: "Space is an enabler of military operations. Forces depend on information." It went on to predict an even greater use of space for military co-ordination and command in the future. To "attain the Vision" it proposed "four operational concepts." The first was the "control of space," meaning that the United States would defend a monopoly of control over the use of space. The second was "global engagement," which in a phrase amounted to "worldwide situational awareness," particularly aimed at missile attacks but including a more general surveillance of global activity. The third was "full force integration," which meant "the integration of space forces and information with air, land, sea forces and information." The whole of the U.S. military apparatus and the resources of the so-called "coalition partners" were to be integrated into a single command structure. The fourth concept was the building of "global partnerships," which constituted the "strengthening of military space capabilities through the leveraging of civil, commercial, intelligence, national and international space efforts."[62]

As evident in these "vision" statements, the control of space had become part of U.S. military strategy in the 1990s. Well aware of the U.S. plans, the nations of the world have consistently voted in the United Nations to express their opposition to the militarization of space. Among many other similar resolutions, in the year 2000, 163 nations in the UN General Assembly voted in favour of a resolution to prevent an arms race in outer space; there were no negative votes, but the United States and Israel (and the Federated States of Micronesia) abstained. In the same year the UN General Assembly also voted by overwhelming majority in favour of a resolution for the "preservation of and compliance with the Anti-Ballistic Missile Treaty," which was related to the prevention of the arms race in space.[63] With the election of President Bush, however, the Pentagon pushed ahead with its plans. In 2001 a four-star general was appointed to be in charge of space matters; the new government unilaterally opted out of the ABM Treaty of 1972; and the secretary of defense, Donald Rumsfeld, said, "More than any other country, the United States relies on space for its security and well-being."[64] Before becoming defense secretary in the Bush administration, Rumsfeld was the chair of the Space Commission, which recommended in its report of January 2001 that the U.S. president "have the option to deploy weapons in space to deter threats to and, if necessary, defend against attacks on U.S. interests." The report stressed that "the U.S. must develop the means both to deter and defend against hostile acts in and from space." In one of the few admissions from any quarter in the U.S. government that there may be a legal barrier to their plans, the report stated, "There is no blanket prohibition in international law on placing or using weapons in space."[65]

The United States is experimenting with space weapons and is planning to militarize space, to deploy space weapons, if it has not done so already,[66] but the various "vision" documents do not address or even raise the legal issue of militarizing space – except for the Rumsfeld report, which raises the issue in order to dismiss it. Outer space is not, however, a legal void that allows unrestricted activity; the use of space is governed not only by the 1967 Outer Space Treaty, but also by a host of legal instruments, resolutions, conventions, and other treaties. As well, the recognized principles of international law also apply to outer space. At the very least, the idea of military control over space and the deployment of weapons there violate the spirit and the letter of the 1967 treaty. Its preamble speaks of the "use of outer space for peaceful purposes," for the "benefit of all peoples," and of developing "mutual understanding and … strengthening of friendly relations." Article I states that outer space is "the province of all mankind"; Article II declares that space is "not subject to national appropriation" by any means, including "use or occupation"; Article III says that the use of space shall be "in accordance with international law"; Article IV prohibits the weaponization of space; and Article V asserts that astronauts shall be regarded "as envoys of mankind." These magnanimous principles and the prohibitions to guard them are nowhere to be seen in the Pentagon documents; in fact, the language and rules of the 1967 treaty stand in stark contrast to the military doctrine of "full spectrum dominance."

The Expansion of NATO

In 1990 the imminent demise of the Soviet Union and the recently dissolved Warsaw Pact caused NATO's heads of government, meeting in London that year, to call for a review of the future role of NATO in Europe. Towards the end of 1991 they agreed on a vision set out in a document entitled "The Alliance's New Strategic Concept." In rather general terms the organization searched for a new rationale, citing ill-defined and uncertain new threats, and a change in its practice, but it would require the events of the 1990s and the clarification of U.S. global military strategy before there would be a clear idea of the new role of NATO.

In 1999 NATO released a second "Strategic Concept" document that incorporated its activities and new strategies in the aftermath of the Cold War.[67] If NATO had originally been formed to forestall the spread of socialism, consolidate capitalism in Western Europe, and provide the mechanism for U.S. military dominance there, by 1991 the first of these purposes disappeared and with it one abiding rationale for NATO's existence. The absence of an obvious and singular threat, however, did not inhibit the relatively rapid expansion of NATO in the 1990s, because the other two original purposes took on a new life. NATO would remain the key means by which the United States would maintain and ensure its dominance over Europe. To this end, the terms of the founding treaty did not change, leaving a U.S.-appointed officer as the perennial Supreme Allied Commander Europe, NATO. The "Strategic Concept" of the new Alliance actually gave the United States more leverage than before over the increasingly integrated and expanded European armed forces and countered the prospect of a strictly European military alliance. There was to be no potential European bloc separate from U.S. control.

With the establishment of the European Union, the capitalist integration of Western Europe was largely complete, but after 1991 there was the immediate task of consolidating capitalism in the former Soviet republics and Eastern Bloc countries. This task became one of the preoccupations of NATO in the 1990s; the organization was to play a central part in the capitalization of the dissolved Soviet Bloc. To do this, it began to admit new members and to bring together the nations of Eastern Europe and Central Asia in NATO-related accords and councils. In 1997 three former members of the Warsaw Pact – the Czech Republic, Hungary, and Poland – were invited to join NATO; and "aspirant" countries were assured that if they met the requirements for membership – a semblance of democracy and rule of law, free markets, the protection of private property (commonly referred to as "individual rights"), a willingness to integrate and standardize their armed forces, and "English-language capability" – NATO would be open to expanded membership.[68]

Bringing the former Warsaw Pact countries and Soviet Central Asian republics into the fold of NATO was part of the strategy to consolidate the incipient capitalism of the dissolved Soviet Bloc. To prevent any attempt to re-establish an alternative regional power bloc or socialism, the Alliance's Strategic Concept went beyond this new role of establishing a political coherence amongst its members and "partners." It also set forth the principle of "collective security," the achievement of which meant the integration of the armed forces of NATO countries. This integration, moreover, was meant to be a one-way move; the "principle of collective effort," the paper stated, would "prevent the renationalization [sic] of defense policies." Despite lip service paid to the sovereignty of its members, given the "open markets" demanded with membership and the integration of armed forces, the new concept of NATO meant that, for the most part, national armed forces would be one joint force and that once a member always a member – of an organization that gave pre-eminence to the political and military leadership of the United States.[69]

It is difficult to escape the conclusion that the new Strategic Concept was intended to translate into the growth of a political entity and the consolidation of control over the military forces of Europe and hence over the industrial world by the United States. This is not to say unmitigated control, because there is an allowance for consultation, discussion, and decision-making procedures; and NATO documents refer to the necessity of consensus in the approval of its actions. Indeed, many NATO countries have been sceptical of Bush's proclaimed "war on terrorism." But the U.S. prosecution of the wars in the Balkans from 1995 through to 1999 makes it clear that the conflict was waged under the jurisdiction of the U.S. presidency without the approval of Congress and by means of executive orders and presidential directives. This was the structure of command, even though the actions probably had little to do with the incumbent President Clinton. The point is that the wars were prosecuted by means of the assertion of U.S. presidential authority as commander-in-chief of U.S. forces that extended through to NATO.

In general, moreover, Washington sees its NATO partners as its subordinates, given that the United States funds about one-quarter of the NATO military and civil budgets and the Security Investment Program, which is intended to upgrade equipment and to "enhance interoperability with U.S. forces." In 2002 General J.W. Ralston, the Supreme Allied Commander Europe, NATO, summed up the perspective arising from this overriding financial weight: it allowed the "U.S. access to new member militaries, governments and bases."[70] By the sheer weight of its military financing, the United States exercises a far more than equal say in NATO affairs. According to one report, the increased Pentagon budget of $48 billion in 2002 and a projected $120 billion over the following five years would make the U.S. military budget greater than the "total military budget of the world's next 14 biggest defense spenders put together." Even before these increases, the U.S. ambassador to NATO said that the "capabilities gap" between the United States and the other NATO members was creating "a two-tiered alliance." The gap raised the "risk" that the United States and its allies "may no longer have the ability to fight together in the future."[71]

The Alliance's Strategic Concept also strongly suggests that NATO now sees itself as the organization for the promotion of security, stability, and dispute resolution, not only in Europe and Central Asia but also outside these borders. It implies, moreover, that NATO will become an active political force in its own right. While the document mentions that it will "seek the peaceful resolution of disputes as set out in the Charter of the United Nations," and it uses the wording of Article 24 of the UN Charter, giving "primary responsibility for the maintenance of international peace and security" to the UN Security Council, it nevertheless strongly intimates in many places that no mandate for its actions in or outside of NATO borders is needed beyond the Council of Ministers of NATO itself and that the determination of security risks is a matter for NATO alone.[72]

In the spring of 2003, NATO operational control, previously divided between Atlantic and European commands, was merged into a single Allied command structure under the authority of a U.S. commander. NATO's strategic goals were formally shifted from the defence of Europe to preparations for possible global missions.[73]

The new definition of NATO goes well beyond its previous role; the organization has been expanding not only in size but also in purpose and activity. In effect it is intended to be the guarantee of U.S. dominance over the military machines of the industrial world, and so over the ability to act independently of the United States, and to be the means by which the United States could intervene in the affairs of sovereign states under the guise of an alliance of "democratic" nations.

New Technology for Civilian Repression

With the growing efforts by states to enact neo-liberal policies throughout the 1980s and 1990s, and the consequent greater economic insecurity, declining living standards, and unresponsive government, the problem of civilian control began to loom in a way that it had not since the 1930s. New technology began to be applied to civilian policing.

In part, these applications were and remain a reflection of the mere fact that the technology for repression has been developed. In other words, because the technology is there, its development ongoing, and its manufacture and proliferation encouraged by state policies, it will be adopted, and likely justified as more "efficient" or "cost-effective," by governments and their police departments.

In part, the applications are also a response to the changing nature of class contradictions. Since the 1980s the systematic dismantling of the welfare state has exposed government policy more than ever as class-based. The limited social rights that protected the working classes from the depredations of corporations have been reduced or eliminated, leaving the majority more and more vulnerable to the inequities of the system. It can be said unequivocally that nowhere in the world does global capitalism offer a hopeful future for the majority of people. Everywhere there is increasing homelessness, hopelessness, unemployment; there are growing food bank lines, and relative incomes decline as poorly paid, dead-end jobs increase in number.

Where once the system possessed a certain legitimacy, however grounded, its leaders, politicians, and corporate managers increasingly are exposed as corrupt, dishonest, and impotent. Where once a change of party in government could parade as democracy, now alternations of the party in power offer more or less the same policies. Where once social control was largely an unintended consequence of the operation of the system itself, now it is increasingly a matter for coercive measures. When governments act against the interests of the majority of people, the police or military are required in ways not necessary when political compromises or concessions were possible. This is the context that demands that the task of policing shift increasingly to overall social control relying on coercion and threat.

As a spin-off from military and Third World applications, repressive technology began to find its way into civilian control in the industrial world in the 1970s. In 1977 one of the first documents to bring attention to the use of technology for civil repression was published by the British Society for Social Responsibility in Science. A report entitled *The Technology of Political Control* identified "a whole class of technology whose principal function was to achieve social and political control."[74] Some twenty years later, in the late 1990s, the European Parliament received a report on the further development of these technologies for controlling civil unrest.[75] It began by stating, "Throughout the Nineties, many governments have spent huge sums on the research, development, procurement and deployment of new technology for their police, para-military, and internal security forces." The new technologies were expanding in three main areas: physical control, surveillance, and policing.

A major category of new means for crowd control comes under the rubric of "non-lethal weapons" or, more often now, "less-lethal weapons," an implicit acknowledgement of their frequently lethal consequences. Included here are the now worldwide-deployed plastic or rubber bullets and a new range of chemical "incapacitants" or "irritants" that can cause damage to the lungs, nose, eyes, skin, and internal organs, as well as death in high doses. While most of these gases are outlawed for use in war, this prohibition does not extend to domestic use. Electrified shields and truncheons and Taser guns are among the equipment employed in the new uses of electric shock as a means of social control, along with so-called "kill-fences." Torture techniques have been refined so that investigators find it difficult to see any evidence of the abuse on the body of the tortured. The range of these new technologies is limited only by the imaginations of the researchers in the corporations that do the research and development; and there are hundreds of such companies around the world, although most are American, and the proliferation of their products is merely a matter of business, of profits.

Another category includes rapidly evolving surveillance technologies. Although secret informers are hardly a thing of the past (the U.S. government encourages such behaviour),[76] the new technology in this field of surveillance appears little short of science fiction.[77] The new devices for listening to and intercepting communications that are electronic or direct, anywhere in the world, are without precedent; and to prevent the circumventing of this potential violation of privacy right, governments around the world have been introducing similar legislation to make all communication network providers ensure that voice and print networks are "interception-capable."[78] Illegal and covert telephone wiretapping is practised widely the world over. New photographic technology allows for space-based monitoring and for isolating individuals in photographs of massive demonstrations. Recognition technologies can identify individual faces, odour, genes, irises, signatures. Computer programs can now produce "entire life profiles of virtually anyone in a state having an official existence."[79]

Much of this collected information is stored in computer data banks over which there is very little government regulation and few if any oversight bodies.[80] Even the location of and degree of exchange between these data banks is poorly documented. But there is no dispute that there are computer files on political dissidents and opposition parties, and on critical journalists, teachers, students, politicians, and social movements.

Another application of new technology is found in the changing nature of policing. One of these changes is the militarization of police, meaning the introduction of new weapons for social control, new training and the formation of special tactical squads or paramilitary police, the transformation of personal protective equipment, and the legislative facilitation of police activity overriding a broad range of civil and political rights. Another is the rise of "proactive policing," which includes the tracking of social classes, races, groups, political parties, social movements, and individuals, the surveillance of specified areas, the collection of huge data bases, and the global co-ordination of police work.

Global Surveillance: Echelon

In its strategic plan *Joint Vision 2020*, the Pentagon asserts that "a key enabler of victory" is "information superiority," which is defined as "the capability to collect, process, and disseminate an uninterrupted flow of information while exploiting or denying an adversary's ability to do the same." While the document speaks in the future tense, a comprehensive system of global surveillance mainly for military purposes has been evolving since the 1940s. During World War II, the United States and Great Britain collaborated on intelligence-gathering and espionage, but it is thought that in 1947 or 1948, with the coming of the Cold War, those countries, along with Canada, Australia, and New Zealand, entered into a secret agreement, referred to as UKUSA. After the development of satellite technology for communication and reconnaissance, the UKUSA treaty expanded in the early 1970s into a global system, sometimes referred to as Echelon, for tracking all forms of electronic communication. The U.S. National Security Agency (NSA) has been the lead partner in financing, research, design, co-ordination, and provision of the technology, but the four associated national agencies are thought to be "the largest intelligence organizations in their respective countries."[81]

The system comprises a series of receivers in stations located mainly but not only in the treaty countries that target land-based transmission systems, international communication satellites (Intelsats), and Russian, Chinese, and regional satellites. In effect, they intercept communications that are transmitted across the world by satellite, all forms of electrical impulse, microwave, radio-wave, cellular technology, and optical fibres. These would include e-mail, Internet, telex, telephone, radio, and fax messages. Although there are several estimates of how many communications the system intercepts each hour or day, the total number of communications made each day and the percentage checked will always remain in some flux; the point, however, is that NSA strives for complete comprehensiveness and by all accounts it is not far off. Messages are "vacuumed" from all sources and processed through state-of-the-art, interconnected computers that include "voice recognition" and "optical character recognition" capabilities and that are coded to look for words, phrases, names, or whatever the agency is asked to look for, and then sent to the pertinent authority. The "flagged messages" are "recorded and transcribed" for analysis in real time or in the future. No communication anywhere in the world is free of the possibility and high probability that it will pass through this process.

The main targets of the system in the Cold War period were the military, political, and economic activities of the "socialist" countries, particularly the USSR and China. After 1991 the targets remained more or less the same activities, but the focus shifted to internal threats to the dominant global relations of corporate private property. There continue to be recalcitrant countries with restrictions on foreign investment, contentious social movements, opposition parties, critical writers and leaders, the proliferation of weapons of mass destruction, local and regional conflicts, commercial espionage, and the question of "regime change." All of these have been subject to ongoing or specific intelligence-gathering by one or another part of Echelon; it is not clear that any one of them is singularly pre-eminent.

Although the expanding activities of Echelon have been extensive, intrusive, and shrouded in secrecy, after January 2000 declassified NSA documents confirmed its existence.[82] From the beginning the treaty governments refused to admit to its existence, probably because of the questionable legality of this sort of espionage under international and national laws and the importance of obscurity for subterfuge. But the governments of both Australia and New Zealand admitted to its existence in the 1980s, the European Parliament subjected it to two studies in the 1990s,[83] and NSA partially opened its archives in 2000, and so its reality, structure, and operation are now quite well documented.

Still, very little is done to question the meaning or challenge the legality of its pervasive intrusion. Governments in the industrial world are for the most part highly compromised in the area of secret surveillance; they are either party to the UKUSA treaty, or they run their own surveillance systems,[84] making them unwilling to participate in, indeed perhaps active opponents to, the investigation of the meaning, legality, morality, and desirability of monitoring all global communications. This is not a world of disinterested parties.

It must be stressed, however, that secret, globally comprehensive, surveillance of communications without legal authority or rationale stands prima facie as a violation of most constitutions and many bilateral and multilateral international laws and conventions. The UDHR, the International Covenant on Civil and Political Rights, the European Convention of Human Rights, OECD Guidelines – indeed, all national human rights legislation – clearly provide "a robust protection for natural persons against unlawful interception by the State of communications."[85] Despite these international legal prohibitions, Echelon covertly siphons the majority of the world's communications of all sorts and processes them in search of secretly designated names, organizations, topics, and activities. Its clandestine nature and operation are not only a probable violation of international and national laws, but also leave it open to abuse by governments and its operating personnel, and indeed there is convincing evidence that it has been misused for patently partisan commercial, political, and even personal purposes. Echelon has no international oversight or appeal body; whatever national mechanisms exist are generally compromised, being part of the system of corporate right; and if they do exist their jurisdictional powers extend no further than declining national sovereignty. Echelon is part of a global system of control that is dominated by the United States and that operates in the interests of global corporate private property.

A New Role for Nuclear Weapons

Plans to rebuild the U.S. nuclear arms program began under President Clinton. In 2000 the U.S. Congress mandated a review of the program, and on December 31, 2001, the "nuclear posture review" (NPR) was submitted by Bush's secretary of defense, Donald Rumsfeld. Portions of this document were released in the following month, and they spelled out plans to develop a new class of smaller nuclear weapons. "Mini-nukes," "bunker busters," and neutron bombs were proposed not simply as deterrents, as weapons of last resort, but as useable weapons in conventional warfare.

The news of those plans was greeted with consternation the world over because the program would reverse an almost ten-year ban on research and development of "low-yield" nuclear weapons, something that the Bush administration had begun to lobby for on assuming power. The initiative also implied that U.S. obligations under both the Nuclear Non-Proliferation Treaty (NPT) "to take concrete steps toward eliminating its nuclear arsenal" and the Comprehensive Test Ban Treaty (CTBT) would be violated because the new plans would require the production and testing of new nuclear weapons. Critics argued, moreover, that plans to develop useable nuclear bombs, to resume testing, and to incorporate these weapons in conventional battle strategies would lead to a nuclear arms race.

Within a few months international alarm and dismay over the implications of the NPR dissipated as attention shifted to other actions of the Bush regime. But Washington did not relent; the proposed U.S. military budget for 2004 included hundreds of millions of dollars to be spent on the resumption of nuclear weapons production.[86]

Unmentioned in the NPR and in the commentaries and critiques that followed was the already wide use of "armour-piercing" depleted uranium (DU) ammunition. Its use in Iraq, Bosnia, Kosovo, and elsewhere resulted in the radiation contamination of thousand of troops and civilians, as well as of the environment.[87]

The Spread of Depleted Uranium

According to the Pentagon, over 300 tons of depleted uranium munitions were used in the Gulf War in 1991. In 1995 DU weapons were employed in Bosnia; in 1995-96 U.S. Marines trained with them near Okinawa, Japan; in 1999 the U.S. Navy deployed DU ammunition on Vieques, an island test zone for the U.S. military, recently returned to Puerto Rican jurisdiction; in the same year DU ammunition was used in Kosovo, and it was revealed that the Canadian navy fired several tons of DU shells, much of it into a fishing zone off Halifax. In 2003 the weapons appeared again in Iraq.

Chronic illness, birth defects, and cancer are widely associated with its use. The Pentagon, by far the largest procurer and user of DU, has not commissioned any independent study into the actual consequences for human health or the environment and has obstructed a UN attempt to investigate the use of DU in Kosovo.

• For more information on DU, see the Military Toxics Project web site.

"Benevolent Global Hegemony"

An early recognition of the need to affirm a single dominant authority over the globalized economy in the post-Cold War era came in 1996, in the U.S. journal *Foreign Affairs*, in a widely discussed article by William Kristol and Robert Kagan.[88] In "Toward a Neo-Reaganite Foreign Policy," the authors called for the United States to assert a "benevolent global hegemony" over the new world order of prevailing corporate private property, stating: "A hegemon is nothing more than a leader with a preponderant influence and authority over all others in its domain. That is America's position in the world today." While it is difficult to disagree with this statement, it is another matter to call the U.S. role in the past or present "benevolent." Its violations of the entire range of political, civil, and social rights around the world are a matter of numerous well-documented reports and studies.

The authors suggested that to achieve this goal of "benevolent hegemon," the United States would have to pursue "three imperatives." The one they most emphasized was an increase in military spending – sufficient to maintain the current amount, which was more than "the next six major powers combined." Another imperative was the militarization of American culture by "educating the citizenry to the responsibilities of global hegemony," by clarifying "America's global mission," and by giving "many more Americans experience of the military and an appreciation of military virtues." The third imperative came under the rubric of "moral clarity" and amounted to "actively promoting American principles of governance abroad – democracy, free markets, respect for liberty."

At least one of these "imperatives" was soon realized. Under the Bush administration, military spending increased significantly. Another was advanced in several programs that began to further military-civilian co-operation in U.S. society – an effort to advance what has been a part of American culture since at least 1945. The third point would prove more difficult to achieve given that democracy and respect for liberty are not generally compatible with an increase in military spending and the militarization of culture. More specifically, the questions surrounding the legitimacy of the Bush election in 2000, the undemocratic rule of the global agencies representing the interests of TNCs and dominated by the United States, and the patently unfair trade agreements between the United States and the rest of the world and between the industrial and less developed worlds mean that this final imperative could be not be more than a rhetorical flourish.

The authors go on to say that if "the American people will not support the burdens of such a policy" – referring to the three imperatives – that will enable the United States to pursue its role as "benevolent hegemon," there are "two answers" to this problem. They present one of those answers indirectly by means of a discussion of past instances when the government needed public support for new foreign policy initiatives, such as the post-World War II use of anti-communism and President Reagan's arms race in the 1980s. With these references, the authors make it clear that fear of an enemy allowed the administration of the day "to rally support" for policies to increase military budgets and to use U.S. armed forces overseas – policies that otherwise the American people would not have accepted. To make acceptable a "foreign policy vision" of anti-communism and the Cold War required the Korean War, the actual origin of which has always been in doubt.[89] And to make "the military buildup of the 1980s" possible there were at least two manufactured crises: "the Soviet invasion of Afghanistan," which Zbigniew Brzezinski, former national security advisor to President Carter, has said was the product of U.S. covert actions,[90] and the notion of the "missile gap" with the Soviet Union.[91]

The second answer was to create "an elevated patriotism" that would serve the "task of preparing and inspiring the nation to embrace the role of global leadership." This bit of conscious deception was not to be the narrow nationalism of an "America First" position, but a belief in Americans as a sort of "chosen people." The authors cite George Kennan, who wrote that Americans should feel a "certain gratitude to a Providence" for making "history" give them "the responsibilities of moral and political leadership." Of course, all dominant or aspiring powers in the past have created beliefs about themselves as exceptional, chosen, destined, or just superior; such notions are simply the ideological counterparts of economic and political ascendancy. This is an ideology that comes easily to Americans because the United States is the dominant power in an age of capital and was the first nation to be born of capitalist relations and defined by the same.

If these authors mapped out the nature of the predicament that a globalized economy presented to the United States in the 1990s, it would seem that they mistook the problem as a strictly American issue rather than as the need for the global enabling framework to have a single guarantor of the new world order. In other words, a global economy without a central authority and policing mechanism is a problem for world capitalist relations and not simply for U.S. interests. It is true to say that the United States is the only power capable of guaranteeing those relations, and that to do so it must maintain military supremacy, but its role in this regard is as a guarantor for the hegemony of transnational capital. The U.S. government is central to the global quasi-state and all its functions, but it is not an American imperium that it is defending and advancing; rather it is the imperium of transnational capital, a large part of which, but not all, is American.

The authors do not clarify just what new crisis or event would serve "to rally support" for the pursuit of this proposed role as "benevolent global hegemon." They did, however, argue that such a galvanizing event or threat might be necessary; and they did know that crises had been invented in the past to serve as justification for the policies they thought necessary for the role of global hegemon.

THE QUESTION OF PRETEXTS

Throughout the history of capitalism pretexts have certainly been used to justify military spending and action, but it is not often asked why such pretexts are needed in the first place. In their article Kristol and Kagan answer by implying that "the American people" may not "support the burdens" of the policy they were proposing. Although they do not inquire why that might be the case, the answer has to be that their proposed role for the U.S. government and military is not necessarily in the interests of "the American people." Divided interests in a society always mean that not all interests are equally served by state policies or practices – in particular, military action – or indeed that some interests may suffer so that other interests may benefit. Here lies the general reason for the need for pretexts.

More specifically, contrived excuses may be needed to justify actions that are not in the interests of certain strata of the working classes or some other segment of civil society, including corporate subsectors. In other words, state operations may advance certain narrow class, strata, or particular interests but not the interests of other subsectors, in particular those who will have to fight the battles and risk life and livelihood. Keeping the capitalist world open to corporate investment and resisting the socialization of capital have always been a question of a particular class interest. The defence of the system does not necessarily serve all classes within it.

There is now a well-recorded history of the use of pretexts for military action by the U.S. government over the last hundred years.[92] The reasons for past pretexts are still present: a divided society whose contradictions belie the existence of any single inherent national interest. For state actions to be undertaken in the guise of the national interest, which can only be class interest, the working-class majority must be convinced by means of pretexts and manufactured patriotism, as Kristol and Kagan argue.

With the demise of the Soviet Union in 1991, the U.S. government lost the main rationale for its military interventions around the world and attempted suppression of dissent and resistance at home and abroad. During the 1990s, Pentagon documents referred repeatedly to the problem of the loss of the military threat of the Soviets and the need to find a replacement. In the absence of specific threats, they invented generalized rationales such as "uncertainty" – which given its banality could not be anything but a temporary measure. The idea of peace, of a world without war, was not and could not be put on the agenda.

The United States had two main continuing obligations to pursue, but without a convincing rationale it would be clear that the absence of peace in the world was due to the iniquitous nature of the system and the U.S. role in defending it. One obligation was the need for a single authoritative force to oversee the regional and global enabling frameworks and to enforce the accompanying relations of economic domination. Associated with this burden was the need to complete the subordination of the world to capital, and to threaten and confront all resistance to the assertion of transnational corporate rights. The other obligation concerned the political economy of military action and production. Unequal property relations are inherently unstable and, in the long run, insupportable; wherever they exist they need defending. For this reason, the maintenance of war industries is essential to the continuance of a divided and unequal system; but the support of the military-industrial complex also performs the functions of stabilizing and guaranteeing the profits of a sizable sector of U.S. industry and subordinating the state to corporate ends. These functions are a product of keeping production outside the marketplace – the provision of the capital for the production and use of military goods is safely within the realm of the state.

THE MEANING OF SEPTEMBER 11: ITS AFTERMATH

There are numerous examples of invented rationales, staged incidents, and illegal acts planned and carried out by the U.S. government to justify its interventions over many years around the world; for that reason alone a great many people are sceptical of the official version of the events of September 11.[93] The question of who actually planned and executed the attacks is important in confirming or denying the scepticism, but we may never know how they were planned and executed. What we do know is that the official explanation is not credible; it has only been asserted, never argued, and only the barest of circumstantial evidence has been offered.

To discover who was responsible for the attacks, moreover, will not necessarily reveal what is most important about the terror of September 11 – that is, its subsequent use. No amount of study of the assassination of Archduke Ferdinand in 1914, for example, will explain why the murder became the pretext for World War I. And to identify those responsible for the burning of the Reichstag in 1933 will not help to understand the use made of that suspect event. Uncovering those who were culpable would never explain the implacable political and economic contradictions that were waiting for an excuse to find their "resolution" in the only way possible, through war and dictatorship. And it cannot explain the following declaration of and preparation for war, or the outcome. The objective in analyzing 9/11, then, should focus on how opportune that terror was – that is, on the nature of the contradictions of the 1990s and beyond that the terror has been used to address, and on the particular interests served and how.

Above all, the terror of 9/11 served to replace the threat that was lost with the demise of the Soviet Union – the danger that justified massive U.S. military expenditures and interventions around the world. Like the Cold War, the declared war on terrorism provided the means to sanction the defence and advance of class inequalities at home, to assert U. S. dominance abroad, and to pre-empt the possibilities of national or regional challenges to U. S. hegemony.

Class War at Home

Within weeks of 9/11, the Bush administration intensified the domestic class war in several arenas. One field of continuous contest has been the configuration of fiscal policy – the struggle over the size, number, and kinds of taxes, the magnitude of the debt, and the disposition of expenditures. Among many other tax measures passed since 9/11, a number included large giveaways to wealthy individuals and the corporate sector. Ostensibly to address the economic impact of 9/11, on October 24, 2001, the Republican majority in the House of Representatives "rammed through its first 'stimulus' bill" (the Economic Security and Recovery Act), which provided an estimated $160 billion by and large in "special interest tax cuts." A repeal of one tax gave $7.4 billion in rebates to several of the largest U.S. corporations, including a rebate for Enron of $254 million. On December 20, 2001, the House passed its second "stimulus" bill, which included a further $157 billion in tax cuts. On February 14, 2002, it pushed its third "stimulus" bill through to increase corporate tax breaks by another $157 billion.[94] These tax cuts continued in 2002 and 2003.

In addition to these enormous tax refunds and cuts, the Bush administration awarded large military contracts to a handful of the biggest military companies, even though many of them had a long record of lawbreaking involving Pentagon contracts. The case that stood out was a contract to Lockheed Martin, which received the most expensive contract in history to build the United States' "next-generation" jet – over $200 billion, albeit spread over several years, with billions more promised in foreign sales over twenty-five years.[95]

The events of September 11 also provided the opportunity for the government to increase the size of the budget dedicated to "defence" and "security." They justified the massive public debt that the Bush administration incurred in cutting taxes, granting rebates, and selectively increasing the budget. In 2003-4, the projected deficits were $455 billion and $475 respectively, when in 2001 the same administration projected a surplus of $334 billion.[96] The public debt entails the use of the state to spread the costs of certain class benefits and priorities in capital accumulation across the whole of the working class and over many years.

Another arena of class conflict encompasses the sphere of social rights. Here the Bush government continued the policies of the Clinton administration to cut back or transform every aspect of the welfare state. The Bush budget proposed for 2004 would, if passed, continue the process of eliminating health insurance for low-income families, cancelling school lunches, abolishing benefits for thousands of neglected and abused children, and continuing to curtail food stamp benefits. By 2003 the federal tax cuts and growing deficits had already led to state and local budget shortfalls resulting in cutbacks in education, health care, and social welfare, which in turn resulted in the large-scale firing of teachers and welfare and health-care workers and in the closing of schools, clinics, hospitals, shelters, and other services. Even the budgets of some police and fire departments were severely cut. Large corporations were allowed to cancel their "defined benefit pension" plans, to eliminate corporate health insurance or cut benefits and increase employee contributions, to disencumber themselves of unions, and to circumvent employment standards.[97] The Social Security Trust Fund, moreover, has been under attack by successive administrations since the Reagan years in the early 1980s.[98]

Another arena of contestation concerns the law. The constitution lays out the fundamental property relations and structures of the state; and law in the form of statutes, codes, and regulations embodies the specific prevailing property relations that obtain in civil society. The form and content of law and the nature of judicial decisions and state activities, then, by and large reflect relations that exist outside themselves, and, it follows, they change to correspond more or less with the balance of contested power in civil society in a given period. When organized countervailing interests are weak or non-existent, when trade unions, social movements, or alternative political parties no longer present a significant challenge to the prevailing property relations, and when the structure of corporations has become increasingly oligopolistic and cartelized, the shape of the law will reflect this dominance of large capital. Every aspect of law succumbs in due time to these changes.

Even before the events of 9/11, the Bush administration had a bill before Congress "to establish the National Homeland Security Agency" – long the ambition of the Pentagon to create "a new domestic military command to combat terrorism."[99] This militarized oversight agency for the United States lacked the rationale at that time for its smooth passing through Congress. But on October 8, 2001, the Office of Homeland Security (OHS) was established by executive order with the mission "to develop and coordinate the implementation of a comprehensive national strategy to secure the United States from terrorist threat or attack." The Office was given vast new powers to co-ordinate "all executive departments and agencies" that carry out intelligence work and to maintain an executive office of oversight over all activities under the guise of threats of terror.[100] This overarching military command structure was nothing short of the creation of a single national structure, premised on a continuous war against terror at home and abroad, with executive powers able to co-ordinate and oversee every aspect of American society.

In the weeks following 9/11 Congress did not question the actions of the Bush administration, and at the end of October 2001 it passed a significant bill, the United States Patriot Act, without taking time to debate or digest its contents. The legislation granted incisive executive powers to act in ways that usurped the usual guarantees of the Constitution. It allowed the executive branch to criminalize protest movements and to suppress dissent; it enhanced the powers of arbitrary surveillance throughout civil society; it permitted the detention and deportation of non-citizens for political activities and membership in associations. It gave the executive branch the power to commit a wide range of acts counter to the rule of law, such as preventative detention, secret detention, and non-disclosure of identities of detainees, and it provided the rationale for the illegal use of torture and harsh conditions of confinement. Here are all the fundamentals of a police state.[101]

On November 13, 2001, the White House issued an "Executive Order on the Detention, Treatment, and Trial of Certain Non-Citizens in the War on Terrorism," which allowed the government to arrest and detain non-Americans on grounds that were sweeping and extremely vague. Those arrested could be tried in military tribunals, thereby limiting or abolishing legal safeguards outlined in domestic and international law. Habeas corpus, due process, the separation of judge, jury, and prosecution, and judicial review were eclipsed by executive fiat. Fundamental aspects of rule of law came to an end for non-Americans within U.S. political or military reach.[102] The world's pre-eminent power had arrogated to itself the right to detain, prosecute, and punish any non-American it considered suspect and was able to arrest. The poverty of response by U.S. organizations and citizens suggests not only that Americans accept a vision of the world as divided between the United States and the rest, but also that the same law could be applied to them without much resistance.[103]

These executive edicts and rushed legislation were only some of the many decrees and legislative bills brought into law in the weeks and months following September 11.[104] As a whole they provide the government with the powers necessary to keep all forms of resistance and criticism in check, to veil the decline of alternative political policies, and to create an atmosphere of chronic tension and danger that goes far to justify the executive circumscription of the rule of law.

Global Assertion of Dominance

The events of 9/11 did not change the general position that the United States had taken over the years on international law and multilateral treaties. As becoming the power and status of a superpower that can march to its own tune, the United States has made it clear that it does not intend to subordinate itself to the obligations implied in agreements, conventions, or treaties that the majority of the world's nations have signed and ratified, and does not intend to be accountable to the UN and its conventions and treaties. Even before September 11, the Bush administration was busy abrogating, rejecting, and withdrawing from a number of multilateral agreements.

In March 2001 President Bush declared the 1997 Kyoto Protocol to be "dead." Although in April the United States lost its position on the UN Human Rights Commission, for some time in that body it had been alone in opposing proposals for low-cost access to AIDS drugs, food as a basic human right, and a moratorium on the death penalty. In May 2001 the United States declined to meet with representatives of the European Union to review the surveillance of vast numbers of electronic messages that it was vacuuming up through the Echelon system. In the same month it rejected participation in the OECD talks on curbing offshore and other money-laundering and tax havens. In July it alone opposed the UN Agreement to Curb the International Flow of Illicit Small Arms; in the same month it stood again as the sole opposing voice to the International Plan for Cleaner Energy. In August Bush repudiated former President Clinton's statement that the United States would "eventually" sign the Land Mines Treaty agreed to in Ottawa in 1997.

After 9/11, the pattern continued. In November the United States declared a protocol to the 1972 Biological and Toxin Weapons Convention to be "dead," and in the same month it voted in the UN against revitalizing the Comprehensive Test Ban Treaty, although it had never ratified it. In December Washington renounced its commitment to the 1972 Antiballistic Missile Treaty.[105]

It is difficult to imagine any clearer set of statements indicating that the U.S. government would hereafter follow only its own direction in world affairs and that in principle it was no longer willing to subordinate itself to multilateral rules and regulations, or to respect international law, or to honour the rule of law and the constitution at home – unless certain interests were served. With September 11 as rationale, Washington carried out a wide range of arbitrary actions that violated many clauses of the UN Charter, other embodiments of international law, and the national forms of civil, political, and social rights of the UDHR, all a matter of recent public record.

The Transformation of International Relations and Human Rights

Although this show of contempt for international law was hardly new for Washington, what needs to be explained is why the structure of the relations outlined in these international agreements, conventions, and treaties increasingly appears as an ideal from a past age. The explanation begins with the assumption of state sovereignty that underlies the UN Charter and, more broadly, international relations. The history of the modern state, however, has always been the history of particular configurations of capital; or to emphasize the independent variable, the development of capital has given rise to different political shells – the modern state being the evolving political form of capital from the late eighteenth to the late twentieth centuries. But capital does not stop growing, and after World War II the mechanisms were set up for its expansion as global capital. With the establishment of the World Bank, the IMF, GATT, common markets and free trade agreements, military pacts, and later the WTO, among many other supranational agencies and organizations, capital continued to evolve, but increasingly without a national character or interest. In this light, the UN Charter of 1945 may be seen as both the culminating statement of the principles of relations between national capitals and the beginning of the end of such relations.

In the twenty-first century the world is no longer a place of independent national capitals with their own sovereign political expression. It is a world dominated by global agencies, organizations, and regulations, with an increasingly unified set of property relations defended by multilateral military pacts and agreements. And because after World War II U.S capital emerged as dominant, the political expression of this capital, the U.S. state, dominated the development of the global framework for the transnational expansion of capital.

International law and the UN Charter lay out the rules of conduct pertaining to relations between states, international institutions and organizations, and the behaviour of individuals and non-state entities outside the confines of the nation-state. Their presupposition, however, is a world of sovereign states, and for this reason these bodies of law have begun to lose their relevance to a world in which states are increasingly subordinate to regional and global quasi-states, in which sovereignty has become more rhetorical than real, in which national armed forces are tied to multilateral pacts, and over which the United States prevails, with its military might superior to all of the others put together.

While never fully respected, the principles of liberal democracy and the rule of law have become more open to challenge in the twenty-first century. The "war on terrorism" has merely served to renew the justifications for a wide range of violations of these principles. Although both liberal democracy and the rule of law rest on a civil society characterized and dominated by competing national capitals, the civil societies of contemporary nation-states are distinguished less by competition and more by oligopoly and cartelization of national and global capital; increasingly the dominant corporations exert pressure from a supranational level outside national civil society.

This transformation of national civil society means that the practice of liberal democracy becomes increasingly meaningless. The possibility of alternating parties representing different factions of capital in civil society within a given framework of private property, allowing for a degree of citizen participation and the possibility of countervailing rights and a certain national accountability for corporations, is characteristic of an earlier age. With the decline of competing factions, mainstream parties increasingly and necessarily advocate more or less the same policies; and working-class parties, where they exist, can only conform to the prevailing demands or demand revolutionary change to the system; the preconditions for reform are more and more circumscribed. Liberal democracy succumbs to one-party rule or alternating political parties with largely the same policies. From the point of view of cartelized or transnational capital there is no need for alternating political parties and no tolerance for accountability at the national level.

The principle of the rule of law in the history of political systems stands as an important step in resistance to political arbitrariness.[106] But this principle of subordinating procedure and conduct to the law does not address the question of the nature of the law. In liberal democracy the constitution presupposes individual rights – fundamentally, the rights of private property. Given this, the rule of law in a capitalist society has always meant subordination to the principles of private property. Since at least the 1980s the increasingly dominant manifestation of private property has been the transnational corporation. If national law more and more reflects the interests of TNCs formalized into rules and regulations at the regional and global levels, then rule of law at the national level implies subordination to demands from another level.

Circumventing Principles of Human Rights

United Nations Resolution 1373, passed by the Security Council on Sept. 28, 2001, merely days after 9/11, and drafted by the United States, called upon all nations to co-operate in countering terrorism in a wide variety of ways. It also established a Security Council committee "to monitor implementation of this resolution" and to which all member states were requested to report within ninety days of the date of the resolution "on the steps they have taken to implement" it. Many of the members of the committee were well-known counterterrorist experts.

Amnesty International issued an "open letter" on Jan. 17, 2002, expressing concern that the monitoring committee was "not tasked ... with ensuring that measures taken by states to combat 'terrorism' are in conformity with their UN Charter obligations."

• See the Amnesty International web site, Library Online documentation archive.

The existence of two fundamental levels of law, national and international, with overlapping jurisdictions and mechanisms means that all aspects of the principles of rule of law are compromised. The tenets that no individual or entity is above the law, that all legal process must take place in the ordinary courts of the land and in the ordinary manner, and that the judiciary must be independent are all jeopardized by the contradiction between global and national rules and regulations, the overlapping jurisdictions, and by the many arbitrary and *in camera* processes that pass for due process at the transnational level.

The Coming End of Liberal Democracy

Since September 11, 2001, at the national and global levels numerous well-documented violations of all the fundamental principles of the rule of law, the full range of the rights of the UDHR, and international law have occurred. Almost all of the world's nations have passed similar emergency legislation under the auspices of the United Nations – legislation allowing the executive branch and police to circumvent the accepted principles of human rights, including liberal democracy and the rule of law. At the international level, arbitrary military actions by the United States and other industrial powers have been carried out against smaller nations. Since 9/11, these actions have been and continue to be justified by the "war on terror."

The world, moreover, is now divided between the United States and the rest. The United States is in a position to assert that the world will conform to its demands – the 2002 National Security Strategy (NSS) spells this out clearly.[107] It stresses, "The United States possesses unprecedented – and unequalled – strength and influence in the world." This military and economic pre-eminence is construed as "leadership," on the basis of which it is declared that the United States will advance a "distinctly American internationalism" for the world. The vision is defined as nothing more than the world as a free market and human intercourse as free trade; and Washington pledges to promote programs and policies that advance these goals.

The document states, however, that there is a new threat to "open societies": "shadowy networks of individuals" – in a word, terrorists. Accordingly, there is a need to confront this danger. "The enemy is terrorism," the NSS declares, and the war against it will be indefinite. "The war against terrorists of global reach is a global enterprise of uncertain duration," discloses the document. "There will be no quick or easy end to this conflict." The war "will be fought on many fronts against a particularly elusive enemy over an extended period of time." Besides emphasizing the undefined extent of the battles to come, the NSS affirms Washington's determination: "To defeat this threat we must make use of every tool in our arsenal."

The Strategy insists that the United States will undertake this war unilaterally ("We will not hesitate to act alone, if necessary"), but its preference is to act with "coalitions of the willing," or other alliances, and through multinational institutions. "Coalition warfare" amounts to the use of NATO and other military pacts, subordinating the military forces of all European industrial powers and others to the will of the United States and integrating them with the U.S. forces. Again, this policy of uniting the world's armed forces under the direction of the United States has been part of the Pentagon's strategy since at least the early 1990s.

Another significant change of U.S. military policy appearing in the NSS is the policy of pre-emptive strikes: "We cannot let our enemies strike first." Although this is a continuation of its de facto policy of unilateral and pre-emptive action, Washington is now declaring openly that it would determine what groups and nations constitute a threat to its interests and take action accordingly. In the document, Washington announced this unilateralism as its formal policy.

To meet the challenge of terrorism, the NSS insists that the main security institutions of the United States have to be "transformed." The U.S. military must be capable of "long-distance deployment" around the world and in outer space to defend the interests of transnational corporations. The CIA would also have to be strengthened, with more powers given to its director and the establishment of new networks and means for collecting information. As self-appointed defender of free enterprise in the world, moreover, the United States is not about to subordinate its personnel to international rule of law. On this question, the document pointedly states that the United States would not tolerate any investigation or prosecution of Americans by the newly established International Criminal Court.

It rightly concludes, "The distinction between domestic and foreign affairs is diminishing." The point holds true for the whole world but particularly for the United States as the pre-eminent global power whose domestic interests are now simultaneously global.

September 11 and its aftermath allowed everything to be put in place for ruling a world in which oligopolies, monopolies, and cartels have reached a certain point of concentration. There is no longer a foundation, and therefore a need, for national sovereignty, for alternating parties, for the "checks and balances" of liberal democracy, or for the rule of law that reflects contradictory national interests; in fact, all of the elements of liberal democracy, the political system that corresponds to the age of national competitive capital, begin more and more to appear as impediments to the rule of transnational law in an age of global conglomerates. The imperatives of capital to expand as global capital – to penetrate all corners of the world and every aspect of human existence and to become increasingly monopolistic at the same time – have moved corporations beyond the political shell that they required during their long development as national entities.

If the preconditions of the principles and institutions of liberal democracy have been transformed, this political form – which allowed for a range of social rights to be won and has been idealized as democracy itself – is simply no longer appropriate; indeed, it is an encumbrance to the new conditions of the global economy. The institutions of liberal democracy are not, however, dismantled, but rather modified to reflect the prevailing interests. The structures representative of global capital have grown to dominate and govern in more arbitrary ways, especially in the absence of any other organized force at the global level demanding countervailing rights. As implied in the National Security Strategy, the near future will likely see a consolidation, defence, and expansion of these structures under the aegis of the United States and the accompanying growth and concentration of TNCs.

Capital has constructed whole frameworks for itself at the global and regional levels; it has given itself powers that rival and indeed subordinate national states; it competes within these frameworks with little necessity to make concessions to national political entities; it has designated numerous ports and other centres and even whole regions of countries to be free of restrictions to the rights of capital; and it has promoted legislative attacks on union rights and employment protection everywhere. The labour movement, by contrast, has failed to establish a meaningful transnational presence; where it does have an international presence, formal union activity for the most part follows or promotes the interests of global capital or the states that represent them, or advocates modest reforms. By and large, trade unions remain nationally fragmented and largely preoccupied with the national labour laws that define their existence and have at best managed to slow down the attacks on workers' rights at this level.

It would be a mistake, however, to characterize U.S. unilateralism and the political/legal pre-eminence of the regional and global enabling frameworks as fascism.[108] It is true that fascism brings the abandonment of formally legitimized rule and the resort to overt coercion to bolster the privileges of corporate private property. It transforms the state into a one-party dictatorship that abolishes most political rights, disallows many social reforms, abrogates trade union laws, and restricts civil liberties. To compensate for these breaches, the new state takes a role in creating an exaggerated national chauvinism, militarizing social life, and preoccupying the working classes with spectator sports, pornography, other forms of cultural escapism, as well as fears of war or terror. But there is a defining dimension to fascism that is not always drawn out. It is the repudiation of the fundamental principle of capitalism; fascism violates the principle of what it is intended to save; in a word, the principle of absolutism negates the rule of law. As long as capitalism remains somewhat competitive, it demands the rule of law. By contrast, fascist leaders/governments more or less dance to their own tune; they are not mere managers of a framework for private property. The arbitrary personal powers associated with fascist leaders displace the objective rules and regulations of constitutional or negotiated power relations that frame the exercise of corporate rights. For this reason, fascism can only be considered as a temporary solution to threats to competitive capitalism.[109]

In the post-9/11 era, the world order is still characterized by the rule of law, but the content of the law has changed: it is determined by multilateral institutions and other corporate and military organizations at the global and regional levels. There is usually little or no pretence of democracy in these organizations. They exist to facilitate, defend, and expand global relations of capital; and they provide venues for deliberations between the representatives of capital. Resting on the principle of pre-eminent power, the United States asserts for itself the executive role.

This structure of global power relations allows for legal frameworks at the national and global levels, with their content and limits determined by these multinational institutions, and under sufferance of executive fiat (emergency laws for use with apprehended terror) at both national and global levels. The structure, then, provides for a restricted reality to the rule of law: transnational corporate rights are given a primacy, while the rights of all other sectors of national civil society are restricted. Social rights are retrenched, political rights become less meaningful, and civil rights for transnational corporations prevail.

This arrangement fulfils the operational exigencies of global corporations. The law remains supreme, albeit as law for corporations determined at supranational levels, while governments retain degrees of executive power to ensure the primacy of corporate right over countervailing demands. The arbitrariness of personal power, as it defines fascist states, is not tolerated except as a temporary measure. Indeed, when the United States refers to a country as a "rogue state" – a term applied at one time or another to Iran, Syria, Libya, North Korea, and (before the 2003 invasion) Iraq – the one common characteristic of those states is precisely the subordination of capital to the particular power of leaders or to a rule of law that is not that of global capital.

For the overwhelming majority of the people of the world, the passing of the rule of law of national corporations to global corporations signifies the decline of the range of human rights that they may once have enjoyed. With the end of meaningful alternative political choices, cynicism about national politics sets in. With the restrictions to social rights and decline of union powers and membership, it is economic coercion in the form of the dull compulsion of poor jobs and poor wages and the threat or reality of unemployment that increasingly acts as the main form of social control. Daily life for the majority everywhere is life in the workplace, which means subjection to a form of dictatorship; that corporations are anything but democracies becomes more evident the more that the democratic pretensions of national political systems succumb to global demands. As the process of global capital accumulation proceeds apace – producing vast increases in wealth at one end and widespread poverty at the other – it exposes both its intolerance of national sovereignty and its democratic shortfall at the global level.

The immediate problem that arises is the question of legitimacy. At best, national governments in the twenty-first century can pretend to be representative of their constituencies, but over time the lack of alternative policies and political options becomes obvious. The increasingly oligopolistic structure of global capital allows for few if any significant development alternatives. Consciousness of this condition is already widespread, but without organization, leadership, forums, or plans for the future, the people of the world can do little to change the direction of transnational corporate growth beyond public protests to make manifest their understanding and rejection of the changes in rule of law and the assertion of U.S. executive powers over global development.

As the pre-eminent power, the United States had to find an excuse for the lack of legitimacy of this structure and for its dominance over global affairs. For transnational capital and U.S. stewardship over the development of that capital, there is no alternative to maintaining these global relations that increase inequality and necessarily violate their own declared principles; and there is no alternative to enforcing increasingly self-evident unjust relations by means other than the compulsion of economic necessity and coercive force. For these reasons, it is necessary to have a credible threat that at once requires and justifies the violation of the very principles that capitalism asserted when it first assumed its pre-eminence on the world stage in the form of liberal democracy. The same threat becomes the reason to declare permanent war, to attempt to militarize the society that must do the enforcing, and to convince a people that it is selected for a divine purpose. [110]

Although the powers that be have few alternatives but to pursue this course, in response the people of the world have few alternatives but to resist. To succumb is not only to accept subordination to a global plutocracy but also to abandon the struggle for forms of democracy. For only so long can the threat of terror veil the lack of democracy, obscure class war, and conceal the coercive subordination of nations, peoples, classes, strata, and individuals to the demands of capital. A government can violate its own purported principles only until the majority of people understand the transgressions and their rationale for what they are. It is difficult to perform a charade when the audience can no longer suspend disbelief. The answer to the riddle of declining human rights becomes self-evident when people no longer believe the lies.

Appendix

Universal Declaration of Human Rights

Adopted and proclaimed by the United Nations General Assembly Resolution 217 A (III) of 10 December 1948

Preamble

Whereas recognition of the inherent dignity and of the equal and inalienable rights of all members of the human family is the foundation of freedom, justice and peace in the world,

Whereas disregard and contempt for human rights have resulted in barbarous acts which have outraged the conscience of mankind, and the advent of a world in which human beings shall enjoy freedom of speech and belief and freedom from fear and want has been proclaimed as the highest aspiration of the common people,

Whereas it is essential, if man is not to be compelled to have recourse, as a last resort, to rebellion against tyranny and oppression, that human rights should be protected by the rule of law,

Whereas it is essential to promote the development of friendly relations between nations,

Whereas the peoples of the United Nations have in the Charter reaffirmed their faith in fundamental human rights, in the dignity and worth of the human person and in the equal rights of men and women and have determined to promote social progress and better standards of life in larger freedoms,

Whereas member States have pledged themselves to achieve, in co-operation with the United Nations, the promotion of universal respect for and observance of human rights and fundamental freedoms,

Whereas a common understanding of these rights and freedoms is of the greatest importance for the full realization of this pledge,

Now therefore,

The General Assembly

Proclaims this Universal Declaration of Human Rights as a common standard of achievement for all peoples and all nations, to the end that every individual and every organ of society, keeping this Declaration constantly in mind, shall strive by teaching and education to promote respect for these rights and freedoms and by progressive measures, national and international, to secure their universal and effective recognition and observance, both among the peoples of member States themselves and among the peoples of territories under their jurisdiction.

Article 1

All human beings are born free and equal in dignity and rights. They are endowed with reason and conscience and should act towards one another in a spirit of brotherhood.

Article 2

1. Everyone is entitled to all the rights and freedoms set forth in this Declaration, without distinction of any kind, such as race, colour, sex, language, religion, political or other opinion, national or social origin, property, birth or other status.

2. Furthermore, no distinction shall be made on the basis of the political, jurisdictional or international status of the country or territory to which a person belongs, whether it be independent, trust, non-self-governing or under any other limitation of sovereignty.

Article 3

Everyone has the right to life, liberty and security of person.

Article 4

No one shall be held in slavery or servitude; slavery and the slave trade shall be prohibited in all their forms.

Article 5

No one shall be subjected to torture or to cruel, inhuman or degrading treatment or punishment.

Article 6

Everyone has the right to recognition everywhere as a person before the law.

Article 7

All are equal before the law and are entitled without any discrimination to equal protection of the law. All are entitled to equal protection against any discrimination in violation of this Declaration and against any incitement to such discrimination.

Article 8
Everyone has the right to an effective remedy by the competent national tribunals for acts violating the fundamental rights granted him by the constitution or by law.

Article 9
No one shall be subjected to arbitrary arrest, detention or exile.

Article 10
Everyone is entitled in full equality to a fair and public hearing by an independent and impartial tribunal, in the determination of his rights and obligations and of any criminal charge against him.

Article 11
1. Everyone charged with a penal offence has the right to be presumed innocent until proved guilty according to law in a public trial at which he has had all the guarantees necessary for his defence.

2. No one shall be held guilty of any penal offence on account of any act or omission which did not constitute a penal offence, under national or international law, at the time when it was committed. Nor shall a heavier penalty be imposed than the one that was applicable at the time the penal offence was committed.

Article 12
No one shall be subjected to arbitrary interference with his privacy, family, home or correspondence, nor to attacks upon his honour and reputation. Everyone has the right to the protection of the law against such interference or attacks.

Article 13
1. Everyone has the right to freedom of movement and residence within the borders of each State.

2. Everyone has the right to leave any country, including his own, and to return to his country.

Article 14
1. Everyone has the right to seek and to enjoy in other countries asylum from persecution.

2. This right may not be invoked in the case of prosecutions genuinely arising from non-political crimes or from acts contrary to the purposes and principles of the United Nations.

Article 15
1. Everyone has the right to a nationality.

2. No one shall be arbitrarily deprived of his nationality nor denied the right to change his nationality.

Article 16

1. Men and women of full age, without any limitation due to race, nationality or religion, have the right to marry and to found a family. They are entitled to equal rights as to marriage, during marriage and at its dissolution.

2. Marriage shall be entered into only with free and full consent of the intending spouses.

3. The family is the natural and fundamental group unit of society and is entitled to protection by society and the State.

Article 17

1. Everyone has the right to own property alone as well as in association with others.

2. No one shall be arbitrarily deprived of his property.

Article 18

Everyone has the right to freedom of thought, conscience and religion; this right includes freedom to change his religion or belief, and freedom, either alone or in community with others and in public or private, to manifest his religion or belief in teaching, practice, worship and observance.

Article 19

Everyone has the right to freedom of opinion and expression; this right includes freedom to hold opinions without interference and to seek, receive and impart information and ideas through any media and regardless of frontiers.

Article 20

1. Everyone has the right to freedom of peaceful assembly and association.

2. No one may be compelled to belong to an association.

Article 21

1. Everyone has the right to take part in the government of his country, directly or through freely chosen representatives.

2. Everyone has the right to equal access to public service in his country.

3. The will of the people shall be the basis of the authority of government; this will shall be expressed in periodic and genuine elections which shall be by universal and equal suffrage and shall be held by secret vote or by equivalent free voting procedures.

Article 22

Everyone, as a member of society, has the right to social security and is entitled to realization, through national effort and international co-operation and in accordance with the organization and resources of each State, of the economic, social and cultural rights indispensable for his dignity and the free development of his personality.

Article 23

1. Everyone has the right to work, to free choice of employment, to just and favourable conditions of work and to protection against unemployment.

2. Everyone, without any discrimination, has the right to equal pay for equal work.

3. Everyone who works has the right to just and favourable remuneration ensuring for himself and his family an existence worthy of human dignity, and supplemented, if necessary, by other means of social protection.

4. Everyone has the right to form and to join trade unions for the protection of his interests.

Article 24

Everyone has the right to rest and leisure, including reasonable limitation of working hours and periodic holidays with pay.

Article 25

1. Everyone has the right to a standard of living adequate for the health and well-being of himself and of his family, including food, clothing, housing and medical care and necessary social services, and the right to security in the event of unemployment, sickness, disability, widowhood, old age or other lack of livelihood in circumstances beyond his control.

2. Motherhood and childhood are entitled to special care and assistance. All children, whether born in or out of wedlock, shall enjoy the same social protection.

Article 26

1. Everyone has the right to education. Education shall be free, at least in the elementary and fundamental stages. Elementary education shall be compulsory. Technical and professional education shall be made generally available and higher education shall be equally accessible to all on the basis of merit.

2. Education shall be directed to the full development of the human personality and to the strengthening of respect for human rights and fundamental freedoms. It shall promote understanding, tolerance and friendship among all nations, racial or religious groups, and shall further the activities of the United Nations for the maintenance of peace.

3. Parents have a prior right to choose the kind of education that shall be given to their children.

Article 27

1. Everyone has the right freely to participate in the cultural life of the community, to enjoy the arts and to share in scientific advancement and its benefits.

2. Everyone has the right to the protection of the moral and material interests resulting from any scientific, literary or artistic production of which he is the author.

Article 28

Everyone is entitled to a social and international order in which the rights and freedoms set forth in this Declaration can be fully realized.

Article 29

1. Everyone has duties to the community in which alone the free and full development of his personality is possible.

2. In the exercise of his rights and freedoms, everyone shall be subject only to such limitations as are determined by law solely for the purpose of securing due recognition and respect for the rights and freedoms of others and of meeting the just requirements of morality, public order and the general welfare in a democratic society.

3. These rights and freedoms may in no case be exercised contrary to the purposes and principles of the United Nations.

Article 30

Nothing in this Declaration may be interpreted as implying for any State, group or person any right to engage in any activity or to perform any act aimed at the destruction of any of the rights and freedoms set forth herein.

Notes

Introduction

1. That individuals as well as states could be subjects in international law was established in the Nuremberg Tribunals after World War II.
2. Humphrey, "Universal Declaration of Human Rights."
3. For an interesting review of the continuing debate in the American Anthropological Association, see Engle, "From Skepticism to Embrace." See also Preis, "Human Rights as Cultural Practice."
4. Espiell, "Evolving Concept of Human Rights."
5. "Amnesty Puts US in the Dock over Human Rights Record," *London Telegraph*, Oct. 4, 1998. Amnesty International has a series of reports of human rights violations by state officials in the United States (see: www.web.amnesty.org). Human Rights Watch, *Unfair Advantage*; Human Rights Watch/American Civil Liberties Union, *Human Rights Violations in the United States*.
6. There is, of course, the UN High Commission on Human Rights, and similar regional and national commissions, but their mandates, budgets, and procedures do not allow for the systematic universal upholding of human rights. There is also the International Criminal Court, but its mandate and powers are highly circumscribed. See Chapter VI.
7. For a definition of "Third World," see Chapter IV, note 6.

Chapter I The Diverse Origins

1. Marshall, "Citizenship and Social Class." This seminal work poses the coming of these rights as the development of civil, political, and social "citizenship." See also Marshall, *Class, Citizenship, and Social Development*.
2. Marshall, "Citizenship and Social Class," p.74.
3. It is often asserted that civil rights are "chiefly rights *against* the state, that is, claims for individual freedoms which the state cannot invade." C.B. Macpherson, "Problems of Human Rights in the Late Twentieth Century," in his *Rise and Fall of Economic Justice*, p.23. Such a view was valid at the time of the emergence of liberal democracy, when the civil rights of the ascendant bourgeoisie had to be secured constitutionally in opposition to the monarchy, which embodied "national" property with associated arbitrary rights. To argue that civil rights stand opposed to the state today assumes the capitalist state to be rather more than what it is; it misconceives the relation between civil society and the state. Our argument sees the state as having no "content" other than the property relations of civil society, relations abstracted in the form of law and advanced and protected by the state. Civil society is the sphere of private property whose principles are expressed as civil rights and, by upholding these rights, the liberal-democratic state is defending private property and associated relations. This is its raison d'être. Such a state, however, may contradict civil rights in three main instances. First, in defending the civil rights of one class or fraction of a class against the rights of another, the state necessarily violates the rights of part of civil society in favour of another. Second, where the liberal-democratic state socializes some of the processes of capital or social reproduction (or threatens to) it is seen as a threat to civil rights and may be overturned in order to restore the premise (private property and civil rights) of liberal

democracy. Third, when a political/bureaucratic elite employs the state for its own purposes, as in fascist or state capitalist regimes, civil rights will be violated, but here we are no longer dealing with a liberal-democratic state.

4. See the American "Declaration of Independence," the French Constitution of 1793, and the Preamble to the Universal Declaration of Human Rights (see Appendix).

5. Tilly, "Emergence of Citizenship in France and Elsewhere," and Ikegami, "Citizenship and National Identity in Early Meiji Japan." See also Turner, "Citizenship and Capitalism"; Turner, ed., *Citizenship and Social Theory*.

6. A relatively recent addition to social rights is *affirmative action*. Premised on the unequal structure of civil society, affirmative action is government policy intended to offset or rectify structural inequalities, parading as the consequence of equal rights. Those who believe that civil rights are equal in reality, and not merely abstractly, oppose affirmative action as unfair – as an unfair advantage for some in a world conceived as characterized by equality. The real world, however, is patently unequal, and it is structured so, and ipso facto favours those who are privileged by wealth or ownership or position within the structure. Affirmative action is a form of privilege to counter the structural privileges disguised by abstractly equal civil rights.

7. Rosenblatt, "Legal Entitlement and Welfare Benefits."

8. Morsink, "World War Two and the Universal Declaration."

9. Moore, *Social Origins of Democracy and Dictatorship*. See also Norman, *Origins of the Modern Japanese State*.

10. Guerin, *Fascism and Big Business*; Salvemini, *Under the Axe of Fascism*; Sohn-Rethel, *Economy and Class Structure of German Fascism*; Neumann, *Behemoth*.

11. Authoritarian regimes, by contrast to totalitarian ones, are dictatorships that arise to defend the rule of capital against possible alternatives but remain subordinate to the demands of capital.

12. In 1968 the UN Conference on Human Rights adopted the Declaration of Tehran, which states: "The United Nations Declaration of Human Rights ... constitutes an obligation for the members of the International Community." See also Skogly and Gibney, "Transnational Human Rights Obligations." As with local and national laws, transnational obligations do not necessarily translate into respect for or compliance with laws and customs.

13. For a brief review of the debates regarding the covenants, see Evans, *US Hegemony and the Project of Universal Human Rights*, pp.125-32. For a description of the attempts to abort or minimize the effectiveness of this mechanism, see Robertson and Merrills, *Human Rights in the World*, pp.55-69.

14. The same can be said for the other commissions established by the European Convention for the Protection of Human Rights (1950), the American Human Rights Convention (1969), and the African Charter on Human Rights and the Rights of Peoples (1981). Between 1953 and 1969, for instance, the European Court of Human Rights "declared only 52 applications by individuals admissible out of 3,797 applications considered." Brownlie, ed., *Basic Documents on Human Rights*, p.338.

15. Forsythe, "United States and International Criminal Justice," p.976.

16. There is a large body of literature analyzing the nature of these global agencies, but there is not a lot of work that analyzes their interactions or joint effect on the world. Some of the early work remains among the best; see, for example: Hayter, *Aid as Imperialism*; Payer, *Debt Trap*; Payer, *World Bank*; George and Sabelli, *Faith and Credit*; Wallach and Sforza, *Whose Trade Organization?*; Barker and Mander, *Invisible Government*.

Chapter II The Absolutes

1. See, among many examples, Slack, "Operation Condor and Human Rights."

2. Dohnal, "Structural Adjustment Programs." See also Wallace and Sforza, *Whose Trade Organization?*

3. Many works detail the inherent violations of human rights in global trade relations. See Madeley, *Big Business, Poor Peoples*; Walton and Seddon, *Free Markets and Food Riots*; Conklin and Davidson, "The IMF and Economic and Social Human Rights."
4. UN Human Development Programme, *Human Development Report*, 1997, p.86.
5. Williams, ed., *Global Codes of Conduct*. See also Rothstein, *Global Bargaining*.
6. Blum, *Killing Hope*.
7. See, for example, Article 29 (2) of the UDHR, which recognizes the self-contradictory nature of individual exclusive rights and limits the exercise of these rights to "meeting the just requirements of morality, public order and general welfare in a democratic society."

   See also Clements and Young, "Human Rights." The authors write (p.2): "All rights are limited and may be subject to restriction. This ... is accepted in all countries which profess to protect human rights, but this is generally either implicitly understood, as in the Constitution of the United States of America, or made the subject of a general clause, reminding the users that rights are not absolute and may be subject to certain limits." (See appendix.)
8. Cook, "Women's International Human Rights Law." See also United Nations Development Programme, *Human Development Report*, 1995.
9. Pollis, "Cultural Relativism Revisited," p.330. See also Perry, "Are Human Rights Universal?" pp.481ff. At this same conference, several "Islamic states" criticized the UN and the industrial nations for their double standards, violations of human rights, neglect of certain rights, and ethnocentrism. About the same conference, *The New York Times* reported, "Washington warned 'that it would oppose any attempt to use religious and cultural traditions to weaken the concept of universal human rights.'" Quoted in Chomsky, *Umbrella of U.S. Power*, p.11.
10. Chomsky, *Deterring Democracy*, p.109.
11. *The Economist*, Feb. 8, 1992.
12. Pollis, "Cultural Relativism Revisited." See also Donnelly, "Cultural Relativism and Universal Human Rights"; Pannikar, "Is the Notion of Human Rights a Western Concept?"; and Renteln, "Unanswered Challenge of Relativism."
13. Szeftel, "Ethnicity and Democraticization in South Africa," pp.187-88.
14. Petras and Morley, *United States and Chile*; Johnson, ed., *Chilean Road to Socialism*.
15. See various articles in Tomas, ed., *Collective Human Rights of Pacific Peoples*. For a good overview of the evolution (hence relativism) of indigenous rights, see Stamatopoulou, "Indigenous Peoples and the United Nations."
16. The U.S. ambassador to the UN, J. Kirkpatrick, referred to social rights as "a letter to Santa Claus." Cited in Chomsky, "Umbrella of U.S. Power," p.21.
17. For a somewhat similar view, see Donnelly, "Social Construction of International Human Rights," pp.80-85. For one of the better arguments on the relativity of human rights, see Pollis and Schwab, "Human Rights: A Western Construct with Limited Applicability."

Chapter III The Contradictions

1. American Convention on Human Rights, 1969, in Brownlie, ed., *Basic Documents on Human Rights*, p.413. Implicitly, Article 29 (2) of the UDHR recognizes this point by acknowledging the need for legal protection for "the rights and freedoms of others." (See appendix.)
2. For some of the arguments in this section, see Tushnet, "Corporations and Free Speech"; Friedmann, *Legal Theory* (especially ch. 26, "Theories of Corporate Personality and Legal Practice"); Berle and Means, *Modern Corporation and Private Property*; Berle, *20th Century Capitalist Revolution*; and Scott, *Corporations, Classes, and Capitalism*.
3. The poorer people are, the more their civil rights to possessions are usurped by corporations. See Hudson, ed., *Merchants of Misery*.

4. In the United States this point has led to a call for the circumscription of the power of corporations and the assertion of a populist belief in a "return" to a mythical past of a government by, for, and of the "people." See Program on Corporations, Law and Democracy <www.poclad.org>. Even if we allow for a reality behind the myth, because of competition private property, no matter how small and dispersed, always moves in the direction of greater monopolies. The state of corporate rule that now exists is the inevitable consequence of a system of private property.

5. Analysts have long made the connection between militarism and the violation or denial or paucity of human rights, but unless they also understand the contradictory nature of the rights that constitute human rights they have trouble grasping the growing conflict between military expenditures and human rights. W.F. Felice ably outlines "the enduring tension between militarism and human rights" but cannot fathom why it not only endures but also grows. Felice, "Militarism and Human Rights."

6. Article II reads: "A well regulated Militia, being necessary to the security of a free State, the right of the people to keep and bear Arms shall not be infringed." Although the wording is somewhat ambiguous, the subject is clearly the militia; and the article would appear to be a reference to the arms required by a militia, in an age without a standing military or police force, and not to a right extended to all individuals as such.

7. Small-arms trafficking exists in conjunction with the widespread military training of both regular and irregular armed forces. Mercenary groups, death squads, and paramilitary units often act as the defenders of corporate rights, organized and financed by, but without direct links to, governments or corporations.

8. See various reports from Project Underground <www.moles.org>.

9. Conservative political commentators understand that a contradiction exists here, but they do not grasp why or what it reflects. The reformist left has little or no understanding of this point, believing that these two categories of right are compatible. See Cranston, "What Are Human Rights?"; and compare with Marshall, "Citizenship and Social Class."

10. Even in jurisdictions governed by supposedly democratic states, political rights may be suppressed or restricted to allow for the most advantageous conditions for capital accumulation. Hong Kong under the British is the most obvious example. And even as China enters the global market, the concern of Western governments about human rights in China is over the guarantee for corporate civil rights – political rights help in this guarantee, but social rights are by and large secondary.

11. Greider, "Right and US Trade Law"; Public Citizen, "NAFTA, Chapter 11."

12. *The Economist*, Nov. 4, 2000, p.68.

13. See Deckard, *Women's Movement*, pp.7-8. Here are a few of the passages she has drawn out: from the Old Testament, Genesis 2-3, "And thy desire shall be to thy husband, and he shall rule over thee"; and Job 25:4, "How can he be clean that is born of a woman?"; from an Orthodox Jewish prayer, "Blessed art Thou, oh Lord our God ... that I was not born a woman"; from the Koran, "Men are superior to women on account of the qualities in which God has given them pre-eminence"; from the Hindu Code of Manu, "In childhood a woman must be subject to her father; in youth to her husband; when her husband is dead, to her sons. A woman must never be free of subjugation"; from a Confucian saying, "Such is the stupidity of woman's character, that it is incumbent upon her, in every particular, to distrust herself and to obey her husband."

14. All sorts of grave abuses of human rights are regularly committed today in the name of religion. In the name of Islam, certain transgressors can be stoned to death, hands and feet can be amputated, and public beheadings carried out. In the name of maintaining a Jewish state, Israelis have legalized torture, carried out systematic assassinations, meted out collective punishments, and killed and maimed thousands of children. The Catholic Church, among other things, has systematically worked to deny women around the world access to abortion and birth control.

15. *The Independent*, April 28, 2001.

16. "The sexual abuse scandal engulfing the Roman Catholic Church, far from being nearly over, has only begun," stated one account. "The hierarchy regularly moved accused priests from parish to parish, treated victims without compassion, used lay offerings for legal fees and lawsuits, and systematically covered-up." "As Scandal Keeps Growing, Church and Its Faithful Reel," *The New York Times*, March 17, 2002.

17. Israeli Information Center for Human Rights <www.btselem.org>; Rabbis for Human Rights <www.rhr.israel.net>; Israeli Women for Peace <www.batshalom.org>.

18. Inter-Parliamentary Union, "Women in National Parliaments" web site.

19. Dines, Jensen, and Russo, *Pornography*.

20. Other sources of the data for these assertions come from: United Nations Population Fund, *State of the World's Population 2000*; Fraser, "Becoming Human"; Cook, "Women's International Human Rights Law"; Charlesworth, "What Are 'Women's International Human Rights'?"; Russell and Van de Ven, eds., *Crimes against Women*.

21. "UNFPA: Report Paints Grim Picture for World's Women," press release, UN Wire, Sept. 20, 2000.

22. World Conference of the United Nations for Women, Copenhagen, 1980.

23. United Nations, *Human Development Report*, 1995, pp.iii, 2, 6. The authors of this report state (p.6): "A major index of neglect is that many of women's economic contributions are grossly undervalued or not valued at all – on the order of $11 trillion a year."

24. Scott, *Does Socialism Liberate Women?*.

25. In revolutions made in the name of the people, women had their lot improved but they never did find genuine equality in all rights because of one form or another of patriarchy. See Tetreault, ed., *Women and Revolution in Africa, Asia, and the New World*. On the Chinese revolution, see Maloney, "Women in the Chinese Communist Revolution"; and Crook and Crook, *Revolution in a Chinese Village*. See also Farnsworth, "Communism and Feminism"; and Casal, "Revolution and Consciencia," both in *Women, War, and Revolution*, ed. Berkin and Lovett.

26. The early rubric of "the woman question" made the victim of male/female inequality, rather than the cause, into the object of analysis. "The woman question" should really have been phrased as "the question of patriarchy" or "the question of gender inequality."

27. Equal rights for one part of a population to the exclusion of another creates "equal rights" for the former as a privilege. The achievement of universal male suffrage without female suffrage, as an obvious example, constituted enfranchisement as a privilege for men.

28. Even the earliest of the national declarations of liberal-democratic rights (in the United States and France) referred implicitly only to men; women were not granted equal rights despite the language of universality in those declarations. None of the other bourgeois revolutions of the eighteenth and nineteenth centuries conferred equal rights to men and women. Not until the twentieth century (with minor exceptions) and, for the most part, the second half of the twentieth century did the women in the capitalist liberal-democratic nations find even the formalities of equality of right, accompanied by certain concessions in practice.

29. Fraser, "Becoming Human," pp.857, 888. For another discussion of this point, see Charlesworth, "What Are 'Women's International Human Rights'?" p.68.

30. Humphrey, *Human Rights and the United Nations*.

31. Hevener, *International Law and the Status of Women*.

32. United Nations, World Conference on Human Rights, "Vienna Declaration and Programme of Action," June 25, 1993.

33. Similar but more recent struggles have been fought in Europe within the European Commission of Human Rights and European Court of Human Rights, in Latin America within the Inter-American Commission on Human rights, and in Africa within the African Charter of Human and Peoples Rights (1981). On Latin America see, Medina, "Toward a More Effective Guarantee of the Enjoyment of Human Rights by Women in the Inter-American System"; and on Africa, see Beyani, "Toward a More Effective Guarantee of

Women's Rights in the African Human Rights System." See also United Nations, *United Nations and the Advancement of Women*.

34. Amnesty International, "20th Anniversary of Women's Convention."

35. Aslanbeigui, Pressman, and Summerfield, eds., *Women in the Age of Economic Transformation*; Kuenyehia, "Impact of Structural Adjustment Programs on Women's International Human Rights"; Adu-Kofi, "Impact of the International Monetary Fund and the World Bank's Structural Adjustment Policies."

36. When women struggle for more *social rights*, they are challenging the principles of the system, but then these rights are not necessarily specific to women.

37. For a good analysis of how women are "discounted," see Waring, *Counting for Nothing*.

38. Undervalued labour refers to labour-power that receives a wage or salary insufficient to allow for the social reproduction of the recipient (and dependants) in a manner to maintain his/her given knowledge, skills, health, and well-being.

39. From the late 1960s to its defeat in 1982, the Equal Rights Amendment (ERA) dominated the women's rights movement in the United States. This seemingly innocuous proposed amendment to the U.S. Constitution ("Equality of rights under the law shall not be denied or abridged by the United States or by any State on account of sex.") had been introduced as an amendment "in every session of Congress since 1923," but the concerted effort in the 1970s failed to achieve its adoption after it met with massive well-financed resistance. Underlying the debates about the many laws discriminatory against women was the issue of pay equity. See Deckard, *Women's Movement*.

About the same time in Europe the issue of equal pay met with similar resistance. In 1976 the EEC Court of Justice ruled that "only workers with cases actually pending" could appeal for enforcement of the Treaty of Rome provisions on retroactive equal pay. Two governments made the reason clear: the British government warned that predating equal pay might "overturn the economic and social situation in the UK"; and the Irish government stated that the costs "would constitute a burden on the Irish economy which it would not be in a position to bear." See *Financial Times*, April 9, 1976, and *The Sunday Times*, April 11, 1976.

These statements suggest the enormous importance of women's undervalued (and unpaid) labour to corporate viability – or to the "economy." Just why women should bear this burden through unequal pay is not addressed.

40. After the means of production are socialized, among the first acts in transforming society is to restrict the laws of inheritance and to begin to socialize the domestic realm.

41. The Preamble to the Convention on the Rights of the Child (1989) states, following assertions about the primacy of the institution of the family, that "the child should be fully prepared to live an *individual* life in society" (my emphasis).

42. If the nuclear family were "natural" and "fundamental," it is not clear why it would need to be "protected" by the state – unless it were to ensure its role in reproducing the system as a system of private property and to protect it against the socialization of its functions.

43. One of the "first defining moments" of the new President Bush in 2001 was "a ban on [U.S.] funds for any international family planning organizations that even dare to give women information about abortion." *Guardian Weekly*, Feb. 1-7, 2001. Another of his "first official acts was to propose that religiously sponsored organizations should get public money to provide social services." *The New York Times Book Review*, March 25, 2001.

44. See United Nations Population Fund, *State of the World Population 2000* , ch. 3; von Struensee, "Globalized, Wired, Sex Trafficking in Women and Children"; Global Alliance against Traffic in Women.

45. Reed, *Woman's Evolution*, pp.428ff.

46. This resistance includes the United Nations, if in no other way than through its neglect of the issue. In Afghanistan, for instance, when the Taliban forces between 1995 and 2000 had conquered most of the country and stripped women of their public roles in society and subjected them to a strict and brutal subordination to men, allegedly in adherence to Islamic

law, the United Nations found itself able to mount relief efforts for Afghan refugees and to impose a U.S.-sponsored Security Council resolution in 2000 with diplomatic and political sanctions for the regime's alleged support of Washington's most wanted international "terrorist," Osama bin Laden, but the UN did not take similar action to counter the harsh suppression of women that had become the subject of worldwide condemnation.

47. Part of the Preamble of the Convention on the Rights of the Child states: "Convinced that the family, as the fundamental group of society and the natural environment for the growth and well-being of all its members and particularly children, should be afforded the necessary protection and assistance so that it can fully assume its responsibilities within the community." And another part states, "The child should be prepared to live an individual life in society." The Convention can be found on the United Nations High Commissioner for Human Rights web site.

48. In particular, the notion of "the best interests of the child" that appears in the Convention on the Rights of the Child allows state authorities to make judgments regarding the well-being of the child in opposition to the rights of the parents. This impingement on the rights of the parents was one of the reasons for the U.S. refusal to ratify the Convention of the Rights of the Child. In 1999, with qualifications, the U.S. ratified the Convention.

49. Amnesty International, "Hidden Scandal, Secret Shame." This report notes that while torture and ill treatment take place commonly in detention centres and juvenile homes, "the most dangerous place for children can be their home, where they should be safest.... They are more likely to be beaten, sexually abused, abducted or subjected to harmful traditional practices or mental violence by family members than by anyone else."

50. See Hawes, *Children's Rights Movement*; Gross and Gross, eds., *Children's Rights Movement*; and Marx, *Capital*, vol.1, p. 620.

51. This need for children's rights in opposition to, or in the absence of, parental rights arises only in systems of private property. Theoretically, in societies characterized by socialized capital, the need for rights of this sort are subsumed in the fact of socialized wealth that obviates social reproduction through the institution of the nuclear family and gives everyone access to the socialized means of personal development.

52. ILO Convention 182 is formally entitled "Convention Concerning the Prohibition and Immediate Action for the Elimination of the Worst Forms of Child Labour," June 1999. The full text may be found in the ILO magazine *World of Work*, no. 30 (1999).

53. The rights to free elementary education and "health and well-being" are everywhere being circumscribed and compromised by the introduction of neo-liberal policies.

54. ILO, *World of Work*, no.22 (1997), p.18.

55. This would include family enterprises, seasonal work, "home work," street trades, prostitution, and so on.

56. See various issues of ILO, *World of Work*, no.16 (1996), no.22 (1997), no.30 (1999), no.37 (2000). See also ILO, *Child Labour: Targeting the Intolerable*.
It must be acknowledged that considerable ambiguity exists surrounding the definition of "child" and "labour" in these UN and ILO documents. The ambiguity may well stem from a reluctance to admit to the enormity of the problem. It is not difficult, however, to provide acceptable definitions: according to UN documents, a child is anyone not over the age of majority, which for the UN is eighteen; and labour in a capitalist mode of production refers only to work that is directly or indirectly subordinate to an employer. For an interesting discussion of some of these issues, see Smolin, "Strategic Choices in the International Campaign against Child Labour."

57. Freeman, "Introduction: Children as Persons," p.2.

58. Ibid., p.1.

59. Ennew, "Outside Childhood," p.202. She writes: "It is no coincidence, I would claim, that the Convention on the Rights of the Child was drafted during the same decade as an unprecedented increase in interest in groups of children called 'street children.'"

In 1985 the Brazilian Movement of Street Children was formed, and in 1986 a national meeting of street children was convened in Brazilia; in 1989 a second one took place.

60. Ibid., pp.210-13.

61. The Convention defines the "worst forms of child labour" as slavery or slave-like practices, exploitation in prostitution or pornography, use in illicit activities, and work that might harm children's health, safety, or morals.

62. These same points can be found in the earlier ILO conventions on child labour, the most comprehensive of which was the Minimum Age Convention of 1973. That document instituted a variable minimum age reaching down to twelve for some kinds of work in countries with a "struggling economy." Despite its lax standards, the 1973 Convention failed to be ratified by the majority of the world's governments. The nations in Asia with the largest number of child labourers did not sign.

63. Wallach and Sforza, *Whose Trade Organization?* p.172.

64. UN Committee on the Rights of the Child, "State Violence Against Children." Almost one-half of all U.S. states allow the death penalty for those under eighteen – a practice outlawed in the UN Convention on Children, and one reason that the United States has refused, along with Somalia, to ratify the Convention. This U.S. position was reasserted by the Bush II administration in 2002 when Washington insisted that the UN General Assembly Special Session on Children, in May 2002, not endorse a call for "reproductive health services" because that might be construed to include abortion or sex education beyond promoting abstinence and to imply opposition to the death penalty for minors.

Other reasons for the U.S. refusal to sign might include the U.S. position as the country with the highest rate of adolescent industrial accidents in the developed world; it has an estimated 800,000 children under sixteen working in the agricultural sector, and the Convention stresses a state responsibility to ensure the rights to health, welfare, and education where parents are unable to provide. For some of these points, see National Consumers League, "Child Labour Abuses Remain a Problem in the U.S.," press release, February 1999.

65. Amnesty International, *Hidden Scandal, Secret Shame*. In 2002 the UN estimated that about 300,000 children were engaged in fighting wars. *The New York Times*, May 8, 2002.

66. For an examination of some of these issues, see Arat, "Analyzing Child Labour as a Human Rights Issue."

67. The assertion of the universality of individual rights in the UDHR contradicts the sovereignty of the state and so then a fundamental premise of the Charter and UDHR.

68. Under the League of Nations, the colonial territories of the nations defeated in World War I were divided among the victorious nations in the form of "mandates" or "protectorates" – to be ruled by the new colonial power, albeit with vague provisos to move the "protected" peoples towards independence.

69. All UN peacekeeping operations have by and large resulted in strategic advantages for the United States, a point on which most commentators agree. In 1969 the U.S. United Nations Association reported: "Each UN peacekeeping operation to date has ... been clearly in the United States' interests." U.S. United Nations Association, *Controlling Conflicts in the 1970s*, p.48. J. Stoessinger stated: "The main reason why the Americans have been the chief supporters of the peace-keeping functions is because each and every one of these fourteen UN operations has been a direct extension of the American national interest." Stoessinger, "Payments Dispute," p.29. And A.M. Cox concurred: "The U.S. commitment to UN peacekeeping has been extensive not for altruistic reasons, but because these operations have served the national interest." Cox, *Prospects for Peacekeeping*, pp.9-10.

70. Brownlie, ed., *Basic Documents on Human Rights*, p.113. No country voted against this resolution, but nine abstained – among them all the former colonial powers except Holland; namely, Portugal, Spain, United Kingdom, United States, Belgium, and France.

71. Green, *Taking Sides*; see also Haim, *Quicksand*; and Chomsky, "Israel's Role in US Foreign Policy."

72. The numerous postcolonial attempts at socialism in Africa are often forgotten today in the midst of the current widespread destruction. See, for example, Friedland and Rosberg, eds., *African Socialism*; Rosberg and Callaghy, eds., *Socialism in Sub-Saharan Africa*; Muslow, ed., *Africa*; and Ottaway and Ottaway, *Afro-Communism*.

73. Blum, *Killing Hope* (p.209 for the quote by Kissinger); Agee and Wolf, eds., *Dirty Work*; Petras and Morley, *United States and Chile*; Ray et al., eds., *Dirty Work 2*. The United States, in particular, has had its hand in the formation and maintenance of almost every dictatorship since World War II; increasingly it cannot deny its role. See Herman and Brodhead, *Demonstration Elections*; Chomsky and Herman, *Political Economy of Human Rights*, vol.1; Herman and Sullivan, *"Terrorism" Industry*; Bar-Joseph, *Intelligence Intervention in the Politics of Democratic States*.

74. The enabling framework has since evolved and continues to do so. Today certain broad policy matters are determined by the heads of the major national governments in the G-3/7/8 forums. Matters of supranational regulation, policy formation, standardization, and credit facilitation, for example, are dealt with by several agencies, such as the UN, WTO, IMF, World Bank, Organization for Economic Cooperation and Development (OECD), and Bank for International Settlements (BIS). Common markets or trading blocs such as the European Union (EU), North American Free Trade Agreement (NAFTA), and MERCOSUR (Common Market of the South) establish supranational control over many economic issues. Other multilateral agreements such as OPEC and UNCTAD commodity agreements also pre-empt national control over the production and distribution of key staples. International law has become well established, and increasingly national law must conform or submit to its principles. Bilateral and multilateral military pacts more or less complete the picture of a global system controlled beyond the powers of the nation-state.

75. Noam Chomsky does not question human rights in and of themselves or, indeed, the United States as a model of liberal democracy. In his article "The United States and the Challenge of Relativity," he states (p.24) that the United States "has the most stable and long standing democratic institutions and unparalleled advantages in every sphere, including the economy and security concerns.... It has long been as good a model as one can find of a sociopolitical order in which basic rights are upheld." And later (p.51): "The USA is a world leader in defense of freedom of speech, perhaps uniquely so since the 1960s. With regard to civil-political rights, the U.S. record at home ranks high by comparative standards." This position would likely not be shared, in the past or present, with Afro-Americans, Native peoples, trade unionists, Hispanic immigrants, or large parts of the working class.

Chomsky's incisive and principled critique of U.S. foreign policy can only be praised, although much of it remains on the level of exposing the atrocities and hypocrisy of the United States and the West. The point, however, is to explain the hypocrisy; and then the problematic nature of human rights can begin to be exposed. Chomsky appears to hold the position that human rights are universal and that the United States is exemplary in upholding them domestically, despite some shortcomings. Such a position does not alter his trenchant critique of the United States abroad, but it is counterproductive to understanding the limited nature of human rights. Chomsky, "The United States and the Challenge of Relativity," in *Human Rights Fifty Years On: A Reappraisal*, ed. T. Evans, 1998.

Chapter IV Rights Outside Capitalist Relations

1. This argument rests on the work of Charles Bettelheim; see his *Economic Calculation and Forms of Property*; and *Transition to Socialist Economy*. For a good review of the debate on the character of the Soviet political economy, see Bellis, *Marxism and the USSR*.

2. Because organized religion in Eastern Europe remained separate from the party and state and as a remnant of pre-revolutionary civil society, it was well placed to become involved in the demands for capitalist political and civil rights that parade as universal and inalienable human rights.

3. For an interesting analysis of the USSR along these lines, see Lefort, "Politics and Human Rights," and "Logic of Totalitarianism."

4. For a review of the accord, see Robertson, "Helsinki Agreement and Human Rights."

5. There was always some truth to this claim. The whole point of the Cold War, the arm's race, ever-present espionage, and the formation of NATO in the late 1940s was to counter and undermine the existence of socialism.

6. To be sure, the concept of Third World as used here remains rather broad, but then again it has a more precise meaning than many other concepts used to delineate the countries of the less industrialized part of the world. The concept of "North/South" is certainly suggestive but hardly exact; and the notions of "underdevelopment" and "less developed countries" obscure the effects of colonialism and the biases of global trade regimes and national indebtedness. For the time being, the definition of Third World used here continues to have a corresponding reality; but in due course there may be no differentiated "worlds," that is, no significant notion of a national economy, just global classes in a global economy.

7. Harris, *New Untouchables* and *End of the Third World*; Foerstal, ed., *Creating Surplus Populations*.

8. See Mandela, *Struggle Is My Life*. About the ANC's Freedom Charter, Mandela wrote (pp.173, 180): "It is by no means a blueprint for a socialist state. It calls for redistribution, but not for nationalization, of land; it provides for nationalization of mines, banks and monopoly industry, because big monopolies are owned by one race only, and without such nationalization racial domination would be perpetuated despite the spread of political power.... Under the Freedom Charter, nationalization would take place in an economy based on private enterprise.... The ANC has never at any period of its history advocated a revolutionary change in the economic structure of the country, nor has it, ever condemned capitalist society.... Above all, we want equal political rights."

   Mandela, like Nkrumah, Nyerere, Kenyata, Mugabe, and others, led an organized resistance movement against forms of colonial domination, but in the end their efforts were sabotaged or the possibilities for real change for the people were exchanged for the illusion of democracy in the form of human rights, party politics, and personal wealth and power for a few Africans within a system of private property controlled, by and large, by former colonists and often foreign interests.

9. Adam and Moodley, *Opening of the Apartheid Mind*; and Adam, Van Syl Slabbert, and Moodley, *Comrades in Business*.

10. Chomsky and Herman made this point many years ago. Indeed, they faced publishing difficulties for writing this statement: "The leadership in the United States, as a result of its dominant position and wide-ranging counterrevolutionary efforts, has been the most important single instigator of serious bloodbaths in the years that followed World War II." Chomsky and Herman, *Political Economy of Human Rights*, vol.1, p.xiv.

    There is much written on the role of U.S. foreign policy and the overriding of human rights. See, for example: Brown, *With Friends Like These*; Lernoux, *Cry of the People*; Mower, *Human Rights and American Foreign Policy*; and Wright, *Destruction of a Nation*.

11. See, for example, Cohen, Hyden, and Nugan, eds., *Human Rights and Governance in Africa*; and Shepard and Ankipo, eds., *Emerging Human Rights*. For an interesting critique of such arguments, see Howard, "African Concept of Human Rights?"; and Cobbah, "African Values and the Human Rights Debate."

12. One of the earliest books to make this case is Davidson, *Lost Cities of Africa*. See also Wolpe, ed., *Articulation of Modes of Production*; and Crummey and Stewart, eds., *Modes of Production in Africa*.

13. Fitch and Oppenheimer, *Ghana*.

14. For an overview of the destructive role of the United States in providing massive amounts of arms and military training to the majority of African countries, see Hartung and Moix, "Deadly Legacy." See also Wright, *Destruction of a Nation*; Ray, ed., *Dirty Work 2*.

    For a critical review of what passes for democratic constitutions in Africa, see Ihonvbere, "How to Make an Undemocratic Constitution: The Nigerian Example." For examples of continuing interference in African affairs by the former colonial countries, see Ogbu and Akunna, "Nigeria"; and various Amnesty International reports: "Africa and the G8," "Britons Involved in Africa Gun-Running," "Canada, Oil and Sudan," "Following the Oil: French Arms Deals in Africa," "Italian Arms Fuel African Suffering," "The USA and Rwanda," "Russian Weapons Fuel African Conflicts." <amnesty.org>.

15. Quoted in Ray, "NAFTA for Africa and the National Summit on Africa," p.14.

16. For sceptical views on this "new partnership," see Bond, ed., *Fanon's Warning.*

17. See, for instance, Human Rights Watch, "Double Standards." For an excellent analysis of one aspect of the fate of women in Africa, see Ewelukwa, "Post-Colonialism, Gender and Customary Injustice."

18. The attempt also casts light on the efforts of the International Commission of Jurists, largely U.S.-funded, urging the newly independent African (and Asian) states in the late 1950s and early 1960s to adopt the principle of "rule of law." At the African Conference on the Rule of Law, in Lagos in 1961, it was stressed that individual rights were all-important and that the rule of law was the principal means for their protection. In individual rights and rule of law are the ethical/legal foundations of capitalism, that is, subordination to the principles of private property – a set of premises distinctly different from the premises of socialism or various forms of indigenous communalism. See Brownlie, ed., *Basic Documents on Human Rights*, p.440.

19. See the web site for the Organization of African Unity. For a review of human rights practice in Africa, see Allain and O'Shea, "African Disunity." With respect to the rights in the African Charter, the authors conclude (p.124) that African states have "united in their failure to implement these same rights." This "failure" in Africa is little different throughout the Third World and increasingly in the industrial world.

20. African Union 2002: Documents and Speeches.

21. Arzt, "Religious Human Rights in Muslim States of the Middle East and North Africa," p.1.

22. For a good review of this question, see Afshari, "Essay on Islamic Cultural Relativism in the Discourse of Human Rights."

23. Amnesty International, "Broken Lives"; Chomsky, *Fateful Triangle*; Green, *Taking Sides*; Said, *Question of Palestine*, and *Politics of Dispossession*; Lockman and Beinin, eds., *Intifada.*

24. After World War I, with the collapse of the Ottoman Empire, not one Middle East country was without external interference in its affairs. For a good review of many of these interventions, see *Press for Conversion!* Issue no.51, "The U.S. Role in Wars and Regime Changes in the Middle East and North Africa since World War II"; and Quigley, *Ruses for War.*

25. Blum, *CIA.*

26. Bakhash, *Reign of the Ayatollahs.*

27. Nasr, *Ideals and Realities of Islam,* pp.106-7.

28. Rodinson, *Islam and Capitalism*; Ahmad, "Islam, Market Economy and the Rule of Law." Ahmad contends that the Koran does not oppose the market and indeed has been consistent with clearing away the impediments to commercial exchange. See also Ahmad, "Islam and Hayek."

29. See, for instance, Tarock, "Politics of the Pipeline."

30. Mayer, *Islam and Human Rights*. Mayer writes (pp.53-54): "The authors [of Islamic human rights] lack any clear theory of what rights should mean in an Islamic context or how to derive their content from Islamic sources in a consistent and principled fashion." Of course, there should be no illusions that human rights are free of debate over interpretation.

31. Amnesty International, "Arab Convention for the Suppression of Terrorism."

32. Eshghipour, "Islamic Revolution's Impact on the Legal and Social Status of Iranian Women."

33. R.J. Aldrich, "America Used Islamists to Arm the Bosnian Muslims," *The Guardian*, April 22, 2002; R. Olivier, "Fundamentalists without a Common Cause," *Le Monde Diplomatique* (English edition), October 1998.

34. The interpretation of religious tenets evolves in relation to social and economic change, and this is no less true for Islam than for other religions. In recent times, it is said, Islam has been in the midst of "the Islamic Reformation," and Muslim countries are widely debating the case for democratizing and modernizing Islam. For an interesting review of this "reformation," see Eickelmann, "Inside the Islamic Reformation." See also An-Na'im, *Toward an Islamic Reformation*; Mayer, *Islam and Human Rights*; and Tibi, "Islamic Law/Shari'a, Human Rights, Universal Morality and International Relations."

35. The higher figure comes from Clay, "Looking Back to Go Forward," p.67. The International Labour Organization uses the number of 300 million "indigenous and tribal peoples" – this is a conservative estimate, but no universally accepted definition and no authoritative census exist. See *World of Work*, no.40 (August 2001), p.14.

36. For a good review of the current status of the rights of Aboriginal peoples, see Wickliffe, "Overview of Collective Human Rights in the Pacific Region."

37. See Article 1 of the 1993 Draft Declaration on the Rights of Indigenous Peoples. For a good review of some of the key difficulties in the draft and other UN positions on Aboriginal peoples, see Corntassel and Primeau, "Indigenous 'Sovereignty' and International Law."

38. Shiva, *Biopiracy*, and *Protect or Plunder?*

39. Gedicks, *New Resource Wars*; Wadden, *Nitassinan*; Leger, *Aboriginal Peoples*; Foerstel, ed., *Creating Surplus Populations*.

40. A review of some of these cases can be found in Miller, ed., *State of the Peoples*; Dyck, ed., *Indigenous Peoples and the Nation-State*.

41. A good survey of the continuing history of "enclosures" of common property can be found in *The Ecologist*, "Whose Common Future?"

42. Barsh, "Indigenous Peoples and the UN Commission on Human Rights."

43. Sengupta, "On the Theory and Practice of the Right to Development."

44. This is a reference to the multilayered bargaining that surrounded the proposal for the New International Economic Order and the Charter of the Economic Rights and Duties of States, both adopted by the UN General Assembly in 1974. See Rothstein, *Global Bargaining*; and Ferguson, "Third World."

Chapter V The Curious Unanimity

1. Moynihan, "Politics of Human Rights," p.33. For a more critical view of the U.S. position on social rights, see Alston, "U.S. Ratification of the Covenant on Economic, Social and Cultural Rights."

2. Tomuschat, "Clarification Commission in Guatemala."

3. Examples can be found around the world. Nigeria under the generals gave full rights to Shell Oil while persecuting the Ogoni people. The Mexican state helped to suppress the indigenous people of Chiapas while giving rights to ranchers and mining and lumber companies. Burma has used coerced labour to build roads and pipelines for Western gas and mining companies, while attacking indigenous groups and allowing the destruction of the environment. The Canadian provincial and federal states ignore or override Innu rights with military exercises and the granting of rights to mining and oil companies.

4. *The Economist*, Dec. 11, 1999. For a broad, uncritical overview of the history and rationale of NGOs, see: Korey, *NGOs and the Declaration of Human Rights*.

5. For a trenchant and critical appraisal of the relation between neo-liberalism and the proliferation of NGOs, see Petras, "Imperialism and NGOs in Latin America," and "NGOs in the Service of Imperialism."

6. For an interesting short survey of the concept of NGO, see Gudynas, "NGOs Facing Democracy and Globalization."

7. See Alston, "U.S. Ratification of the Covenant on Economic, Social and Cultural Rights," pp.389-92. Human Rights Watch and Washington have adopted this position despite the 1968 Proclamation of Tehran (International Conference on Human Rights), which declared: "Since human rights and fundamental freedoms are indivisible, the full realization of civil and political rights without the enjoyment of economic, social and cultural rights is impossible." The 1986 UN Declaration of the Right to Development, moreover, integrated these three aspects of human rights. The United States was the only nation to vote against it. Sengupta, "On the Theory and Practice of the Right to Development," pp.839-40.

8. Thomas, "Helsinki Accords and Political Change in Eastern Europe," p.205.

9. Dixon, ed., *On Trial*.

10. Brownlie, ed., *Basic Documents on Human Rights*, pp.387-88.

11. Given the central role of the U.S. government in the violation of human rights in the United States and around the world, directly or through surrogates, it is not a difficult argument to make that socially and politically aware citizens of the United States should see no other task before them other than the critical analysis of their own government. In this regard, Noam Chomsky, Ralph Nader, Edward Herman, and Michael Parenti, among others, whatever their limits, have led the way. By contrast, U.S. human rights NGOs such as HRW have only recently and cautiously turned their attention to their own country. See Human Rights Watch, "Unfair Advantage." See also Amnesty International, "United States of America: Rights for All."

12. Human Rights Watch, "Cuba's Repressive Machinery."

13. The "Cuban Liberty and Democratic Act," or the Helms-Burton Act, of 1996 is more or less universally recognized as contravening international law. HRW, however, does not address the illegal acts committed by the U.S. government or its agencies. For a review of Helms-Burton, see Stern, "How to Regulate Globalization."

14. Such a critique remains on the level of measuring the disjuncture between theory and practice; it does not pretend to ask why there is such discontinuity or why theory and practice in liberal democracy can never be matched.

15. To help them get started, we suggest the following. On the FBI, see Blackstock, *COINTELPRO*; Gelbspan, *Break-ins, Death Threats and the FBI*; Goldstein, *Political Repression in Modern America*; Keller, *Liberals and J. Edgar Hoover*; Washburn, *Question of Sedition*; Foerstal, *Surveillance in the Stacks*; Robins, *Alien Link*; Davis, *Assault on the Left*; Theoharis and Cox, *Boss*; Olmsted, *Challenging the Secret Government*; Diamond, *Compromised Campus*.

On the CIA, see Johnson, *America's Secret Power*; Rodriguez, *Bay of Pigs and the CIA*; Marchetti and Marks, *CIA and the Cult of Intelligence*; Immerman, *CIA in Guatemala*; Nutter, *CIA's Black Ops*; Chester, *Covert Network*; Ray, ed., *Dirty Work 2*; CIA, *CIA Targets Fidel*; Westerfield, ed., *Inside CIA's Private World*; Buncher, ed., *CIA and the Security Debate*; Wise and Ross, *Invisible Government*; Wise, *American Police State*; U.S. Congress, Senate Select Committee to Study Government Operations with Respect to Intelligence Activities: Covert Action in Chile, 1963-1973.

16. This list was drawn from the Statute of Amnesty International, Cape Town, 1997. The facts were taken from Amnesty International, "Facts and Figures."

17. Amnesty International, "Facts and Figures," p.10 (emphasis added).

18. Paraphrased from Amnesty International, "Statute of Amnesty International," and "Brief History."

19. Power, *Against Oblivion*, p.39.

20. Amnesty International, "Brief History," p.2.

21. See Blum, *Killing Hope*; Chomsky, *Deterring Democracy*; and Agee and Wolfe, eds., *Dirty Work*.

22. Mandela, *Struggle Is My Life*, p.166.

23. The Vienna Declaration shifted the intent of this preamble when it stated: "Taking into account the particular situation of peoples under colonial or other forms of alien domination or foreign occupation, the World Conference on Human Rights recognizes the right of peoples *to take any legitimate action*, in accordance with the Charter of the United Nations, to realize their inalienable right of self-determination." (Emphasis added.) The right to act against violations of political rights apparently has to be taken up in a legitimate manner; resistance against an illegal government, or government committing illegal acts, has to be done legally. If there were any doubt as to this point, the Vienna Declaration states clearly: "The World Conference on Human Rights also deplores the continuing acts of violence aimed at undermining the quest for a peaceful dismantling of apartheid." It did not deplore the continuing acts of violence that were apartheid itself.

24. "Amnesty Puts US in the Dock over Human Rights Record," *London Telegraph*, Oct. 4, 1998.

25. AI began belatedly to make reports on the question of women's rights as "human rights," but it has done so within its framework of prisoners of conscience and violations of civil and political rights. See Amnesty International, "Women on the Front Line." Still, AI has made no statement on the violation of social rights as human rights.

26. Hayner, "Fifteen Truth Commissions"; Ensalaco, "Truth Commission for Chile and El Salvador"; Adam, "Divided Memories."

Chapter VI The Future of Human Rights

1. Although the high degree of comprehensiveness of this framework has often gone unnoticed, several authors have been reviewing and summarizing it for some time. See, for instance, these early assessments: Jacobson, *Networks of Interdependence*; and various articles in Jutte and Grosse-Jutte, eds., *Future of International Organization*.

2. Cutler, "Global Capitalism and Liberal Myths."

3. Shrybman, *World Trade Organization*; Sinclair, *GATS*; Barker and Mander, *Invisible Government*.

4. There is an extensive literature on these issues. The following contain good summaries: Otting, "International Labour Standards"; Charnovitz, "Influence of International Labour Standards on the World Trading Regime"; van Liemt, "Minimum Labour Standards and International Trade." See also Harvey, Collingsworth, and Athreya, "Developing Effective Mechanisms for Implementing Labour Rights"; Dorman, "Worker Rights and International Trade"; and Lee, "Globalization and Labour Standards."

5. Alston, "Critical Appraisal of the United Nations Human Rights Regime," pp.10-11.

6. For a series of articles examining the whole range of human rights mechanisms, see Hannum, ed., *Guide to International Human Rights Practice*.

7. Bircham and Charlton, eds., *Anti-Capitalism*; Danaher, ed., *Democratising the Global Economy*; Collier and Quaratiello, *Basta! Land and the Zapatista*; Zapatista website <www.ezln.org/>; Madres de la Plaza de Mayo <www.madres.org>; Permanent Peoples' Tribunal <www.law.warwick. ac.uk/lawschool/>.

8. Otto, "Nongovernmental Organizations in the United Nations System."See also Korey, *NGOs and the Universal Declaration of Human Rights*.

9. Although the structure of the EU is closer in form than in content to the structure of a national liberal democracy, the pretence of transnational liberal democracy is implicit in the European Parliament. For other regional frameworks, such as NAFTA and MERCUSOR, there is no such charade; as at the global level, the structures of governance are for TNCs alone.

10. The principle of territorial sovereignty, the question of retroactive law, their ad hoc nature (special courts for special groups), and the argument that the trials were political and not judicial in nature were among the issues raised in opposition to the tribunals. It is also possible to argue that in part these trials were intended as "show" trials; they could not be allowed to interfere with the tasks of rebuilding capitalism in Germany and Japan and resisting socialism. To fulfil these tasks many of those in government, business, and the military who

were complicit in the war crimes had to be recruited for these postwar struggles. For an interesting insight into this issue in Japan, see Davis and Roberts, *Occupation without Troops*. See also Silverstein, "Our Nazi Allies."

11. Woetzel, *Nuremberg Trials in International Law*, p.233; Starke, *Introduction to International Law*, p.59.

12. Amadiume and An-Na'im, eds., *Politics of Memory*; Hayner, "Fifteen Truth Commissions," and "Commissioning the Truth"; Adam, "Divided Memories"; Gourevitch, *We Wish to Inform You*; Mamdami, *When Victims Become Killers*; Tomuschat, "Clarification Commission in Guatemala."

13. Ensalaco, "Truth Commissions for Chile and El Salvador." The Rettig Commission in Chile took no position on the coup itself; but it "extolled" the role of the military in the country's history, and it "cautioned" the use of human rights violations to "sully" the reputation of the military or its contribution to the nation (p.662). On Chile, see also Chile, *Report of the National Truth and Reconciliation Commission*.

14. Chapman and Ball, "Truth of Truth Commissions." This is an interesting article on the question of the "truth" of these commissions, but the authors do not relate it to the necessity of not finding the truth.

15. Amnesty International, "South Africa: Compensate Victims of the Past."

16. United Nations, Security Council Resolution 827, May 25, 1993; and Security Council Resolution 955, Nov. 8, 1994.

17. Forsyth, *Human Rights in International Relations*, pp.93-102.

18. Hitchens, "Case against Henry Kissinger," Parts 1 and 2. These articles, originally published in *Harper's Magazine*, also appear in book form: Hitchens, *Trial of Henry Kissinger*.

19. The indictment of Milosevic and his extradition to The Hague should be seen not so much as the fate of a leader alleged to be responsible for a range of serious crimes, but the fate of a leader who dared to thwart the interests and goals of transnational corporations and their embodiment in U.S. foreign policy.

20. Concerning allegations of such crimes by U.S. officials in the former Yugoslavia, see, for example, International Action Center (IAC), "Text of the Indictment Prepared by Ramsay Clark."

21. See Amnesty International, "'Collateral Damage' or Unlawful Killings?"

22. See Kirchheimer, *Political Justice*. This classic text on "the use of legal procedure for political ends" is very pertinent to these tribunals.

23. U.S. military and economic pre-eminence after World War II made the Security Council highly responsive to Washington's foreign policy interests. The failure of the United States and Britain to secure a majority of votes on the Security Council to sanction its invasion of Iraq is a rare exception in the history of the Council. But this "failure" of the Council to bend to U.S. demands will also probably make it "irrelevant," to use the Bush administration's term, in the future. Its supposed relevance in the past depended on its consistent tendency to follow U.S. interests.

24. For an interesting survey of the limits of the Security Council, see Nolte, "Limits of the Security Council's Powers."

25. Power, "Bystanders to Genocide."

26. Chossudovsky, *Globalisation of Poverty*; Woodward, *IMF, the World Bank and Economic Policy in Rwanda*; Storey, "Economics and Ethnic Conflict."

27. By contrast, see Melvern, *People Betrayed*. See also Organization for African Unity, "International Panel of Eminent Personalities."

28. Central Intelligence Agency, "CIA Activities in Chile." For a good review of the issues surrounding the attempt to prosecute Pinochet, see Wilson, "Prosecuting Pinochet."

29. Collins and Lear, *Chile's Free-Market Miracle*.

30. Philpot, "Colonialism and Injustice," pp.8-10.

31. Woetzel, *Nuremberg Trials in International Law*, pp.190-217.

32. Young, *Rise and Fall of Alfried Krupp*. Twelve key officials of I.G. Farben were imprisoned for slavery and mistreatment of concentration camp inmates at the Nuremberg trials. In the 1950s, after short periods in prison, some of them were hired back to Hoechst and Bayer – two of the three companies into which the Allied powers divided I.G. Farben after the war. See Borkin, *Crime and Punishment of I. G. Farben.*

    Forced to recognize their complicity in these crimes during the war and the benefits arising, several German corporations and the German government are now contributing to a restitution fund for those who were forced to work in their factories. In August 2000 the German Foundation Act was passed, establishing a fund to help compensate for losses in property, personal injury, or harm to children of those taken as slaves or forced labourers. See <www.compensation-for-forced-labour.org>.

33. "Crimes against humanity" as defined in the Rome Statute of the ICC, adopted in 1998, states clearly that they "must have been committed pursuant to a 'a state or organizational policy,'" and so committed by state agents or representatives of some organization.

34. The focus on individual culpability and the associated limitations on the pursuit of justice should be compared to the focus of the Permanent Peoples' Tribunals (PPTs). For the PPTs, crimes are not seen as singular events perpetuated by a deviant actor or actors victimizing a particular subject, but as a form of violence perpetuated by certain structures or organizations with victims being categories of people, such as workers, women, children, neighbourhoods, communities, regions, and even countries. See <www.law.warwick.ac.uk/lawschool/>.

35. "Clinton Offers His Apologies to Guatemala," *The New York Times*, March 11, 1999.

36. Gilbert, "El Salvador's Death Squads"; Walker, ed., *Reagan versus the Sandinistas.* The Truth Commission in El Salvador found that 73 per cent of the soldiers cited in human rights abuses in that country were trained in the School of the Americas at Fort Benning, Georgia; see Farenthold, "Militarization of United States Foreign Policy," p.234.

37. McWhinney, *International Court of Justice*, pp.99-133.

38. See Hemisphere Institute for Security Cooperation web sites.

39. See Korea Truth Commission; the tribunal was held in New York in July 2001.

40. See, for instance, Novick, *Holocaust in American Life.* See also Matzpun web site <www.matzpun.com>. The Matzpun appeal for a boycott of Israeli goods by Israelis and Jews is an example of the limits of the human conscience to tolerate inhumanity, in this case the repression by Israelis of the Palestinians. Even what passes for democracy in Israel comes into question. See Negbi, "Murderers Are Still Free."

    Every major human rights organization over many years has consistently condemned Israel for numerous and extreme violations of the rights of the Palestinian people. The crimes documented by the Israeli Committee Against House Demolition, Rabbis for Human Rights <www.rhi.israel.net>, Public Committee Against Torture <www.stoptorture.org.il>, among others, include political repression, assassinations, labour exploitation, collective punishment, demolition of homes and other buildings, administrative detention, indeterminate curfews over whole towns and cities, destruction of the Palestinian economic base, denial of education and medical services, systematic torture, and the use of military weapons against unarmed civilians. All of these charges have been confirmed by other organizations and the United Nations as continuing over several decades.

    The Israeli Information Center for Human Rights <www.btselem.org> has compared the illegal occupation of the Palestinian Territories to the apartheid regime in South Africa. The degree of oppression in South Africa, however, was rarely so brutal as the ongoing oppression in Palestine.

    On the question of human rights, the Israelis face several contradictions of their own making. While Jews were the victims of unprecedented crimes in World War II, in the name of this suffering Israel has committed massive new suffering; and in the name of what passes for democracy in Israel, moreover, the Palestinians are denied self-rule, facilitating their occupation and perhaps eventual creation of Bantustans in the West Bank and Gaza. More generally, the Israelis make the human tragedy of the Holocaust into a Jewish tragedy alone – they conflate the massive crimes of the Nazis against numerous groups, peoples, and individuals into solely crimes against Jews – and so diminish the extent of the crimes of the Nazis and obfuscate the full import of the lessons of World War II. In short, in the name of the crimes committed against Jews, Israel commits similar crimes against the Palestinians and obscures for the world the broader implications and meaning of the crimes of the Nazi regime. The Israeli government has changed lessons for humanity into an instrument to justify its occupation of Palestine and ruthlessness towards the Palestinians. Palestinian violence towards Israelis must be seen as the response to a brutal and illegal occupation of their land.

41. International People's Tribunal to Judge the G-7, *Report.* The Permanent Peoples' Tribunal evolved out of the Bertrand Russell Tribunal on War Crimes in Vietnam and the movement that give rise to the Algiers Declaration on the Rights of Peoples in 1976. For this document, see Falk, *Human Rights and State Sovereignty*, pp.192-93; and for more on the Tribunal, see <www.grisnet.it/flib/tribu>.

42. See Amnesty International web site for a good review of the events of this legal battle.

43. See Réseau Damoclès, "Debate over Belgium's Law of Universal Jurisdiction," Feb. 12, 2003; BBC News, "Belgium Rethinks War Crimes Law," Feb. 26, 2003; ABC Online, "Belgium Revises 'Universal Competence' Law," April 6, 2003; Human Rights Watch, "Rumsfeld Wrong to Attack Belgium Human Rights Law," June 13, 2003; International Campaign for Justice for the victims of Sabra and Shatila <indictsharon.net>.

44. *Daily Telegraph*, June 24, 2003.

45. International Theological Commission, "Memory and Reconciliation." To do justice to the extent of their sins, the Church might need as many volumes as pages in this document. But this beginning is remarkable in itself.

46. See, for instance, Vistica, "What Happened in Thanh Phong."

47. Gibney and Roxstrom, "Status of State Apologies."

48. See various position papers and fact sheets on the ICC by Amnesty International <www.amnesty.org>; and for the documents and commentary, see *The American Journal of International Law*, "Developments in International Criminal Law."

49. As the world's pre-eminent violator of human rights, the U.S. government would almost certainly find itself confronted by an independent criminal court. Washington has been condemned on many occasions for its unilateral actions: in 1984 by the International Court of Justice for its blockade of Nicaragua; by many nations for its embargo of Cuba; in 1986 for its bombing of Tripoli; in 1989 for its invasion of Panama. Other examples are interventions in Granada, Guatemala, El Salvador, and the embargo and continuous bombing of Iraq in the 1990s. See, for instance, Latin American Bureau, *Grenada*; Thompson, Kaldor, et al., *Mad Dogs*; Chomsky, *Year 501*; Chomsky and Herman, *Political Economy of Human Rights*, vol.1.

50. Kissinger, "Pitfalls of Universal Jurisdiction"; see also Hitchens, *Trial of Henry Kissinger*.

51. "U.S. Fears Prosecution of President in World Court," Reuters, Nov. 15, 2002.

52. In a letter from HRW to President Bush on Dec. 26, 2002, HRW explicitly warned the U.S. administration that reports of its treatment of detainees at Bagram air base in Afghanistan, the U.S. base at Diego Garcia, and elsewhere constituted violations of the prohibition of torture. It reminded the president of the concept of "command responsibility" – "the responsibility of superior officers for atrocities [committed] by their subordinates" – making it clear that this responsibility extended to "civil authorities for abuses committed by persons" under direct orders or within their jurisdiction. The letter concluded with a further reminder that violations of the international laws against torture can be prosecuted by any state regardless of the place of the crime, or nationality of the victim or perpetrator. All of these could be considered good reasons to frustrate the formation of an international court explicitly charged with prosecuting international criminal acts.

53. Scharf, "Politics behind the U.S. Opposition to the International Criminal Court."

54. Kissinger, "Pitfalls of Universal Jurisdiction," p.87.

55. Forsyth, *Human Rights in International Relations*, pp.103-6; Vanda, "Establishment of a Permanent International Criminal Court"; *The American Journal of International Law*, "Developments in International Criminal Law."

56. Amnesty International, "International Criminal Court."

57. Donegan, "The United States' Extraterritorial Abduction of Alien Fugitives." Unilateral abductions and prosecutions of alleged international criminals rest by and large on the principle of might is right and not on international law. It is not possible to imagine the government of Panama abducting President Bush I to try him on charges of crimes against the Panamanian people; yet in early January 1990 the United States was able to abduct the president of Panama, General Manuel Noriega, take him to the United States, prosecute him in a U.S. court, and imprison him.

In the last few decades there has been an increasing use of U.S. courts to settle international disputes. The likely explanation is not difficult to fathom: the largest number of TNCs are U.S.-based and U.S.-controlled, and the U.S. government actively protects these interests by employing the world's largest military forces and diplomatic and other means. Given this reality, the U.S. legal system and concept of law actually accompany the process of globalization, or Americanization, of the world's economic activities. See W. Glaberson, "U.S. Courts Become Arbiters of Global Rights and Wrongs," *The New York Times*, June 21, 2001.

Ironically, U.S. law has been used for some years to prosecute violations of human rights as found in international declarations. See Drinan and Kuo, "Putting the World's Oppressors on Trial"; and Lillich, "Damages for Gross Violations of International Human Rights."

58. E. Becker, "US Issues Warning to Europeans in Dispute over New Court," *The New York Times*, Aug. 26, 2002.

59. "Total immunity for all American citizens and U.S.-connected personnel" was what the United States was demanding from the EU in 2002. Human Rights Watch, "EU Decision on ICC Sets 'Vague Benchmarks.'" By 2003, after a "year-long campaign" during which U.S. ambassadors were "acting like schoolyard bullies," the Bush administration had managed to blackmail about forty-eight countries, for the most part "small and poor," to sign bilateral agreements with the United States, agreeing not "to hand over U.S. personnel to the ICC." Human Rights Watch, "U.S.: End Bully Tactics against Court – Letter to Colin Powell."

60. Amnesty International, "'Collateral Damage' or Unlawful Killings?"

61. Human Rights Watch, "Opposition Mounting on US Arm-Twisting on ICC."

62. "Human Rights, American Wrongs," *Financial Times*, July 1, 2002. The problem with this view is that the Bush administration was doing nothing different from the Clinton government or other earlier U.S. regimes concerning respect for international law.

Chapter VII Principles for the Future?

1. Even the arbitrary rights of the employer over the employee are disguised by the notion of the formal equality of contractual exchange, the right to change employer, and certain social (including trade union) rights.

2. Fukuyama, *End of History and the Last Man*.

3. United Nations, World Conference on Human Rights, "Vienna Declaration and Programme of Action."

4. Among many other sources, for a quick survey of the extent of government corruption, see the numerous reports of Transparency International on that organization's web site.

5. See Corporate Watch web site; see also Weisman, "Money Trail"; and Centre for Responsive Politics web site.

6. Starke, *Introduction to International Law*, p.53. Article 2.2 of the Convention Against Torture states: "No exceptional circumstances whatsoever, whether a state of war or a threat of war, internal political instability or any other public emergency, may be invoked as a

justification of torture." For a constructive critique of the principle, see Charlesworth and Chinkin, "Gender of *Jus Cogens*."

7. See various reports by Amnesty International and Human Rights Watch. In May 2000 the UN Committee Against Torture "expressed concern over cases of abuse involving people arrested or imprisoned in the United States." Amnesty International reported to the UN Committee its concern over "brutality, beatings and shootings by police officers, sexual abuse of female prisoners and cruel conditions in isolation units as violations of the torture convention." *The Globe and Mail*, Oct. 1, 2000.

8. Priest and Gellman, "U.S. Decries Abuse but Defends Interrogations – 'Stress and Duress' Tactics Used on Terrorism Suspects Held in Secret Overseas Facilities," *Washington Post*, Dec. 26, 2002. Directly after the publication of this article, HRW sent a letter to President Bush laying out the laws against torture and warning, "Direct involvement or complicity in torture, as well as the failure to prevent torture, may subject U.S. officials to prosecution under international law." See HRW, "United States: Reports of Torture of Al-Qaeda Suspects."

9. HRW, "U.S. Should Renounce Torture before Powell Speech to U.N."

10. J. Turley, "Rights on the Rack," *Los Angeles Times*, Feb. 6, 2003.

11. A. Dershowitz, "A Choice among Evils," *The Globe and Mail*, March 5, 2003. In this article the Harvard law professor argues that "no democracy has ever, or would ever, actually live by" the position that "torture should never be employed." The implication, he outlines, is that the democratic state can then remain "hypocritical" in practising but denying torture, or it can "'legalize' limited torture in special circumstances." The author deftly avoids taking a stand but leaves the reader no logical choice but the last. Once the door is open to officially sanctioned torture, the question is also opened as to who can be tortured, when, how much, and what for. See also Cockburn, "Wide World of Torture."

12. See Blum, *Rogue State*, in particular Chapters 4, 5, and 9. See also D. Saunders, "Foreign Torturers Enjoy the Good Life in Florida," *The Globe and Mail*, Feb. 18, 2003.

13. "Cut Off Fingers until They Talk," *National Post*, March 10, 2003. This article reviewed some of the acknowledged practices at the U.S. air base at Bagram and U.S. public acceptance of these techniques.

14. As with the establishment of the ICC, even though the United States voted against the Protocol, it did much in the preceding discussions to make it more or less ineffectual. "U.S. Moves to Undermine New Torture Treaty, Bush Administration Again Defies Allies on Human Rights," *Human Rights News*, July 20, 2002 <hrw.org/press/2002/07/torture-treaty>.

15. Amnesty International, *Stopping the Torture Trade*.

16. World Policy Institute, "WTO and the Globalization of the Arms Industry." The WTO is actually structured in a way that facilitates the trade in arms.

17. See Campbell and Brenner, eds., *Death Squads in Global Perspective*; Barak, ed., *Crimes by the Capitalist State*; and Mason and Krane, "Political-Economy of Death Squads." There is now a vast amount of official data, especially from the CIA, on state-run and -financed death squads available on the Internet; simply use "death squads" as entry with any search engine. (See in particular: CIABASE files on death squads for a list of CIA-facilitated death squads around the world.

18. Berrigan, "Beyond the School of the Americas." See also Huggins, *Political Policing*.

19. In 1998 Amnesty International "for the first time ... made the US the target of its worldwide campaign, accusing it of double standards and creating a climate 'in which human rights violations thrive.'... The report accuses the US of refusing to recognize the primacy of international law, reserving the right to use death penalty against juveniles, not paying its dues to the UN, to which it now owes over a billion dollars, and being one of only two countries (along with Somalia) that has failed to ratify the UN Convention on the Rights of the Child." *London Telegraph*, Oct. 4, 1998. With qualifications, the United States ratified the Convention in 1999.

20. See United Nations Human Rights Commission, Subcommittee for the Promotion and Protection of Human Rights, for a wide number of reports on these issues. See also Bales, *Disposable People*.

21. See material published by Project Underground.

22. Inter-Parliamentary Union, "Women in National Parliaments" web site.

23. According to the United Nations, *Human Development Report 1997*, p.7, "The share of the poorest 20% of the world's people in global income now stands at a miserable 1.1%, down from 1.4% in 1991 and 2.3% in 1960. It continues to shrink. And the ratio of the income of the top 20% to that of the poorest 20% rose from 30 to 1 in 1960, to 61 to 1 in 1991 – and to a startling new high of 78 to 1 in 1994."

24. Churchill, "Like Sand in the Wind"; Fellman, *Citizen Sherman*, p.271; Marszalek, *Sherman*, p.379; DiLorenzo, *Real Lincoln*; Geddicks, *New Resource Wars*.

25. See Miller (Project Director), *State of the Peoples*; see also various issues of *Cultural Survival Quarterly*.

26. There are many works on both of these issues. On the question of destruction or degradation, see Greenpeace, *International Trade in Wastes*; and United Nations, *Climate Change and Transnational Corporations*. On the question of the commodification of the environment, see Lohmann and Clochester, eds., *Struggle for Land and the Fate of the Forests*; Shiva, *Biotechnology and the Environment*, and *Monocultures of the Mind*; and Kimbrell, "Biocolonization."

27. See Rich, *Mortgaging the Earth*; Princen and Finger, eds., *Environmental NGOs in World Politics*; Hynes, *Recurring Silent Spring*; Rogers, *Oceans Are Emptying*; and Suter, *Antarctica*.

28. In an infamous memo, a former chief economist of the World Bank and now president of Harvard University, Larry Summers, wrote: "The argument that moral obligation to future generations demands special treatment of environmental investments is fatuous." *The Economist*, Feb. 8, 1992, May 30, 1992. On the question of just how fatuous the argument is, see O'Connor, ed., *Is Capitalism Sustainable?*

29. According to the *Financial Post*, March 29, 2001, "The new [U.S.] administration [2001] had been lobbied heavily by the coal and oil industry to chop out the Kyoto agreement." This was only one of several reversals that the new president took on environment issues.

30. See Dommen, "Raising Human Rights Concerns in the World Trade Organization"; Dohnal, "Structural Adjustment Programs"; Rich, *Mortgaging the Earth*; Conklin and Davidson, "IMF and Economic and Social Human Rights"; Oloka-Onyango and Udagama, "Realization of Economic, Social and Cultural Rights"; and McCorquordale, "Globalization and Human Rights." See also various articles in Mander and Goldsmith, eds., *Case against the Global Economy*.

31. Hannum, ed., *Guide to International Human Rights Practice*.

32. Anderson and Cavanagh, "Rise of Corporate Global Power." Another study reported, "The market capitalization of Nokia, Finland's global telecommunications giant, is now higher than the country's gross domestic production." Kearney, "Measuring Globalization." Corporate sales and market capitalization are, of course, not strictly comparable to national GDPs; but the point of the comparison is to provide a certain measure of corporation size and power. See also Ietto-Gillies, *Transnational Corporations*.

33. Farenthold, "Militarization of United States Foreign Policy."

34. Raboy and Dagenais, eds., *Media, Crisis and Democracy*; Lorimer (with Scannell), *Mass Communications*; Schiller, *Information and the Crisis Economy*; Schiller, *Culture, Inc.*

35. Magdoff, Foster, and Buttel, eds., *Hungry for Profit*; McMichael and Raynolds, "Capitalism, Agriculture and World Economy."

36. United Nations Commission on Transnational Corporations, *Transnational Corporations, Services and the Uruguay Round*. For a good early review of the issues, see Nixson, "Controlling the Transnationals?"

37. Bruno and J. Karliner, "Tangled up in Blue."

38. Tesmer, *United Nations and Business*, p.xxi.

39. United Nations, Address of Secretary-General Kofi Annan.

40. Elsewhere Annan was to make the same points. "The United Nations I am asking you to support is *in fundamental respects a changed organization*." [Emphasis added.] "Confrontation has taken a back seat to cooperation. Polemics have given way to partnerships." "The voice of business is now heard in United Nations policy debates." United Nations, "Secretary-General, Addressing the United States Chamber of Commerce."

41. Robinson, "Business and Human Rights," p.9.

42. United Nations, "The Nine Principles."

43. CorpWatch, *TRAC Facts*, November 1999; Sustainable Energy and Economy Network, "Fossil Fuels and Human Rights Fact Sheet."

44. Robinson, "Business and Human Rights," p.12.

45. CorpWatch, "Citizens Compact on the United Nations and Corporations."

46. Robinson, "Business and Human Rights," p.8.

47. The United Nations Development Programme, *Human Development Report, 1999*, pp. 25-26, states, "Nearly 1.3 billion people live on incomes of less than $1 a day. The same number of people are without access to clean water." And "The assets of the top three billionaires are more than the combined GNP of all 48 least developed countries and their 600 million people." As well the report states that "a yearly contribution of 1 percent of the wealth of the 200 richest people could provide universal access to primary education for all."

48. Simai, "Politics and Economics of Global Unemployment," pp.4-5.

49. *The Ecologist*, "Whose Common Future?" See also World Commission on Environment and Development (United Nations), *Our Common Future*, 1987, often referred to as the "Brundtland Report" on sustainable development. For a short critical review see De La Court, *Beyond Brundtland*.

50. We are already more or less there; world production in all commodity groups is in excess of demand. See Cottrell, *Sacred Cow*; and McMichael and Raynolds, "Capitalism, Agriculture, and the World Economy." The UN *Human Development Report, 1998* states (p.30): "It is estimated that the additional cost of achieving and maintaining universal access to basic education for all, basic health care for all, reproductive care for all women, adequate food for all and safe water and sanitation for all is roughly $50 billion a year. This is less than 4% of the combined wealth of the 225 richest people in the world."

51. Walton and Seddon, *Free Markets and Food Riots*; Bello et al., *Does Globalization Help the Poor?*

Chapter VIII September 11 and the New Behemoth

1. "Wrestling for the Truth of 9/11," *The New York Times*, editorial, July 9, 2003; L. Arnold, "Sept. 11 Panel Rips Lack of Cooperation," Associated Press, July 9, 2003.

2. See various articles in Miliband, Saville, and Liebman, eds., *Socialist Register 1984: The Uses of Anti-Communism*.

3. Gleditsch et al., eds., *Peace Dividend*; Bonn International Center for Conversion, *Conversion Survey 1996*.

4. Most analysts agree that all spheres of the economy show overcapacity, which means that far more can be produced than can be consumed, given the current level of demand. In February 1999, for instance, *The Economist* stated that the world was "awash with excess capacity in computer chips, steel, cars, textiles, and chemicals." It could easily have added a long list of basic foods to eliminate hunger and malnutrition, and medicines to eradicate or ameliorate the world's most prevalent diseases.

5. International Forum on Globalization, *Does Globalization Help the Poor?*

6. Adams, *Odious Debts*. Originally, the concept of "odious debt" arose as Washington's rationalization for refusing to pay Cuba's debts to Spain after U.S. troops took the island in

1898. The United States argued that the debt was forced on the people of Cuba without their consent and therefore did not have to be honoured. On the same grounds, the Bolshevik government refused to honour the Tsar's debts after the revolution.

7. Walton and Seddon, *Free Markets and Food Riots*. See also the earlier work by Payer, *Debt Trap*; and her *World Bank*.

8. World Bank, *World Development Report, 2000/2001: Attacking Poverty*. One recent study stated: "In 1998-99, with the world gross output per capita growing at the rate of 1.5-1.8 per cent, more than eighty countries have lower per capita incomes than a decade or more ago, and at least fifty-five countries have consistently declining per capita incomes. The income gap between the fifth of the world's people living in the richest countries and the fifth in the poorest was 74 to 1 in 1997, up from 60 to 1 in 1990 and 30 to 1 in 1960. The income inequalities have also risen sharply within the rich countries – particularly in the US and UK – and the global poor are now as poor or more poor than they were in 1820." Patomaki, *Democratising Globalization*, p.100. See also Forrester, *Economic Horror*.

9. *Business Wire*, Jan. 3, 2002; <www.BankruptcyData.com>. On Jan. 21, 2003, the *Financial Times* reported: "Corporate bankruptcies in Japan reached their second highest postwar level last year.... The total liabilities reached almost 179 billion dollars."

10. International Labour Organization (ILO), Global Employment Trends, Geneva, January 2003. For the complete report, see <www.ilo.org/public>.

11. Eatwell and Taylor, *Global Finance at Risk*, p.107.

12. *The Wall Street Journal*, March 8, 2000.

13. World Bank, *Annual Report 2000*.

14. Glasbeek, *Wealth by Stealth*; Pearce and Snider, eds., *Corporate Crime*; Zey, *Banking on Fraud*; Tonry and Reiss, eds., *Beyond the Law*; Transparency International <www.transparency.de/>.

15. OECD, *Behind the Corporate Veil*; della Porta and Vannucci, *Corrupt Exchanges*; Glasberg and Skidmore, *Corporate Welfare Policy and the Welfare State*; Jacoby, Nehemkis, and Eells, *Bribery and Extortion in World Business*; and Epstein, *Corporation in American Politics*.

16. For surveys of state and corporate corruption around the world, see the web site of "Transparency International" <www.transparency.de/>. For insight into the degree of corporate-political linkages in the United States, see World Policy Institute, "Dirty Dozen Corporations."

17. Welton and Wolf, *Global Uprising*.

18. This is not the place for a critique of the World Social Forum, which has yet to be done; we are merely pointing to the reason why it had to evolve. <www.forumsocialmundial.org>.

19. See Rothstein, *Global Bargaining*.

20. U.S. Trade Representative Robert B. Zoellick, Evening Press Conference, WTO Fifth Ministerial Meeting, Cancun, Mexico, Sept. 14, 2003 <www.ustr.gov>.

21. In an uncommon revelation of awareness of the causes of conflict in the 1990s, the U.S. Space Command Long Range Plan admitted, "Widespread communications will highlight disparities in resources and quality of life – contributing to unrest in developing countries"; and "The gap between the 'have' and 'have-not' nations will widen – creating regional unrest." Quoted in Grossman, "Space Corps."

22. Conetta and Knight, "New US Military Strategy." Most of these figures represent an absolute decline in the physical presence of U.S. military forces overseas compared to earlier decades, but the decline is due not to a lessening interest in control by the United States but to new technology (especially in missiles, satellite surveillance, submarines, aircraft carriers, and long-range aircraft), the development of proxy armed forces, and the demise of the immediate threat of socialism.

23. Lumpe, "U.S. Foreign Military Training." Most of this police and military training is carried on under special military training programs, but increasingly training is conducted by covert

intelligence organizations and private companies financed in less than transparent ways by the U.S. government. The human rights record of many of these U.S. trained troops is appalling, and U.S. Congressional oversight over these training programs is more or less absent.

24. Hillman, "Top Seven Reasons Why We Need to Increase Military Spending." According to the article, "While total global military spending has decreased from $1.6 trillion in 1985 to $797 billion in 1996, the US share of the global military budget has increased from 30% to 33%."

25. Conetta and Knight, "Inventing Threats."

26. Cited in Wrigley, "Arms Industry," p.10.

27. The figures used in this section come from two main sources: Stockholm International Peace Research Institute and Center for Defense Information. Despite the problems of definition of the phenomena under consideration and the collection of statistics from multiple sources, these numbers do not seem to be in dispute. We use them simply as a guide to the general size and extent of military spending in the world.

28. Conetta and Knight, "New US Military Strategy."

29. Center for Defense Information web site, "World Military Expenditures."

30. Ciarrocca and Hartung, "Star Wars Revisited."

31. Center for Defense Information, *Weekly Defense Monitor*, Feb. 10, 2000. On receiving this request, bipartisan budget committees in both the U.S. Senate and House of Representatives declared that it was inadequate and called for more money to be given to the military.

32. About the Clinton budget in 2000, retired Rear Admiral Eugene Carroll said: "The US already spends substantially more for military force than any other nation, with no significant threats to our national security. This is a time when we should be seriously addressing urgent national needs, not adding billions to the Pentagon's budget." Center for Defense Information, press release, Feb. 7, 2000.

33. Center for Defense Information, "Highlights of the FY '03 Budget Request," Feb. 4, 2002, and "Bush Budget Stalls Transformation Drive," Feb. 4, 2002.

34. These points are based on the arguments in DeGrasse, *Military Expansion Economic Decline*, Appendix C; and are also made by the U.S. War Resister's League pamphlet, "Where Your Income Tax Money Really Goes" <warresisters.org>.

35. Melman, *Permanent War Economy*, p.23. See also Barnet, *Economy of Death*.

36. Center for Defense Information web site, "Military Costs: The Real Total."

37. Cited in Wrigley, "Arms Industry," p.10.

38. Friedman, *Lexus and the Olive Tree*, p.373.

39. Feffer, "Globalization and Militarization."

40. Hartung with J. Reingold, "About Face."

41. World Policy Institute, "Dirty Dozen Corporations."

42. Spinney, "Defense Power Games," p.6; see also Spinney, "Defense Spending Time Bomb."

43. Spinney, "Defense Power Games," p.6.

44. Morgan, "Threats to Use Nuclear Weapons."

45. Conetta and Knight, "Inventing Threats." Unless otherwise indicated, other quotations on the question of a threat are taken from this article.

46. Aspin, "Report on the Bottom-Up Review." The citations below are from "Section I: National Security in the Post-Cold War Era."

47. Hellman, "Top Seven Reasons Why We Need to Increase Military Spending."

48. Conetta and Knight, "Inventing Threats," p.5. Others were more blunt; military analyst Frank Spinney stated, "The Pentagon's two war strategy is just a marketing device to justify a high budget." Quoted in Hartung, "Military-Industrial Complex Revisited." Michael Klare suggests that this "two-war" scenario was Colin Powell's strategy for finding a new

justification for maintaining the Pentagon budget in the absence of obvious threats. See Klare, *Rogue States and Nuclear Outlaws*.

49. U.S. Air Force, "New World Vistas," citations from the Foreword and Chapter 1.

50. Huntington, "The Clash of Civilizations?"

51. See Rashid, *Taliban*.

52. *The Washington Post*, March 11, 1992; *The New York Times*, May 23, 1992; this edition of the *NYT* published original parts of both documents.

53. Israel is Washington's main guarantor over the region; in many ways it is an extension of the United States in the Middle East, where its military might prevails and its intelligence service is second to none. This central geo-political rationale for its existence is obscured by the abject use of the moral weight of a historic crime against humanity in which the Jews suffered disproportionately. The very existence of Israel *as a Jewish state*, moreover, stands as a violation of human rights. It has, furthermore, repeatedly violated United Nations resolutions, it has supported apartheid in South Africa, and it has a long record of inhuman treatment of the Palestinians. In world affairs Israel and the United States have worked together to suppress a wide variety of progressive and democratic movements in the Middle East, Central America, and Africa. Criticism of its long-standing violations of human rights and other aspects of international law has long been countered with the spurious charge of anti-Semitism.

54. Lumpe, "U.S. Foreign Military Training Global Reach, Global Power." She writes: "U.S. government-run or supported training programs for foreign and police forces have grown dramatically since the end of the cold war, both in size and number. In recent years, the U.S. forces have trained 100,000 or more foreign police and soldiers annually. This training takes place in some 200 institutions within the United States, as well as in at least 150 countries around the world."

55. Canada, National Defence, Vice-Chief of the Defence Staff Group Canada, Joint Experimentation Discussion Paper,' Section 2: "Operationalizing JV2010: J-7."

56. Cohen, *Report of the Quadrennial Defense Review*, Washington, D.C.: U.S. Department of Defense, May 1997.

57. Conetta and Knight, "Military Strategy under Review."

58. United States, Director for Strategic Plans and Policy, *Joint Vision 2020*.

59. Faulkenberry, "Global Reach – Global Power," pp.16-19.

60. United States Air Force, Air University, *SPACECAST 2020*, vol.1, p. 2.

61. Ibid., "Introduction."

62. United States Space Command, "U.S. Spacecom Unveils Long Range Plan," news release, April 7, 1998.

63. See United Nations Office for Outer Space Affairs at the United Nations web site.

64. Rothschild, "Lasers from Heaven."

65. Material on the Space Commission (Commission to Assess United States National Security Space Management and Organizations) taken from Grossman, "Space Corps."

66. Grossman, "Star Wars."

67. "The Alliance's Strategic Concept," approved by the Heads of State and Government participating in the meeting of the North Atlantic Council, Washington, D.C., April 23, 24, 1999.

68. In February 2002, U.S. forces arrived in the former Soviet Republic of Georgia, ostensibly to train the Georgian military to fight "terrorists" in that country. The Partnership for Peace program called for NATO exercises in autumn 2002; it is probably fair to say that NATO will be in Georgia for a long time.

69. D. Priest, "U.S. Military Builds Alliances across Europe," *Washington Post*, Dec. 14, 1998.

70. Ralston, "Successfully Managing NATO Enlargement," p.3.

71. S. Erlanger, "Military Gulf Separates U.S. and European Allies," *The New York Times*, March 16, 2002.

72. Here are a few passages to illustrate the points: "In pursuit of its policy of preserving peace, preventing war … NATO will seek, in cooperation with other organizations, to prevent conflict …" (pp.9-10); "Alliance forces must safeguard NATO's military effectiveness and freedom of action …" (p.13); "The Alliance should also be prepared to support … operations under the political control and strategic direction of either the WEU [Western European Union] or as otherwise agreed …" (p.15); "The forces of the Alliance must continue to be adapted to meet the requirements of the full range of Alliance missions effectively and to respond to future challenges" (p.16).

73. "NATO Overhaul Boosts U.S. Role," *The Globe and Mail*, June 13, 2003.

74. European Parliament, STOA, "Special Report to the European Parliament." See also "The Globalization of Repression: A Special Report to the European Parliament," a short version, which can be found at <www.thenation.com>.

75. European Parliament, *Appraisal of Technologies of Political Control*, European Parliament, January 6, 1998.

76. Redden, *Snitch Culture*.

77. For several decades the U.S. government has used a vast array of surveillance means; see Donner, *Age of Surveillance*.

78. "The Government [of New Zealand] will pay about $3 million so calls from all land and mobile phone networks, as well as e-mail, can be intercepted…. The legislation would bring New Zealand into line with legal requirements already in place in such countries as the United States, Australia, Germany, the Netherlands and Britain." *The New Zealand Herald*, April 22, 2002.

79. European Parliament, *Appraisal of the Technology of Political Control*.

80. See the Statewatch web site for analysis of the "Schengen Information System" (SIS) in Europe; the system now collects information on political protesters as well as "third country nationals." See <www.statewatch.org/>. Based in Strasbourg, the SIS had information on an estimated six million people in 2002.

81. Hagar, "Exposing the Global Surveillance System." See also Echelon Watch web site.

82. Richelson, ed., *National Security Agency Declassified*. "In the last several decades some of the secrecy surrounding NSA has been stripped away by Congressional hearings and investigative research. Most recently NSA has been the subject of criticism for failing to adjust to the post-Cold War technological environment as well as for operating a 'global surveillance network' alleged to intrude on the privacy of individuals across the world. The following documents provide insight into the creation, evolution, management and operations of NSA, including the controversial ECHELON program."

83. European Parliament, "Appraisal of Technologies for Political Control," and "Interception Capabilities 2000."

84. A good example, but no means the only one, is RISSNET (Regional Information Sharing System Network), a database of information on activist groups throughout the United States and parts of Canada. For a survey of some recent U.S. developments, see Madsen, "Homeland Security, Homeland Profits."

85. Elliot, "Legality of the Interception of Electronic Communications."

86. The information on Echelon is drawn from: American Civil Liberties Union "Echelonwatch"web site; Hagar, *Secret Power*; Frost and Gratton, *Spyworld*; Poole, "Echelon"; Campbell, "Somebody's Listening"; and P. Goodspeed, "The New Space Invaders: Spies in the Sky," *The National Post*, Feb. 19, 2000.

87. For this section, see W. Arkin, "Secret Plan Outlines the Unthinkable," *The Los Angeles Times*, March 10, 2002; J. Sterngold, "Bush's Nuclear Arms Plan," *San Francisco Chronicle*, May 11, 2003; Physicians for Social Responsibility Center for Global Health and Security, "'Dr. Strangelove' Meets the Pentagon"; J. Borger, "U.S. Plan for New Nuclear Arsenal," *The Guardian*, Feb. 18, 2003; and Ciarrocca, "The Nuclear Posture Review."

88. Kristol and Kagan, "Toward a Neo-Reaganite Foreign Policy."

89. Stone, *Hidden History of the Korean War*. See also Fleming, *Cold War and Its Origins*.

90. Interview with Zbigniew Brzezinski in *Le Nouvel Observateur*, Jan. 15-21, 1998. "That secret operation [the U.S. involvement in the 1970s in Afghanistan] was an excellent idea. It had the effect of drawing the Russians into the Afghan trap.... Indeed for almost 10 years, Moscow had to carry on a war unsupportable by the government, a conflict that brought about the demoralization and finally the breakup of the Soviet empire" (p.76). See also "Anatomy of a Victory: CIA's Covert Afghan War," *The Washington Post*, July 19, 1992.

91. See Cahn, *Killing Detente*; and Johnson, *Improbable Dangers*.

92. The details are readily available in a number of sources and there is no need to review them here. See, for example, Bamford, *Body of Secrets*; Stinnett, *Day of Deceit*; Ahmed, *War On Freedom*; Blum, *Killing Hope*; and Shalom, *Imperial Alibis*. See also Kwitney, *Endless Enemies*; Sanders, *Peddlers of Crisis*; and Blum, *Rogue State*.

    Other false pretexts were employed to maintain "defence" spending – the "bomber gap" in the 1950s, the "missile gap" in the 1960s, and the "window of vulnerability" in the 1970s – all invented in part to ensure that arms industries continued to receive large percentages of annual government expenditures. Johnson, *Improbable Dangers*. See also Cahn, *Killing Detente*.

93. One of the best sceptical analyses of 9/11 is by Ahmed, *War on Freedom*.

94. U.S. Democratic Policy Committee, March 7, 2002; G. Morgenson, "An Economic Stimulus Bill with the Corporations in Mind," *The New York Times*, Oct. 27, 2001; "Political Donors Profiteering in the Name of Economic Stimulus," *Common Cause*, Oct. 25, 2001.

95. C.H. Schmitt, "Wages of Sin," *U.S. News and World Report*, May 13, 2002.

96. P. Krugman, "Passing It Along," *The New York Times*, July 18, 2003.

97. Blau, *Illusions of Prosperity*; Institute for Public Accuracy, "Bush's Tax Cuts."

98. D. Baker, "Nine Misconceptions about Social Security."

99. *The New York Times*, Jan. 13, 1999.

100. The White House, "Executive Order Establishing Office of Homeland Security," Washington, Oct. 8, 2001.

101. One of the few comprehensive analyses of the U.S.A Patriot Act is by Chang, *Silencing Political Dissent*.

102. Olshansky, *Secret Trials and Executions*.

103. Leone, "The Quiet Republic."

104. Schulhofer, *Enemy Within*.

105. The U.S. record on international treaties is outlined in Du Boff, "Rogue Nation"; and R. Du Boff and E.S. Hermann, "In Its Unilateralist Disregard, U.S. Is the Real 'Rogue State,'" *The Philadelphia Inquirer*, Feb. 25, 2002.

106. For a brief definition, see Chapter I, p.25.

107. "The National Security Strategy of the United States," full text in *The New York Times*, Sept. 20, 2002.

108. Shivani, "Is America Becoming Fascist?"

109. Liberal democracy, by contrast, allows for the dominance of a framework of private property within which more or less social reform is sanctioned. In other words, class conflict and consciousness are contained with sufficient concessions, compromises, and coercion to maintain the stability of the system and to ensure that the economy remains by and large open to competitive capital within and between nations. By the 1950s, and after fascism had been defeated in World War II, all the industrial nations had adopted the welfare state in their national social formations as the main method for ensuring the future of capitalism.

110. While this sort of Israelification of the United States has begun, it is unlikely that Americans will succumb as completely as Israelis have to such patent manipulation.

Bibliography

Adam, H. "Divided Memories: Confronting the Crimes of Previous Regimes." *Telos* 118, Winter 2000.

Adam, H. and K. Moodley. *The Opening of the Apartheid Mind*. Berkeley and Los Angeles: University of California Press, 1993.

Adam, H., F. Van Syl Slabbert and K. Moodley. *Comrades in Business*. Cape Town: Tafelberg, 1997.

Adams, P. *Odious Debts: Loose Lending, Corruption, and the Third World's Environmental Legacy*. London/Toronto: Earthscan/Probe International, 1991.

Adu-Kofi, L. "The Impact of the International Monetary Fund and the World Bank's Structural Adjustment Policies on Sub-Saharan African Women." *New England International and Comparative Law Annual*, 1998.

Afshari, Reza. "An Essay on Islamic Cultural Relativism in the Discourse of Human Rights." *Human Rights Quarterly* 16 (1994).

Agee, P. and L. Wolf, eds. *Dirty Work: The CIA in Western Europe*. London: Zed Press, 1981.

Ahmad, I. "Islam, Market Economy and the Rule of Law." *Minaret of Freedom*, Preprint Series 96-1, May 1996.

———. "Islam and Hayek." *Economic Affairs* 13,3 (1993).

Ahmed, N.M. *The War on Freedom*. Brighton: Institute for Policy Research and Development, 2002.

Allain, J. and A. O'Shea. "African Disunity: Comparing Human Rights Law and Practice of North and South African States." *Human Rights Quarterly* 24,1 (2002).

Alston, P. "US Ratification of the Covenant on Economic, Social and Cultural Rights: The Need for an Entirely New Strategy." *The American Journal of International Law* 94 (1990).

———. "Critical Appraisal of the United Nations Human Rights Regime." In *The United Nations and Human Rights: A Critical Appraisal*, ed. P. Alston. Oxford: Oxford University Press, 1992.

Amadiume, I. and A. An-Na'im, eds. *The Politics of Memory*. London: Zed Books, 2000.

Anderson, S. and J. Cavanagh. "The Rise of Corporate Global Power." Institute for Policy Studies, Washington, D.C., December 2000.

An-Na'im, A.A. *Toward an Islamic Reformation: Civil Liberties, Human Rights, and International Law*. Syracuse, N.Y.: Syracuse University Press, 1990.

Arat, Z.F. "Analyzing Child Labour as a Human Rights Issue: Its Causes, Aggravating Policies, and Alternative Proposals." *Human Rights Quarterly* 24,2 (2002).

Arzt, D.E. "Religious Human Rights in Muslim States of the Middle East and North Africa." <www.law.emory.edu/EILR/volumes/Spring96/>

Aslanbeigui, N., S. Pressman, and G. Summerfield, eds. *Women in the Age of Economic Transformation: Gender Impact of Reforms in Post-Socialist and Developing Countries*. London: Routledge, 1994.

Aspaturian, V.V. "The Soviet Union." In *Modern Political Systems: Europe*, ed. R.C. Macridis and R.E. Ward. Engelwood Cliffs, N.J.: Prentice-Hall, 1963.

Aspin, Les. "Report on the Bottom-Up Review." Washington, D.C.: Department of Defense. October 1993.

Baker, D. "Nine Misconceptions about Social Security." *The Atlantic Online*, July 1998.

Bakhash, S. *The Reign of the Ayatollahs: Iran and the Islamic Revolution*. New York: Basic Books, 1984.

Bales, K. *Disposable People: Neo-Slavery in the Global Economy*. Los Angeles: University of California Press, 1999.

Bamford, J. *Body of Secrets: Anatomy of the Ultra-Secret National Security Agency from the Cold War through the Dawn of a New Century*. New York: Doubleday, 2001.

Barak, G. ed. *Crimes by the Capitalist State*. New York: State University of New York, 1991.

Bar-Joseph, U. *Intelligence Intervention in the Politics of Democratic States: The United States, Israel and Britain*. University Park, P.A.: Penn State University Press, 1995.

Barker, D. and J. Mander. *Invisible Government: The World Trade Organization*. San Francisco: International Forum on Globalization, 1999.

Barnet, R.J. *The Economy of Death*. New York: Atheneum, 1970.

Barsh, R.L. "Indigenous Peoples and the UN Commission on Human Rights: A Case of the Immovable Object and the Irresistible Force." *Human Rights Quarterly* 18,4 (1996).

Bellis, Paul. *Marxism and the USSR*. Atlantic Highlands, N.J.: Humanities Press, 1979.

Bello, W. et al. *Does Globalization Help the Poor?* San Francisco: International Forum on Globalization, 2001.

Berle, A.A. *The 20th Century Capitalist Revolution*. New York: Harcourt and Brace, 1954.

Berle, A.A. and G.C. Means. *The Modern Corporation and Private Property*. New York: Harcourt, Brace and World, 1968.

Berrigan, F. "Beyond the School of the Americas: U.S. Military Training Programs Here and Abroad." Arms Trade Resources Center, Washington, D.C., 2000.

Bettelheim, Charles. *Economic Calculation and Forms of Property*. New York: Monthly Review Press, 1975.

———. *The Transition to Socialist Economy*. Hassocks, U.K.:Harvester Press, 1978.

Beyani, C. "Toward a More Effective Guarantee of Women's Rights in the African Human Rights System." In *Human Rights of Women*, ed. R. Cook. Philadelphia: University of Pennsylvania Press, 1994.

Bircham, E. and J. Charlton, eds. *Anti-Capitalism: A Guide to the Movement*. London: Bookmarks, 2001.

Blackstock, N. *COINTELPRO: The FBI's Secret War on Political Freedom*. New York: Vintage Books, 1975.

Blau, J. *Illusions of Prosperity: America's Working Families in an Age of Economic Insecurity*. New York: Oxford University Press, 1999.

Bobbio, N. *The Age of Rights*. Cambridge: Polity Press, 1996.

Bond, P., ed. *Fanon's Warning: A Civil Society Reader on the New Partnership for Africa's Development*. Lawrenceville, N.J.: Africa World Press, 2002.

Bonn International Center for Conversion. *Conversion Survey 1996*. Oxford: Oxford University Press, 1996.

Borkin, J. *The Crime and Punishment of I.G. Farben*. New York: The Free Press, 1978.

Blum, Wm. *The CIA: A Forgotten History*. London: Zed Books, 1986.

———. *Killing Hope: US Military and CIA Interventions since WWII*. Montreal: Black Rose Books, 1998.

———. *Rogue State: A Guide to the World's Only Superpower*. Monroe, Maine: Common Courage Press 2000.

Brock, R. and S.B. Thistlethwaite. *Casting Stones: Prostitution and Liberation in Asia and the United States*. Minneapolis: Fortress Press, 1996.

Brown, C. *With Friends Like These: The Americas Watch Report on Human Rights and US Foreign Policy in Latin America*. New York: Pantheon Books, 1985.

Brownlie, I., ed. *Basic Documents on Human Rights*. Oxford: Clarendon Press, 1971.

Bruno, K. and J. Karliner. "Tangled up in Blue: Corporate Partnerships at the United Nations." Transnational Resource and Action Center, Berkeley, Ca., 2000 <www.corpwatch.org>.

Cahn, A.H. *Killling Detente: The Right Attacks the CIA*, University Park: Pennsylvania State University, 1998.

Campbell, B.B. and A.D. Brenner, eds. *Death Squads in Global Perspective*. New York: St. Martin's Press, 2000.

Campbell, D. "Somebody's Listening." *New Statesman*. Aug. 12, 1988.

Casal, L. "Revolution and Consciencia: Women in Cuba." In *Women, War, and Revolution*, ed. C.R. Berkin and C.M. Lovett. New York: Holmes and Meier, 1980.

Center for Defense Information. "Highlights of the FY '03 Budget Request," Feb. 4, 2002; and "Bush Budget Stalls Transformation Drive," Feb. 4, 2002. See also their web site.

Chang, N. *Silencing Political Dissent: How Post-September Anti-Terrorism Measures Threaten Our Civil Liberties*. New York: Seven Stories Press, 2002.

Chapman, A.R. and P. Ball. "The Truth of Truth Commissions: Comparative Lessons from Haiti, South Africa, and Guatemala." *Human Rights Quarterly* 23,1 (2001).

Charnovitz, S. "The Influence of International Labour Standards on the World Trading Regime." *International Labour Review* 126, 5 (1987).

Charlesworth, H. "What Are 'Women's International Human Rights'?" In *Human Rights of Women*, ed. R. Cook. Philadelphia: University of Pennsylvania Press, 1994.

Charlesworth, H. and C. Chinkin. "The Gender of *Jus Cogens*." *Human Rights Quarterly* 15 (1993).

Chester, E.T. *Covert Network: Progressives, the International Rescue Committee and the CIA.* Armonk, N.Y.: M.E. Sharpe, 1985.

Chomsky, N. *The Fateful Triangle: Israel, the United States and the Palestinians.* Montreal: Black Rose Books, 1984.

——. "Israel's Role in US Foreign Policy." In *Intifada: The Palestinian Uprising against Israeli Occupation.*, ed. Z. Lockman and J. Beinin. Toronto: Between the Lines, 1989.

——. *Deterring Democracy.* New York: Hill and Wang, 1992.

——. *Year 501: The Conquest Continues.* Montreal: Black Rose Books, 1993.

——. "The United States and the Challenge of Relativity." In *Human Rights Fifty Years On: A Reappraisal*, ed. T. Evans. Manchester: Manchester University Press, 1998. [Reprinted as Chomsky, N., "The Umbrella of US Power: The Universal Declaration of Human Rights and the Contradictions of US Policy." Open Media Pamphlet Series. New York: Seven Stories Press, 1999.]

Chomsky, N. and E. Herman. *The Political Economy of Human Rights.* Vol.1. Boston: South End Press, 1979.

Chossudovsky, M. *The Globalisation of Poverty: Impacts of IMF and World Bank Reforms.* London: Zed Books, 1997.

Churchill, W. "Like Sand in the Wind: The Making of an American Indian Diaspora in the United States." In *Creating Surplus Populations: The Effect of Military and Corporate Polices on Indigenous Peoples*, ed. L. Foerstal. Washington: Maisonneuve Press, 1996.

CIA. *CIA Targets Fidel: The Secret Assassination Report.* With a commentary by Fabian Escalante. New York: Ocean Press, 1996.

Ciarrocca, M. "The Nuclear Posture Review: Reading Between the Lines." *Common Dreams*, May 17, 2002.

Ciarrocca, M. and W. Hartung. "Star Wars Revisited." *Foreign Policy in Focus* 6,25 (June 2001).

Clay, J.W. "Looking Back to Go Forward: Protecting and Preventing Human Rights Violations." In *State of the Peoples*, ed. M. Miller. Boston: Beacon Press, 1993.

Clements, L. and J. Young. "Human Rights: Changing the Culture." *Journal of Law and Society*, 26,1 (1999).

Cobbah, J.A.M. "African Values and the Human Rights Debate: An African Perspective." *Human Rights Quarterly* 9 (1987).

Cockburn, A. "The Wide World of Torture." *The Nation*, Nov. 26, 2001.

Cohen, R., G. Hyden, and W. Nugan, eds. *Human Rights and Governance in Africa.* Gainsville: University of Florida, 1993.

Cohen, Wm. S. *Report of the Quadrennial Defense Review.* Washington: D.C.: U.S. Department of Defense, May 1997.

Collier, G.A. and E.L. Quaratiello. *Basta! Land and the Zapatista Rebellion in Chiapas.* Oakland, Cal.: Food First, 1999.

Collins, J. and J. Lear. *Chile's Free-Market Miracle: A Second Look.* Oakland, Cal.: A Food First Book, 1995.

Conklin, M. and D. Davidson. "The IMF and Economic and Social Human Rights: A Case Study of Argentina, 1958-1985." *Human Rights Quarterly* 8 (1986).

Conetta, C. and C. Knight. "Inventing Threats." *Bulletin of the Atomic Scientists* 54,2 (March/April 1998).

——. "Military Strategy under Review." *Foreign Policy in Focus* 4,3 (January 1999).

——. "New US Military Strategy: Issues and Options." Project on Defense Alternatives Briefing Memo, May 20, 21, 2001.

Cook, R., ed. *Human Rights of Women.* Philadelphia: University of Pennsylvania Press, 1994.

——. "Women's International Human Rights Law: The Way Forward." *Human Rights Quarterly* 15 (1993).

Corntassel, J.J. and T.H. Primeau. "Indigenous 'Sovereignty' and International Law: Revised Strategies for Pursuing 'Self-Determination.'" *Human Rights Quarterly* 17 (1995).

Cottrell, R. *The Sacred Cow: The Folly of Europe's Food Mountains.* London: Grafton Books, 1987.

Cox, A.M. *Prospects for Peacekeeping.* Washington, 1967.

Cranston, M. "What Are Human Rights?" In *The Human Rights Reader*, ed. W. Laqueur and B. Rubin. Philadelphia: Temple University Press, 1977.

Crook, D. and I. Crook. *Revolution in a Chinese Village.* London: Routledge and Paul, 1959.

Crummey, C. and C.C. Stewart, eds. *Modes of Production in Africa: The Pre-Colonial Era.* London: Sage Publications, 1981.

Cutler, A.C. "Global Capitalism and Liberal Myths: Dispute Settlement in Private International Trade Relations." *Millennium: Journal of International Studies* 24,3 (1995).

Danaher, K., ed. *Democratising the Global Economy.* Philadelphia: Common Courage Press, 2001.

Davidson, B. *The Lost Cities of Africa.* Boston: Little, Brown and Co., 1959.

Davis, G. and J. G. Roberts. *An Occupation without Troops.* Tokyo: Yen Books, 1996.

Davis, J.K. *The Assault on the Left: The FBI and the 60's Antiwar Movement.* Westport, Conn.: Praeger, 1997.

Deckard, B. *The Women's Movement.* New York: Harper and Row, 1983.

DeGrasse, R. *Military Expansion, Economic Decline: The Impact of Military Spending on US Economic Performance.* Armonk, N.Y.: M.E. Sharpe, 1983.

De La Court, T. *Beyond Brundtland.* London: Zed Books, 1990.

Della Porta, D. and A. Vannucci. *Corrupt Exchanges: Actors, Resources, and Mechanisms of Political Corruption.* New York: Aldine De Gruyter, 1999.

De Tocqueville, A. *The Old Regime and the French Revolution.* New York: Anchor Books, 1955.

Diamond, S. *Compromised Campus: The Collaboration of Universities and the Intelligence Community, 1945-1955.* New York: Oxford University Press, 1992.

DiLorenzo, T. *The Real Lincoln: A New Look at Abraham Lincoln, His Agenda, and an Unnecessary War.* New York: Random House, 2002.

Dines, G., Jensen, R., and A. Russo, *Pornography: The Production and Consumption of Inequality.* New York and London: Routledge, 1998.

Dixon, M., ed. *On Trial: Reagan's War against Nicaragua.* San Francisco: Synthesis Publications, 1985.

Dohnal, J. "Structural Adjustment Programs: A Violations of Rights." *Australian Journal of Human Rights* 57 (1994).

Dommen, C. "Raising Human Rights Concerns in the World Trade Organization." *Human Rights Quarterly* 24,1 (2002).

Donegan, A. "The United States' Extraterritorial Abduction of Alien Fugitives: A Due Process Standard." *New England International and Comparative Law Annual*, 1997.

Donnelly, J. "The Social Construction of International Human Rights." In *Human Rights and Global Politics*, ed. T. Dunne and N. Wheeler. Cambridge: Cambridge University Press, 1999.

——. "Cultural Relativism and Universal Human Rights." *Human Rights Quarterly* 6 (1984).

Donner, F.J. *The Age of Surveillance.* New York: Vintage, 1981.

Dorman, P. "Worker Rights and International Trade: A Case for Intervention." *Review of Radical Political Economy* 20,2/3 (1988).

Drinan, R.F., S.J. and T.T. Kuo. "Putting the World's Oppressors on Trial: The Torture Victim Protection Act." *Human Rights Quarterly* 15,3 (1993).

Du Boff, R. "Rogue Nation." <www.greenpeacemed.org.mt/international_treaties>.

Dyck, N., ed. *Indigenous Peoples and the Nation-State.* St. John's: Institute of Social and Economic Research, Memorial University of Newfoundland, 1985.

Eatwell, J. and L. Taylor. *Global Finance at Risk.* London: Polity Press, 2000.

Eickelmann, D. "Inside the Islamic Reformation." *Wilson Quarterly* 22,1 (Winter 1998).

Elliot, C. "The Legality of the Interception of Electronic Communications: A Concise Survey of the Principal Legal Issues and Instruments under International, European and National Law." European Parliament, STOA Programme, April 1999, p.15. See also <www.statewatch.org/news/2002>.

Engle, K. "From Skepticism to Embrace: Human Rights and the American Anthropological Association from 1947-1999." *Human Rights Quarterly* 23,3 (2001).

Ennew, J. "Outside Childhood: Street Children's Rights." In *The Handbook of Children's Rights*, ed. B. Franklin. New York: Routledge, 1995.

Ensalaco, M. "Truth Commissions for Chile and El Salvador: A Report and Assessment." *Human Rights Quarterly* 16 (1994).

Epstein, E.M. *The Corporation in American Politics*. Englewood Cliffs, N.J.: Prentice-Hall, 1969.

Eshghipour, K. "The Islamic Revolution's Impact on the Legal and Social Status of Iranian Women." *New England International and Comparative Law Annual*, 1997.

Espiell, H.G. "The Evolving Concept of Human Rights: Western, Socialist and Third World Approaches." In *Human Rights: Thirty Years after the Universal Declaration*, ed. B.G. Ramcharan. The Hague: Martinus Nijhoff, 1979.

Evans, T. *US Hegemony and the Project of Universal Human Rights*. London: Macmillan Press, 1996.

———., ed. *Human Rights Fifty Years On: A Reappraisal*. Manchester: Manchester University Press, 1998.

Ewelukwa, U.U. "Post-Colonialism, Gender and Customary Injustice: Widows in African Societies." *Human Rights Quarterly* 24,2 (2002).

Falk, R.S. *Human Rights and State Sovereignty*. New York: Holmes and Meier, 1991.

———. "False Universalism and the Geopolitics of Exclusion: The Case of Islam." *Third World Quarterly* 18,1 (1997).

———. *Human Rights Horizons*. London: Routledge, 2000.

Farenthold, S. "The Militarization of United States Foreign Policy." In *Creating Surplus Populations: The Effect of Military and Corporate Polices on Indigenous Peoples*, ed. L. Foerstel. Washington, D.C.: Maisonneuve Press, 1996.

Farnsworth, B.B. "Communism and Feminism: Its Synthesis and Demise." In *Women, War, and Revolution*, ed. C.R. Berkin and C. M. Lovett. New York: Holmes and Meier, 1980.

Faulkenberry, B.J. "Global Reach – Global Power." Unpublished thesis, School of Advanced Airpower Studies, Air University, Alabama, 1995.

Feffer, J. "Globalization and Militarization." *Foreign Policy in Focus* 7,1 (February 2002).

Felice, W.F. "Militarism and Human Rights." *International Affairs* 74,1 (1998).

Fellman, M. *Citizen Sherman*. New York: Random House, 1995.

Ferguson, J.A. "The Third World." In *Foreign Policy and Human Rights*, ed. R.J. Vincent. Cambridge: Cambridge University Press, 1986.

Fielding, L.R. "Japan's Sex Slaves." *New England International and Comparative Law Annual* 5 (1999).

Fields, A.B. and Wolf-Dieter Narr. "Human Rights as a Holistic Concept." *Human Rights Quarterly* 14 (1992).

Fitch, B. and M. Oppenheimer. *Ghana: End of an Illusion*. New York: Monthly Review Press, 1966.

Fleming, D.F. *The Cold War and Its Origins*. Vol. 2. London: George Allen and Unwin, 1961.

Foerstal, H.N. *Surveillance in the Stacks: The FBI's Library Awareness Program*. New York: Greenwood Press, 1991.

Foerstal, L., ed. *Creating Surplus Populations: The Effect of Military and Corporate Polices on Indigenous Peoples*. Washington, D.C.: Maisonneuve Press, 1996.

Forrester, V. *The Economic Horror*. London: Polity Press, 1999.

Forsythe, D.P. *Human Rights in International Relations*. Cambridge: Cambridge University Press, 2000.

———. "The United States and International Criminal Justice." *Human Rights Quarterly* 24, 4 (2002).

Fraser, A. "Becoming Human: The Origins and Development of Women's Human Rights." *Human Rights Quarterly* 21 (1999).

Freeman, M. "Introduction: Children as Persons." In *Children's Rights: A Comparative Perspective*, ed. M. Freeman. Aldershot, U.K.: Dartmouth Publishing, 1996.

Friedland, W.H. and C.G. Rosberg, eds. *African Socialism*. Stanford, Cal.: Stanford University Press, 1964.

Friedman, T. *The Lexus and the Olive Tree*. New York: Farrar, Strauss and Giroux, 1999.

Friedmann, W. *Legal Theory*. London: Stevens and Sons, 1949.

Frost, M. and M. Gratton. *Spyworld: Inside the Canadian and American Intelligence Establishments*. Toronto: Doubleday, 1994.

Fukuyama, F. *The End of History and the Last Man*. New York: Avon Books, 1992.

Gedicks, A. *The New Resource Wars: Native and Environmental Struggles against Multinational Corporations.* Montreal: Black Rose Books, 1994.

Gelbspan, R. *Break-ins: Death Threats and the FBI.* Boston: South End Press, 1991.

George, S. and F. Sabelli. *Faith and Credit: The World Bank's Secular Empire.* London: Penguin, 1994.

Gibney, M. and E. Roxstrom. "The Status of State Apologies." *Human Rights Quarterly* 23,4 (2001).

Gilbert, L. "El Salvador's Death Squads: New Evidence from US Documents." *International Policy Report.* Washington, D.C.: Center for International Policy, March 1994.

Glasbeek, H. *Wealth by Stealth: Corporate Crime, Corporate Law, and the Perversion of Democracy.* Toronto: Between the Lines, 2002.

Glasberg, D. S. and D. Skidmore. *Corporate Welfare Policy and the Welfare State: Bank Deregulation and the Savings and Loan Bailout.* New York: Aldine De Gruyter, 1997.

Gleditsch, N.P. et al., eds. *The Peace Dividend.* Amsterdam: Elsevier, 1996.

Goldstein, R.J. *Political Repression in Modern America: 1870 to the Present.* New York: Schenkman, 1978.

Gordon, Haim. *Quicksand: Israel, the Intifada and the Rise of Political Evil in Democracy.* East Lansing: Michigan State University Press, 1995.

Gourevitch, P. *We Wish to Inform You That Tomorrow We Will Be Killed with Our Families: Stories from Rwanda.* New York: Farrar, Straus, Giroux, 1998.

Green, S. *Taking Sides: America's Secret Relations with a Militant Israel.* New York: Morrow and Co., 1984.

Greenpeace. *The International Trade in Wastes: A Greenpeace Inventory.* Washington, D.C.: Greenpeace USA, 1990.

Greider, William. "The Right and US Trade Law: Invalidating the 20th Century." *The Nation*, Oct. 15, 2001.

Gross, B. and R. Gross, eds. *The Children's Rights Movement.* Garden City, N.Y.: Anchor Press, 1977.

Grossman, K. "Space Corps: The Dangerous Business of Making the Heavens a War Zone." *Covert Action Quarterly*, April/June 2001.

——. "Star Wars: Protecting Globalization from Above." Jan. 18, 2002, <www.corpwatch.org>.

Gudynas, E. "NGOs Facing Democracy and Globalization: The Challenges in Latin America." *Transnational Associations*, 5/1997.

Guerin, D. *Fascism and Big Business.* New York: Pathfinder Press, 1973.

Hagar, N. *Secret Power: New Zealand's Role in the International Spy Network.* Nelson, N.Z.: Craig Potton, 1996.

——. "Exposing the Global Surveillance System." *Covert Action Quarterly*, Spring/Summer 1998.

Halliday, F. "Relativism and Universalism in Human Rights: The Case of the Islamic Middle East." *Political Studies* 43 (1995).

Hannum, H., ed. *Guide to International Human Rights Practice.* Ardsley, N.Y.: Transnational Publishers, 1999.

Harris, N. *The New Untouchables.* London: Penguin, 1995.

——. *The End of the Third World.* London: Penguin, 1990.

Hartung, W. "Military-Industrial Complex Revisited: How Weapons Makers Are Shaping US Foreign and Military Policy." *Foreign Policy in Focus*, 1997 [revised 1999] <www.fpif.org>.

Hartung, W.D. and G. Moix. "Deadly Legacy: U.S. Arms to Africa and the Congo War." World Policy Institute, Washington, D.C. <www.worldpolicy.org>.

Hartung, W. with J. Reingold. "About Face: The Role of the Arms Lobby in the Bush Administration's Radical Reversal of Two Decades of US Nuclear Policy." World Policy Institute, Special Report, May 2002.

Harvey, P., T. Collingsworth, and B. Athreya. "Developing Effective Mechanisms for Implementing Labour Rights in the Global Economy." *International Labour Rights Fund*, Washington, D.C., 1998.

Hayner, P.B. "Commissioning the Truth: Further Research Questions." *Third World Quarterly* 17,1 (1996).

——. "Fifteen Truth Commissions – 1974 to 1994: A Comparative Study." *Human Rights Quarterly* 16 (1994).

Hayter, T. *Aid as Imperialism.* Harmondsworth, U.K.: Penguin Books, 1971.

Hawes, J.M. *The Children's Rights Movement.* Boston: Twayne, 1991.

Hellman, C. "Top Seven Reasons Why We Need to Increase Military Spending (and Why They're Wrong)." Center for Defense Information, Washington, D.C., May 1998.

Herbert, S. *The Fall of Feudalism in France.* London: Methuen, 1921.

Herman, E. and F. Brodhead. *Demonstration Elections.* Boston: South End Press, 1984.

Herman, E. and G. Sullivan. *The "Terrorism" Industry.* New York: Pantheon Books, 1989.

Hevener, N. *International Law and the Status of Women.* Boulder, Col.: Westview Press, 1983.

Hitchens, C. "The Case against Henry Kissinger." Part 1. *Harper's Magazine,* February 2001.

——. "The Case against Henry Kissinger." Part 2. *Harper's Magazine,* March 2001.

——. *The Trial of Henry Kissinger.* London: Verso Books, 2001.

Howard, R. "An African Concept of Human Rights?" In *Foreign Policy and Human Rights,* ed. R. J. Vincent. Cambridge: Cambridge University Press, 1986.

Hudson, M. (ed). *Merchants of Misery: How Corporate America Profits from Poverty.* Monroe, Maine: Common Courage Press, 1996.

Huggins, M.K. *Political Policing: The United States and Latin America.* Durham, N.C. and London: Duke University Press, 1998.

Humphrey, J.P. *Human Rights and the United Nations.* New York: Transnational, 1984.

——. "The Universal Declaration of Human Rights: Its History, Impact and Juridical Character." In *Human Rights: Thirty Years after the Universal Declaration,* ed. B.G. Ramcharan. The Hague: Martinus Nijhoff, 1979.

Huntington, S. "The Clash of Civilizations?" *Foreign Affairs* 72,3 (Summer 1993).

——. *The Clash of Civilizations and the Remaking of World Order.* New York: Touchstone, 1996.

Hynes, P. *The Recurring Silent Spring.* New York: Pergamon Press, 1989.

Ietto-Gillies, G. *Transnational Corporations.* London: Routledge, 2002.

Ihonvbere, J.O. "How to Make an Undemocratic Constitution: The Nigerian Example." *Third World Quarterly* 21,2 (2000).

Ikegami, E. "Citizenship and National Identity in Early Meiji Japan, 1868-1889." In *Citizenship, Identity and Social History,* ed. C. Tilly. Cambridge: Cambridge University Press, 1996.

Immerman, R.H. *The CIA in Guatemala: The Foreign Policy of Intervention.* Austin: University of Texas Press, 1982.

International Forum on Globalization. *Does Globalization Help the Poor?* Special Report. San Francisco, August 2001.

Jacobson, H.K. *Networks of Interdependence: International Organization and the Global Political System.* New York: Alfred A. Knopf, 1979.

Jacoby, N.H., P. Nehemkis, and R. Eells, *Bribery and Extortion in World Business.* New York: Macmillan, 1977.

Johnson, D.L., ed. *The Chilean Road to Socialism.* New York: Anchor Press/Doubleday, 1973.

Johnson, L.K. *America's Secret Power: The CIA in a Democratic Society.* New York: Oxford University Press, 1989.

Johnson, R.H. *Improbable Dangers: US Conceptions of Threat in the Cold War and After.* New York: St. Martin's, 1994.

Jonas, S. "Dangerous Liaisons: The U.S. in Guatemala." *Foreign Policy* 144 (1996).

Jutte, R. and A. Grosse-Jutte, eds. *The Future of International Organization.* London: Frances Pinter, 1981.

Kearney, A.T. "Measuring Globalization." *Foreign Policy,* January/February 2001 <www.foreignpolicy.com>.

Keller, William. *The Liberals and J. Edgar Hoover: Rise and Fall of a Domestic Intelligence State.* Princeton, N.J.: Princeton University Press, 1989.

Kimbrell, A. "Biocolonization: The Patenting of Life and the Global Market in Body Parts." In *The Case against the Global Economy,* ed. J. Mander and E. Goldsmith. San Francisco: Sierra Club Books, 1996.

Kirchheimer, O. *Political Justice.* Princeton, N.J.: University of Princeton Press, 1961.

Kissinger, H.A. "The Pitfalls of Universal Jurisdiction." *Foreign Affairs,* July/August 2001.

Klare, M. *Rogue States and Nuclear Outlaws.* New York: Hill and Wang, 1995.

Korey, W. *NGOs and the Declaration of Human Rights.* New York: St. Martin's Press, 1998.

Kristol, Wm. and R. Kagan. "Toward a Neo-Reaganite Foreign Policy." *Foreign Affairs,* July/August 1996.

Kuenyehia, A. "The Impact of Structural Adjustment Programs on Women's International Human Rights: The Example of Ghana." In *Human Rights of Women*, ed. R. Cook. Philadelphia: University of Pennsylvania Press, 1994.

Kwitney, J. *Endless Enemies*. New York: Penguin Books, 1986.

Laqueur, W. and B. Rubin, eds. *The Human Rights Reader*. Philadelphia: Temple University Press, 1977.

Latin American Bureau. *Grenada: Whose Freedom?* London, 1984.

Lee, E. "Globalization and Labour Standards: A Review of Issues." *International Labour Review* 136,2 (1997).

Lefort, C. "Politics and Human Rights" and "The Logic of Totalitarianism." In *The Political Forms of Modern Society*, ed. C. Lefort. Oxford: Polity Press, [1978] 1986.

Leger, M. *Aboriginal Peoples: Towards Self-Government*. Montreal: Black Rose Books, 1994.

Leone, R.C. "The Quiet Republic: The Missing Debate about Civil Liberties after 9/11." In *The War on Our Freedoms*, ed. R.C. Leone and G. Anrig. New York: The Century Foundation, 2003.

Lernoux, P. *The Cry of the People*. London: Penguin, 1982.

Lillich, R.B. "Damages for Gross Violations of International Human Rights Awarded by US Courts." *Human Rights Quarterly* 15,1 (1993).

Lockman, Z. and J. Beinin, eds. *Intifada: The Palestinian Uprising against Israeli Occupation*. Toronto: Between the Lines,1989.

Lohmann, L. and M. Clochester, eds. *The Struggle for Land and the Fate of the Forests*. London: Zed Books, 1992.

Lorimer, R. (with P. Scannell). *Mass Communications*. Manchester: Manchester University Press, 1994.

Lumpe, L. "U.S. Foreign Military Training: Global Reach, Global Power, and Oversight Issues." *Foreign Policy in Focus*, Special Report. May 2002 <www.foreignpolicy-infocus.org>.

———. "US Foreign Military Training: Global Reach, Global Power, and Oversight Issues." *Foreign Policy in Focus*, May 2002.

Macpherson, C.B. "Problems of Human Rights in the Late Twentieth Century." In Macpherson, *The Rise and Fall of Economic Justice*. Oxford: Oxford University Press, 1985.

Madeley, J. *Big Business, Poor Peoples: The Impact of Transnational Corporations on the World's Poor*. London: Zed Books, 1999.

Madsen, W. "Homeland Security, Homeland Profits." Dec. 21, 2001 <www.corpwatch.org>.

Magdoff, F., J.B. Foster, and F. Buttel, eds. *Hungry for Profit: The Agribusiness Threat to Farmers, Food, and the Environment*. New York: Monthly Review Press, 2000.

Maloney, J.M. "Women in the Chinese Communist Revolution: The Question of Political Equality." In *Women, War, and Revolution*, ed. C.R. Berkin and C.M. Lovett. New York: Holmes and Meier, 1980.

Mamdami, M. *When Victims Become Killers: Colonialism, Nativism, and the Genocide in Rwanda*. Princeton, N.J.: Princeton University Press, 2001.

Mandela, N. *The Struggle Is My Life*. London: Canon Collins House, 1986.

Mander, J. and E. Goldsmith, eds. *The Case against the Global Economy*. San Francisco: Sierra Club Books, 1996.

Marchetti, J. and G.D. Marks. *The CIA and the Cult of Intelligence*. New York: Knopf, 1974.

Marshall, T.H. "Citizenship and Social Class." In Marshall, *Sociology at the Crossroads and Other Essays*. London: Heinemann, 1963.

———. *Class, Citizenship, and Social Development*. New York: Anchor Books, 1965.

Marszalek, J.F. *Sherman: A Soldier's Passion for Order*. New York: Free Press, 1993.

Marx, K. *Capital*. Vol.1. New York: Vintage, 1977.

Marx, K. and F. Engels. *The German Ideology*. In Marx and Engels, *Collected Works*. Vol.5. London: Lawrence and Wishart, 1976.

Mason, T.D. and D.A. Krane. "The Political-Economy of Death Squads: Towards a Theory of the Impact of State-Sponsored Terror." *International Studies Quarterly* 33 (1989).

Mayer, A. *Islam and Human Rights: Tradition and Politics*. Boulder, Col.: Westview Press, 1991.

McCorquordale, R. "Globalization and Human Rights." *Human Rights Quarterly* 21 (1999).

McMichael, P. and D. Myhre. "Global Regulation versus the Nation-State: Agro-Food Systems and the New Politics of Capital." *Capital and Class* 43 (1991).

McMichael, P. and L.T. Raynolds. "Capitalism, Agriculture, and the World Economy." In *Capitalism and Development*, ed. L. Sklair. London: Routledge, 1994.

McWhinney, E. *The International Court of Justice and the Western Tradition of International Law*. Dordrecht: Martinus Nijhoff, 1987.

Medina, C. "Toward a More Effective Guarantee of the Enjoyment of Human Rights by Women in the Inter-American System." In *Human Rights of Women*, ed. R. Cook. Philadelphia: University of Pennsylvania Press, 1994.

Melman, S. *The Permanent War Economy*. New York: Simon and Schuster, 1974.

Melvern, L.R. *A People Betrayed: The Role of the West in Rwanda's Genocide*. London: Zed Books, 2000.

Miliband, R., J. Saville, and M. Liebman, eds. *The Uses of Anti-Communism: Socialist Register 1984*. London: Merlin Press, 1984.

Miller, M. (Project Director). *State of the Peoples: A Global Human Rights Report on Societies in Danger*. Boston: Beacon Press, 1993.

Moon, K. *Sex among Allies: Military Prostitutes in US-Korean Relations*. New York: Columbia University Press, 1997.

Moore, Jr., Barrington. *The Social Origins of Dictatorship and Democracy: Lord and Peasant in the Making of the Modern World*. Boston: Beacon Press, 1966.

Morgan, D.R. "Threats to Use Nuclear Weapons: The Sixteen Known Nuclear Crises of the Cold War, 1946-1985." March 6, 1996 <www.vana.ca/> .

Morsink, J. "World War Two and the Universal Declaration." *Human Rights Quarterly* 15 (1993).

Mower, G. *Human Rights and American Foreign Policy*. New York: Greenwood Press, 1987.

Moynihan, D.P. "The Politics of Human Rights." In *The Human Rights Reader*, ed. W. Laqueur and B. Rubin. Philadelphia: Temple University Press, 1977.

Muslow, B., ed. *Africa: Problems in the Transition to Socialism*. London: Zed Books, 1986.

Nasr, S.H. *Ideals and Realities of Islam*. London: Harper-Collins, [1966] 1974.

Negbi, M. "The Murderers Are Still Free; Israeli Democracy Is Dying of Fear." *Haaretz*, Nov. 4, 2002.

Neumann, F. *Behemoth*. London: Victor Gollancz, 1942.

Nixson, F.I. "Controlling the Transnationals? Political Economy and the United Nations Code of Conduct." *International Journal of the Sociology of Law* 11 (1983).

Nolte, G. "The Limits of the Security Council's Powers and Its Functions in the International Legal System: Some Reflections." In *The Role of Law in International Politics*, ed. M. Byers. Oxford: Oxford University Press, 2000.

Norman, E.H. *Origins of the Modern Japanese State*. New York: Pantheon Books, 1975.

Novick, P. *The Holocaust in American Life*. Boston and New York: Houghton Mifflin, 2000.

Nutter, J.J. *The CIA's Black Ops: Covert Action, Foreign Policy, and Democracy*. Amherst, N.Y.: Prometheus Books, 2000.

O'Connor, M., ed. *Is Capitalism Sustainable?* New York: Guildford Press, 1994.

Ogbu, A. and C. Akunna. "Nigeria: Ogonis Say Arms Were Sponsored by Shell." Jan. 25, 2001 <corpwatch.org>.

Olmsted, K.S. *Challenging the Secret Government: The Post-Watergate Investigations of the CIA and FBI*. Chapel Hill: University of North Carolina Press, 1996.

Oloka-Onyango, J. and D. Udagama. "The Realization of Economic, Social and Cultural Rights: Globalization and Its Impact on the Full Enjoyment of Human Rights." Report for the Subcommittee on the Promotion and Protection of Human Rights, United Nations, New York, June 15, 2000.

Olshansky, B. *Secret Trials and Executions: Military Tribunals and the Threat to Democracy*. New York: Seven Stories Press, 2002.

Organization for Economic Cooperation and Development (OECD). *Behind the Corporate Veil: Using Corporate Entities for Illicit Purposes*. Paris: OECD, 2001.

Ottaway, M. and D. Ottaway. *Afro-Communism*. New York: Africana Publishing Co., 1981.

Otting, A. "International Labour Standards: A Framework for Social Security." *International Labour Review* 132,2 (1993).

Otto, D. "Non-governmental Organizations in the United Nations System: The Emerging Role of International Civil Society." *Human Rights Quarterly* 18 (1996).

Pannikar, R. "Is the Notion of Human Rights a Western Concept?" *Diogenes* 120 (1982).

Patomaki, H. *Democratising Globalization*. London: Zed Books, 2001.

Payer, C. *The Debt Trap: The IMF and the Third World*. Harmondsworth, U.K.: Penguin Books, 1974.

———. *The World Bank: A Critical Analysis*. New York: Monthly Review Press, 1982.

Pearce, P. and L. Snider, eds. *Corporate Crime*. Toronto: University of Toronto Press, 1995.

Penna, D.R. and P.J. Campbell. "Human Rights and Culture: Beyond Universality and Relativism." *Third World Quarterly* 19,1 (1998).

Perry, M.J. "Are Human Rights Universal? The Relativism Challenge and Related Matters." *Human Rights Quarterly* 19 (1997).

Petras, J. "Imperialism and NGOs in Latin America." *Monthly Review* 7 (December 1997).

———. "NGOs in the Service of Imperialism." *Journal of Contemporary Asia* 29,4 (1999).

Petras, J. and M. Morley. *The United States and Chile*. New York: Monthly Review Press, 1975.

Philpot, J. "Colonialism and Injustice: The International Criminal Tribunal for Rwanda." *Canadian Dimension*, March-April 1997.

Pollis, A. "Cultural Relativism Revisited: Through a State Prism." *Human Rights Quarterly* 18 (1996).

Pollis, A. and P. Schwab. "Human Rights: A Western Construct with Limited Applicability." In *Human Rights: Cultural and Ideological Perspectives*, ed. A. Pollis and P. Schwab. New York: Praeger, 1979.

Poole, P.S. "Echelon: America's Secret Global Surveillance Network." <fly.hiwaay.net/~pspoole/echelon>.

Power, J. *Against Oblivion*. Glasgow: Fontana, 1981.

Power, S. "Bystanders to Genocide: Why the United States Let the Rwandan Tragedy Happen." *The Atlantic Monthly*, September 2001.

Preis, A-B. S. "Human Rights as Cultural Practice: An Anthropological Critique." *Human Rights Quarterly* 18 (1996).

Princen, T. and M. Finger, eds. *Environmental NGOs in World Politics*. New York: Routledge, 1994.

Public Citizen. "NAFTA, Chapter 11: Investor-to-State Cases: Bankrupting Democracy." <www.citizen.org/publications/>.

Quigley, J. *The Ruses for War: American Interventions since World War II*. Buffalo, N.Y.: Prometheus, 1992.

Raboy, M. and B. Dagenais, eds. *Media, Crisis and Democracy: Mass Communication and the Disruption of Social Order*. Newbury Park, Cal.: Sage Publications, 1992.

Ralston, General J.W. "Successfully Managing NATO Enlargement." *U.S. Foreign Policy Agenda*, March 2002.

Rashid, A. *Taliban: Militant Islam, Oil and Fundamentalism in Central Asia*. New Haven, Conn.: Yale University Press, 2000.

Ray, E. "NAFTA for Africa and the National Summit on Africa." *CovertAction Quarterly* 69 (Spring/Summer 2000).

Ray, E. et al., eds. *Dirty Work 2: The CIA in Africa*. Secaucus, N.Y.: Lyle Stuart, 1979.

Redden, J. *Snitch Culture: How Citizens Are Turned into the Eyes and Ears of the State*. Venice, Cal.: Feral House Books, 2000.

Reed, E. *Woman's Evolution*. New York: Pathfinder Press, 1975.

Renteln, A.D. "The Unanswered Challenge of Relativism and the Consequences for Human Rights." *Human Rights Quarterly* 7 (1985).

Rich, B. *Mortgaging the Earth: The World Bank, Environmental Impoverishment, and the Crisis of Development*. Boston: Beacon Press, 1994.

Richelson, J.T., ed. *The National Security Agency Declassified*. National Security Archive Electronic Briefing Book no. 24. Jan. 13, 2000.

Robertson, A.H. "The Helsinki Agreement and Human Rights." In *Human Rights and American Foreign Policy*, ed. D. Kommers and G. Loescher. Notre Dame, Ind.: University of Notre Dame Press, 1979.

Robertson, A.H. and J.G. Merrills. *Human Rights in the World*. Manchester: Manchester University Press, 1989.

Robins, N.S. *Alien Link: The FBI's War in Intellectual Freedom*. New York: W. Morris, 1992.

Robinson, Mary. "Business and Human Rights: A Progress Report." <www.unhchr.ch>.

Rodinson, M. *Islam and Capitalism*. Austin: University of Texas Press, 1974.

Rodriguez, J.C. *The Bay of Pigs and the CIA*. New York: Ocean Press, 1999.

Rogers, R.A. *The Oceans Are Emptying: Fish Wars and Sustainability*. Montreal: Black Rose Books, 1995.

Rosberg, C.G. and T.M. Callaghy, eds. *Socialism in Sub-Saharan Africa*. Berkeley, Ca.: Institute of International Studies, University of California, 1979.

Rosenblatt, R.E. "Legal Entitlement and Welfare Benefits." In *The Politics of Law*, ed. D. Kairys. New York: Pantheon Books, 1982.

Rothschild, M. "Lasers from Heaven."*The Progressive*, May 10, 2001.

Rothstein, R.L. *Global Bargaining: UNCTAD and the Quest for a New International Economic Order*. Princeton, N.J.: Princeton University Press, 1979.

Russell, D. and N. Van de Ven, eds. *Crimes against Women*. Millbrae, Cal.: Les Femmes, 1976.

Said, E.W. *The Question of Palestine*. New York: Times Books, 1979.

——. *The Politics of Dispossession: The Struggle for Palestinian Self-Determination, 1969-1994*. New York: Pantheon Books, 1994.

Salvemini, G. *Under the Axe of Fascism*. London: Victor Gollancz, 1936.

Sanders, J.W. *Peddlers of Crisis*. Boston: South End Press, 1983.

Schmitt, C.H. "Wages of Sin." *US News and World Report*, May 13, 2002.

Schulhofer, S.J. *The Enemy Within: Intelligence Gathering, Law Enforcement, and Civil Liberties in the Wake of September 11*. New York: The Century Foundation, 2002.

Scott, H. *Does Socialism Liberate Women?* Boston: Beacon Press, 1974.

Scott, J. *Corporations, Classes, and Capitalism*. London: Hutchinson, 1985.

Scharf, M.P. "The Politics behind the U.S. Opposition to the International Criminal Court." *New England International and Comparative Law Annual*, 1999.

Schiller, H. *Information and the Crisis Economy*. New York: Oxford University Press, 1986.

——. *Culture, Inc.* New York: Oxford University Press, 1989.

Sengupta, A. "On the Theory and Practice of the Right to Development." *Human Rights Quarterly* 24,4 (2002).

Shalom, S. *Imperial Alibis: Rationalizing U.S. Intervention after the Cold War*. Boston: South End Press, 1993.

Shepard, G. and Ankipo, M., eds. *Emerging Human Rights: The African Political Economy Context*. New York: Greenwood Press, 1990.

Shiva, V. *Biotechnology and the Environment*. Penang, Malaysia: Third World Network, 1993.

——. *Monocultures of the Mind: Biodiversity, Biotechnology, and the Third World*. Penang, Malaysia: Third World Network, 1993.

——. *Biopiracy: The Plunder of Nature and Knowledge*. Toronto: Between the Lines, 1998.

——. *Protect or Plunder? Understanding Intellectual Property Rights*. London: Zed Books, 2001.

Shivani, A. "Is America Becoming Fascist?" *CounterPunch*, Oct. 26, 2002.

Shrybman, S. *The World Trade Organization: A Citizen's Guide*. Ottawa and Halifax: Canadian Centre for Policy Alternatives and James Lorimer, 1999.

Silverstein, K. "Our Nazi Allies." May 3, 2000 <www.salon.com>.

Simai, M. "The Politics and Economics of Global Unemployment." In *Global Unemployment: An International Investigation into the Future of Work*, ed. M. Simai. London: Zed Books, 1995.

Sinclair, S. *GATS: How the World Trade Organization's New 'Services' Negotiations Threaten Democracy*. Ottawa: Canadian Centre for Policy Alternatives, 2000.

Skar, E. "Truth Commissions: Trials – or Nothing? Policy Options in Democratic Transitions." *Third World Quarterly* 20,6 (1999).

Skogly, S.I. and M. Gibney. "Transnational Human Rights Obligations." *Human Rights Quarterly* 24 (2002).

Slack, K.M. "Operation Condor and Human Rights: A Report from Paraguay's Archive of Terror." *Human Rights Quarterly* 18 (1996).

Sluka, J.A. *Death Squad: The Anthropology of State Terror*. Philadelphia: University of Pennsylvania Press, 1999.

Smith, Adam. *Wealth of Nations*. London: The Standard Library Co., nd.

Smolin, D. "Strategic Choices in the International Campaign against Child Labour." *Human Rights Quarterly* 22,4 (2000).

Sohn-Rethel, A. *Economy and Class Structure of German Fascism*. London: CSE Books, 1978.

Speed, S. and J. Collier. "Limiting Indigenous Autonomy in Chiapas, Mexico: The State Government's Use of Human Rights." *Human Rights Quarterly* 22,4 (2000).

Spinney, F.C. "Defense Power Games." Report, The Fund for Constitutional Government, Washington, D.C., October 1990.

———. "Defense Spending Time Bomb." *Challenge: The Magazine of Economic Affairs*, July-August 1996 (also available at: <www.infowar.com>).

Starke, J.G. *An Introduction to International Law*. London: Butterworths, 1967.

Stamatopoulou, E. "Indigenous Peoples and the United Nations: Human Rights as a Developing Dynamic." *Human Rights Quarterly* 16 (1994).

Stern, B. "How to Regulate Globalization." In *The Role of Law in International Politics*, ed. M. Byers. Oxford: Oxford University Press, 2000.

Stinnett, R.B. *Day of Deceit: The Truth about FDR and Pearl Harbor*. New York: Touchstone Books, 2001.

Stoessinger, J. "The Payments Dispute." In *The Future of UN Peacekeeping*, ed. W. Woodside. Toronto, 1965.

Stone, I.F. *The Hidden History of the Korean War: America's First Vietnam*. New York: Monthly Review, [1952] 1970.

Storey, A. "Economics and Ethnic Conflict: Structural Adjustment in Rwanda." *Development Policy Review* 17,1 (1999).

Suter, K. *Antarctica: Private Property or Public Heritage?* London: Zed Books, 1991.

Szeftel, M. "Ethnicity and Democratization in South Africa." *Review of African Political Economy*, 1994.

Tarock, A. "The Politics of the Pipeline: The Iran and Afghanistan Conflict." *Third World Quarterly* 20, 4 (1999).

Tesmer, S. *The United Nations and Business*. New York: St. Martin's Press, 2000.

Tetreault, M.A., ed. *Women and Revolution in Africa, Asia, and the New World*. Columbia: University of South Carolina Press, 1994.

Theoharis, A.G. and J.S. Cox. *The Boss: J. Edgar Hoover and the Great American Inquisition*. Philadelphia: Temple University Press, 1988.

Thomas, D.C. "The Helsinki Accords and Political Change in Eastern Europe." In *The Power of Human Rights*, ed. T. Risse, S.C. Ropp, and K. Sikkink. Cambridge: Cambridge University Press, 1999.

Thompson, E.P., M. Kaldor, et al. *Mad Dogs: The US Raids on Libya*. London: Pluto Press, 1986.

Tibi, B. "Islamic Law/Shari'a, Human Rights, Universal Morality and International Relations." *Human Rights Quarterly* 16 (1994).

Tilly, C. "The Emergence of Citizenship in France and Elsewhere." In *Citizenship, Identity and Social History*, ed. C. Tilly. Cambridge: Cambridge University Press, 1996.

Tomas, N., ed. *Collective Human Rights of Pacific Peoples*. Auckland, N.Z.: University of Auckland, 1999.

Tomuschat, C. "Clarification Commission in Guatemala." *Human Rights Quarterly* 23, 2 (2001).

Tonry, M. and A.J.Reiss, eds. *Beyond the Law: Crime in Complex Organizations*. Chicago: University of Chicago Press, 1993.

Turner, B.S. *Citizenship and Capitalism*. London: Allen and Unwin, 1986.

———. ed. *Citizenship and Social Theory*. Newbury Park: Sage Publications, 1993.

Turshen, M. and B. Holcomb, eds. *Women's Lives and Public Policy: The International Experience*. Westport, Conn.: Praeger, 1993.

Tushnet, M. "Corporations and Free Speech." In *The Politics of Law*, ed. D. Kairys. New York: Pantheon Books, 1982.

Vanda, V.P. "The Establishment of a Permanent International Criminal Court: Challenges Ahead." *Human Rights Quarterly* 20 (1998).

van Liemt, G. "Minimum Labour Standards and International Trade: Would a Social Clause Work?" *International Labour Review* 128, 4 (1989).

Vincent, R.J., ed. *Foreign Policy and Human Rights*. Cambridge: Cambridge University Press, 1986.

Vistica, G. "What Happened in Thanh Phong." *The New York Times Magazine*, April 29, 2001.

von Struensee, V. "Globalized, Wired, Sex Trafficking in Women and Children." *Murdock University Electronic Journal of Law* 7, 2 (June 2000) <www.murdock.edu.au/elaw/>.

Wadden, M. *Nitassinan: The Innu Struggle to Reclaim Their Homeland*. Vancouver: Douglas and McIntyre, 1996.

Walker, T.W., ed. *Reagan Versus the Sandinistas*. Boulder, Col.: Westview Press, 1987.

Wallach, L. and M. Sforza. *Whose Trade Organization? Corporate Globalization and the Erosion of Democracy*. Washington, D.C.: Public Citizen, 1999.

Walton, J. and D. Seddon. *Free Markets and Food Riots: The Politics of Global Adjustment.* Cambridge, Mass.: Blackwell, 1994.

Waring, M. *Counting for Nothing.* Toronto: University of Toronto Press, 1999.

——. *Three Masquerades.* Toronto: University of Toronto Press, 1998.

Washburn, P.S. *A Question of Sedition: The Federal Government Investigation of the Black Press during World War II.* New York: Oxford University Press, 1986.

Weisman, R. "The Money Trail." *Multinational Monitor,* October 2000.

Welton, N. and L. Wolf. *Global Rising: Confronting the Tyrannies of the Twenty-First Century.* Gabriola Island, B.C.: New Society Publishers, 2002.

Westerfield, H.B., ed. *Inside CIA's Private World.* New Haven, Conn.: Yale University Press, 1995.

Wickliffe, C. "An Overview of Collective Human Rights in the Pacific Region." In *Collective Human Rights of Pacific Peoples,* ed. N. Tomas. Auckland, N.Z.: University of Auckland, 1999.

Williams, O. F., ed. *Global Codes of Conduct.* Notre Dame, Ind.: University of Notre Dame Press, 2000.

Wilson, R.J. "Prosecuting Pinochet: International Crimes in Spanish Domestic Law." *Human Rights Quarterly* 21,4 (1999).

Wise, D. *The American Police State: The Government against the People.* New York: Random House, 1976.

Wise, D. and T.P. Ross. *The Invisible Government.* New York: Random House, 1964.

Woetzel, R.K. *The Nuremberg Trials in International Law.* New York: Praeger, 1960.

Wolpe, H., ed. *The Articulation of Modes of Production.* London: Routledge and Kegan Paul, 1980.

Woodward, D. *The IMF, the World Bank and Economic Policy in Rwanda: Economic and Social Implications.* Oxford: Oxford University Press, 1996.

World Bank. *Attacking Poverty: World Development Report, 2000/2001.* New York: Oxford University Press, 2001.

Wright, G. *The Destruction of a Nation: United States Policy toward Angola since 1945.* London: Pluto Press, 1997.

Wrigley, C. "The Arms Industry." March 2001 <www.caat.uk/research/ArmsIndustry>.

Young, G. *The Rise and Fall of Alfried Krupp.* London: Cassell, 1960.

Zey, M. *Banking on Fraud: Drexel, Junk Bonds, and Buyouts.* New York: Aldine De Gruyter, 1993.

Reports

Amnesty International <www.amnesty.org>

Amnesty International. "A Brief History." 1999.

——. "The Arab Convention for the Suppression of Terrorism: A Serious Threat to Human Rights." AI Index: IOR 51/001/2002.

——. "Broken Bodies, Shattered Minds – The Torture of Women Worldwide." May 2001.

——. "Broken Lives: A Year of Intifada, Israel/Occupied Territories/Palestinian Authority." AI Index: MDE 15/083/2000.

——. "'Collateral Damage' or Unlawful Killings? Violations of the Laws of War by NATO during the Operation Allied Force." 2000.

——. "Facts and Figures about Amnesty International." 1999.

——. "Guatemala's Legal Legacy: Past Impunity and Renewed Human Rights Violations." 2002.

——. "Hidden Scandal, Secret Shame: Torture and Ill-treatment of Children." London, 2000.

——. "International Criminal Court – 'Crippled at Birth.'" July 17, 1998.

——. "South Africa: Compensate Victims of the Past." Joint Statement by Amnesty International and Human Rights Watch. New York and London, Feb. 13, 2003.

——. "Statute of Amnesty International." 1997.

——. "Stopping the Torture Trade." London, 2001.

——. "20th Anniversary of Women's Convention: Time to Take Women's Human Rights Seriously." Dec. 17, 1999.

——. "United States of America: Rights for All." <www.rightsforall-usa.org/info/report>.

——. "Women on the Front Line." 1991.

Human Rights Watch (HRW)/ Asia Watch/ Africa Watch/ etc.

Human Rights Watch. "Cuba's Repressive Machinery: Human Rights Forty Years after the Revolution. June 1999. <www.hrw.org/hrw/reports/1999/cuba/>.

——. "Double Standards: Women's Property Rights Violations in Kenya." March 2003. <hrw.org/reports/2003/kenya0303>.

——. "EU Decision on ICC Sets 'Vague Benchmarks.'" Sept. 30, 2002.

——. "Opposition Mounting on US Arm-Twisting on ICC." Aug. 13, 2002.

——. "Unfair Advantage." 2000 <www.hrw.org/reports/2000/>.

——. "United States: Reports of Torture of Al-Qaeda Suspects." Dec. 27, 2002.

——. "U.S.: End Bully Tactics against Court – Letter to Colin Powell." July 2003.

——. "U.S. Should Renounce Torture before Powell Speech to U.N." Feb. 3, 2003.

Human Rights Watch/American Civil Liberties Union. "Human Rights Violations in the United States: A Report on US Compliance with the International Covenant on Civil and Political Rights." New York, 1993.

Peoples' Tribunals

Korea Truth Commission <www.koreatruthcommission.org.>.

Permanent Peoples' Tribunals <www.grisnet.it/flib/tribu>.

International People's Tribunal to Judge the G-7. *Report: The People vs. Global Capital*. Tokyo: Pacific Asia Center, July 1993.

School of the Americas – renamed in 2001; now called Western Hemisphere Institute for Security Cooperation. <www.geocities.com> and <www.soaw.org>.

Women's International War Crimes Tribunal. "Japan's Military Sexual Slavery." Tokyo. December 2000.

United Nations

United Nations <www.unhchr.ch/>

United Nations. Address of Secretary-General Kofi Annan to the World Economic Forum, in Davos, Switzerland, Jan. 31, 1999. <www.unglobalcompact.org>.

——. Children's Watch <www.unicef-icdc.org/>.

——. *Climate Change and Transnational Corporations*. New York, 1992.

——. Historical Clarification Commission. *Guatemala: Memory of Silence*. 1999. <www.unhrc.org>; see also <www.seas.gwu.edu/nsarchive/>; <www.motherjones.com/scoop>.

——. "The Nine Principles." <www.unglobalcompact.org>.

——. "Secretary-General, Addressing the United States Chamber of Commerce, Highlights Fundamental Shift of United Nations Attitude towards the Private Sector." UN Press Release, June 1999, SG/SM/7022. <www.un.org/partners/business>.

——. *The United Nations and the Advancement of Women, 1945-1996*. New York, 1995.

——. Women Watch <www.un.org/women watch/>.

——. World Conference on Human Rights. "Vienna Declaration and Programme of Action." Vienna, 1993.

——. World Conference of the United Nations for Women. Copenhagen, 1980.

United Nations Commission on Transnational Corporations. *Transnational Corporations, Services and the Uruguay Round*. New York, 1990.

United Nations Committee on the Rights of the Child. "State Violence Against Children." Report and General Recommendations, September 2000.

United Nations Development Fund for Women <www.unifem.org.jo/humanrights>.

United Nations High Commissioner for Human Rights <www.unhchr.ch>.

United Nations Human Development Programme. *Human Development Report 1995*. New York: Oxford University Press, 1995.

——. *Human Development Report 1997*. New York: Oxford University Press, 1997.

——. *Human Development Report 1999*. New York: Oxford University Press, 1999.

United Nations Human Rights Commission. Subcommittee for the Promotion and Protection of Human Rights – for a wide number of reports on these issues. <www.unhchr.ch>.

United Nations Population Fund. *The State of the World's Population 2000 – Lives Together, World's Apart: Men and Women in a Time of Change*. Washington, 2000. <www.unfpa.org/swp/swp/2001>.

World Commission on Environment and Development. *Our Common Future*. Oxford and New York: Oxford University Press, 1987.

Other Sources

African Union 2002: Documents and Speeches <www.au2002.gov.za/docs/>.

The American Journal of International Law. "Developments in International Criminal Law" (on the International Criminal Court) 93,2 (1999).

Chile. *Report of the National Truth and Reconciliation Commission.* May 1991. <www.derechoschile.com>.

Central Intelligence Agency (CIA). "CIA Activities in Chile." Report, Sept. 18, 2000. <www.cia.gov/cian/publications/chile/>.

CorpWatch. "Citizens Compact on the United Nations and Corporations." Davos, Switzerland, Jan. 28, 2000. <www.corpwatch.org>.

——. *TRAC Facts.* San Francisco. November 1999. <www.corpwatch.org>.

The Ecologist. "Whose Common Future?" 22, 4 (1992).

European Parliament, Directorate General for Research. *An Appraisal of Technologies of Political Control.* Luxembourg, Jan. 6, 1998.

European Parliament, Department of Scientific and Technological Options Assessment (STOA). "Special Report to the European Parliament." Prepared by the Omega Foundation. Luxembourg, September 1998. <www.europarl.eu.int/stoa/publi>.

European Parliament. *Interception Capabilities 2000.* STOA report. April 1999.

Institute for Public Accuracy. "Bush's Tax Cuts: Who Benefits?" Feb. 9, 2001 <ipa.accuracy.org>.

International Action Center (IAC). "Text of the Indictment Prepared by Ramsay Clark." New York, July 30, 1999. <www.iacenter.org/warcrime/indictment.htm>.

International Labour Organization. "Convention Concerning the Prohibition and Immediate Action for the Elimination of the Worst Forms of Child Labour." June 1999.

International Theological Commission. "Memory and Reconciliation: The Church and the Faults of the Past." Rome, December 1999. <www.vatican.va>.

Organization for African Unity. "The International Panel of Eminent Personalities to Investigate the 1994 Genocide in Rwanda and the Surrounding Events. Rwanda: The Preventable Genocide 2000." Commissioned by the OAU. <www.oau-oua.org/Document/ipep/report/rwanda-e/>.

Physicians for Social Responsibility, Center for Global Health and Security. "'Dr. Strangelove' Meets the Pentagon: The U.S. Nuclear Posture Review." Factsheet, 2002.

Press for Conversion! Issue no.51 (May 2003). "The U.S. Role in Wars and Regime Changes in the Middle East and North Africa since World War II." Coalition to Oppose the Arms Race, Ottawa <www.ncf.ca/coat>.

Sustainable Energy and Economy Network (SEEN). "Fossil Fuels and Human Rights Fact Sheet." <www.seen.org>.

United States Air Force, Air University. *SPACECAST 2020.* Vol. 1. Maxwell Air Force Base, Alabama, June 1994.

——. Air Force, Scientific Advisory Board. "New World Vistas: Air and Space Power for the Twenty-First Century." Washington, D.C. December 1995.

——. Director for Strategic Plans and Policy. *Joint Vision 2020.* Washington, D.C. June 2000.

——. Space Command. "US Spacecom Unveils Long Range Plan." News Release, April 7, 1998.

——. United Nations Association. *Controlling Conflicts in the 1970s.* New York, 1969.

——. The White House. "Executive Order Establishing Office of Homeland Security." Oct. 8, 2001.

U.S. War Resister's League pamphlet. "Where Your Income Tax Money Really Goes." <warresisters.org>.

The World Bank. *Annual Report 2000.* Washington, D.C.

World Policy Institute. *Child Labour: Targeting the Intolerable.* Report VI (1), 1998.

——. "The WTO and the Globalization of the Arms Industry." Washington, D.C., 1999. <www.worldpolicy.org/>.

——. "The Dirty Dozen Corporations: Partners in Mass Destruction." Joint project of Arms Trade Resource Center and Reaching Critical Will <www.worldpolicy.org/projects/arms>.

International Labour Organization. *World of Work* 16 (1996), 22 (1997), 30 (1999), 37 (2000).

Web Sites

American Civil Liberties Union: Echelon Watch <www.echelonwatch.org>.

Anti-Landmine Resources (Vietnam Veterans of America Foundation) <www.vvaf.org/landmine>.

BankruptcyData.com (New Generation Research, Inc., Boston) <www.Bankruptcydata.com>.
Center for Defense Information <www.cdi.org>.
Centre for Responsive Politics <www.opensecrets.org>.
Center for World Indigenous Studies <www.cwis.org/>.
CIABASE files on death squads for a list of CIA facilitated death squads around the world. <come.to/
    CIABASE>. See also <www.cia.gov/cia/publications/chile>.
Corporate Watch <www.corpwatch.org>.
Counterpunch (on-line journal) <www.counterpunch.org>.
Concise Guide to Human Rights on the Internet <www.derchos.org/human-rights/manual.htm>.
Council on International and Public Affairs (Program on Corporations, Law and Democracy) <www.cipa-
    apex.org/>.
Derechos Human Rights <www.derechos.org/>.
Foreign Policy in Focus <www.fpif.org>.
Gendercide Watch <www.gendercide.org>.
Global Alliance Against Traffic in Women <www.inet.co.th/org/70>.
Global March <www.globalmarch.org>.
Global Trade Watch <www.citizen.org/trade/>.
Institute for Global Communications (IGC) <www.igc.org> – for human rights links.
International Helsinki Federation for Human Rights <www.ihf-hr.org/>.
International Labour Organization (ILO) <www.ilo.org>.
Inter-Parliamentary Union, "Women in National Parliaments" <www.ipu.org/wmn-e/world.>.
Israeli Information Center for Human Rights <www.btselem-org>.
Law, Social Justice and Global Development <elj.warwick.ac.uk/global>.
Military Toxics Project <www.miltoxproj.org>.
Project Underground <www.moles.org>.
Public Committee Against Torture <www.stoptorture.org.il>.
Public Education for Peace Society, and End the Arms Race <www.peacewire.org/>.
Madres de la Plaza de Mayo <www.madres.org>.
Matzpun <www.matzpun.com>.
Rabbis for Human Rights <www.rhi.israel.net>.
SOA Watch <www.soaw.org>.
Statewatch: monitoring the state and civil liberties in the European Union <www.statewatch.org>.
Swans (on-line journal) <www.swans.com/>.
The Human Rights Directory (Europe) <www.echr.net>.
The Fire This Time <www.firethistime.org>.
Transparency International <www.transparency.de/documents/newsletter/>.
Truth and Reconciliation Commission (South Africa) <www.doj.gov.za/trc/>.
United Nations Office for Outer Space Affairs <www.un.org>.
What Really Happened <www.whatreallyhappened.com>.
Women's Human Rights Resources <www.law_lib.utoronto.ca/Diana>.
Women, Law and Development <www.wld.org/>.
World Social Forum <www.forumsocialmundial.org>.
Yale Human Rights and Development Law Journal <www.yale.edu/yhrdlj>.
Zapatista website <www.ezln.org/>.

Index

Recently Published Titles from Garamond Press

Yildiz Atasoy & William K. Carroll, eds.
Global Shaping and its Alternatives
1-55193-043-9

Deborah Barndt
**Tangled Routes: Women,
Work and Globalization on
the Tomato Trail**
1-55193-042-0

John Bratton, Jean Helms-Mills, Timothy
Pyrch, Peter Sawchuk
**Workplace Learning: A Critical
Introduction**
1-55193-047-1

Marie Campbell & Francis Gregor
**Mapping Social Relations:
A Primer in Doing Institutional
Ethnography**
1-55193-034-X

Grant, Amaratunga, Armstrong, Boscoe,
Pederson, Willson
**Caring For / Caring About:
Women, Home Care, and
Unpaid Caregiving**
1-55193-048-X

D.W. Livingstone
**The Education-Jobs Gap:
Underemployment or Economic
Democracy**
(re-issued with new Introduction, 2004)
1-55193-017-X

D. W. Livingstone & Peter Sawchuk
**Hidden Knowledge: Organized
Labour in the Information Age**
1-55193-045-5

Leo Panitch & Donald Swartz
**From Consent to Coercion:
The Assault on Trade Union
Freedoms, 3rd ed.**
1-55193-048-x

Alan Sears
**Retooling the Mind Factory:
Education in a Lean State**
1-55193-044-7

Gary Teeple
The Riddle of Human Rights
1-55193-039-0 pb
1-55193-041-2 hc

Garamond Press Ltd., 63 Mahogany Court, Aurora ON L4G 6M8
(905) 841-1460 • Fax (905) 841-3031 • garamond@web.ca • www.garamond.ca